John Payne Collier

Shakespeare's Library

A Collection of Plays. Vol. 4

John Payne Collier

Shakespeare's Library
A Collection of Plays. Vol. 4

ISBN/EAN: 9783744710480

Printed in Europe, USA, Canada, Australia, Japan

Cover: Foto ©Thomas Meinert / pixelio.de

More available books at **www.hansebooks.com**

SHAKESPEARE'S LIBRARY.

PART I.—VOL. IV.

———o———

THE TEMPEST.   THE WINTER'S TALE.
KING HENRY VIII.
TWO NOBLE KINSMEN.
PERICLES, PRINCE OF TYRE.
TIMON OF ATHENS.
THE TAMING OF A SHREW.

Shakespeare's Library

A COLLECTION OF THE

PLAYS ROMANCES NOVELS POEMS
AND HISTORIES

EMPLOYED BY

SHAKESPEARE

IN THE COMPOSITION OF HIS WORKS

With Introductions and Notes

SECOND EDITION

CAREFULLY REVISED AND GREATLY ENLARGED

The Text now First formed
from a New Collation of the Original Copies

VOLUME THE FOURTH

LONDON
REEVES AND TURNER 100 CHANCERY LANE W.C.
1875

THE TEMPEST.

AFTER the most persevering researches of all the writers on Shakespeare, during more than a century, it is strange that no story has come to light which can have supplied the great poet with his raw material, even to the extent that Green's "Pandosto" served his purpose in the "Winter's Tale," or Lodge's "Rosalind" in "As You Like it." It seems likely that he drew his facts and the thread of his story from several publications and occurrences of or about the time, and was not considerably indebted to any single original. Thus Florio's Montaigne, published in 1603—a book, of which Shakespeare's own copy is in the British Museum [1]—has been followed pretty implicitly as regards the speech of Gonzalo in act ii., scene 1 ; and the passage is for that reason reprinted below ; and again it appears to me worth suggesting that another volume which Shakespeare in all probability read—or at any rate which was very well known to the author (or authors) of "Pericles," the "Pattern of Painful Adventures," may have supplied a hint, where the description is so vividly given, in the fourth chapter, of the shipwreck of Apollonius, Prince of Tyre, on the coast of Pentapolis. Douce's remark ("Illustr. of Shakespeare," i. 5), seems to me much to the purpose here :—"Several contemporary narratives of the above event [voyage of Sir George Somners] were published, which Shakespeare might have consulted, and the *conversation of the time* might have furnished, or at least suggested, some particulars, that are *not to be found in any of the printed accounts.*"

In "Green's Tu Quoque," 1614 (Hazlitt's Dodsley, xi. 187), Bubble says, when his master speaks of going to sea :—

"To sea? Lord bless us! *methinks I hear of a tempest already.*"

It seems to have been a *tempestuous* period. The play here cited was written and acted some time before 1614.

---

[1] An account of this precious volume was given in a pamphlet published by Sir Frederic Madden, 8º, 1838.

The case seems very different with respect to Jacob Ayrer's "Die Schöne Sidea," which there is not the most distant pretence for treating as a foundation-play, or even an analogue, since any resemblances which are to be observed between it and the "Tempest" are readily to be explained, as Mr Dyce pointed out, "by supposing that, so far as the incidents in question are concerned, both dramas had a common source." But it has occurred to me as possible that the resemblances between the English and German plays may have arisen from Ayrer having had access to some MS. copy of Shakespeare's drama transmitted abroad, or taken there by an English company for representation.

Mr Dyce, in his revised edition, speaks of the "Tempest" as written in the author's "latest style;" and it is not quite easy therefore to understand why it was allowed to occupy the earliest place in the series.

Of course, Mr Hunter's admirable and charming "Disquisition on the Tempest," as incorporated with his "New Illustrations of Shakespeare," 1845, ought to be always read by all students of the play. But it is proper to point out that one of the arguments brought to bear by Mr Hunter upon the subject, when he is trying to establish the "Tempest" as an early play—namely, that Shakespeare would not have alluded to Raleigh's tract on Guiana, printed in 1596, if it had not been then a quite recent publication—seems to be controverted somewhat by the circumstance that in the complete text of the "Merry Wives of Windsor," as first printed in 1623, the poet inserts a reference to this very Guiana, which does not occur in the first sketch of 1602.

1. *Search for the Island of Lampedusa.*

[*From Harington's "Ariosto,"* 1591, *Canto* xli.]

A FRENDLY gale at first their iourney fitted,
    And bare them from the shore full farre away :
But afterward within a little season,
The wind discouerd his deceipt and treason.

First from the poop, it changed to the side,
Then to the prore, at last it wherled round,
In one place long it neuer would abide,
Which doth the Pilots wit and skill confound :
The surging waues swell still in higher pride,
While Proteus flocke did more and more abound,
And seeme to them as many deaths to threaten,
As that ships sides with diuers waues are beaten.

Now in their face the wind, straight in their backe,
And forward this, and backward that it blowes,
Then on the side it makes the ship to cracke,
Among the Mariners confusion growes ;
The Master ruine doubts, and present wracke,
For none his will, nor none his meaning knowes,
To whistle, becken, crie, it nought auailes,
Somtime to strike, somtime to turne their sailes.

But none there was could heare, nor see, nor marke,
Their eares so stopt, so dazeld were their eyes,
With weather so tempestuous and so darke,
And black thick clouds, that with the storme did rise
Frõ whence somtime great gastly flames did sparke,
And thunderclaps, that seemd to rend the skies:
Which made them in a manner deafe and blind,
That no man vnderstood the Masters mind.

Nor lesse, nor much lesse fearfull is the sound,
The cruell tempest in the tackle makes,
Yet each one for himselfe some busnesse found,
And to some speciall office him betakes:
One this vntide, another that hath bound,
He the Main bowling, now restraines, now slakes:
Some take an oare, some at the pumpe take paine,
And powre the sea into the sea againe.

Behold a horrible and hideous blast,
That Boreas from his frozen lips doth send,
Doth backward force the sayle against the mast,
And makes the waues vnto the skies ascend:
Then brake their oares and rudder eke at last,
Now nothing left from tempest to defend,
So that the ship was swaid now quite aside,
And to the waues laid ope her naked side.

Then all aside the staggring ship did reele,
For one side quite beneath the water lay,
And on the tother side the verie keele,
Aboue the water plaine discerne you may.
Then thought they al hope past, & down they kneele
And vnto God to take their soules they pray,
Worse danger grew then this, when this was past,
By meanes the ship gan after leake so fast.

The wind, the waues, to them no respite gaue,
But readie eu'rie houre to ouerthrow them,

Oft they wer hoist so high vpon the waue,
They thought the middle region was below them;
Oft times so low the same their vessel draue,
As though that Caron there his boat would show thē
Scant had they time and powre to fetch their breath,
All things did threaten them so present death.

Thus all that night they could haue no release,
But when the morning somewhat nearer drew,
And that by course, the furious wind should cease,
(A strange mishap) the wind then fiercer grew,
And while their troubles more and more increase,
Behold a rocke stood plainly in their vew,
And right vpon the same the spitefull blast,
Bare them perforce, which made them all agast.

Yet did the master by all meanes assay,
To steare out roomer, or to keepe aloofe,
Or at the least to strike sailes if they may,
As in such danger was for their behoofe.
But now the wind did beare so great a sway,
His enterprises had but little proofe:
At last with striuing yard and all was torne,
And part thereof into the sea was borne.

Then each man saw all hope of safetie past,
No meanes there was the vessell to direct,
No helpe there was, but all away are cast,
Wherefore their common safetie they neglect,
But out they get the ship-boat, and in hast,
Each man therein his life striues to protect,
Of King, nor Prince no man taks heed or note,
But well was he could get him in the bote.

2. *The supposed original of the Speech of Gonzalo, Act ii., Scene* 1.

[*From Florio's Montaigne*, 1603, *p.* 102.]

———o———

" THEY [Lycurgus and Plato] could not imagine a genuitie so pure and simple, as we see it by experience, nor ever beleeve our societie might be maintained with so little arte and humane combination. It is a nation, would I answere Plato, that hath no kinde of traffike, no knowledge of letters, no intelligence of numbers, no name of magistrate, nor of politike superioritie; no vse of service, of riches, or of poverty; no contracts, no successions, no dividences, no occupation but idle; no respect of kinred, but common; no apparrell but naturall, no manuring of lands, no vse of wine, corne, or mettle. The very words that import lying, falsehood, treason, dissimulation, covetousnes, envie, detraction, and pardon, were never heard of amongst them. How dissonant would hee finde his imaginary commonwealth from this perfection?

Hos natura modos primum dedit.

  Nature at first vprise
  These manners did devise.

Furthermore, they live in a country of so exceeding pleasant and temperate situation, that as my testimonies have tolde me it is very rare to see a sicke body amongst them; and they have further assured me, they never saw any man there, shaking with the palsie, toothlesse, with eyes dropping, or crooked and stooping through age."

THE WINTER'S TALE.

"The History of Pandosto," by that greatly over-estimated writer, Robert Greene, formed the skeleton groundwork out of which Shakespeare constructed his own very different production. Pandosto first appeared in 1588.

But there is little doubt that, in writing the "Winter's Tale," the author had also an eye to Gascoigne's paraphrase of the "Phœnissæ" of Euripides, presented at Gray's Inn in 1566, and printed among the works of that interesting old Maker, 1573, 1575, 1587, and as edited in 1869-70.

As regards the character of Autolycus, it is a matter for speculation whether Shakespeare had not in his recollection that extraordinarily curious production by Thomas Newbery, "The Book of Dives Pragmaticus," 1563, reprinted in Mr Huth's "Fugitive Tracts," 1875.

MR COLLIER'S INTRODUCTION.

THE more we become acquainted with the sources from which Shakespeare derived the plots of his dramas, the more room we find to wonder at the extent, power, and variety of his genius. We cannot justly estimate his excellence without the knowledge which this publication is intended to furnish.

Those who are best informed regarding the productions of his contemporaries and rivals are most ready to admit his immeasurable superiority to all of them. He seems greater by comparison than when judged of by his own positive and separate merits; and this position will be completely established by the instance before us.

Robert Greene was a man who possessed all the advantages of education: he was a graduate of both universities, he was skilled in ancient learning and in modern languages, he had, besides, a prolific imagination, a lively and elegant fancy, and a grace of expression rarely exceeded; yet let any person well acquainted with "The Winter's Tale" read the novel of "Pandosto," upon which it was founded, and he will be struck at once with the vast pre-eminence of Shakespeare, and with the admirable manner in which he has converted materials supplied by another to his own use. The bare outline of the story (with the exception of Shakespeare's miraculous conclusion) is nearly the same in both; but this is all they have in common, and Shakespeare may be said to have scarcely adopted a single hint for his descriptions, or a line for his dialogue;[1] while in point of passion and sentiment Greene is cold, formal, and artificial: the very opposite of everything in Shakespeare.

It is fair to observe, however, that Greene ceased to write not long after Shakespeare had commenced his career. Greene died in September 1592, and the plausible conjecture seems to be, that by this date Shakespeare had not composed any of his great works, and had probably not written anything original for the stage prior to the year 1588 or 1589. All the known facts regarding the life of Greene may be found in the preliminary matter to the Rev. Mr Dyce's excellent edition of Greene's Poetical Works. He was certainly an author in 1584, and perhaps before that date. It is a point not hitherto touched, that there was, perhaps, an earlier impression of "Pandosto" than any yet discovered; but it depends not upon obvious facts or inferences, but upon minute circumstances not worth detailing, and upon a close

---

[1] Some verbal resemblances and trifling obligations have been incidentally pointed out by the commentators in their notes to "The Winter's Tale." One of the principal instances occurs in Act iv. sc. 3, where Florizel says—

"The gods themselves,
Humbling their deities to love, have taken
The shapes of beasts upon them: Jupiter
Became a bull and bellow'd; the green Neptune
A ram and bleated; and the fire-rob'd god,
Golden Apollo, a poor humble swain,
As I seem now. Their transformations
Were never for a piece of beauty rare,
Nor in a way so chaste."

"This (says Malone) is taken almost literally from the novel," when, in fact, the resemblance merely consists in the adoption by Shakespeare of part of the mythological knowledge supplied by Greene. "The Gods above disdaine not to love women beneath. Phœbus liked Sibilla; Jupiter, Io; and why not I then Fawnia?" The resemblance is anything but literal.

observation of the errors of the press which, in the edition of 1588, appear to be those which would be made by a compositor engaged rather upon a reprint than upon a manuscript.[1] It is a well ascertained fact, that there must have been an earlier edition of one of the same author's pieces (a "Quip for an Upstart Courtier") than any that has come down to us.

As the means of comparison, page by page, and scene by scene, are now afforded to the reader, it is not necessary to point out the particular instances in which Shakespeare follows or differs from his original. The variation in the conclusion has already been mentioned: nothing can well be more lame, unsatisfactory, and even offensive than the winding up of Greene's novel, where he makes Pandosto first fall desperately and grossly in love with his own daughter, and then, without any adequate motive, commit suicide. Here the genius of Shakespeare triumphed over all competition: he saw at once how the preceding incidents might be converted to a great dramatic and moral purpose, the most pathetic and the most beautiful. In other places the skill and judgment of our great dramatist are scarcely less conspicuous: as, for instance, in the very outset of his play, where he represents Polixenes (the Egistus of the novel) as previously prepared to take his departure in his ships, which had only, therefore, to weigh anchor; while, in Greene's novel the determination of the visitor to quit the kingdom of his royal friend is sudden, and all his vessels have to be got ready on the instant. The variation in the time of the disclosure of the decision

---

[1] Mr Dyce (Greene's Works, ii. 242) prints from an edition of "Pandosto," as late as 1694 a "love-passion," addressed by Dorastus to Fawnia, observing that he had met with it in no earlier impression. The poem is unquestionably old, and it may possibly have been taken from the earliest, and now lost, edition of "Pandosto."

of the Oracle may also be noticed as a proof of the knowledge Shakespeare possessed of dramatic effect. It is, nevertheless, to be admitted, that a mere prose narrative and an acting drama would require different treatment.

Steevens correctly stated ("Prel. Rem. to the Winter's Tale") that "the parts of Antigonus, Paulina, and Autolicus, are of Shakespeare's own invention;" but he ought to have added the Shepherd's son to the list, and he committed a strange blunder (which shews that he had read Greene's work with very little attention), when he asserted that the Leontes of Shakespeare is the Egistus of the novel. Pandosto is Leontes, and Egistus is Polixenes. None of the other commentators corrected the error, or, perhaps, were able to do so, from not having taken the trouble to go through the incidents in the original story, and to compare them with those of the play.

There is one circumstance that ought not to be passed over without observation; and it will serve to strengthen the position, that "The Tempest" was produced anterior to the "Winter's Tale." The Rev. Mr Hunter, if he has not established that "The Tempest" was written in 1596 ("Disquisition on the Scene, Origin, Date, &c. of The Tempest," p. 87), has at all events shewn that it was written earlier than 1611, to which year Malone assigns both it and "The Winter's Tale." ("Shakespeare," by Boswell, ii. 296.) Now, the reason for the opinion, that "The Winter's Tale" was posterior in composition to "The Tempest" is this—that, in his novel of "Pandosto," Greene describes the turning adrift of Fawnia (the Perdito of Shakespeare) at sea in a boat, very much in the same manner as Prospero describes what had happened to himself and Miranda under similar circumstances. Shakespeare having already employed this species of incident in "The Tempest," was obliged to vary it in "The Winter's

Tale," or he would probably have followed Greene's description, which is certainly one of the prettiest and most natural portions of his narrative. Shakespeare, also, without any very apparent reason, reverses the scene: his play opens in Sicily, and Perdita is exposed on the coast of Bohemia; while Greene's novel begins in Bohemia, and Fawnia is found by the old Shepherd on the coast of Sicily. Bohemia is, however, over and over again spoken of by Greene as a maritime country, and Shakespeare, supposing he knew better, did not think it worth while to disturb the popular notion. We have the evidence of Taylor, the water-poet, in his "Travels to Prague," that in 1620 it was not considered a piece of very unusual ignorance in an Alderman of London not to be aware that "a fleet of ships" could not arrive at a port of Bohemia.

"Pandosto" appears to have been extraordinarily popular, and Mr Dyce enumerates twelve editions: to these at least two others are to be added, with which he was not acquainted, viz. in 1609 and 1632. No doubt several more have been lost, as we do not find it to have been reprinted between 1588 and 1607, a period during which it would probably have been most attractive. The only known copy of the edition of 1588 is in the British Museum; but it is defective in one place, and we have necessarily been compelled to complete our impression from a later copy. Whether the story were the invention of Greene, or whether, as was not unusual with him, he adopted it from a foreign language, cannot now be ascertained; but it is not known abroad in any other form than that in which it has been received from this country.

It will not be out of place to take some notice here of a production, which is asserted by the bookseller to have come from the pen of this prolific author; but at all events he could have had nothing to do with the title-page, which runs thus:—" Greenes Vision: Written at the instant of his death. Conteyning a penitent passion for the folly of his Pen. sero sed serio. Imprinted at London for Thomas Newman, and are to be sould at his shop in Fleetestreete, in Saint Dunstons Churchyard." It is in 4°, and in black letter, but without date, though we need not hesitate in assigning it to the close of 1592. It is autobiographical, which renders the tract more interesting, and in the address to the readers, Greene expresses deep regret that his lighter pieces had ever been published, adding, "Many things I have wrote to get money, which I could otherwise wish supprest: povertie is the father of innumerable infirmities." The first poem[1] is called "Greenes Ode on the Vanitie of Wanton Writings," which after six introductory lines, thus speaks of himself under the name of Tytirus:—

> " Telling in his song how faire
> Phillis eie-browes and hir haire:
> How hir face past all supposes
> For white Lillies: for red Roses.
> Though he sounded on the hils
> Such fond passions as loue wils,
> That all the Swaines that foulded by
> Flockt to heare his harmonie,
> And vowed by Pan that Tytirus
> Did Poet-like his loues discusse;
> That men might learne mickle good
> By the verdict of his mood,
> Yet olde Menalcas ouer-ag'd,
> That many winters there had wag'd,
> Sitting by and hearing this,
> Said, their wordes were all amisse," &c.

The ode is followed by a prayer full of self-reproach, and afterwards the author represents himself as lying down upon his bed, and in a vision seeing

---

[1] [The poems in "Greene's Vision" not printed by Dyce are given in Mr Huth's volume of Prefaces, 1874, pp. 128-37.]

Chaucer and Gower, both of whom he describes in verse. The portrait of Chaucer runs thus:—

> "His stature was not very tall;
> Leane he was, his legs were small,
> Hosd within a stock of red;
> A buttond bonnet on his head,
> From under which did hang, I weene,
> Silver haires both bright and sheene.
> His beard was white, trimmed round,
> His countenance blithe and merry found.
> A sleevelesse jacket, large and wide,
> With many pleights and skirts side,
> Of water chamlet did he weare.
> A whittell by his belt he beare.
> His shoes were corned, broad before;
> His inckhorne at his side he wore,
> And in his hand he bore a booke:
> Thus did this auntient poet looke."

The "Description of John Gower" may be found extracted in "Farther Particulars regarding Shakespeare and his Works," p. 35. Both are curious, as they were probably derived from some then existing painting or illumination, not now known. In the course of the tract Greene acknowledges various works, but he especially repudiates "The Cobbler of Canterbury," which had been falsely attributed to him. He speaks of his "Never too Late," printed in 1590, and of his "Mourning Garment," as if it were then in the press; but according to Mr Dyce it had been printed two years before. Greene's "Repentance," the title of which is also introduced, bears date in 1592. Chaucer and Gower discuss the merits and vices of Greene's productions, and King Solomon is called in as an umpire, who exhorts Greene to abandon folly and to seek wisdom.

PANDOSTO.

¶ THE TRIUMPH OF TIME.

WHEREIN IS DISCOVERED

by a pleasant Historie, that although by the meanes of sinister fortune, Truth may be concealed *yet by Time in spight of fortune it is most manifestly reuealed.*

Pleasant for age to auoyde drowsie thoughts, profitable for youth to eschue other wanton *pastimes, and bringing to both a desired content.*

Temporis filia veritas.

¶ *By Robert Greene*, Maister of Artes in *Cambridge*.

Omne tulit punctum qui miscuit vtile dulci.

Imprinted at London by *Thomas Orwin* for *Thomas Cadman*, dwelling at the Signe of the *Bible*, neere vnto the North doore of Paules, 1588.

TO THE GENTLEMEN READERS HEALTH.

———o———

THE paultring Poet *Aphranius*, being blamed for troublinge the Emperor Trajan with so many doting *Poems*, adventured notwithstanding, stil to present him with rude and homely verses, excusing himselfe with the courtesie of the Emperour, which did as friendly accept, as he fondly offerd. So Gentlemen, if any condemne my rashnesse for troubling your eares with to many unlearned Pamphlets: I will straight shroud my selfe under the shadowe of your courtesies, and with *Aphranius* lay the blame on you as well for frendly reading them, as on my selfe for fondly penning them: Hoping though fond curious, or rather currish backbiters breathe out slaunderous speeches: yet the courteous Readers (whom I feare to offend) wil requite my travell, at the least with silence: and in this hope I rest wishing you health and happines.

ROBERT GREENE.

TO THE

RIGHT HONORABLE GEORGE CLIFFORD,

EARLE OF CUMBERLAND,

ROBERT GREENE

Wisheth increase of Honour and Vertue.

———o———

THE Rascians (right honorable) when by long gazing against the Sunne, they become halfe blinde, recover their sightes by looking on the blacke Loade-stone. Unicornes being glutted with brousing on roots of Licquoris, sharpen their stomacks with crushing bitter grasse.

Alexander vouchsafed as well to smile at the croked picture of Vulcan, as to wonder at the curious counterfeite of Venus. The minde is sometimes delighted as much with small trifles as with sumptuous triumphs; and as wel pleased with hearing of Pans homely fancies, as of Hercules renowmed laboures.

Syllie Baucis coulde not serve Jupiter in a silver plate, but in a woodden dish. Al that honour Esculapius, decke not his shrine with Iewels. Apollo gives Oracles as wel to the poor man for his mite, as to the rich man for his treasure. The stone Echites is not so much liked for the colour, as for vertue, and giftes are not to be measured by the worth, but by the will. *Mison* that unskilfull Painter of Greece, adventured to give unto *Darius* the shielde of Pallas, so roughlie shadowed, as he smiled more at the follie of the man, then at the imperfection of his arte. So I present unto your honour the triumph of time, so rudelie finished, as I feare your honour wil rather frowne at my impudencie, then laugh at my ignorancie: But I hope my willing minde shal excuse my slender skill, and your honours curtesie shadowe my rashnes.

They which feare the biting of vipers do carie in their hands the plumes of a Phœnix. Phydias drewe Vulcan sitting in a chair of Ivory. Cæsars crow durst never cry, *Ave*, but when she was pearked on the Capitoll. And I seeke to shroude this imperfect Pamphlet under your honours patronage, doubting the dint of such invenomed vipers, as seeke with their slaunderous reproches to carpe at al, being oftentimes, most unlearned of all; and assure myselfe, that your honours renowmed valure, and vertuous disposition shall be a sufficient defence to protect me from the Poysoned tongues of such scorning Sycophants, hoping that as Jupiter vouchsafed to lodge in Philemons thatched Cotage: and Phillip of Macedon, to take a bunche of grapes of a country pesant, so I hope your honour, measuring my worke by my will, and wayghing more the mind than the matter, will when you have cast a glaunce at this toy, with Minerva, under your golden Target couer a deformed Owle. And in this hope I rest, wishing unto you, and the vertuous Countesse your wife, such happy successe as your honours can desire, or I imagine.

Your Lordships most duetifully to commaunde:

ROBERT GREENE.

The Historie of Dorastus and Fawnia.

AMONG al the passions wherewith humane mindes are perplexed, there is none that so galleth with restlesse despight, as the infectious soare of Iealousie : for all other griefes are eyther to bee appeased with sensible perswasions, to be cured with wholesome counsel, to be relieved in want, or by tract of time to be worne out, (Iealousie only excepted) which is so sawsed with suspitious doubtes, and pinching mistrust, that whoso seekes by friendly counsaile to rase out this hellish passion, it foorthwith suspected that he geveth this advise to cover his owne guiltinesse. Yea, who so is payned with this restlesse torment doubteth all, dystrusteth him-selfe, is alwayes frosen with feare, and fired with suspition, having that wherein consisteth all his joy to be the breeder of his miserie. Yea, it is such a heavy enemy to that holy estate of matrimony, sowing betweene the married couples such deadly seedes of secret hatred, as Love being once rased out by spightful distrust, there oft ensueth bloudy revenge, as this ensuing Hystorie manifestly prooveth : wherein Pandosto (furiously incensed by causelesse Iealousie) procured the death of his most loving and loyall wife, and his owne endlesse sorrow and misery.

In the Countrey of Bohemia there raygned a King called Pandosto, whose fortunate successe in warres against his foes, and bountifull curtesie towardes his friendes in peace, made him to be greatly feared and loved of all men. This Pandosto had to Wife a Ladie called Bellaria, by birth royall, learned by education, faire by nature, by vertues famous, so that it was hard to judge whether her beautie, fortune, or vertue, wanne the greatest commendations. These two lincked together in perfect love, led their lives with such fortunate content, that their Subjects greatly rejoyced to see their quiet disposition. They had not beene married long, but Fortune (willing to increase their happines) lent them a sonne, so adorned with the gifts of nature, as the perfection of the Childe greatly augmented the love of the parentes, and the joys of their commons; in so much that the Bohemians, to shewe their inward joyes by outwarde actions, made Bonefires and triumphs throughout all the Kingdome, appointing Justes and Turneyes for the honour of their young Prince: whether resorted not onely his Nobles, but also divers Kings and Princes which were his neighbours, willing to shewe their friendship they ought to Pandosto, and to win fame and glory by their prowesse and valour. Pandosto, whose minde was fraught with princely liberality, entertayned the Kings, Princes, and noble men with such submisse curtesie and magnifical bounty, that they all sawe how willing he was to gratifie their good wils, making a feast for Subjects, which continued by the space of twentie dayes; all which time the Justes and Turneys were kept to the great content both of the Lordes and Ladies there present. This solemne tryumph being once ended, the assembly, taking their leave of Pandosto and Bellaria: the young sonne (who was called Garinter) was nursed up in the house to the great joy and content of the parents.

Fortune envious of such happy successe, willing to shewe some signe of her inconstancie, turned her wheele, and darkned their bright sunne of prosperitie, with the mistie cloudes of mishap and misery. For it so happened that Egistus, King of Sycilia, who in his youth had bene brought up with Pandosto, desirous to shewe that neither tracte of time, nor distance of place could diminish their former friendship, provided a navie of ships, and sayled into Bohemia to visite his old friend and companion, who hearing of his arrivall, went himselfe in person, and his wife Bellaria, accompanied with a great traine of Lords and Ladies, to meete Egistus; and espying him, alighted from his horse, embraced him very lovingly, protesting that nothing in the world could have happened more acceptable to him then his comming, wishing his wife to welcome his olde friend and acquaintance: who (to shewe how she liked him whom her husband loved) intertayned him with such familiar curtesie, as Egistus perceived himselfe to bee verie well welcome. After they had thus saluted and embraced eche other, they mounted againe on horsbacke and rode towards the Citie, devising and recounting, howe being children they had passed their youth in friendely pastimes: where, by the meanes of the Citizens, Egistus was recevyed with triumphs and showes in such sort, that he marvelled how on so small a warning they coulde make such preparation.

Passing the streetes thus with such rare sightes, they rode on to the Pallace, where Pandosto entertained Egistus and his Sycilians with such banqueting and sumptuous cheare, so royally, as they all had cause to commend his princely liberality; yea, the verie basest slave that was knowne to come from Sycilia was used with such curtesie, that Egistus might

easily perceive how both hee and his were honored
for his friendes sake. Bellaria (who in her time was
the flower of curtesie), willing to show how unfaynedly
shee looved her husband by his friends intertainement, used him likewise so familiarly that her countenance bewraied how her minde was affected towardes
him; oftentimes comming her selfe into his bed
chamber, to see that nothing should be amis to mislike him. This honest familiarity increased dayly
more and more betwixt them; for Bellaria, noting in
Egistus a princely and bountifull minde, adorned
with sundrie and excellent qualities, and Egistus,
finding in her a vertuous and curteous disposition,
there grew such a secret uniting of their affections,
that the one could not well be without the company
of the other: in so much that when Pandosto was
busied with such urgent affaires, that hee could not
bee present with his friend Egistus, Bellaria would
walke with him into the Garden, where they two in
privat and pleasant devises would passe away the
time to both their contents. This custome still continuing betwixt them, a certaine melancholy passion
entring the minde of Pandosto drave him into sundry
and doubtfull thoughts. First, he called to minde
the beauty of his wife Bellaria, the comelines and
braverie of his friend Egistus, thinking that Love was
above all Lawes and therefore to be staied with no
Law; that it was hard to put fire and flaxe together
without burning; that their open pleasures might
breede his secrete displeasures. He considered with
himselfe that Egistus was a man, and must needes
love: that his wife was a woman, and therefore subject unto love, and that where fancy forced, friendship was of no force.

These and such like doubtfull thoughtes a long
time smoothering in his stomacke, beganne at last to
kindle in his minde a secret mistrust, which increased

by suspition, grewe at last to be a flaming Iealousie, that so tormented him as he could take no rest. He then began to measure all their actions, and to misconstrue of their too private familiarite, judging that it was not for honest affection, but for disordinate fancy, so that hee began to watch them more narrowely to see if hee coulde gette any true or certaine proofe to confirme his doubtfull suspition. While thus he noted their lookes and gestures, and suspected their thoughtes and meaninges, they two seely soules who doubted nothing of this his treacherous intent, frequented daily eache others companie, which drave him into such a franticke passion, that he beganne to beare a secret hate to Egistus, and a lowring countenance to Bellaria, who marveiling at such unaccustomed frownes, began to cast beeyond the Moone, and to enter into a thousand sundrie thoughtes, which way she should offend her husband: but finding in her selfe a cleare conscience, ceassed to muse, until such time as she might find fit opportunitie to demaund the cause of his dumps. In the meane time Pandostoes minde was so farre charged with Iealously, that he did no longer doubt, but was assured (as he thought) that his Friend Egistus had entered a wrong pointe in his tables, and so had played him false play: wherupon desirous to revenge so great an injury, he thought best to dissemble the grudge with a faire and friendly countenance: and so under the shape of a friend, to shew him the tricke of a foe. Devising with himself a long time how he might best put away Egistus without suspition of treacherous murder, hee concluded at last to poyson him: which opinion pleasing his humour, he became resolute in his determination, and the better to bring the matter to passe he called unto him his cupbearer, with whom in secret he brake the matter: promising to him for the performance thereof to geve him a

thousande crownes of yearely revenues: his cup-
bearer, eyther being of a good conscience, or willing
for fashion sake, to deny such a bloudy request,
began with great reasons to perswade Pandosto from
his determinate mischief: shewing him what an
offence murther was to the Gods: how such unnaturall actions did more displease the heavens, than
men, and that causelesse cruelty did seldome or
never escape without revenge: he layd before his
face, that Egistus was his friend, a King, and one that
was come into his Kingdome, to confirme a league of
perpetuall amitie betwixt them; that he had, and did
shew him a most friendly countenance: how Egistus
was not onely honoured of his owne people by
obedience, but also loved of the Bohemians for his
curtesie. And that if he now should, without any
just or manifest cause, poyson him, it would not
onely be a great dishonour to his Majestie, and a
meanes to sow perpetuall enmity between the Sycilians
and the Bohemians, but also his owne subjects would
repine at such treacherous cruelty. These and such
like perswasions of Franion (for so was his Cup-bearer
called) could no whit prevaile to disswade him from
his divellish enterprize: but remaining resolute in
his determination (his fury so fired with rage, as it
could not be appeased with reason) he began with
bitter taunts to take up his man, and to lay before him
two baites; preferment and death: saying that if he
would poyson Egistus, he would advance him to high
dignities: if he refused to doe it of an obstinate
minde, no torture should be too great to requite his
disobedience. Franion, seeing that to perswade
Pandosto any more, was but to strive against the
streame, consented, as soone as an opportunity would
give him leave, to dispatch Egistus: wherewith
Pandosto remained somewhat satisfied, hoping now
he should be fully revenged of such mistrusted in-

juries, intending also as soon as Egistus was dead, to give his wife a sop of the same sawce, and so be rid of those which were the cause of his restles sorrow. While thus he lived in this hope, Franion being secret in his chamber, began to meditate with himselfe in these terms.

Ah Franion, treason is loved of many, but the Traitor hated of all: unjust offences may for a time escape without danger, but never without revenge. Thou art servant to a King, and must obey at command; yet Franion, against law and conscience, it is not good to resist a tyrant with armes, nor to please an unjust King with obedience. What shalt thou doe? Folly refused gold, and frenzie preferment: wisdome seeketh after dignity, and counsell keepeth for gaine. Egistus is a stranger to thee, and Pandosto thy Soveraigne: thou has little cause to respect the one, and oughtest to have great care to obey the other. Thinke this Franion, that a pound of gold is worth a tunne of Lead, great gifts are little Gods: and preferment to a meane man is a whetstone to courage; there is nothing sweeter than promotion, nor lighter then report: care not then though most count thee a traitor, so all call thee rich. Dignity (Franion) advaunceth thy posteritie, and evil report can but hurt thy selfe. Know this, where Eagles builde, Falcons may prey; where Lyons haunt, Foxes may steale. Kings are knowne to commaund, servants are blamelesse to consent: feare not thou then to lift at Egistus, Pandosto shall beare the burthen. Yea but Franion, conscience is a worme that ever biteth, but never ceaseth: that which is rubbed with the stone Galactites will never bee hot. Flesh dipped in the Sea Ægeum will never bee sweete: the hearbe Trigion beeing once bit with an Aspis, never groweth, and conscience once stayned with innocent blood, is alwaies tyed to a guiltie remorse. Prefer thy content before riches, and a cleare minde before dignity; so beeing poore, thou shalt have rich peace, or else rich, thou shalt enjoy disquiet.

Franion having muttered out these or such like words, seeing either he must die with a cleare minde, or live with a spotted conscience, he was so cumbred with divers cogitations that hee could take no rest: untill at last he determined to breake the matter to Egistus; but fearing that the King should eyther suspect or heare of such matters, he concealed the device till opportunitie would permit him to reveale it. Lingring thus in doubtfull feare, in an evening he went to Egistus lodging, and desirous to breake with him of certaine affaires that touched the King, after all were commaunded out of the Chamber, Franion made manifest the whole conspiracie which Pandosto had devised against him, desiring Egistus not to account him a Traytor for bewraying his Maisters counsaile, but to thinke that he did it for conscience: hoping that although his Maister inflamed with rage, or incensed by some sinister reportes, or slanderous speeches, had imagined such causelesse mischiefe: yet when time should pacifie his anger, and try those talebearers but flattering Parasites, then he would count him as a faithfnll Seruant that with such care had kept his Maisters credite. Egistus had not fully heard Franion tell forth his tale, but a quaking feare possessed all his limmes, thinking that there was some treason wrought, and that Franion did but shaddow his craft with these false colours: wherefore he began to waxe in choller, and saide that he doubted not Pandosto, sith he was his friend, and there had never as yet beene any breach of amity: he had not sought to invade his lands, to conspire with his enemies, to disswade his Subjects from their allegeance; but in word and thought he rested his at all times: he knew not therefore any cause that should moove Pandosto to seeke his death, but suspected it to be a compacted knavery of the Bohemians to bring the King and him to oddes.

Franion staying him the middst of his talke, told him, that to dally with Princes was with the swannes to sing against their death, and that if the Bohemians had intended any such mischiefe, it might have beene better brought to passe then by revealing the conspiracie: therefore his Majesty did ill to misconstrue of his good meaning, sith his intent was to hinder treason, not to become a traytor; and to confirme his promises, if it pleased his Majestie to fly into Sicilia for the safegarde of his life, hee would goe with him, and if then he found not such a practise to be pretended, let his imagined treacherie be repayed with most monstrous torments. Egistus hearing the solemne protestation of Franion, beganne to consider, that in Love and Kingdomes, neither faith, nor lawe is to bee respected: doubting that Pandosto thought by his death to destroy his men, and with speedy warre to invade Sycilia. These and such doubtes throughly weyghed, he gave great thankes to Franion, promising if hee might with life returne to Syracusa, that hee would create him a Duke in Sycilia: craving his Counsell how hee might escape out of the Countrie. Franion, who having some small skill in Navigation, was well acquainted with the Ports and havens, and knew every daunger in the Sea, joyning in counsell with the Maister of Egistus Navie, rigged all their ships, and setting them a flote, let them lie at anchor, to be in the more readines, when time and winde should serve.

Fortune although blind, yet by chaunce favouring this just cause, sent them within six dayes a good gale of winde; which Franion seeing fit for their purpose,

to put Pandosto out of suspition, the night before
they should sayle, he went to him, and promised,
that the next day he would put the device in practise, for he had got such a forcible poyson, as the
very smell thereof wold procure suddain death. Pandosto was joyfull to heare this good newes, and
thought every houre a day, till he might be glutted
with bloudy revenge; but his suit had but ill successe. For Egistus fearing that delay might breede
danger, and willing that the grass should not be cut
from under his feete, taking bagge and baggage, by
the helpe of Franion, conveied himselfe and his men
out of a posterne gate of the Cittie, so secretly and
speedily that without any suspition they got to the
Sea shoare; where, with many a bitter curse taking
their leave of Bohemia, they went aboord. Weighing
their Anchors and hoisting sayle, they passed as fast
as wind and sea would permit towards Sycilia:
Egistus being a joyfull man that he had safely past
such treacherous perils. But as they were quietly
floating on the sea, so Pandosto and his Cittizens were
in an oproare; for seeing that the Sycilians without
taking their leave, were fled away by night, the
Bohemians feared some treason, and the King
thought that without question his suspition was true,
seeing the Cup-bearer had bewrayed the sum of his
secret pretence. Whereupon he began to imagine
that Franion and his wife Bellaria had conspired with
Egistus, and that the fervent affection shee bare him,
was the onely meanes of his secret departure; in so
much that incensed with rage, he commaunded that
his wife should be carried straight to prison, untill
they heard further of his pleasure. The Guarde unwilling to lay their hands one such a vertuous Princesse, and yet fearing the Kings fury, went very
sorrowfull to fulfill their charge: comming to the
Queenes lodging, they found her playing with her

yong sonne Garinter: unto whom with teares doing the message, Bellaria astonished at such a hard censure, and finding her cleere conscience a sure advocate to pleade in her cause, went to the prison most willingly: where with sighes and teares shee past away the time, till she might come to her triall.

But Pandosto whose reason was suppressed with rage, and whose unbridled follie was incensed with fury: seeing Franion had bewrayed his secrets, and that Egistus might well be rayled on, but not revenged: determined to wreake all his wrath on poore Bellaria. He therefore caused a generall proclamation to be made through all his Realme, that the Queene and Egistus had by the helpe of Franion, not onely committed most incestuous adultery, but also had conspired the Kings death; whereupon the Traitor Franion was fled away with Egistus, and Bellaria was most justly imprisoned. This proclamation being once blazed through the country, although the vertuous disposition of the Queene did halfe discredit the contents, yet the suddaine and speedy passage of Egistus, and the secret departure of Franion, induced them (the circumstances throughly considered) to thinke that both the proclamation was true, and the King greatly injured: yet they pityed her case, as sorrowful that so good a Lady should be crossed with such adverse fortune. But the King, whose restlesse rage would remit no pitty, thought that although he might sufficiently requite his wives falshood with the bitter plague of pinching penury, yet his minde should never be glutted with revenge, till he might have fit time and opportunity to repay the treachery of Egistus with a totall injury. But a curst Cow hath oftentimes short hornes, and a willing minde but a weake arme. For Pandosto although he felt that revenge was a spurre to warre, and that envy alwaies proffereth steele, yet he saw, that Egistus was not onely of great puissance and prowesse to withstand him, but had also many Kings of his alliance to ayde him, if neede should serve: for he married the Emperours daughter of Russia. These and the like considerations something daunted Pandosto his courage, so that hee was content rather to put up a manifest injurie with peace, then hunt after revenge, dishonor and losse; determining since Egistus had escaped scot-free, that Bellaria should pay for all at an unreasonable price.

Remayning thus resolute in his determination, Bellaria continuing still in prison and hearing the contents of the Proclamation, knowing that her minde was never touched with such affection, nor that Egistus had ever offered her such discurtesie, would gladly have come to her answere, that both shee might have knowne her just accusers, and cleared her selfe of that guiltlesse crime.

But Pandosto was so inflamed with rage, and infected with Jelousie, as he would not vouchsafe to heare her, nor admit any just excuse; so that shee was faine to make a vertue of her neede and with patience to beare those heavie injuries. As thus shee lay crossed with calamities (a great cause to increase her griefe) she found her selfe quicke with childe: which as soone as she felt stirre in her body, she burst forth into bitter teares, exclayming against fortune in these termes.

Alas, Bellaria, how infortunate art thou, because fortunate: Better thou hadst beene borne a beggar, then a Prince, so shouldest thou have bridled Fortune with want, where now shee sporteth her selfe with thy plentie. Ah happy life, where poore thoughts, and meane desires live in secure content, not fearing Fortune because too low for Fortune.[1] Thou seest

---

[1] [Edit. 1588 reads, "too low. For Fortune, thou seest now," &c.; but the passage is wrongly pointed.]

now, Bellaria that care is a companion to honor, not to povertie; that high Cedars are crushed with tempests, when low shrubs are not touched with the winde; pretious Diamonds are cut with the file, when despised pibbles lye safe in the sand. Delphos is sought to by Princes, not beggers: and Fortunes Altars smoke with kings presents, not with poore mens gifts. Happie are such Bellaria, that curse Fortune for contempt, not feare: and may wish they were, not sorrow they have beene. Thou art a Princesse Bellaria, and yet a prisoner; borne to the one by descent, assigned to the other by dispite: accused without cause, and therefore oughtest to dye without care: for patience is a shield against Fortune, and a guiltlesse minde yeeldeth not to sorrow. Ah but infamy galleth unto death, and liveth after death: Report is plumed with times feathers, and Envie oftentimes soundeth Fames trumpet: the suspected adultery shall fly in the ayre, and thy knowne vertues shall lye hid in the Earth; one Moale staineth a whole Face: and what is once spotted with infamy can hardly be worne out with time. Die then Bellaria, Bellaria die: for if the Gods should say thou art guiltlesse, yet envie would heare the Gods, but never beleeve the Gods. Ah haplesse wretch, cease these tearmes: desperate thoughtes are fit for them that feare shame, not for such as hope for credite. Pandosto hath darkened thy fame, but shall never discredite thy vertues. Suspition may enter a false action, but proofe shall never put in his plea: care not then for envie, sith report hath a blister on her tongue: and let sorrow baite them which offend, not touch thee that art faultlesse. But alas poore soule, how canst thou but sorrow? Thou art with childe, and by him, that in steed of kind pittie, pincheth thee in cold prison.

And with that, such gasping sighes so stopping her

breath, that shee could not utter more words, but wringing her hands, and gushing forth streames of teares, shee passed away the time with bitter complaints. The Jaylor pitying those her heavie passions, thinking that if the King knew she were with childe, he would somewhat appease his fury and release her from prison, went in al hast, and certified Pandosto, what the effect of Bellarias complaint was ; who no sooner heard the Jailor say she was with childe, but as one possessed with a phranzie, he rose up in a rage, swearing that shee and the basterd brat she was [big] withall should die, if the Gods themselves said no ; thinking that surely by computation of time, that Egistus and not he was father to the childe. This suspitious thought galled a fresh this halfe healed sore, in so much as he could take no rest, untill he might mittigate his choller with a just revenge, which happened presently after. For Bellaria was brought to bed of a faire and beautifull daughter : which no sooner Pandosto hearde, but he determined that both Bellaria and the young infant should be burnt with fire. His Nobles, hearing of the kings cruell sentence, sought by perswasions to divert him from his bloodie determination : laying before his face the innocencie of the childe, and vertuous disposition of his wife, how she had continually loved and honoured him so tenderly, that without due proofe he could not, nor ought not to appeach her of that crime. And if she had faulted, yet it were more honourable to pardon with mercy, then to punish with extremity, and more kingly, to be commended of pitty, than accused of rigour : and as for the childe, if he should punish it for the mothers offence, it were to strive against nature and justice ; and that unnatural actions doe more offend the Gods then men : how causelesse cruelty, nor innocent blood never scapes without revenge. These and such like reasons could not appease his rage, but he rested resolute in this, that Bellaria beeing an Adultresse, the childe was a Bastard, and he would not suffer that such an infamous brat should call him Father. Yet at last (seeing his Noble men were importunate upon him) he was content to spare the childes life, and yet to put it to a worse death. For he found out this devise, that seeing (as he thought) it came by fortune, so he would commit it to the charge of Fortune, and therefore caused a little cock-boat to be provided, wherein he meant to put the babe, and then send it to the mercies of the Seas and the destenies. From this his Peeres in no wise could perswade him, but that he sent presently two of his guard to fetch the childe: who being come to the prison, and with weeping teares recounting their Maisters message: Bellaria no sooner heard the rigorious resolution of her mercilesse husband, but she fell downe in a swound, so that all thought she had bin dead: yet at last being come to her selfe, shee cryed and screeched out in this wise.

Alas sweete infortunate babe, scarce borne, before envied by fortune, would the day of thy birth had beene the terme of thy life: then shouldest thou have made an ende to care and prevented thy Fathers rigour. Thy faults cannot yet deserve such hatefull revenge, thy dayes are too short for so sharpe a doome, but thy untimely death must pay thy Mothers Debts, and her guiltlesse crime must bee thy gastly curse. And shalt thou, sweete babe be committed to Fortune, when thou art already spited by Fortune? Shall the Seas be thy harbour, and the hard boate thy cradle? Shall thy tender Mouth, in steede of sweete kisses, be nipped with bitter stormes? Shalt thou have the whistling windes for thy Lullabie, and the salt Sea fome in steede of sweete milke? Alas, what destinies would assigne such hard hap? What Father would be so cruell? or what Gods will not revenge such rigor? Let me kisse thy lippes (sweete Infant) and wet thy tender cheekes with my teares, and put this chayne about thy necke, that if fortune save thee, it may helpe to succour thee. This,[1] since thou must goe to surge in the gastfull Seas, with a sorrowfull kisse I bid thee farewell, and I pray the Gods thou maist fare well.

Such, and so great was her griefe, that her vitall spirits being suppressed with sorrow, she fell againe downe into a trance, having her sences so sotted with care, that after she was revived yet shee lost her memorie, and lay for a great time without moving, as one in a trance. The guard left her in this perplexitie, and carried the child to the King, who quite devoide of pity commanded that without delay it should bee put in the boat, having neither saile nor rudder to guid it, and so to bee carried into the midst of the sea, and there left to the wind and wave as the destinies please to appoint. The very shipmen, seeing the sweete countenance of the yong babe, began to accuse the King of rigor, and to pity the childs hard fortune: but feare constrayned them to that which their nature did abhorre; so that they placed it in one of the ends of the boat, and with a few green bows made a homely cabben to shrowd it as they could from wind and weather: having thus trimmed the boat they tied it to a ship, and so haled it into the mayne Sea, and then cut in sunder the coarde, which they had no sooner done, but there arose a mighty tempest, which tossed the little Boate so vehemently in the waves, that the shipmen thought it could not long continue without sincking, yea the storme grewe so great, that with much labour and perill they got to the shoare.

But leaving the Childe to her fortunes. Againe to

---

[1] [Thus.]

Pandosto, who not yet glutted with sufficient revenge, devised which way he should best increase his Wives calamitie. But first assembling his Nobles and Counsellors, hee called her for the more reproch into open Court, where it was objected against her, that she had committed adulterie with Egistus, and conspired with Franion to poyson Pandosto her husband, but their pretence being partely spyed, she counselled them to flie away by night for their better safety. Bellaria, who standing like a prisoner at the Barre, feeling in her selfe a cleare Conscience to withstand her false accusers: seeing that no lesse then death could pacifie her husbands wrath, waxed bolde, and desired that she might have Lawe and Justice, for mercy shee neyther craved nor hoped for; and that those perjured wretches, which had falsely accused her to the King, might be brought before her face, to give in evidence. But Pandosto, whose rage and Jealousie was such, no reason, nor equitie could appease: tolde her, that for her accusers they were of such credite, as their wordes were sufficient witnesse, and that the sodaine and secret flight of Egistus and Franion confirmed that which they had confessed: and as for her, it was her parte to deny such a monstrus crime, and to be impudent in forswearing the fact, since shee had past all shame in committing the fault: but her stale countenance should stand for no coyne, for as the Bastard which she bare was served, so she should with some cruell death be requited. Bellaria no whit dismayed with this rough reply, tolde her Husband Pandosto, that he spake upon choller, and not conscience: for her vertuous life had beene ever such, as no spot of suspition could ever staine. And if she had borne a friendly countenaunce to Egistus, it was in respect he was his friende, and not for any lusting affection: therefore if she were condemned without any further proofe, it was rigour, and not Law.

The noble men which sate in judgement, said that Bellaria spake reason, and intreated the king that the accusers might be openly examined, and sworne, and if then the evidence were such, as the Jury might finde her guilty (for seeing she was a Prince she ought to be tryed by her peeres) then let her have such punishment as the extremitie of the Law will assigne to such malefactors. The king presently made answere, that in this case he might, and would dispence with the Law, and that the Jury being once panneld, they should take his word for sufficient evidence, otherwise he would make the proudest of them repent it. The noble men seeing the king in choler were all whist, but Bellaria, whose life then hung in the ballaunce, fearing more perpetuall infamie then momentarie death, tolde the king, if his furie might stand for a Law that it were vaine to have the Jury yeeld their verdit; and therefore she fell downe upon her knees, and desired the king that for the love he bare to his young sonne Garinter, whome she brought into the world, that hee woulde graunt her a request, which was this, that it would please his majestie to send sixe of his noble men whome he best trusted, to the Isle of Delphos, there to enquire of the Oracle of Apollo, whether she had committed adultery with Egistus, or conspired to poyson with Franion: and if the God Apollo, who by his devine essence knew al secrets, gave answere that she was guiltie, she were content to suffer any torment, were it never so terrible. The request was so reasonable, that Pandosto could not for shame deny it, unlesse he would bee counted of all his subjects more wilfull then wise, he therefore agreed, that with as much speede as might be there should be certaine Embassadores dispatched to the Ile of Delphos; and in the meane season he commanded that his wife should be kept in close prison.

Bellaria having obtained this graunt was now more

carefull for her little babe that floated on the Seas, then sorrowful for her owne mishap. For of that she doubted: of her selfe shee was assured, knowing if Apollo should give Oracle according to the thoughts of the hart, yet the sentence should goe one her side, such was the clearenes of her minde in this case. But Pandosto (whose suspitious heade still remained in one song) chose out six of his Nobility, whom hee knew were scarse indifferent men in the Queenes behalfe, and providing all things fit for their journey, sent them to Delphos: they willing to fulfill the Kinges commaund, and desirous to see the situation and custome of the Iland, dispatched their affaires with as much speede as might be, and embarked themselves to this voyage, which (the wind and weather serving fit for their purpose) was soone ended. For within three weekes they arrived at Delphos, where they were no sooner set on lande, but with great devotion they went to the Temple of Apollo, and there offring sacrifice to the GOD, and giftes to the Priest, as the custome was, they humbly craved an aunswere of their demaund: they had not long kneeled at the Altar, but Apollo with a loude voice saide: Bohemians, what you finde behinde the Alter take and depart. They forthwith obeying the Oracle founde a scroule of parchment, wherein was written these words in letters of Golde,—

THE ORACLE.

SUSPITION IS NO PROOFE: JEALOUSIE IS AN UNEQUALL JUDGE: BELLARIA IS CHAST; EGISTUS BLAMELESSE: FRANION A TRUE SUBJECT; PANDOSTO TREACHEROUS: HIS BABE AN INNOCENT, AND THE KING SHAL LIVE WITHOUT AN HEIRE: IF THAT WHICH IS LOST BE NOT FOUNDE.

As soone as they had taken out this scroule, the Priest of the God commaunded them that they should not presume to read it, before they came in the presence of Pandosto: unlesse they would incurre the displeasure of Apollo. The Bohemian Lords carefully obeying his commaund, taking their leave of the Priest, with great reverence departed out of the Temple, and went to their ships, and assoone as wind would permit them, sailed toward Bohemia, whither in short time they safely arrived, and with great tryumph issuing out of their Ships went to the Kinges pallace, whom they found in his chamber accompanied with other Noble men: Pandosto no sooner saw them, but with a merrie countenaunce he welcomed them home, asking what newes: they told his Majestie that they had received an aunswere of the God written in a scroule, but with this charge, that they should not read the contents before they came in the presence of the King, and with that they delivered him the parchment: but his Noble men entreated him that sith therein was contayned either the safetie of his Wives life, and honesty, or her death, and perpetuall infamy, that he would have his Nobles and Commons assembled in the judgement Hall, where the Queene brought in as prysoner, should heare the contents: if shee were found guilty by the Oracle of the God, then all should have cause to thinke his rigour proceeded of due desert: if her Grace were found faultlesse, then shee should bee cleared before all, sith she had bene accused openly. This pleased the King so, that he appointed the day, and assembled al his Lords and Commons, and caused the Queene to be brought in before the judgement seat, commaunding that the inditement shoulde bee read, wherein she was accused of adultery with Egistus, and of conspiracy with Franion: Bellaria hearing the contentes, was no whit astonished, but made this chearefull aunswer:

If the devine powers bee privy to humane actions (as no doubt they are) I hope my patience shall make fortune blushe, and my unspotted life shall staine spightful discredit. For although lying Report hath sought to appeach mine honor, and Suspition hath intended to soyle my credit with infamie: yet where Vertue keepeth the Forte, Report and suspition may assayle, but never sack: how I have led my life before Egistus comming, I appeale Pandosto to the Gods and to thy conscience. What hath past betwixt him and me, the Gods only know, and I hope will presently reveale: that I loved Egistus I can not denie: that I honored him I shame not to confesse: to the one I was forced by his vertues, to the other for his dignities. But as touching lascivious lust, I say Egistus is honest, and hope my selfe to be found without spot: for Franion, I can neither accuse him nor excuse him, for I was not privie to his departure, and that this is true which I have heere rehearsed, I referre myself to the devine Oracle.

Bellaria had no sooner sayd, but the King commaunded that one of his Dukes should read the contentes of the scroule; which after the commons had heard, they gave a great showt, rejoysing and clapping their hands that the Queene was cleare of that false accusation: but the king whose conscience was a witnesse against him of his witlesse furie, and false suspected Iealousie, was so ashamed of his rashe folly, that he entreated his nobles to perswade Bellaria to forgive, and forget these injuries: promising not onely to shew himselfe a loyall and loving husband, but also to reconcile himselfe to Egistus, and Franion: revealing then before them all the cause of their secrete flighte, and how treacherously hee thought to have practised his death, if the good minde of his Cupbearer had not prevented his purpose. As thus he was relating the whole matter, there was worde brought him that his young sonne Garinter was sodainly dead, which newes so soone as Bellaria heard, surcharged before with extreame joy, and now suppressed with heavie sorrowe, her vital spirites were so stopped, that she fell downe presently dead, and could never be revived. This sodaine sight so appalled the Kings Sences, that he sancke from his seat in a sound, so as he was fayne to be carried by his nobles to his Pallace, where hee lay by the space of three dayes without speech: his commons were as men in dispaire, so diversely distressed: there was nothing but mourning and lamentation to be heard throughout al Bohemia: their young Prince dead, their vertuous Queene bereaved of her life, and their King and Soveraigne in great hazard: this tragicall discourse of fortune so daunted them, as they went like shadowes, not men; yet somewhat to comfort their heavie hearts, they heard that Pandosto was come to himselfe, and had recovered his speache, who as in a fury brayed out these bitter speaches:

O miserable Pandosto, what surer witnesse then conscience? what thoughts more sower then suspition? What plague more bad then Iealousie? Unnaturall actions offend the Gods more than men, and causelesse crueltie never scapes without revenge: I have committed such a bloudy fact, as repent I may, but recall I cannot. Ah Iealousie, a hell to the minde, and a horror to the conscience, suppressing reason, and inciting rage; a worse passion then phrensie, a greater plague than madnesse. Are the Gods just? Then let them revenge such brutishe crueltie: my innocent Babe I have drowned in the Seas; my loving wife I have slaine with slaunderous suspition; my trusty friend I have sought to betray, and yet the Gods are slacke to plague such offences. Ah unjust Apollo, Pandosto is the man that hath committed the faulte: why should Garinter, seely childe, abide the paine? Well sith the Gods meane to prolong my dayes, to increase my dolour, I will offer my guiltie bloud a sacrifice to those sackles[1] soules, whose lives are lost by my rigorous folly.

And with that he reached at a Rapier, to have murdered himselfe, but his Peeres being present, stayed him from such a bloudy acte: perswading him to think, that the Commonwealth consisted on his safetie, and that those sheep could not but perish, that wanted a sheepheard; wishing that if hee would not live for himselfe, yet he should have care of his subjects, and to put such fancies out of his minde, sith in sores past help, salves do not heale, but hurt: and in things past cure, care is a corrosive:[2] with these and such like perswasions the Kinge was overcome, and began somewhat to quiet his minde: so that assoone as he could goe abroad, hee caused his wife to be embalmed, and wrapt in lead with her young sonne Garinter; erecting a rich and famous Sepulchre, wherein hee intombed them both, making such solemn obsequies at her funeral, as al Bohemia might perceive he did greatly repent him of his forepassed folly: causing this Epitaph to be ingraven on her Tombe in letters of Gold:

¶ The Epitaph.

HERE LYES ENTOMBDE BELLARIA FAIRE,
FALSLY ACCUSED TO BE UNCHASTE:
CLEARED BY APPOLLOS SACRED DOOME,
YET SLAINE BY JEALOUSIE AT LAST.

WHAT ERE THOU BE THAT PASSEST BY,
CURSSE HIM, THAT CAUSDE THIS QUEENE TO DIE.

This epitaph being ingraven, Pandosto would once a day repaire to the Tombe, and there with watry plaintes bewaile his misfortune; coveting no other companion but sorrowe, nor no other harmonie, but repentance. But leaving him to his dolorous passions,

---

[1] [Guiltless.]   [2] [*Corrasive* in text.]

at last let us come to shewe the tragicall discourse of the young infant.

Who beeing tossed with Winde, and Wave, floated two whole daies without succour, readie at every puffe to bee drowned in the Sea, till at last the Tempest ceassed and the little boate was driven with the tyde into the Coast of Sycilia, where sticking uppon the sandes it rested. Fortune minding to be wanton, willing to shewe that as she hath wrinckles on her browes : so shee hath dimples in her cheekes ; thought after so many sower lookes, to lend a fayned smile, and after a puffing storme, to bring a pretty calme : shee began thus to dally. It fortuned a poore mercenary Sheepheard, that dwelled in Sycilia, who got his living by other mens flockes, missed one of his sheepe, and thinking it had strayed into the covert, that was hard by, sought very diligently to find that which he could not see, fearing either that the Wolves or Eagles had undone him (for hee was so poore, as a sheepe was halfe his substaunce), wandered downe toward the Sea cliffes, to see if perchaunce the sheepe was browsing on the sea Ivy, whereon they greatly doe feede, but not finding her there, as he was ready to returne to his flocke, hee heard a child crie : but knowing there was no house nere, he thought he had mistaken the sound, and that it was the bleatyng of his Sheepe. Wherefore looking more narrowely, as he cast his eye to the Sea, he spyed a little boate, from whence as he attentively listened, he might heare the cry to come : standing a good while in a maze, at last he went to the shoare, and wading to the boate, as he looked in, he saw the little babe lying al alone, ready to die for hunger and colde, wrapped in a Mantle of Scarlet, richely imbrodered with Golde, and having a chayne about the necke.

The Sheepeheard, who before had never seene so faire a Babe, nor so riche Iewels, thought assuredly,

that it was some little God, and began with great
devocion to knock on his breast. The Babe, who
wrythed with the head, to seeke for the pap, began
againe to cry a fresh, whereby the poore man knew
that it was a Childe, which by some sinister meanes
was driven thither by distresse of weather; marvailing
how such a seely infant, which by the Mantle, and the
Chayne, could not be but borne of Noble Parentage,
should be so hardly crossed with deadly mishap. The
poore sheepheard perplexed thus with divers thoughts,
tooke pitty of the childe, and determined with himselfe to carry it to the King, that there it might be
brought up, according to the worthinesse of birth; for
his ability coulde not afforde to foster it, though his
good minde was willing to further it. Taking therefore the Chylde in his armes, as he foulded the mantle
together, the better to defend it from colde, there fell
downe at his foote a very faire and riche purse, wherein
he founde a great summe of golde: which sight so
revived the shepheards spirits, as he was greatly
ravished with joy, and daunted with feare; Ioyfull to
see such a summe in his power, and fearefull if it
should be knowne, that it might breede his further
daunger. Necessitie wisht him at the least, to retaine
the Golde, though he would not keepe the childe: the
simplicity of his conscience scared him from such
deceiptfull briberie. Thus was the poore manne perplexed with a doubtfull Dilemma, until at last the
covetousnesse of the coyne overcame him: for what
will not the greedy desire of Golde cause a man to
doe? So that he was resolved in himselfe to foster
the child, and with the summe to relieve his want:
resting thus resolute in this point he left seeking of
his sheepe, and as covertly, and secretly as he coulde,
went by a by way to his house, least any of his neighbours should perceave his carriage: as soone as he
was got home, entring in at the doore, the childe be-

gan to crie, which his wife hearing, and seeing her
husband with a yong babe in his armes, began to bee
somewhat jelousse, yet marveiling that her husband
should be so wanton abroad, sith he was so quiet at
home : but as women are naturally given to beleeve
the worste, so his wife thinking it was some bastard :
beganne to crowe against her goodman, and taking
up a cudgel (for the most maister went breechles)
sware solemnly that shee would make clubs trumps,
if hee brought any bastard brat within her dores.
The goodman, seeing his wife in her majestie with her
mace in her hand, thought it was time to bowe for
feare of blowes, and desired her to be quiet, for there
was non such matter ; but if she could holde her
peace, they were made for ever: and with that he
told her the whole matter, how he had found the
childe in a little boat, without any succour, wrapped
in that costly mantle, and having that rich chaine
about the neck : but at last when he shewed her the
purse full of gold, she began to simper something
sweetely, and taking her husband about the neck,
kissed him after her homely fashion : saying that she
hoped God had seene their want, and now ment to
relieeve their poverty, and seeing they could get no
children, had sent them this little babe to be their
heire. Take heede in any case (quoth the shepherd)
that you be secret, and blabbe it not out when you
meete with your gossippes, for if you doe, we are like
not only to loose the Golde and Iewels, but our other
goodes and lives. Tush (quoth his wife), profit is a
good hatch before the doore: feare not, I have other
things to talke of then of this ; but I pray you let us
lay up the money surely, and the Iewels, least by any
mishap it be spied.

After that they had set all things in order, the shepheard went to his sheepe with a merry note, and the
good wife learned to sing lullaby at home with her

yong babe, wrapping it in a homely blanket in sted of
a rich mantle; nourishing it so clenly and carefully as
it began to bee a jolly girle, in so much that they
began both of them to be very fond of it, seeing, as it
waxed in age, so it increased in beauty. The shepheard every night at his comming home, would sing
and daunce it on his knee, and prattle, that in a short
time it began to speake, and call him Dad, and her
Mam: at last when it grew to ripe yeeres, that it was
about seven yeares olde, the shepheard left keeping of
other mens sheepe, and with the money he found in
the purse, he bought him the lease of a pretty farme,
and got a smal flocke of sheepe, which when Fawnia
(for so they named the child) came to the age of ten
yeres, hee set her to keepe, and shee with such diligence performed her charge as the sheepe prospered
marveilously under her hand. Fawnia thought Porrus
had been her father, and Mopsa her mother, (for so
was the shepheard and his wife called) honoured and
obeyed them with such reverence, that all the neighbours praised the duetifull obedience of the child.
Porrus grewe in a short time to bee a man of some
wealth, and credite; for fortune so favoured him in
having no charge but Fawnia, that he began to purchase land, intending after his death to give it to his
daughter; so that diverse rich farmers sonnes came as
woers to his house: for Fawnia was something clenly
attired, beeing of such singular beautie and excellent
witte, that whoso sawe her, would have thought shee
had bene some heavenly nymph, and not a mortal
creature: in so much, that when she came to the age
of sixteene yeeres, shee so increased with exquisite
perfection both of body and minde, as her natural disposition did bewray that she was borne of some high
parentage; but the people thinking she was daughter
to the shephard Porrus, rested only amazed at hir
beauty and wit; yea she won such favour and com-

mendations in every mans eye, as her beautie was not only praysed in the countrey, but also spoken of in the Court: yet such was her submisse modestie, that although her praise daily increased, her mind was no whit puffed up with pride, but humbled her selfe as became a country mayde and the daughter of a poore sheepheard. Every day she went forth with her sheepe to the field, keeping them with such care and diligence, as al men thought she was verie painfull, defending her face from the heat of the sunne with no other vale, but with a garland made of bowes and flowers; which attire became her so gallantly, as shee seemed to bee the Goddesse Flora her selfe for beauty.

Fortune, who al this while had shewed a frendly face, began now to turne her back, and to shewe a lowring countenance, intending as she had given Fawnia a slender checke, so she would give her a harder mate: to bring which to passe, she layd her traine on this wise. Egistus had but one only son called Dorastus, about the age of twenty yeeres: a prince so decked and adorned with the gifts of nature: so fraught with beauty and vertuous qualities, as not onely his father joyed to have so good a sonne, and al his commons rejoyced that God had lent them such a noble Prince to succeede in the Kingdom. Egistus placing al his joy in the perfection of his sonne: seeing that he was now mariage-able, sent Embassadors to the king of Denmarke, to intreate a mariage betweene him and his daughter, who willingly consenting, made answer, that the next spring, if it please Egistus with his sonne to come into Denmarke, hee doubted not but they should agree upon reasonable conditions. Egistus resting satisfied with this friendly answer, thought convenient in the meane time to breake with his sonne: finding therefore on a day fi opportunity, he spake to him in these fatherly tearmes:

Dorastus, thy youth warneth me to prevent the worst, and mine age to provide the best. Oportunities neglected, are signes of folly: actions measured by time, are seldome bitten with repentance: thou art young, and I olde: age hath taught me that, which thy youth cannot yet conceive. I therefore will counsell thee as a father, hoping thou wilt obey as a childe. Thou seest my white hayres are blossomes for the grave,[1] and thy freshe colour fruite for time and fortune, so that it behooveth me to thinke how to dye, and for thee to care how to live. My crowne I must leave by death, and thou enjoy my Kingdome by succession, wherein I hope thy vertue and prowesse shall bee such, as though my subjectes want my person, yet they shall see in thee my perfection. That nothing either may faile to satisfie thy minde, or increase thy dignities: the onely care I have is to see thee well marryed before I die, and thou become olde.

Dorastus, who from his infancy, delighted rather to die with Mars in the Fielde then to dally with Venus in the Chamber, fearing to displease his father, and yet not willing to be wed, made him this reuerent answere.

Sir, there is no greater bond then duetie, nor no straiter law then nature: disobedience in youth is often galled with despight in age. The commaund of the father ought to be a constraint to the childe: so parentes willes are laws, so they passe not all laws: may it please your Grace therefore to appoint whome I shall love, rather then by deniall I should be appeached of disobedience: I rest content to love, though it bee the only thing I hate.

---

[1] Percy, in his "Reliques," ii. 177, ed. 1812, quotes the following as part of an old song on the story of the Beggar's Daughter of Bethnal Green:—

"His reverend lockes in comelye curles did wave,
And on his aged temples grewe the blossomes of the grave."

Egistus hearing his sonne to flie so farre from the marke, began to be somewhat chollericke, and therefore made him this hastie aunswere.

What Dorastus canst thou not love? Commeth this cynicall passion of prone desires or peevish frowardnesse? What durst thou thinke thy selfe to good for all, or none good inough for thee? I tell thee, Dorastus, there is nothing sweeter then youth, nor swifter decreasing while it is increasing. Time past with folly may bee repented, but not recalled. If thou marrie in age, thy wives freshe couloures will breede in thee dead thoughtes and suspition, and thy white hayres her lothesomnesse and sorrowe. For Venus affections are not fed with Kingdomes, or treasures, but with youthfull conceits and sweet amours. Vulcan was allotted to shake the tree, but Mars allowed to reape the fruite. Yeelde Dorastus to thy Fathers perswasions, which may prevent thy perils. I have chosen thee a Wife, faire by nature, royall by birth, by vertues famous, learned by education and rich by possessions, so that it is hard to judge whether her bounty, or fortune, her beauty, or vertue bee of greater force: I mean, Dorastus, Euphrania daughter and heire to the King of Denmarke.

Egistus pausing here a while, looking when his son should make him answere, and seeing that he stoode still as one in a trance, he shooke him up thus sharply.

Well Dorastus take heede, the tree Alpya wasteth not with fire, but withereth with the dewe: that which love nourisheth not, perisheth with hate: if thou like Euphrania, thou breedest my content, and in loving her thou shalt have my love, otherwise; and with that hee flung from his sonne in a rage, leaving him a sorrowfull man, in that he had by deniall displeased his Father, and halfe angrie with him selfe that hee could not yeelde to that passion, whereto both reason

and his Father perswaded him: but see how fortune
is plumed with times feathers, and how shee can
minister strange causes to breede straunge effects.

It happened not long after this that there was a
meeting of all the Farmers Daughters in Sycilia,
whither Fawnia was also bidden as the mistres of the
feast, who having attired her selfe in her best garments,
went among the rest of her companions to the merry
meeting: there spending the day in such homely
pastimes as shepheards use. As the evening grew on,
and their sportes ceased, ech taking their leave at
other, Fawnia desiring one of her companions to
beare her companie, went home by the flocke, to see
if they were well folded, and as they returned, it
fortuned that Dorastus (who all that daye had bene
hawking, and kilde store of game) incountred by the
way these two mayds, and casting his eye sodenly
on Fawnia, he was halfe afraid, fearing that with
Acteon he had seene Diana: for hee thought such
exquisite perfection could not be founde in any mortall
creature. As thus he stoode in a maze, one of his
Pages told him, that the maide with the garland on
her heade was Fawnia, the faire shepheard, whose
beauty was so much talked of in the Court. Dorastus
desirous to see if nature had adorned her minde with
any inward qualities, as she had decked her body
with outward shape, began to question with her whose
daughter she was, of what age and how she had bin
trained up, who answered him with such modest
reverence and sharpnesse of witte, that Dorastus
thought her outward beautie was but a counterfait to
darken her inward qualities, wondring how so courtly
behaviour could be found in so simple a cottage, and
cursing fortune that had shadowed wit and beauty
with such hard fortune. As thus he held her a long
while with chat, Beauty seeing him at discovert,
thought not to lose the vantage, but strooke him so

deeply with an invenomed shafte, as he wholy lost his libertie, and became a slave to Love, which before contemned love, glad now to gaze on a poore shepheard, who before refused the offer of a riche Princesse; for the perfection of Fawnia had so fired his fancie as he felt his minde greatly chaunged, and his affections altered, cursing Love that had wrought such a chaunge, and blaming the basenesse of his mind, that would make such a choice: but thinking these were but passionat toies that might be thrust out at pleasure, to avoid the Syren that inchaunted him, he put spurs to his horse, and bad this faire shepheard farewell.

Fawnia (who all this while had marked the princely gesture of Dorastus) seeing his face so wel featured, and each lim so perfectly framed, began greatly to praise his perfection, commending him so long, till she found her selfe faultie, and perceived that if she waded but a little further, she might slippe over her shooes: shee therefore seeking to quench that fire which never was put out, went home, and faining her selfe not well at ease, got her to bed: where casting a thousand thoughts in her head, she could take no rest: for if she waked, she began to call to minde his beautie, and thinking to beguile such thoughts with sleepe, she then dreamed of his perfection: pestered thus with these unacquainted passions, she passed the night as she could in short slumbers.

Dorastus (who all this while rode with a flea in his eare) could not by any meanes forget the sweete favour of Fawnia, but rested so bewitched with her wit and beauty, as hee could take no rest. He felt fancy to give the assault, and his wounded mind readie to yeeld as vanquished: yet he began with divers considerations to suppresse this frantick affection, calling to minde, that Fawnia was a shepheard, one not worthy to bee looked at of a Prince, much less to bee loved of such a potentate, thinking what a discredite it were to himself, and what a griefe it would be to his father, blaming fortune and accusing his owne follie, that should bee so fond as but once to cast a glaunce at such a country slut. As thus he was raging against him selfe, Love fearing if shee dallied long, to loose her champion, stept more nigh, and gave him such a fresh wounde as it pearst him at the heart, that he was faine to yeeld, maugre his face, and to forsake the companie and gette him to his chamber: where being solemnly set, hee burst into these passionate tearmes.

Ah, Dorastus, art thou alone? No not alone, while thou art tired with these unacquainted passions. Yeld to fancy, thou canst not by thy fathers counsaile, but in a frenzie thou art by just destinies. Thy father were content, if thou couldest love, and thou therefore discontent, because thou doest love. O devine Love, feared of men because honoured of the Gods, not to be suppressed by wisdome, because not to be comprehended by reason: without Lawe, and therefore above all Law. How now Dorastus, why doest thou blaze that with praises, which thou hast cause to blaspheme with curses? yet why should they curse Love that are in Love? Blush Dorastus at thy fortune, thy choice, thy love: thy thoughts cannot be uttered without shame, nor thy affections without discredit. Ah Fawnia, sweete Fawnia, thy beautie Fawnia. Shamest not thou Dorastus to name one unfitte for thy birth, thy dignities, thy Kingdomes? Dye Dorastus, Dorastus die. Better hadst thou perish with high desires, then live in base thoughts. Yea but, beautie must be obeyed, because it is beauty, yet framed of the Gods to feede the eye, not to fetter the heart. Ah but he that striveth against Love, shooteth with them of Scyrum against the wind, and with the Cockeatrice pecketh against the steele. I will therefore obey, because I must obey. Fawnia, yea Fawnia shall be my fortune, in spight of fortune. The Gods above disdain not to love women beneath. Phœbus liked Sibilla, Jupiter Io, and why not I then Fawnia? one something inferiour to these in birth, but farre superiour to them in beautie, borne to be a Shepheard, but worthy to be a Goddesse. Ah Dorastus, wilt thou so forget thy selfe as to suffer affection to suppresse wisedome, and Love to violate thine honour? How sower will thy choice be to thy Father, sorrowfull to thy Subjects, to thy friends a griefe, most gladsome to thy foes! Subdue then thy affections, and cease to love her whome thou couldst not love, unlesse blinded with too much love. Tushe I talke to the wind, and in seeking to prevent the causes, I further the effectes. I will yet praise Fawnia; honour, yea and love Fawnia, and at this day followe content, not counsaile. Doo Dorastus, thou canst but repent: and with that his Page came into the chamber, whereupon hee ceased from his complaints, hoping that time would weare out that which fortune had wrought. As thus he was pained, so poore Fawnia was diversly perplexed: for the next morning getting up very earely, she went to her sheepe, thinking with hard labours to passe away her new conceived amours, beginning very busily to drive them to the field, and then to shifte the foldes, at last (wearied with toile) she sate her down, where (poore soule) she was more tryed with fond affections: for love beganne to assault her, in so much that as she sate upon the side of a hill, she began to accuse her owne folly in these tearmes.

Infortunate Fawnia, and therefore infortunate because Fawnia, thy shepherds hooke sheweth thy poore state, thy proud desires an aspiring mind: the one declareth thy want, the other thy pride. No bastard hauke must soare so high as the Hobbie, no

Fowle gaze against the Sunne but the Eagle, actions wrought against nature reape despight, and thoughts above Fortune disdaine. Fawnia, thou art a shepheard, daughter to poore Porrus: if thou rest content with this, thou art like to stande, if thou climbe thou art sure to fal. The Herb Anita growing higher then sixe ynches becommeth a weede. Nylus flowing more then twelve cubits procureth a dearth. Daring affections that passe measure, are cut shorte by time or fortune: suppresse then Fawnia those thoughts which thou mayest shame to expresse. But ah Fawnia, love is a Lord, who will commaund by power, and constraine by force. Dorastus, ah Dorastus is the man I love, the woorse is thy hap, and the lesse cause hast thou to hope. Will Eagles catch at flyes, will Cedars stoupe to brambles, or mighty Princes looke at such homely trulles? No, no, thinke this, Dorastus disdaine is greater then thy desire, hee is a Prince respecting his honour, thou a beggars brat forgetting thy calling. Cease then not onely to say, but to thinke to love Dorastus, and dissemble thy love Fawnia, for better it were to dye with griefe, then to live with shame: yet in despight of love I will sigh, to see if I can sigh out love.

Fawnia somewhat appeasing her griefes with these pithie perswasions, began after her wonted maner to walke about her sheepe, and to keepe them from straying into the corne, suppressing her affection with the due consideration of her base estate, and with the impossibilities of her love, thinking it were frenzy, not fancy, to covet that which the very destinies did deny her to obteine.

But Dorastus was more impatient in his passions; for love so fiercely assayled him, that neither companie, nor musicke could mittigate his martirdome, but did rather far the more increase his maladie: shame would not let him crave counsaile in this case,

nor feare of his Fathers displeasure reveyle it to any
secrete friend; but hee was faine to make a Secretarie
of himselfe, and to participate his thoughtes with his
owne troubled mind. Lingring thus awhile in doubtfull suspence, at last stealing secretely from the court
without either men or Page, hee went to see if hee
could espie Fawnia walking abroade in the field; but
as one having a great deale more skill to retrive the
partridge with his spaniels, then to hunt after such
a straunge pray, he sought, but was little the better:
which crosse lucke drave him into a great choler, that
he began to accuse love and fortune. But as he was
readie to retire, he sawe Fawnia sitting all alone under
the side of a hill, making a garland of such homely
flowres as the fields did afoord. This sight so revived
his spirites that he drewe nigh, with more judgement
to take a view of her singular perfection, which hee
found to bee such as in that countrey attyre she
stained al the courtlie Dames of Sicilia. While thus
he stoode gazing with pearcing lookes on her surpassing beautie, Fawnia cast her eye aside, and spyed
Dorastus, with sudden sight made the poore girle to
blush, and to die her christal cheeks with a vermilion
red; which gave her such a grace, as she seemed farre
more beautiful. And with that she rose up, saluting the
Prince with such modest curtesies, as he wondred how
a country maid could afoord such courtly behaviour.
Dorastus, repaying her curtesie with a smiling countenance, began to parlie with her on this manner.

Faire maide (quoth he) either your want is great, or
a shepheards life very sweete, that your delight is in
such country labors. I can not conceive what pleasure
you should take, unless you meane to imitate the
nymphes, being yourself so like a Nymph. To put me
out of this doubt, shew me what is to be commended
in a shepherdes life, and what pleasures you have to
countervaile these drudging laboures.

Fawnia with blushing face made him this ready aunswere. Sir, what richer state then content, or what sweeter life then quiet? we shepheards are not borne to honor, nor beholding unto beautie, the less care we have to feare fame or fortune: we count our attire brave inough if warme inough, and our foode dainty, if to suffice nature: our greatest enemie is the wolfe; our onely care in safe keeping our flock: in stead of courtlie ditties we spend the daies with cuntry songs: our amorous conceites are homely thoughtes; delighting as much to talke of Pan and his cuntrey prankes, as Ladies to tell of Venus and her wanton toyes. Our toyle is in shifting the fouldes, and looking to the Lambes, easie labours: oft singing and telling tales, homely pleasures; our greatest welth not to covet, our honor not to climbe, our quiet not to care. Envie looketh not so lowe as shepheards: Shepheards gaze not so high as ambition: we are rich in that we are poore with content,[1] and proud onely in this, that we have no cause to be proud.

This wittie aunswer of Fawnia so inflamed Dorastus fancy, as he commended him selfe for making so good a choyce, thinking, if her birth were aunswerable to her wit and beauty, that she were a fitte mate for the most famous Prince in the worlde. He therefore beganne to sifte her more narrowely on this manner.

Fawnia, I see thou art content with Country labours, because thou knowest not Courtly pleasures: I commend thy wit, and pitty thy want: but wilt thou leave thy Fathers Cottage and serve a Courtlie Mistresse?

Sir (quoth she) beggers ought not to strive against fortune, nor to gaze after honour, least either their fall be greater, or they become blinde. I am borne to toile for the Court, not in the Court, my nature unfit

---

[1] "Poor and content is rich, and rich enough."
—"Othello," iii. 3.

for their nurture : better live then in meane degree, than in high disdaine.

Well saide, Fawnia (quoth Dorastus) I gesse at thy thoughtes ; thou art in love with some Countrey Shephearde,

No sir (quoth she) shepheards cannot love, that are so simple, and maides may not love that are so young.

Nay therefore (quoth Dorastus) maides must love, because they are young, for Cupid is a child, and Venus, though olde, is painted with fresh coloures.

I graunt (quoth she) age may be painted with new shadowes, and youth may have imperfect affections ; but what arte concealeth in one, ignorance revealeth in the other. Dorastus seeing Fawnia held him so harde, thought it was vaine so long to beate about the bush : therefore he thought to have given her a fresh charge ; but he was prevented by certaine of his men, who missing their maister, came posting to seeke him ; seeing that he was gone foorth all alone, yet before they drewe so nie that they might heare their talke, he used these speeches.

Why Fawnia, perhappes I love thee, and then thou must needes yeelde, for thou knowest I can commaunde and constraine. Trueth sir (quoth she) but not to love ; for constrained love is force, not love : and know this sir, mine honesty is such, as I hadde rather dye then be a concubine even to a King, and my birth is so base as I am unfitte to bee a wife to a poore farmer. Why then (quoth he) thou canst not love Dorastus. Yes saide Fawnia, when Dorastus becomes a shepheard, and with that the presence of his men broke off their parle, so that he went with them to the palace and left Fawnia sitting still on the hill side, who seeing that the night drewe on, shifted her fouldes, and busied her selfe about other worke to drive away such fond fancies as began to trouble her braine. But all this could not prevaile, for the beautie of Dorastus had made such a deepe impression in her heart, as it could not be worne out without cracking, so that she was forced to blame her owne folly in this wise.

Ah Fawnia, why doest thou gaze against the Sunne, or catch at the Winde? starres are to be looked at with the eye, not reacht at with the hande:[1] thoughts are to be measured by Fortunes, not by desires: falles come not by sitting low, but by climing too hie: what then shal al feare to fal, because some happe to fall? No luck commeth by lot, and fortune windeth those threedes which the destinies spin. Thou art favored Fawnia of a prince, and yet thou art so fond to reject desired favours: thou hast deniall at thy tonges end, and desire at thy hearts bottome; a womans fault, to spurne at that with her foote, which she greedily catcheth at with her hand. Thou lovest Dorastus, Fawnia, and yet seemest to lower. Take heede, if hee retire thou wilt repent; for unles hee love, thou canst but dye. Dye then Fawnia; for Dorastus doth but jest: the Lyon never prayeth on the mouse, nor Faulcons stoupe not to dead stales. Sit downe then in sorrow, ceasse to love, and content thy selfe, that Dorastus will vouchsafe to flatter Fawnia, though not to fancy Fawnia. Heigh ho! Ah foole, it were seemelier for thee to whistle as a Shepheard, then to sigh as a lover. And with that she ceassed from these perplexed passions, folding her sheepe, and hying home to her poore Cottage.

But such was the incessant sorrow of Dorastus to thinke on the witte and beautie of Fawnia, and to see how fond hee was being a Prince; and how froward

---

[1] " Wilt thou reach stars, because they shine on thee?"
—" Two Gentlemen of Verona," iii. 1.

she was being a beggar, then he began to loose his
wonted appetite, to looke pale and wan; instead of
mirth, to feede on melancholy; for courtly daunces
to use cold dumpes; in so much that not onely his
owne men, but his father and all the court began to
marvaile at his sudden change, thinking that some
lingring sickenes had brought him into this state:
wherefore he caused Phisitions to come, but Dorastus
neither would let them minister, nor so much as suffer
them to see his urine; but remained stil so oppressed
with these passions, as he feared in him selfe a farther
inconvenience. His honor wished him to ceasse
from such folly, but Love forced him to follow fancy:
yea and in despight of honour, love wonne the conquest,
so that his hot desires caused him to find new devises,
for hee presently made himselfe a shepheards coate,
that he might goe unknowne, and with the lesse suspition to prattle with Fawnia, and conveied it secretly
into a thick grove hard joyning to the Pallace, whether
finding fit time, and opportunity, he went all alone,
and putting off his princely apparel got on those shepheards roabes, and taking a great hooke in his hand
(which he had also gotten) he went very anciently
[sic] to find out the mistres of his affection: but as
he went by the way, seeing himselfe clad in such un-
seemely ragges, he began to smile at his owne folly,
and to reprove his fondnesse, in these tearmes.

Well said Dorastus, thou keepest a right decorum,
base desires and homely attires: thy thoughtes are
fit for none but a shepheard, and thy apparell such as
only become a shepheard. A strange change from a
Prince to a pesant! What is it? thy wretched fortune or thy wilful folly? Is it thy cursed destinies?
Or thy crooked desires, that appointeth thee this pen-
ance? Ah Dorastus thou canst but love, and unlesse
thou love, thou art like to perish for love. Yet fond
foole, choose flowers, not weedes; Diamondes, not

peables; Ladies which may honour thee, not shepheards which may disgrace thee. Venus is painted in silkes, not in ragges; and Cupid treadeth on disdaine, when he reacheth at dignitie. And yet Dorastus shame not at thy shepheards weede: the heavenly Godes have sometime earthly thoughtes: Neptune became a ram, Jupiter a Bul, Apollo a shepheard: they Gods, and yet in love; and thou a man appointed to love.

Devising thus with himselfe, hee drew nigh to the place where Fawnia was keeping her shepe, who casting her eye aside, and seeing such a manerly shepheard, perfectly limmed, and comming with so good a pace, she began halfe to forget Dorastus, and to favor this prety shepheard, whom she thought shee might both love and obtaine: but as shee was in these thoughts, she perceived then, that it was the yong prince Dorastus, wherfore she rose up and reverently saluted him. Dorastus taking her by the hand, repaied her curtesie with a sweet kisse, and praying her to sit downe by him, he began thus to lay the batterie.

If thou marvell Fawnia at my strange attyre, thou wouldest more muse at my unaccustomed thoughtes: the one disgraceth but my outward shape, the other disturbeth my inward sences. I love Fawnia, and therefore what love liketh I cannot mislike. Fawnia thou hast promised to love, and I hope thou wilt performe no lesse: I have fulfilled thy request, and now thou canst but graunt my desire. Thou wert content to love Dorastus when he ceast to be a Prince and to become a shepheard, and see I have made the change, and therefore not to misse of my choice.

Trueth, quoth Fawnia, but all that weare Cooles are not Monkes: painted Eagles are pictures, not Eagles. Zeusis Grapes were like Grapes, yet shadowes: rich clothing make not princes: nor homely attyre beggers: shepheards are not called shepheardes, because they were hookes and bagges, but that they are borne poore, and live to keepe sheepe; so this attire hath not made Dorastus a shepherd, but to seeme like a shepherd.

Well Fawnia, answered Dorastus, were I a shepherd, I could not but like thee, and being a prince I am forst to love thee. Take heed Fawnia be not proud of beauties painting, for it is a flower that fadeth in the blossome. Those which disdayne in youth are despised in age: Beauties shadowes are trickt up with times colours, which being set to drie in the sunne are stained with the sunne, scarce pleasing the sight ere they beginne not to be worth the sight, not much unlike the herbe Ephemeron, which flourisheth in the morning and is withered before the sunne setting: if my desire were against lawe, thou mightest justly deny me by reason; but I love thee Fawnia, not to misuse thee as a Concubine, but to use thee as my wife: I can promise no more, and meane to performe no lesse.

Fawnia hearing this solemne protestation of Dorastus, could no longer withstand the assault, but yeelded up the forte in these friendly tearmes.

Ah Dorastus, I shame to expresse that thou forcest me with thy sugred speeche to confesse: my base birth causeth the one, and thy high dignities the other. Beggars thoughts ought not to reach so far as Kings, and yet my desires reach as high as Princes. I dare not say, Dorastus, I love thee, because I am a shepherd; but the Gods know I have honored Dorastus (pardon if I say amisse) yea and loved Dorastus with such dutiful affection as Fawnia can performe, or Dorastus desire: I yeeld, not overcome with prayers, but with love, resting Dorastus handmaid ready to obey his wil, if no prejudice at all to his honour, nor to my credit.

Dorastus hearing this freendly conclusion of Fawnia embraced her in his armes, swearing that neither distance, time, nor adverse fortune should diminish his affection: but that in despight of the destinies he would remaine loyall unto death. Having thus plight their troath each to other, seeing they could not have the full fruition of their love in Sycilia, for that Egistus consent woulde never bee graunted to so meane a match, Dorastus determined, assone as time and oportunitie would give them leave, to provide a great masse of money, and many rich and costly jewels, for the easier cariage, and then to transporte themselves and their treasure into Italy, where they should leade a contented life, until such time as either he could be reconciled to his Father, or els by sucession come to the Kingdome. This devise was greatly praysed of Fawnia, for she feared if the King his father should but heare of the contract, that his furie would be such as no lesse than death would stand for payment: she therefore tould him, that delay bred daunger: that many mishaps did fall out betweene the cup and the lip, and that to avoid danger, it were best with as much speed as might be to pass out of Sycilia, least fortune might prevent their pretence with some newe despight: Dorastus, whom love pricked forward with desire, promised to dispatch his affaires with as great hast, as either time or oportunitie would geve him leave: and so resting upon this point, after many imbracings and sweete kisses they departed.

Dorastus having taken his leave of his best beloved Fawnia, went to the Grove where hee had his rich apparel, and there uncasing himself as secretly as might be, hiding up his shepheards attire, till occasion should serve againe to use it: he went to the pallace, shewing by his merrie countenaunce, that either the state of his body was amended, or the case of his minde greately redressed: Fawnia poore soule was no less joyful, that being a shepheard, fortune had favoured her so, as to reward her with the love of a Prince, hoping in time to be advaunced from the daughter of a poore farmer to be the wife of a riche King: so that she thought every houre a yeere, till by their departure they might prevent danger, not ceasing still to goe every daye to her sheepe, not so much for the care of her flock, as for the desire she had to see her love and Lord Dorastus: who oftentimes, when oportunitie would serve, repaired thither to feede his fancy with the sweet content of Fawnias presence: and although he never went to visit her, but in his shepheards ragges, yet his ofte repaire made him not onely suspected, but knowne to divers of their neighbours: who for the good will they bare to old Porrus, tould him secretly of the matter, wishing him to keepe his daughter at home, least she went so ofte to the field that she brought him home a yong sonne: for they feared that Fawnia being so beautifull, the yong prince would allure her to folly. Porrus was stricken into a dump at these newes, so that thanking his neighboures for their good will: he hyed him home to his wife, and calling her aside, wringing his handes and shedding foorth teares, he brake the matter to her in these tearmes.

I am afraid wife, that my daughter Fawnia hath made her selfe so fine, that she will buy repentance too deare. I heare newes, which if they be true, some will wish they had not proved true. It is tould me by my neighbours, that Dorastus the Kinges sonne begins to looke at our daughter Fawnia: which if it be so, I will not geve her a halfepeny for her honestie at the yeeres end. I tell thee wife, nowadaies beautie is a great stale to trap yong men, and faire wordes and sweete promises are two great enemies to a maydens honestie: and thou knowest where poore men intreate, and cannot obtaine, there Princes may commaund, and wil obtaine. Though Kings sonnes daunce in nettes, they may not be seene:[1] but poore mens faultes are spied at a little hole: Well, it is a hard case where Kinges lustes are lawes, and that they should binde poore men to that, which they themselves wilfully breake.

Peace husband (quoth his wife) take heede what you say: speake no more than you should, least you heare what you would not: great streames are to be stopped by sleight, not by force: and princes to be perswaded by submission, not by rigor: doe what you can, but no more than you may, least in saving Fawnias mayden-head, you loose your owne head. Take heede I say, it is ill jesting with edged tooles, and bad sporting with Kinges. The Wolfe had his skinne puld over his eares for but looking into the Lions den. Tush wife (quoth he) thou speakest like a foole, if the King should knowe that Dorastus had begotten our daughter with childe (as I feare it will fall out little better) the Kings furie would be such as no doubt we should both loose our goodes and lives: necessitie therefore hath no lawe, and I will prevent this mischiefe with a newe devise that is come into my head, which shall neither offend the King, nor displease Dorastus. I meane to take the chaine and the jewels that I found with Fawnia, and carrie them to the King, letting him then to understand how she is none of my daughter, but that I found her beaten up with the water alone in a little boate wrapped in a riche Mantle, wherein was inclosed this treasure. By

---

[1] Alluding to the old story of the fisherman's daughter, who was ordered to dance before a great lord, so that she might be seen, yet not seen, to effect which she covered herself with one of her father's nets. The Italian fool and jester Gonella for the same purpose is said to have put himself behind a sieve.

this meanes I hope the King will take Fawnia into his service, and we whatsoever chaunceth shal be blamelesse. This device pleased the good wife very well, so that they determined, assoone as they might know the King at leisure, to make him privie to this case.

In the meane time Dorastus was not slacke in his affaires, but applyed his matters with such diligence, that he provided all thinges fitte for their journey. Treasure and Jewels he had gotten great store, thincking there was no better friend then money in a strange countrey: rich attire he had provided for Fawnia, and, because he could not bring the matter to passe without the helpe and advice of some one, he made an old servant of his called Capnio, who had served him from his childhood, privie to his affaires: who seeing no perswasions could prevaile to divert him from his setled determination, gave his consent and dealt so secretly in the cause, that within short space hee had gotten a ship ready for their passage: the Mariners seeing a fit gale of winde for their purpose, wished Capnio to make no delayes, least if they pretermitted this good weather, they might stay long ere they had such a fayre winde. Capnio fearing that his negligence should hinder the journey, in the night time conveyed the trunckes full of treasure into the shippe, and by secrette meanes let Fawnia understand, that the next morning they meant to depart: she upon this newes slept verie little that night, but gotte up very early, and wente to her sheepe, looking every minute when she should see Dorastus, who taried not long, for feare delay might breede daunger, but came as fast as he could gallop, and without any great circumstance took Fawnia up behinde him and rode to the haven, where the shippe lay, which was not three quarters of a mile distant from that place. He no sooner came there, but the Marriners were readie with their Cockboate to set them aboard, where being couch't together in a Cabben they past away the time in recounting their old loves, til their man Capnio should come. Porrus who had heard that this morning the King would go abroad to take the ayre, called in haste to his wife to bring him his holyday hose and his best Iacket, that he might goe like an honest substantiall man to tell his tale. His wife a good cleanly wenche, brought him all things fitte, and spungd him up very handsomlie, giving him the chaines and Iewels in a little boxe, which Porrus for the more safety put in his bosom. Having thus all his trinkets in readines, taking his staffe in his hand he bad his wife kisse him for good lucke, and so hee went towards the Pallace. But as he was going, fortune (who meant to showe him a little false play) prevented his purpose in this wise.

He met by chaunce in his way Capnio, who trudging as fast as he could with a little coffer under his arme to the ship, and spying Porrus whome he knewe to be Fawnias Father, going towardes the Pallace, being a wylie fellow, began to doubt the worst, and therefore crost him the way, and askt him whither he was going so earely this morning. Porrus (who knew by his face that he was one of the Court) meaning simply, told him that the Kings son Dorastus dealt hardly with him; for he had but one daughter who was a little Beautifull, and that his neighboures told him the young Prince had allured her to folly, he went therefore now to complaine to the King how greatly he was abused.

Capnio (who straight way smelt the whole matter) began to soth him in his talke, and said that Dorastus dealt not like a Prince to spoyle any poore manes daughter in that sort: he therefore would doe the best for him he could, because he knew he was an honest man. But (quoth Capnio) you lose your labour in going to the Pallace, for the King meanes this day to take the aire of the Sea, and to goe aboord of a shippe that lies in the haven. I am going before, you see, to provide all things in redinesse, and if you will follow my counsaile, turne back with me to the haven, where I will set you in such a fitte place as you may speake to the King at your pleasure. Porrus giving credit to Capnios smooth tale, gave him a thousand thanks for his frendly advise, and went with him to the haven, making all the way his complaintes of Dorastus, yet concealing secretlie the chaine and the Jewels. Assone as they were come to the Sea side, the marriners seeing Capnio, came a land with their cock-boate, who still dissembling the matter, demaunded of Porrus if he would go see the ship? who unwilling and fearing the worst, because he was not well acquainted with Capnio, made his excuse that he could not brooke the Sea, therefore would not trouble him.

Capnio seeing that by faire meanes hee could not get him aboord, commaunded the mariners that by violence they should carrie him into the shippe, who like sturdy knaves hoisted the poore shepheard on their backes, and bearing him to the boate, lanched from the land.

Porrus seeing himselfe so cunningly betraied durst not crie out, for hee sawe it would not prevaile, but began to intreate Capnio and the mariners to be good to him, and to pittie his estate, hee was but a poore man that lived by his labour: they laughing to see the shepheard so afraide, made as much haste as they could, and set him aboorde. Porrus was no sooner in the shippe, but he saw Dorastus walking with Fawnia, yet he scarse knew her: for she had attired her selfe in riche apparell, which so increased her beauty, that shee resembled rather an Angell then a mortall creature.

Dorastus and Fawnia, were halfe astonished to see the olde shepherd, marvailing greatly what wind had brought him thither, til Capnio told them al the whole discourse; how Porrus was going to make his complaint to the King, if by pollicie he had not prevented him, and therefore now sith he was aboord, for the avoiding of further danger, it were best to carrie him into Italy.

Dorastus praised greatly his mans devise, and allowed of his counsaile; but Fawnia (who stil feared Porrus, as her father) began to blush for shame, that by her meanes he should either incure daunger or displeasure.

The old shephard hearing this hard sentence, that he should on such a sodaine be caried from his Wife, his country, and kinsfolke, into a forraine Lande amongst straungers, began with bitter teares to make his complaint, and on his knees to intreate Dorastus, that pardoning his unadvised folly he would give him leave to goe home; swearing that hee would keepe all thinges as secret as they could wish. But these protestations could not prevaile, although Fawnia intreated Dorastus very earnestly, but the mariners hoisting their maine sailes waied ankers, and hailed into the deepe, where we leave them to the favour of the wind and seas, and returne to Egistus.

Who having appointed this day to hunt in one of his Forrests, called for his sonne Dorastus to go sport himselfe, because hee saw that of late hee began to loure; but his men made answer that hee was gone abroade none knew whither, except he were gone to the grove to walke all alone, as his custome was to doe every day.

The King willing to waken him out of his dumpes sent one of his men to goe seeke him, but in vaine, for at last he returned, but finde him he could not, so that the King went himselfe to goe see the sport; where passing away the day, returning at night from hunting, hee asked for his sonne, but he could not be heard of, which drave the King into a great choler: where upon most of his Noblemen and other Courtiers, poasted abroad to seek him, but they could not heare of him through all Sicilia, onely they missed Capnio his man, which againe made the King suspect that hee was not gone farre.

Two or three daies being passed, and no newes heard of Dorastus, Egistus began to feare that he was devoured with some wilde beastes, and upon that made out a great troupe of men to go seeke him; who coasted through all the Country, and searched in everie daungerous and secrete place, untill at last they mette with a Fisherman that was sitting in a little covert hard by the sea side mending his nettes, when Dorastus and Fawnia tooke shipping; who being examined if he either knewe or heard where the Kings Sonne was, without any secrecie at all revealed the whole matter, how he was sayled two dayes past, and had in his company his man Capnio, Porrus and his faire Daughter Fawnia. This heavie newes was presently caryed to the King, who halfe dead for sorrow commaunded Porrus wife to bee sent for: she being come to the Pallace, after due examination, confessed that her neighbours had oft told her that the Kings Sonne was too familier with Fawnia, her Daughter: whereuppon, her husband fearing the worst, about two dayes past (hearing the King should goe an hunting) rose earely in the morning and went to make his complaint, but since she neither hearde of him, nor saw him. Egistus perceiving the womans unfeyned simplicity, let her depart without incurring further displeasure, conceiving such secret greefe for his Sonnes recklesse follie, that he had so forgotten his honour and parentage, by so base a choise to dishonor his Father, and discredit himselfe, that with very care and thought be fel into a quartan fever, which was so unfit for his aged yeeres and complexion, that he became so weake, as the Phisitions would graunt him no life.

But his sonne Dorastus little regarded either father, countrie, or Kingdome in respect of his Lady Fawnia, for fortune smyling on this young novice, lent him so lucky a gale of winde, for the space of a day and a night, that the maryners lay and slept upon the hatches; but on the next morning about the breake of the day, the aire began to be overcast, the winds to rise, the seas to swel, yea presently there arose such a fearfull tempest, as the ship was in danger to be swallowed up with every sea, the maine mast with the violence of the wind was thrown over boord, the sayles were torne, the tacklings went in sunder, the storme raging still so furiously that poore Fawnia was almost dead for feare, but that she was greatly comforted with the presence of Dorastus. The tempest continued three dayes, at which time the Mariners everie minute looked for death, and the aire was so darkned with cloudes that the Maister could not tell by his compasse in what Coast they were. But upon the fourth day about ten of the clocke, the wind began to cease, the sea to wax calme, and the sky to be cleare, and the Mariners descryed the coast of Bohemia, shooting of their ordnance for joy that they had escaped such a fearefull tempest.

Dorastus hearing that they were arrived at some harbour, sweetly kissed Fawnia, and bad her be of good cheare: when they tolde him that the port belonged unto the cheife Cittie of Bohemia where Pandosto kept his Court, Dorastus began to be sad, knowing that his Father hated no man so much as Pandosto, and that the King himself had sought secretly to betray Egistus: this considered, he was halfe afraide to goe on land, but that Capnio counselled him to chaunge his name and his countrey, until such time as they could get some other barke to transport them into Italy. Dorastus liking this devise made his case privy to the Marriners, rewarding them bountifully for their paines, and charging them to saye that he was a Gentleman of Trapalonia called Meleagrus. The shipmen willing to shew what friendship they could to Dorastus, promised to be as secret as they could, or hee might wish, and uppon this they landed in a little village a mile distant from the Citie, where after they had rested a day, thinking to make provision for their mariage; the fame of Fawnias beauty was spread throughout all the Citie, so that it came to the eares of Pandosto; who then being about the age of fifty, had notwithstanding yong and freshe affections: so that he desired greatly to see Fawnia, and to bring this matter the better to passe, hearing they had but one man, and how they rested at a very homely house; he caused them to be apprehended as spies, and sent a dozen of his garde to take them: who being come to their lodging, tolde them the Kings message. Dorastus no whit dismayed, accompanied with Fawnia and Capnio, went to the court (for they left Porrus to keepe the stuffe) who being admitted to the Kings presence, Dorastus and Fawnia with humble obedience saluted his majestie.

Pandosto amased at the singular perfection of Fawnia, stood halfe astonished, viewing her beauty, so that he had almost forgot himselfe what hee had to doe: at last with stearne countenance he demaunded their names, and of what countrey they were, and what caused them to land in Bohemia, Sir (quoth Dorastus) know that my name Meleagrus is a Knight borne and brought up in Trapalonia, and this gentlewoman, whom I meane to take to my wife is an Italian borne in Padua, from whence I have now brought her. The Cause I have so small a trayne with me is for that her friends unwilling to consent, I intended secretly to convey her into Trapalonia; whither as I was sailing, by distresse of weather I was driven into these coasts: thus have you heard my name, my country, and the cause of my voiage. Pandosto starting from his seat as one in choller, made this rough reply.

Meleagrus, I feare this smooth tale hath but small trueth, and that thou coverest a foule skin with faire paintings. No doubt this Ladie by her grace and beauty is of her degree more meete for a mighty Prince, then for a simple knight, and thou like a perjured traitour hath bereft her of her parents, to their present griefe, and her insuing sorrow. Till therefore I heare more of her parentage and of thy calling, I wil stay you both here in Bohemia.

Dorastus, in whome rested nothing but Kingly valor, was not able to suffer the reproches of Pandosto, but that he made him this answer.

It is not meete for a King, without due proofe to appeach any man of ill behaviour, nor upon suspition to inferre beleefe: straungers ought to bee entertained with courtesie, not to bee intreated with crueltie, least being forced by want to put up injuries: the Gods revenge their cause with rigor.

Pandosto hearing Dorastus utter these wordes, commaunded that he should straight be committed to prison, untill such time as they heard further of his pleasure, but as for Fawnia, he charged that she should be entertained in the Court, with such curtesie as belonged to a straunger and her calling. The rest of the shipmen he put into the dungeon.

Having thus hardly handled the supposed Trapalonians, Pandosto contrarie to his aged yeares began to be somwhat tickled with the beauty of Fawnia, in so much that hee could take no rest, but cast in his old head a thousand new devises: at last he fell into these thoughtes.

How art thou pestred Pandosto with fresh affections, and unfitte fancies, wishing to possesse with an unwilling mynd, and a hot desire troubled with a could disdaine? Shall thy mynde yeeld in age to that thou hast resisted in youth? Peace Pandosto, blabbe not out that which thou maiest be ashamed to reveale to thy self. Ah Fawnia is beautifull, and it is not for thine honour (fond foole) to name her that is thy Captive, and another mans Concubine. Alas, I reach at that with my hand which my hart would fain refuse; playing like the bird Ibys in Egipt, which hateth Serpents, yet feedeth on their egges. Tush, hot desires turne oftentimes to colde disdaine: Love is brittle, where appetite, not reason, beares the sway: Kinges thoughtes ought not to climbe so high as the heavens, but to looke no lower then honour: better it is to pecke at the starres with the young Eagles, then to pray on dead carkasses with the Vulture: tis more honourable for Pandosto to dye by concealing Love, than to enjoy such unfitte Love. Dooth Pandosto then love? Yea: whome? A maide unknowne, yea, and perhapps immodest, stragled out of her owne countrie; beautifull, but not therefore chast; comely in bodie, but perhappes crooked in minde. Cease then Pandosto to looke at Fawnia, much lesse to love her: be not overtaken with a womans beauty, whose eyes are framed by arte to inamour, whose hearte is framed by nature to inchaunt, whose false teares knowe their true times, and whose sweete wordes pearce deeper then sharpe swordes.

Here Pandosto ceased from his talke, but not from his love: although he sought by reason and wisedome to suppresse this franticke affection: yet he could take no rest, the beautie of Fawnia had made such a deepe impression in his heart. But on a day walking abroad into a Parke which was hard adjoyning to his house, he sent by one of his servants for Fawnia, unto whome he uttered these wordes.

Fawnia, I commend thy beauty and wit, and now pittie thy distresse and want; but if thou wilt forsake Sir Meleagrus, whose poverty, though a Knight, is not able to maintaine an estate aunswerable to thy beauty, and yeld thy consent to Pandosto, I will both increase thee with dignities and riches. No sir, answered Fawnia; Meleagrus is a knight that hath wonne me by love, and none but he shal weare me: his sinister mischance shall not diminishe my affection, but rather increase my good will: thinke not though your Grace had imprisoned him without cause, that feare shall make mee yeeld my consent: I had rather be Meleagrus wife, and a begger, then live in plenty, and be Pandostos Concubine. Pandosto hearing the assured aunswere of Fawnia, would, notwithstanding, prosecute his suite to the uttermost; seeking with faire wordes and great promises to scale the fort of her chastitie, swearing that if she would graunt to his desire Meleagrus should not only be set at libertie, but honored in his courte amongst his Nobles: but these alluring baytes could not entise her minde from the love of her newe betrothed mate Meleagrus; which Pandosto seeing, he left her alone for that time to consider more of the demaund. Fawnia being alone by her selfe, began to enter into these solitarie meditations.

Ah infortunate Fawnia thou seest to desire above fortune, is to strive against the Gods, and Fortune. Who gazeth at the sunne weakeneth his sight: they which stare at the skie, fall ofte into deepe pits: haddest thou rested content to have bene a shepheard, thou needest not to have feared mischaunce: better had it bene for thee, by sitting lowe, to have had quiet, then by climing high to have fallen into miserie. But alas I feare not mine owne daunger, but Dorastus displeasure. Ah sweete Dorastus, thou art a Prince, but now a prisoner, by too much love procuring thine owne losse: haddest thou not loved Fawnia thou haddest bene fortunate: shall I then bee false to him that hath forsaken Kingdomes for my cause? no, would my death might deliver him, so mine honor might be preserved. With that fetching a deepe sigh, she ceased from her complaints, and went againe to the Pallace, injoying a libertie without content, and profered pleasure with smal joy. But poore Dorastus lay all this while in close prison, being pinched with a hard restraint, and pained with the burden of colde, and heavie Irons, sorrowing sometimes that his fond affection had procured him this mishappe, that by the disobedience of his parentes, he had wrought his owne despright: an other while cursing the Gods and fortune, that they should crosse him with such sinister chaunce: uttering at last his passions in these words.

Ah unfortunate wretch borne to mishappe, now thy folly hath his desert: art thou not worthie for thy base minde to have bad fortune? could the destinies favour thee, which hast forgot thine honor and dignities? wil not the Gods plague him with despight that payneth his father with disobedience? Oh Gods, if any favour or justice be left, plague me, but favour poore Fawnia, and shrowd her from the tirannies of wretched Pandosto, but let my death free her from mishap, and then welcome death. Dorastus payned with these heavie passions, sorrowed and sighed, but in vaine, for which he used the more patience. But againe to Pandosto, who broyling at the heat of unlawfull lust, coulde take no rest but still felt his minde disquieted with his new love, so that his nobles and subjectes marveyled greatly at this sudaine alteration, not being able to conjecture the cause of this his continued care. Pandosto thinking every hower a yeare til he had talked once againe with Fawnia, sent for her secretly into his chamber, whither though Fawnia unwillingly comming, Pandosto entertained her very courteously using these familiar speaches, which Fawnia answered as shortly in this wise.

Pandosto.

Fawnia are you become lesse wilfull and more wise, to preferre the love of a King before the liking of a poore Knight? I thinke ere this you thinke it is better to be favoured of a King then of a subject.

Fawnia.

Pandosto, the body is subject to victories, but the minde not to be subdued by conquest, honesty is to be preferred before honour, and a dramme of faith weigheth downe a tunne of gold. I have promised Meleagrus to love, and will performe no lesse.

Pandosto.

Fawnia, I know thou art not so unwise in thy choice, as to refuse the offer of a King, nor so ingrateful as to dispise a good turne: thou art now in that place where I may commaunde, and yet thou seest I intreate: my power is such as I may compell by force, and yet I sue by prayers: Yeelde Fawnia thy love to him which burneth in thy love: Meleagrus shall be set free, thy countrymen discharged, and thou both loved and honoured.

Fawnia.

I see Pandosto, where lust ruleth it is a miserable thing to be a virgin, but know this, that I will alwaies preferre fame before life, and rather choose death then dishonour.

Pandosto seeing that there was in Fawnia a determinate courage to love Meleagrus, and a resolution without feare to hate him, flong away from her in a rage: swearing if in shorte time she would not be wonne with reason; he would forget all courtesie, and compel her to graunt by rigour: but these threatning wordes no whit dismayed Fawnia; but that she still both dispited and dispised Pandosto. While thus these two lovers strove, the one to winne love the other to live in hate: Egistus heard certaine newes by the Merchauntes of Bohemia, that his sonne Dorastus was imprisoned by Pandosto, which made him feare greatly that his sonne should be but hardly entreated: yet considering that Bellaria and hee was cleared by the Oracle of Apollo from that crime wherewith Pandosto had unjustly charged him, hee thought best to send with all speed to Pandosto, that he should set free his sonne Dorastus, and put to death Fawnia and her father Porrus: finding this by the advise of Counsaile the speediest remedy to release his sonne, he caused presently too of his shippes to be rigged, and thoroughly furnished with provision of men and victuals, and sent divers of his men and nobles Embassadoures into Bohemia; who willing to obey their King, and relieve[1] their yong Prince: made no delayes, for feare of danger, but with as much speed as might be, sailed towards Bohemia: the winde and seas favored them greatly, which made them hope of some good happe, for within three daies they were landed: which Pandosto no soner heard of their arrivall, but hee in person went to meete them, intreating them with such sumptuous and familiar courtesie, that they might well perceive how sory he was for the former injuries

---

[1] [Old copies, *receiue*. The correction was suggested by Mr Collier.]

hee had offered to their King, and how willing (if it might be) to make amendes.

As Pandosto made report to them, how one Maleagrus, a Knight of Trapolonia, was lately arived with a Lady called Fawnia in his land, comming very suspitiously, accompanied onely with one servant, and an olde shepheard. The Embassadours perceived by the halfe, what the whole tale ment, and began to conjecture, that it was Dorastus, who for feare to bee knowne, had chaunged his name: but dissembling the matter, they shortly arived at the Court, where after they had bin verie solemnly and sumptuously feasted, the noble men of Sicilia being gathered togither, they made reporte of their Embassage: where they certified Pandosto that Meleagrus was sonne and heire to the King Egistus, and that his name was Dorastus: how contrarie to the Kings minde he had privily convaied away that Fawnia, intending to marrie her, being but daughter to that poore shepheard Porrus: whereupon the Kings request was that Capnio, Fawnia, and Porrus, might bee murthered and put to death, and that his sonne Dorastus might be sent home in safetie. Pandosto having attentively and with great mervaile heard their Embassage, willing to reconcile himselfe to Egistus, and to shew him how greatly he esteemed his favour:[1] although love and fancy forbad him to hurt Fawnia, yet in despight of love hee determined to execute Egistus will without mercy; and therefore he presently sent for Dorastus out of prison, who mervailing at this unlooked for curtesie, found at his comming to the Kings presence, that which he least doubted of, his fathers Embassadours: who no sooner sawe him, but with great reverence they honored him: and

---

[1] [Ed. 1588 has *labour*, which is altered, as pointed out by Mr Collier, in the later copies to the word in the text.]

Pandosto embracing Dorastus, set him by him very lovingly in a chaire of estate. Dorastus ashamed that his follie was bewraied, sate a long time as one in a muse, til Pandosto told him the summe of his Fathers embassage: which he had no sooner heard, but he was toucht at the quicke, for the cruell sentence that was pronounced against Fawnia: but neither could his sorrow nor perswasions prevaile, for Pandosto commaunded that Fawnia, Porrus, and Capnio, should bee brought to his presence; who were no sooner come, but Pandosto having his former love turned to a disdainfull hate, began to rage against Fawnia in these tearmes.

Thou disdainfull vassal, thou currish kite, assigned by the destinies to base fortune, and yet with an aspiring minde gazing after honour: how durst thou presume, being a beggar, to match with a Prince? By thy alluring lookes to inchant the sonne of a King to leave his owne countrie to fulfill thy disordinate lusts? O despightfull minde, a proud heart in a beggar is not unlike to a great fire in a smal cottage, which warmeth not the house, but burneth it: assure thy selfe that thou shalt die, and thou old doating foole, whose follie hath bene such, as to suffer thy daughter to reach above thy fortune; looke for no other meede, but the like punishment. But Capnio, thou which hast betrayed the King, and hast consented to the unlawfull lust of thy Lord and maister, I know not how justly I may plague thee: death is too easie a punishment for thy falsehood, and to live (if not in extreme miserie) were not to shew thee equitie. I therefore award that thou shall have thine eyes put out, and continually while thou diest, grinde in a mil like a brute beast. The feare of death brought a sorrowfull silence upon Fawnia and Capnio, but Porrus seeing no hope of life, burst forth into these speeches.

Pandosto, and ye noble Embassadours of Sicilia, seeing without cause I am condemned to die; I am yet glad I have opportunitie to disburden my conscience before my death: I will tel you as much as I know, and yet no more than is true: whereas I am accused that I have bene a supporter of Fawnias pride, and shee disdained as a vilde begger, so it is that I am neither Father unto her, nor she daughter unto me. For so it happened that I being a poore shepheard in Sicilia, living by keeping others mens flockes; one of my sheepe straying downe to the sea side, as I went to seeke her, I saw a little boat driven upon the shoare, wherein I found a babe of sixe daies olde, wrapped in a mantle of skarlet, having about the necke this chaine: I pittying the child, and desirous of the treasure, carried it home to my wife, who with great care nursed it up, and set it to keepe sheepe. Here is the chaine and the Jewels, and this Fawnia is the childe whome I found in the boate, what shee is, or of what parentage I knowe not, but this I am assured that shee is none of mine.

Pandosto would scarce suffer him to tell out his tale, but that he enquired the time of the yeere, the manner of the boate, and other circumstaunces, which when he found agreeing to his count, he sodainelie leapt from his seate, and kissed Fawnia, wetting her tender cheeks with his teares, and crying my daughter Fawnia, ah sweete Fawnia, I am thy Father, Fawnia. This sodaine passion of the King drave them all into a maze, especially Fawnia and Dorastus. But when the King had breathed himselfe a while in this newe joy, he rehearsed before the Embassadours the whole matter, how hee hadde entreated his wife Bellaria for jealousie, and that this was the childe whome hee sent to floate in the seas.

Fawnia was not more joyfull that she had found such a Father, then Dorastus was glad he should get such a wife. The Embassadors rejoyced that their yong prince had made such a choice, that those Kingdomes, which through enmitie had long time bin dissevered, should now through perpetual amitie be united and reconciled. The Citizens and subjects of Bohemia (hearing that the King had found againe his Daughter, which was supposed dead, joyfull that there was an heire apparent to his Kingdome) made Bonfires and showes throughout the Cittie. The Courtiers and Knights appointed Justs and Turneis to signifie their willing mindes in gratifying the Kings hap.

Eighteene daies being past in these princely sports, Pandosto willing to recompence old Porrus, of a shepheard made him a Knight: which done, providing a sufficient Navie to receive him and his retinue, accompanied with Dorastus, Fawnia, and the Sicilian Embassadours, he sailed towards Sicilia, where he was most princelie entertained by Egistus; who hearing this comicall event, rejoyced greatly at his sonnes good happe, and without delay (to the perpetuall joy of the two yong Lovers) celebrated the marriage: which was no sooner ended, but Pandosto (calling to mind how first he betraied his friend Egistus, how his jealousie was the cause of Bellarias death, that contrarie to the law of nature hee had lusted after his owne Daughter) moved with these desperate thoughts, he fell into a melancholie fit, and to close up the Comedie with a Tragicall stratageme, he slewe himselfe, whose death being many daies bewailed of Fawnia, Dorastus, and his deere friend Egistus, Dorastus taking his leave of his father, went with his wife and the dead corps into Bohemia, where after they were sumptuouslie intoombed, Dorastus ended his daies in contented quiet.

FINIS.

KING HENRY VIII.

IN the composition of this play Shakespeare probably derived help, at least in the shape of suggestions, from an earlier drama, now no longer known, on the subject of Cardinal Wolsey. This was written by Chettle and others in 1601-2, or before, and appears to have been in two parts. To Samuel Rowley's "When you see me, you know me," 1605, he was probably under no obligations whatever.

The old Shakespeare Society contemplated a reprint of Rowley's performance from the *editio princeps* of 1605, it is to be presumed on account of its collateral and contemporary interest; but, after all, it does not come legitimately within the category of Shakespeariana.

But as Mr Dyce (edition of Shakespeare, 1868, v. 481), remarks, the poet frequently employs the very words of Holinshed, to whom he almost unquestionably went for his history. That he also consulted Foxe's "Martyrs," the extract hereafter printed will show with tolerable clearness.

We have no precise evidence as to the state in which the drama left the poet's hands; but there can be little doubt that it received interpolations, especially in the concluding portion, from another and very inferior pen.

At the suggestion of Mr Furnivall, select passages from Holinshed, running more or less parallel with the course of the drama, have been given; but there are portions of the latter which appear to have no counterpart in the historical narrative.

1. *Selected Passages from Holinshed's History of the Reign of Henry VIII.*

CARDINALL WOOLSIE being still most highlie in the kings fauour, obteined licence to erect a college at Oxford, and another at Ipswich, the towne where he was borne, the which foundations he began rather of a vaine desire of glorie and worldlie praise, than vpon the instinction of true religion and aduancement of doctrine, and therfore sith he was not mooued thereto in respect of true godlinesse and bountifull liberalitie, he went about to cloth Peter and rob Paule: for he first got licence of the king to suppresse certeine small monasteries, and after got a confirmation of the pope, that he might imploie the goods, lands, and reuenues belonging to those houses, to the maintenance of those his two colleges, whereby not onelie he, but also the pope were euill spoken of through the whole realme.[1] . . . . .

---

[1] "The point in which Shakespeare's wording of the character of Wolsey differs most from Campion's own, is perhaps where Wolsey's colleges at Ipswich and Oxford are declared to 'witness.' This fine expression is, it appears, to be found in Campion, in immediate connection with the subject of these two colleges." — *Appendix to Mr O'Carroll's Inaugural Address,* 1874.

This time a bill was set vp in London, much contrarie to the honour of the cardinall, in the which the cardinall was warned that he should not counsell the king to marrie his daughter into France: for if hée did, he should shew himselfe enimie to the king and the realme, with manie threatning words. This bill was deliuered to the cardinall by Sir Thomas Seimor maior of the citie, which thanked him for the same, & made much search for the author of that bill, but he could not be found, which sore displeased the cardinall. And vpon this occasion the last daie of Aprill at night he caused a great watch to be kept at Westminster, and had there cart guns readie charged, & caused diuerse watches to be kept about London, in Newington, S. Iohns stréet, Westminster, saint Giles, Islington, and other places néere London: which watches were kept by gentlemen & their seruants, with housholders, and all for feare of the Londoners bicause of this bill. When the citizens knew of this, they said that they maruelled why the cardinall hated them so, for they said that if he mistrusted them, he loued them not: and where loue is not, there is hatred: and they affirmed that they neuer intended anie harme toward him, and mused of this chance. For if fiue or six persons had made alarm in the citie, then had entred all these watchmen with their traine, which might haue spoiled the citie without cause. Wherefore they much murmured against the cardinall and his vndiscréet dooings. . . . . .

The place where the cardinals should sit to heare the cause of matrimonie betwixt the king and the quéene, was ordeined to be at the Blacke friers in London, where in the great hall was preparation made of seats, tables, and other furniture, according to such a solemne session and roiall apparance. The court was platted in tables and benches in manner of a consistorie, one seat raised higher for the iudges to sit in. Then as it were in the midst of the said iudges aloft aboue them three degrées high, was a cloth of estate hanged, with a chaire roiall vnder the same, wherein sat the king; and besides him, some distance from him sat the quéene, and vnder the iudges feet sat the scribes and other officers: the chéefe scribe was doctor Stéeuens, and the caller of the court was one Cooke of Winchester.

Then before the king and the iudges within the court sat the archbishop of Canturburie Warham, and all the other bishops. Then stood at both ends within, the counsellors learned in the spirituall laws, as well the kings as the quéenes. The doctors of law for the king (whose names yée haue heard before) had their conuenient roomes. Thus was the court furnished. The iudges commanded silence whilest their commission was read, both to the court and to the people assembled. That doone the scribes commanded the crier to call the king by the name of king Henrie of England, come into the court, &c. With that the king answered and said, Héere. Then called he the queene by the name of Katharine quéene of England, come into the court, &c. Who made no answer, but rose out of hir chaire. *The king and queene called into the court.*

And bicause shée could not come to the king directlie, for the distance seuered betweene them, shée went about by the court, and came to the king, kneeling downe at his féet, to whome she said in effect as followeth: Sir (quoth she) I desire you to doo me iustice and right, and take some pitie vpon me, for I am a poore woman, and a stranger, borne out of your dominion, hauing héere no indifferent counsell, & lesse assurance of fréendship. Alas sir, what haue I offended you, or what occasion of displeasure haue I shewed you, intending thus to put me from you after this sort? I take God to my iudge, I haue beene to you a true & humble wife, euer conformable to your will and pleasure, that neuer contraried or gainesaid *Queene Katharines lamentable and pithie speech in presence of the court.*

any thing thereof, and being alwaies contented with all things wherein you had any delight, whether little or much, without grudge or displeasure, I loued for your sake all them whome you loued, whether they were my freends or enimies.

I haue béene your wife these twentie yeares and more, & you haue had by me diuerse children. If there be anie iust cause that you can alleage against me, either of dishonestie, or matter lawfull to put me from you; I am content to depart to my shame and rebuke: and if there be none, then I praie you to let me haue iustice at your hand. The king your father was in his time of excellent wit, and the king of Spaine my father Ferdinando was reckoned one of the wisest princes that reigned in Spaine manie yeares before. It is not to be doubted, but that they had gathered as wise counsellors vnto them of euerie realme, as to their wisedoms they thought méet, who déemed the marriage betwéene you and me good and lawfull, &c. Wherefore, I humblie desire you to spare me, vntill I may know what counsell my freends in Spaine will aduertise me to take, and if you will not, then your pleasure be fulfilled. With that she arose vp, making a lowe curtesie to the king, and departed from thence.

The queene iustifieth the mariage.

The king being aduertised that shée was readie to go out of the house, commanded the crier to call hir againe, who called hir by these words; Katharine quéene of England, come into the court. With that (quoth maister Griffith) madame, you be called againe. On on (quosh she) it maketh no matter, I will not tarrie, go on your waies. And thus she departed, without anie further answer at that time, or anie other, and neuer would appeare after in anie court. The king perceiuing she was departed, said these words in effect: For as much (quoth he) as the quéene is gone, I will in hir absence declare to you all, that shée hath beene to me as true, as obedient, and as conformable a wife, as I would wish or desire. She

The queene departing out of the court is called againe.

hath all the vertuous qualities that ought to be in a woman of hir dignitie, or in anie other of a baser estate, she is also surelie a noble woman borne, hir conditions will well declare the same.

With that quoth Wolseie the cardinall: Sir, I most humblie require your highnesse, to declare before all this audience, whether I haue béene the chéefe and first moouer of this matter vnto your maiestie or no, for I am greatlie suspected heerein. My lord cardinall (quoth the king) I can well excuse you in this matter, marrie (quoth he) you haue béene rather against me in the tempting héereof, than a setter forward or moouer of the same. The speciall cause that mooued me vnto this matter, was a certeine scrupulositie that pricked my conscience, vpon certeine words spoken at a time when it was, by the bishop of Baion the French ambassador, who had béene hither sent, vpon the debating of a marriage to be concluded betweene our daughter the ladie Marie, and the duke of Orleance, second son to the king of France. *The cardinall required to have that declared which was well enough known.*

Vpon the resolution and determination whereof, he desired respit to aduertise the king his maister thereof, whether our daughter Marie should be legitimate in respect of this my marriage with this woman, being sometimes my brothers wife. Which words once conceiued within the secret bottome of my conscience, ingendered such a scrupulous doubt, that my conscience was incontinentlie accombred, vexed, and disquieted; whereby I thought my selfe to be greatlie in danger of Gods indignation. Which appeared to be (as me seemed) the rather, for that he sent vs no issue male: and all such issues male as my said wife had by me, died incontinent after they came into the world, so that I doubted the great displeasure of God in that behalfe. *The king confesseth that the sting of conscience made him mislike this mariage.*

Thus my conscience being tossed in the waues of a scrupulous mind, and partlie in despaire to haue anie other issue than I had alredie by this ladie now my wife, it behooued me further to consider the state of this realme, and the danger it stood in for lacke of a prince to succéed me, I thought it good in release of the weightie burthen of my weake conscience, & also the quiet estate of this worthie relme, to attempt the law therin, whether I may lawfullie take another wife

<small>The state of the question.</small> more lawfullie, by whom God may send me more issue, in case this my first copulation was not good, without anie carnall concupiscence, and not for anie displeasure or misliking of the queenes person and age, with whome I would be as well contented to continue, if our mariage may stand with the laws of God, as with anie woman aliue.

In this point consisteth all this doubt that we go about now to trie, by the learning, wisedome, and iudgement of you our prelats and pastors of all this our realme and dominions now héere assembled for that purpose; to whose conscience & learning I haue <small>The king submitteth himselfe to the censures of the learned in this case of diuorse.</small> committed the charge and iudgement: according to the which I will (God willing) be right well content to submit my selfe, and for my part obeie the same. Wherein, after that I perceiued my conscience so doubtfull, I mooued it in confession to you my lord of Lincolne then ghostlie father. And for so much as then you your selfe were in some doubt, you mooued me to aske the counsell of all these my lords: wherevpon I mooued you my lord of Canturburie, first to haue your licence, in as much as you were metropolitane, to put this matter in question, and so I did of all you my lords: to which you granted vnder your seales, héere to be shewed. That is truth, quoth the archbishop of Canturburie. After that the king rose vp, and the court was adiorned vntill another daie.

<small>The queene accuseth Cardinal Wolsie.</small> Héere is to be noted, that the quéene in presence of the whole court most gréeuouslie accused the cardinall of vntruth, deceit, wickednesse, & malice, which

had sowne dissention betwixt hir and the king hir husband; and therefore openlie protested, that she did vtterlie abhorre, refuse, and forsake such a iudge, as was not onelie a most malicious enimie to hir, but also a manifest aduersarie to all right and iustice, and therewith did she appeale vnto the pope, committing hir whole cause to be iudged of him. But notwithstanding this appeale, the legats sat weekelie, and euerie daie were arguments brought in on both parts, and proofes alleaged for the vnderstanding of the case, and still they assaied if they could by anie meanes procure the quéene to call backe hir appeale, which she vtterlie refused to doo. The king would gladlie haue had an end in the matter, but when the legats draue time, and determined vpon no certeine point, he conceiued a suspicion, that this was doone on purpose, that their dooings might draw to none effect or conclusion. *She appeleth to the pope.* *The king mistrusteth the legate of seeking delaies.*

The next court daie, the cardinals set againe, at which time the councell on both sides were there readie to answer. The kings councell alleaged the matrimonie not to be lawfull at the beginning, bicause of the carnall copulation had betwéene prince Arthur and the quéene. This matter was verie vehementlie touched on that side, and to prooue it, they alleaged manie reasons and similitudes of truth: and being answered negatiuelie againe on the other side, it séemed that all their former allegations were doubtfull to be tried, and that no man knew the truth. And thus this court passed from sessions to sessions, and daie to daie, till at certeine of their sessions the king sent the two cardinals to the queene (who was then in Bridewell) to persuade with hir by their wisdoms, and to aduise hir to surrender the whole matter into the kings hands by her owne consent & will, which should be much better to hir honour, than to stand to the *The present mariage whie thought vnlawfull.*

triall of law, and thereby to be condemned, which
should séeme much to hir dishonour.

Queene Katharine and the cardinals haue communication in her priuie chamber.

The cardinalls being in the queenes chamber of presence, the gentleman vsher aduertised the quéene that the cardinals were come to speake with hir. With that she rose vp, & with a skeine of white thred about hir necke, came into hir chamber of presence, where the cardinals were attending. At whose comming, quoth she, What is your plesure with me? If it please your grace (quoth cardinall Wolseie) to go into your priuie chamber, we will shew you the cause of our comming. My lord (quoth she) if yée haue anie thing to saie, speake it openlie before all these folke, for I feare nothing that yee can saie against me, but that I would all the world should heare and sée it, and therefore speake your mind. Then began the cardinall to speake to hir in Latine. Naie good my lord (quoth she) speake to me in English.

The queene refuseth to make sudden answer to so weightie a matter as the diuorse.

Forsooth (quoth the cardinall) good madame, if it please you, we come both to know your mind how you are disposed to doo in this matter betwéene the king and you, and also to declare secretlie our opinions and counsell vnto you: which we doo only for verie zeale and obedience we beare vnto your grace. My lord (quoth she) I thanke you for your good will, but to make you answer in your request I cannot so suddenly, for I was set among my maids at worke, thinking full little of anie such matter, wherein there néedeth a longer deliberation, and a better head than mine to make answer, for I néed counsell in this case which toucheth me so néere, & for anie counsell or freendship that I can find in England, they are not for my profit. What think you my lords, will anie Englishman counsell me, or be fréend to me against the K. pleasure that is his subiect? Naie forsooth. And as for my counsell in whom I will put my trust, they be not here, they be in Spaine in my owne countrie.

And my lords, I am a poore woman, lacking wit, to answer to anie such noble persons of wisedome as you be, in so weightie a matter, therefore I praie you be good to me poore woman, destitute of fréends here in a forren region, and your counsell also I will be glad to heare. And therewith she tooke the cardinall by the hand, and led him into hir priuie chamber with the other cardinall, where they tarried a season talking with the quéene. Which communication ended, they departed to the king, making to him relation of hir talke. Thus this case went forward from court to court, till it came to iudgement, so that euerie man expected that iudgment would be giuen the next day. At which daie the king came thither, and set him downe in a chaire within a doore, in the end of the gallerie (which opened directlie against the iudgement seat) to heare the iudgement giuen, at which time all their proceedings were red in Latine. *The king and queenes matter commeth to iudgement.*

That doone, the kings councell at the barre called for iudgement. With that (quoth cardinall Campeius) I will not giue iudgment till I haue made relation to the pope of all our procéedings, whose counsell and commandement in this case I will obserue: the case is verie doubtfull, and also the partie defendant will make no answer here, but dooth rather appeale from vs, supposing that we be not indifferent. Wherefore I will adiourne this court at this time, according to the order of the court of Rome. And with that the court was dissolued, and no more doone. This protracting of the conclusion of the matter, King Henrie tooke verie displeasantlie. Then cardinall Campeius tooke his leaue of the king and the nobilitie, and returned towards Rome. *Cardinall Campeius refuseth to giue iudgement.*

While these things were thus in hand, the cardinall of Yorke was aduised that the king had set his affection vpon a young gentlewoman named Anne, the daughter of Sir Thomas Bullen, viscount Rochford, *The kings affection and good will to the ladie Anne Bullen.*

which did waite vpon the quéene. This was a great griefe vnto the cardinall, as he that perceiued aforehand, that the king would marie the said gentlewoman, if the diuorse tooke place. Wherefore he began with all diligence to disappoint that match, which by reason of the misliking that he had to the woman, he iudged ought to be auoided more than present death. While the matter stood in this state, and that the cause of the queene was to be heard and iudged at Rome, by reason of the appeale which by hir was put in : the cardinall required the pope by letters and secret messengers, that in anie wise he should defer the iudgement of the diuorse, till he might frame the kings mind to his purpose.

<small>The secret working and dissimulation of cardinall Woolsie.</small>

Howbeit he went about nothing so secretlie, but that the same came to the kings knowledge, who tooke so high displeasure with such his cloked dissimulation, that he determined to abase his degrée, sith as an vnthankefull person he forgot himselfe and his dutie towards him that had so highly aduanced him to all honor and dignitie. When the nobles of the realme perceiued the cardinall to be in displeasure, they began to accuse him of such offenses as they knew might be proued against him, and thereof they made a booke conteining certeine articles, to which diuerse of the kings councell set their hands. The king vnderstanding more plainlie by those articles, the great pride, presumption, and couetousnesse of the cardinall, was sore mooued against him; but yet kept his purpose secret for a while. Shortlie after, a parlement was called to begin at Westminster the third of Nouember next insuing.

<small>The king cōceiueth displeasure against the cardinall.</small>

<small>Edw. Hall.</small>

<small>Articles exhibited against the cardinall.</small>

In the meane time the king, being informed that all those things that the cardinall had doone by his power legantine within this realme, were in the case of the premunire and prouision, caused his atturneie Christopher Hales to sue out a writ of premunire

<small>The cardinall sued in a premunire.
Abr. Fl. ex I. S. pag. 956. 967.</small>

against him, in the which he licenced him to make his atturneie. And further the seuentéenth of Nouember the king sent the two dukes of Norffolke and Suffolke to the cardinals place at Westminster, who (went as they were commanded) and finding the cardinall there, they declared that the kings pleasure was that he should surrender vp the great seale into their hands, and to depart simplie vnto Asher, which was a house situat nigh vnto Hampton court, belonging to the bishoprike of Winchester. The cardinall demanded of them their commission that gaue them such authoritie, who answered againe, that they were sufficient commissioners, and had authoritie to doo no lesse by the kings mouth. Notwithstanding, he would in no wise agrée in that behalfe, without further knowledge of their authoritie, saieng; that the great seale was deliuered him by the kings person, to inioy the ministration thereof, with the roome of the chancellor for the terme of his life, whereof for his suertie he had the kings letters patents. *[marginal: The cardinall is loth to part from the great seale.]*

This matter was greatlie debated betwéene them with manie great words, in so much that the dukes were faine to depart againe without their purpose, and rode to Windsore to the king, and made report accordinglie; but the next daie they returned againe, bringing with them the kings letters. Then the cardinall deliuered vnto them the great seale, and was content to depart simplie, taking with him nothing but onelie certeine prouision for his house: and after long talke betwéene him and the dukes, they departed with the great seale of England, and brought the same to the king. Then the cardinall called all his officers before him, and tooke accompt of them for all such stuffe, whereof they had charge. And in his gallerie were set diuerse tables, wherevpon laie a great number of goodlie rich stuffe, as whole péeces of silke of all colours, veluet, sattin, damaske, taffata, *[marginal: The cardinall discharged of the great seale.]* *[marginal: The cardinall calleth all his officers to accounts.]*

grograine, and other things. Also, there laie a thousand peeces of fine Holland cloth.

There was laid on euerie table, bookes reporting the contents of the same, and so was there inuentaries of all things in order against the kings comming. He caused to be hanged the walles of the gallerie on the one side with cloth of gold, cloth of tissue, cloth of siluer, and rich cloth of bodken of diuerse colours. On the other side were hanged the richest sute of coapes of his owne prouision made for his colleges of Oxford and Ipswich, that euer were séene in England. Then had he two chambers adioining to the gallerie, the one most commonlie called the gilt chamber, and the other the councell chamber, wherein were set vp two broad and long tables vpon trestles, whervpon was set such a number of plates of all sorts, as was almost incredible.

In the gilt chamber were set out vpon the table nothing but gilt plate, and vpon a cupbord and in a window was set no plate but gold, verie rich: and in the councell chamber was all white and parcell gilt plate, and vnder the table in baskets was all old broken siluer plate, and bookes set by them purporting euerie kind of plate, and euerie parcell, with the contents of the ounces thereof. Thus were all things prepared, giving charge of all the said stuffe, with all other remaining in euerie office, to be deliuered to the king, to make answer to their charge: for the order was such, that euerie officer was charged with the receipt of the stuffe belonging to his office by indenture. To Sir William Gascoigne, being his treasuror, he gaue the charge of the deliuerie of the said goods, and therwithall, with his traine of gentlemen and yeomen, he tooke his barge at the priuie staires, and so went by water vnto Putneie, where when he was arriued, he tooke his mule, & euerie man tooke their horsses, and rode streight to Asher, where he and his

<small>The cardinall of Yorke goeth to Asher, and hath his plentie turned into penurie.</small>

familie continued the space of three or four weekes, without either beds, shéets, table cloths, or dishes to eat their meat in, or wherewith to buie anie: the cardinall was forced to borrow of the bishop of Carleill, plate and dishes, &c.

After this, in the kings bench his matter for the premunire, being called vpon, two atturneis, which he had authorised by his warrant signed with his owne hand, confessed the action, and so had iudgement to forfeit all his lands, tenements, goods, and cattels, and to be out of the kings protection: but the king of his clemencie sent to him a sufficient protection, and left to him the bishoprikes of Yorke and Winchester, with plate and stuffe conuenient for his degrée. . . . . . *[marginal: Iohn Scute and Edmund Iennie. The cardinall condemned in a premunire.]*

The king, which all this while, since the doubt was mooued touching his marriage, absteined from the quéenes bed, was now aduertised by his ambassadours, whom he had sent to diuerse vniuersities for the absoluing of his doubt, that the said vniuersities were agreed, and cléerelie concluded, that the one brother might not by Gods law marrie the other brothers wife, carnallie knowen by the first marriage, & that neither the pope nor the court of Rome could in anie wise dispense with the same. For ye must vnderstand, that amongst other things alleged for disproofe of the mariage to be lawfull, euidence was giuen of certeine wordes, which prince Arthur spake the morrow after he was first married to the quéene, whereby it was gathered, that he knew her carnallie the night then passed. The words were these, as we find them in the chronicle of master Edward Hall. *[marginal: Iudgement of the Vniversities on the marriage. A speciall argument in disproofe of the marriage.]*

In the morning after he was risen from the bed, in which he had laine with hir all night, he called for drinke, which he before time was not accustomed to doo. At which thing, one of his chamberleines maruelling, required the cause of his drought. To whome he answered merilie, saeing; I haue this night béene in the middest of Spaine, which is a hot region, and that iournie maketh me so drie: and if thou haddest beene vnder that hot climat, thou wouldest haue béene drier than I. Againe, it was alleged, that after the death of prince Arthur, the king was deferred from the title and creation of prince of Wales almost halfe a yeare, which thing could not haue béene doubted, if she had not béene carnallie knowen. Also she hir selfe caused a bull to be purchased, in the which were these words Velforsan cognitam, that is, and peraduenture carnallie knowen: which words were not in the first bull granted by pope Iulie at her second mariage to the king, which second bull with that clause was onelie purchased to dispense with the second matrimonie, although there were carnall copulation before, which bull néeded not to haue béene purchased, if there had béene no carnall copulation, for then the first bull had béene sufficient. To conclude, when these & other matters were laid foorth to prooue that which she denied, the carnall copulation betwixt her and prince Arthur, hir counsellors left that matter, and fell to persuasions of naturall reason. And lastlie, when nothing else would serue, they stood stiffe in the appeale to the pope, and in the dispensation purchased from the court of Rome, so that the matter was thus shifted off, and no end likelie to be had therein.

<small>Disgrace of Wolsey. Rise of Cromwell. *Abr. Flem. in Edw. Hall in H. 8. fol. cxcj. cxcij.*
1530.
The cardinall licenced to repaire into Yorkeshire.</small>

You haue heard before how the cardinall was attainted in the premunire, and how he was put out of the office of the chancellor, & laie at Asher. In this Lent season the king by the aduise of his councell licenced him to go into his diocesse of Yorke, & gaue him commandement to kéepe him in his diocesse, and not to returne southward without the kings speciall licence in writing. So he made great

prouision to go northward, and apparelled his seruants
newlie, and bought manie costlie things for his houshold: and so he might well inough, for he had of
the kings gentlenesse the bishoprikes of Yorke and
Winchester, which were no small things. But at this
time diuerse of his seruants departed from him to the
kings seruice, and in especiall Thomas Crumwell one
of his chiefe counsell, and chiefe dooer for him in the
suppression of abbeies. . . . . .

When night came, the cardinall waxed verie sicke *Death of Wolsey.*
with the laske, the which caused him continuallie to
go to the stoole all that night, in so much that he had
that night fiftie stooles: therefore in consideration of
his infirmities, they caused him to tarrie all that day:
and the next daie he tooke his iournie with master
Kingston, and them of the gard, till he came to an
house of the earle of Shrewesburies called Hardwike
hall, where he laie all night verie euill at ease. The
next daie he rode to Notingham, and there lodged
that night more sicke: and the next daie he rode to
Leicester abbeie, and by the waie waxed so sicke that
he was almost fallen from his mule; so that it was
night before he came to the abbeie of Leicester, where
at his comming in at the gates, the abbat with all his
conuent met him with diuerse torches light, whom
they honorablie receiued and welcomed.

To whome the cardinall said: father abbat, I am
come hither to lay my bones among you, riding so
still vntill he came to the staires of the chamber,
where he allighted from his mule, and master Kingston
led him vp the staires, and as soone as he was in his
chamber he went to bed. This was on the saturday
at night, and then increased he sicker and sicker, vntill
mondaie, that all men thought he would haue died:
so on tuesdaie saint Andrewes euen, master Kingston
came to him and bad him good morrow, for it was
about six of the clocke, and asked him now he did?

Sir (quoth he) I tarrie but the pleasure of God, to render vp my poore soule into his hands. Not so sir (quoth master Kingston) with the grace of God, yée shall liue and doo verie well, if yée will be of good cheere. Nay in good sooth master Kingston, my disease is such, that I can not liue: for I haue had some experience in physicke.

The cardinall affirmeth by his owne experience in physicke that he can not liue.

Thus it is, I haue a flux with a continuall feuer, the nature whereof is, that if there be no alteration of the same within eight daies, either must insue excoriation of the intrailes, or fransie, or else present death, and the best of them is death, and (as I suppose) this is the eight daie, & if yée sée no alteration in me, there is no remedie, saue (though I may liue a daie or twaine after) but death must insue. Sir (quoth maister Kingston) you be in much pensiuenes, doubting that thing, that in good faith yée néed not. Well, well, master Kingston (quoth the cardinall) I sée the matter how it is framed: but if I had serued God as diligentlie as I haue doone the king, he would not haue giuen me ouer in my greie haires: but it is the iust reward that I must receiue for the diligent paines and studie that I haue had to doo him seruice, not regarding my seruice to God, but onely to satisfie his pleasure.

The cardinall ascribeth his fall to the iust iudgement of God.

I prai you haue me most humblie commended vnto his roiall maiestie, & beséech him in my behalfe to call to his princelie remembrance all matters procéeding betwéene him & me from the beginning of the world, and the progresse of the same, &c. Master Kingston farewell, I can no more saie, but I wish all things to haue good successe, my time draweth on fast. And euen with that he began to draw his spéech at length, & his toong to faile, his eies being set, whose sight failed him. Then they did put him in remembrance of Christ his passion, & caused the yeomen of the gard to stand by to sée him die, and to witnesse

Manifest indication of death in the cardinall.

of his words at his departure : & incontinent the clocke stroke eight, and then he gaue vp the ghost, and departed this present life : which caused some to call to remembrance how he said the daie before, that at eight of the clocke they should loose their master.

Here is the end and fall of pride and arrogancie of men exalted by fortune to dignitie : for in his time he was the hautiest man in all his proceedings aliue, hauing more respect to the honor of his person, than he had to his spirituall profession, wherein should be shewed all meekenes, humilitie, and charitie. [An example (saith Guicciardin, who handleth this storie effectuallie, and sheweth the cause of this cardinals ruine) in our daies woorthie of memorie, touching the power which fortune and enuie hath in the courts of princes.] He died in Leicester abbie, & in the church of the same abbie was buried. Such is the suertie of mans brittle state, doubtfull in birth, & no lesse féeble in life, which is as vncerteine, as death most certeine, and the meanes thereof manifold, which as in number they excéed ; so in strangenesse they passe : all degrees of ages and diuersities of sexes being subiect to the same. In consideration whereof, it was notablie said by one that wrote a whole volume of infirmities, diseases, and passions incident to children : *Example of pride and arrogancie.* *Guic. page 1139.*

A primo vitæ diuersos stamine morbos *Sebast. Austarius.*
  Perpetimur, diris afficimúrque malis:
Donac in occasum redeat qui vixit ab ortu,
  Antea quàm discat viuere, vita cadit.

This **cardinall** (as Edmund Campian in his historie of Ireland describeth him) was a man vndoubtedly born to honor : I thinke (saith he) some princes bastard, no butchers sonne, excéeding wise, fair spoken, high-minded, full of reuenge, vitious of his bodie, loftie to his enimies, were they neuer so big, *The description of cardinall Wolselé set downe by Edmund Campian.*

to those that accepted and sought his fréendship woonderfull courteous, a ripe schooleman, thrall to affections, brought a bed with flatterie, insatiable to get, and more princelie in bestowing, as appeareth by his two colleges at Ipswich and Oxenford, the one ouerthrowne with his fall, the other vnfinished, and yet as it lieth for an house of students, considering all the appurtenances incomparable thorough Christendome, whereof Henrie the eight is now called founder, bicause he let it stand. He held and inioied at once the bishopriks of Yorke, Duresme, & Winchester, the dignities of lord cardinall, legat, & chancellor, the abbie of saint Albons, diuerse priories, sundrie fat benefices In commendam, a great preferrer of his seruants, an aduancer of learning, stout in euerie quarell, neuer happie till this his ouerthrow. Wherein he shewed such moderation, and ended so perfectlie, that the houre of his death did him more honor, than all the pompe of his life passed. Thus far Campian.[1] . . . . .

Birth and baptism of Queen Elizabeth. The seuenth of September, being Sundaie, betwéene thrée and foure of the clocke in the afternoone, the

---

[1] The following slip is attached to an *Inaugural Address* delivered before the Clongowes Wood College Historical Debating Society, by the Rev. J. J. O'Carroll, 8°, Dublin, 1874, and gives in parallel columns the passages from Shakespeare, act v, sc. 2, and Campion :

CAMPION.	SHAKESPEARE.
The Cardinal, a man undoubtedly born to honour. I think some prince's—no butcher's son. A ripe schoolman. Exceedingly wise, fair spoken, high-minded. Lofty to his enemies were they never so big; to those who accepted and sought his friendships wonderful courteous. Insatiable to get, and more prince-like in bestowing.	This Cardinal, though from an humble stock, undoubtedly was fashioned to much honour from the cradle. He was a scholar and a ripe and good one. Exceeding wise, fair spoken, and persuading. Lofty and sour to those men that loved him not; but to those men that sought him sweet as summer. And though he were unsatisfied in getting (which was a sin), yet in bestowing, madam, he was most princely.

queene was deliuered of a fine yong ladie, on which daie the Duke of Norffolke came home to the christening, which was appointed on the wednesdaie next following, and was accordinglie accomplished on the same daie, with all such solemne ceremonies as were thought conuenient. The godfather at the font, was the lord archbishop of Canturburie, the godmothers, the old dutches of Norffolke, & the old marchionesse Dorset widow: and at the confirmation the ladie marchionesse of Excester was godmother: the child was named Elizabeth.

CAMPION.

As appeareth by his two Colleges at Ipswich and at Oxenford. The one suppressed with his fall; the other unfinished, and yet, as it lieth, an house of students incomparable through Christendom.

Never happy till his overthrow; therein he showed such moderation and ended so patiently, that the hour of his death did him more honour than all the pomp of life passed.

SHAKESPEARE.

Ever witness to him those twins of learning that he raised in you. Ipswich and Oxford. One of which fell with him, unwilling to survive the good that did it; the other, though unfinished, yet so famous, so excellent in art, and still so rising, that Christendom shall ever speak his virtue.

His overthrow heaped happiness upon him; and then, and not till then, he felt himself and found the blessedness of being little; and to add more honour to his age than man could give him, he died fearing God.

2. *Extract from Fox's "Book of Martyrs," directly Illustrative of a Passage in Henry VIII., v., 1.*[1]

———o———

"WHEN night came, the King sent Sir Anthonie Denie about midnight to the archbishop [Cranmer], willing him forthwith to resort unto him at the court. The message done, the archbishop speedily addressed himself to the court, and comming into the galerie where the King walked and taried for him, his highnesse said, Ah, my lorde of Canterbury, I can tell you newes. For divers weighty considerations it is determined by me and the counsaile that you to-morrowe at nine of the clocke shall be

---

[1]   *Enter* SIR ANTHONY DENNY.
K. Hen. Well, sir, what follows?
Den. Sir, I have brought my lord the archbishop, as you commanded me." .... &c.
    Shakespeare (or at least the writer of the fifth act of Henry VIII.) has made great use of Fox here, but has distributed the speeches differently, and (for instance) what Henry is made to say in the prose work about the heresy of Munster in Germany is in the drama put into the mouth of Gardiner:
"——————— as of late days, our neighbours,
The Upper Germany, can dearly witness."

committed to the Tower, for that you and your chaplaines (as information is given us) have taught and preached, and thereby sown within the realme such a number of execrable heresies, that it is feared the whole realme being infected with them, no small contention and commotion will rise thereby amongst my subjects, as of late daies the like was in divers parts of Germanie; and therefore the counsell have requested me for the triall of the matter to suffer them to commit you to the Tower, or else no man dare come forthe, as witnesse in those matters, you being a counsellor. When the King had said his mind, the archbishop kneeled down, and said, I am content, if it please your grace, with al my hart, to go thither at your highness commandment; and I most humbly thank your majesty that I may come to my triall, for there be that have many waies slandered me, and now this way I hope to trie myselfe not worthy of such reporte. The King perceiving the mans uprightnesse, joyned with such simplicitie, said, Oh Lorde, what maner of man be you? What simplicitie is in you? I thought that you would rather have sued to us to have heard you and your accusers together for your triall, without any such indurance.[1] Do you not know what state you be in with the whole world, and how many great enemies you have? Do you not consider what an easie thing it is to procure three or four false knaves to witnesse against you? Thinke you to have better lucke that waie than your master Christ had? I see by it you will run headlong to your ending, if I would suffer you.

---

[1] So in the play:

"*K. Hen.* . . . . What manner of man are you? My lord, I look'd
You would have given me your petition, that
I should have ta'en some pains to bring together
Yourself and your accusers; and to have heard you
Without indurance further."

Your enemies shall not so prevaile against you;[1] for I have otherwise devised with my selfe to keep you out of their handes. Yet notwithstanding to-morrow when the counsaile shall sit, and send for you, resort unto them, and if in charging you with this matter, they do commit you to the Tower, require of them, because you are one of them, a counsailer, that you may have your accusers brought before them without any further indurance, and use for your selfe as good persuations that way as you may devise; and if no intreatie or reasonable request will serve, then deliver unto them this my ring (which then the King delivered unto the archbishop) and saie unto them, 'if there be no remedie, my lords, but that I must needs go to the Tower, then I revoke my cause from you, and appeale to the Kinges own person by this token unto you all, for (saide the King then unto the archbishop) so soone as they shall see this ring, they knowe it so well, that they shall understand that I have reserved the whole cause into mine owne handes and determination, and that I have discharged them thereof.' The archbishop perceiving the Kinges benignity to him wards, had much ado to forbeare teares. 'Well,' said the King, 'go your waies, my lord, and do as I have bidden you.' My lord, humbling himselfe with thankes, tooke his leave of the Kinges highnesse for that night.

"On the morrow, about nine of the clocke before noone, the counsaile sent a gentleman usher for the archbishop who, when he came to the counsaill

---

[1] Here, in the play, we have an interrupting remark by Cranmer, which might with advantage have been omitted:—

"*Cran.* God and your majesty
Protect mine innocence, or I fall into
The trap is laid for me ——."

This hardly reads like Shakespeare. The prose narrative is superior and more poetical.

chamber doore, could not be let in, but of purpose (as it seemed) was compelled to waite among the pages, lackies, and serving-men all alone. D. Buts the Kings physician resorting that way, and espying how my lord of Canterbury was handled, went to the King's highnesse, and said: 'My lord of Canterbury, if it please your grace, is well promoted; for now he is become a lackey or a serving man, for yonder hee standeth this halfe hower at the counsaile chamber doore amongste them.' 'It is not so (quoth the King), I trowe, nor the counsail hath not so little discretion as to use the metropolitane of the realme in that sorte, specially being one of their own number. But let them alone (said the King), and we shall heare more soone.' Anone the archbishop was called into the counsaile chamber, to whom was alleadged as before is rehearsed. The archbishop answered in like sort, as the King had advised him; and in the end when he perceived that no maner of persuasion or intreatie could serve, he delivered them the Kings ring, revoking his cause into the Kings hand. The whole counsaile being thereat somewhat amazed, the Erle of Bedford with a loud voice confirming his words with a solemne othe said, 'When you first began the matter, my lordes, I told you what would come of it. Do you thinke that the King would suffer this mans finger to ake? Much more will he defend his life (I warrant you) against brabling varlets. You doe but cumber yourselves to hear tales and fables against him.' And incontinently upon the receipt of the Kings token, they all rose, and carried to the King his ring, surrendring the matter, as the order and use was, into his own hands.

"When they were all come to the Kings presence, his highnesse with a severe countenance said unto them: 'Ah, my lordes, I thought I had wiser men of my counsaile than now I find you. What discretion was this in you thus to make the primate of the realme, and one of you in office, to waite at the counsaille chamber doore amongst serving men? You might have considered that he was a counsailer as wel as you, and you had no such commission of me so to handle him. I was content that you should trie him as a counsellor, and not as a meane subject. But now I well perceive that things be done against him maliciouslie, and if some of you might have had your minds, you would have tried him to the uttermost. But I do you all to wit, and protest, that if a prince may bee beholding unto his subject (and so solemnlie laying his hand upon his brest, said) by the faith I owe to God I take this man here, my lord of Canterburie, to be of all other a most faithful subject unto us, and one to whom we are much beholding,' giving him much commendations otherwise. And with that one or two of the chiefest of the counsaile, making their excuse, declared that in requesting his indurance, it was rather ment for his triall and his purgation against the common fame and slander of the worlde, than for any malice conceived against him. 'Well, well, my lords' (quoth the King), take him, and well use him, as hee is worthy to bee, and make no more ado.' And with that every man caught him by the hand, and made faire weather of altogethers, which might easilie be done with that man."

TWO NOBLE KINSMEN.

THIS drama was founded on the "Knight's Tale" of Chaucer, which (again) is built on Boccaccio's "Teseide." The modern editors are unanimous, or nearly so, in assigning a portion of this interesting drama to our great poet, and scarcely any two agree as to the share which he had in its composition, or in the parts which we ought to treat as from his pen. The opening act, and first scene of the concluding one, it seems to be thought, are Shakespeare's, the rest, Fletcher's.

It is to be regretted, that the play on the same tale ("Palamon and Arcite"), written by Richard Edwards, and performed at Christ Church, Oxford, in 1566, should have perished, as well as that (unless they were substantially identical), which Henslowe quotes as exhibited at the Newington Theatre in 1594. His extant play proves Edwards to have been a writer of some ability; and such a production by him was at any rate surely capable of yielding hints and other occasional help to a follower in his track.

Assuming the first, and portions of the last, act to be Shakespeare's, we are perhaps authorised to assume that the poet died, leaving this much written, and that for the rest we are debtors to the pen of Fletcher. This position might be curious and even important, if it could be established, since we should have then some material for forming a notion of the way in which the great dramatist worked.

Sir Thomas Wyat, in his Epistle to John Poines, says :—

"I am not he, such eloquence to bost :
To make the crow in singyng as the swanne . .
Praise Syr Topas for a noble tale,
And scorne the story that the Knight tolde."

We have given Tyrrhitt's abstract of Boccaccio's "Teseide," as his edition of Chaucer is not readily accessible. He furnishes some account of the earlier version (it is supposed, in the heroic stanza) made by the English poet, but no longer known, except that there are occasional traces of it in the existing "Knight's Tale," as if portions of it had been worked into the latter, and the remainder cancelled. It is not known whence Boccaccio derived the incidents; but he speaks of it in his time (the fourteenth century) as "una antichissima storia."

1. *Abstract of the Teseide of Boccaccio.*

[*From Tyrwhitt's* " *Chaucer,*" 1822, i. 114-20.]

THE "Theseida" is distributed into twelve Books or Cantoes.

Book I. Contains the war of Theseus with the Amazons; their submission to him; and his marriage with Hippolyta.

Book II. Theseus, having spent two years in Scythia, is reproached by Perithons in a vision, and immediately returns to Athens with Hippolyta and her sister Emilia. He enters the city in triumph; finds the Grecian ladies in the temple of Clemenzia; marches to Thebes; kills Creon, &c.; and brings home Palemone and Arcita, who are

Damnati—ad eterna presone.

Book III. Emilia, walking in a garden and singing, is heard and seen first by Arcita, who calls Palemone. They are both equally enamoured of her, but without any jealousy or rivalship. Emilia is supposed to see them at the window, and to be not displeased at their admiration. Arcita is released at the request of

Perithons; takes his leave of Palemone, with embraces, &c.

Book IV. Arcita, having changed his name to *Pentheo*, goes into the service of Menelaus at Mycenæ, and afterwards of Peleus at Ægina. From thence he returns to Athens, and becomes a favourite servant of Theseus, being known to Emilia, though to nobody else; till after some time he is overheard making his complaint in a wood, to which he usually resorted for that purpose, by Pamphilo, a servant of Palemone.

Book V. Upon the report of Pamphilo, Palemone *begins* to be jealous of Arcita, and is desirous to get out of prison in order to fight with him. This he accomplishes with the assistance of Pamphilo, by changing clothes with Alimeto, a Physician. He goes armed to the wood in quest of Arcita, whom he finds sleeping. At first they are very civil and friendly to each other. Then Palemone calls upon Arcita to renounce his pretensions to Emilia, or to fight with him. After many long expostulations on the part of Arcita, they fight, and are discovered first by Emilia, who sends for Theseus. When he finds who they are, and the cause of their difference, he forgives them, and proposes the method of deciding their claim to Emilia, by a combat of an hundred on each side, to which they gladly agree.

Book VI. Palemone and Arcita live splendidly at Athens, and send out messengers to summon their friends; who arrive; and the principal of them are severally described, viz. Lycurgus, Peleus, Phocus, Telamon, &c. Agamemnon, Menelaus, Castor and Pollux, &c. Nestor, Evander, Perithons, Ulysses, Diomedes, Pygmalion, Minos, &c. with a great display of ancient history and mythology.

Book VII. Theseus declares the laws of combat, and the two parties of an hundred on each side are formed. The day before the combat, Arcita, after having visited the temples of all the Gods, makes a formal prayer to Mars. The prayer, *being personified*, is said to go and find Mars in his temple in Thrace, which is described; and Mars, upon understanding the message, causes favourable signs to be given to Arcita. In the same manner Palemone closes his religious observances with a prayer to Venus. His Prayer, *being also personified*, sets out for the temple of Venus on Mount Citherone, which is also described; and the petition is granted. Then the sacrifice of Emilia to Diana is described; her prayer; the appearance of the Goddess; and the signs of the two fires. In morning they proceed to the Theatre with their respective troops, and prepare for the action. Arcita puts up a private prayer to Emilia, and harangues his troop publickly; and Palemone does the same.

Book VIII. Contains a description of the battle, in which Palemone is taken prisoner.

Book IX. The horse of Arcita, being frighted by a Fury, sent from hell at the desire of Venus, throws him. However he is carried to Athens in a triumphal chariot with Emilia by his side; is put to bed dangerously ill; and there by his own desire espouses Emilia.

Book X. The funeral of the persons killed in the combat. Arcita, being given over by his Physicians, makes his will, in discourse with Theseus, and desires that Palemone may inherit all his possessions and also Emilia. He then takes leave of Palemone and Emilia, to whom he repeats the same request. Then lamentations. Arcita orders a sacrifice to Mercury, (which Palemone performs for him,) and dies.

Book XI. Opens with the passage of Arcita's soul to heaven, imitated from the beginning of the 9th Book of Lucan. The funeral of Arcita. Description of the wood felled takes up six stanzas. Palemone builds a temple in honour of him, in which his whole history is painted. The description of this painting is an abridgement of the preceding part of the Poem.

Book XII. Theseus proposes to carry into execution Arcita's will by the marriage of Palemone and Emilia. This they both decline for some time in formal speeches, but at last are persuaded and married. The Kings, &c. take their leave, and Palemone remains " in gioia e in diporto con la sua dona nobile e corteuse."

2. *The Knightes Tale.*

WHILOM, as olde stories tellen us,
  Ther was a duk that highte Theseus;
Of Athenes he was lord and governour,
And in his tyme swich a conquerour,
That gretter was ther non under the sonne.
Ful many a riche contré hadde he wonne;
That with his wisdam and his chivalrie
He conquerede al the regne of Femenye,
That whilom was i-cleped Cithea;
And weddede he the queen Ipolita,
And broughte hire hoom with him in his contré
With mochel glorie and gret solempnité,
And eek hire yonge suster Emelye.
And thus with victorie and with melodye
Lete I this noble duk to Athenes ryde,
And al his host, in armes him biside.
And certes, if it nere to long to heere,
I wolde han told yow fully the manere,
How wonnen was the regne of Femenye
By Thesus, and by his chivalrye;
And of the grete bataille for the nones
Bytwixen Athenes and the Amazones;
And how aseged was Ypolita,
The faire hardy quen of Cithea;

And of the feste that was at hire weddynge,
And of the tempest at hire hoom comynge;
But al that thing I mot as now forbere.
I have, God wot, a large feeld to ere,
And wayke ben the oxen in my plough,
The remenaunt of the tale is long inough;
I wol not lette eek non of al this rowte,
Lat every felawe telle his tale aboute,
And lat see now who schal the soper wynne,
And ther I lafte, I wol agayn begynne.
   This duk, of whom I make mencioun,
Whan he was come almost unto the toun,
In all his wele and in his moste pryde,
He was war, as he caste his eyg*h*e aside,
Where that ther knelede in the hye weye
A companye of ladies, tweye and tweye,
Ech after other, clad in clothes blake;
But such a cry and such a woo they make,
That in this world nys creature lyvynge,
That herde such another weymentynge,
And of this cry they nolde nevere stenten,
Til they the reynes of his bridel henten.
'What folk ben *y*e that at myn hom comynge
Pertourben so my feste with crying*e*?'
Quod Theseus, 'have *y*e so gret envye
Of myn honour, that thus compleyne and crie?
Or who hath *y*ow misboden, or offended?
And telleth me if it may ben amended;
And why that *y*e ben clothed thus in blak?'
   The eldeste lady of hem alle spak,
When sche hadde swowned with a dedly chere,
That it was routhe for to seen or heere;
And seyde, 'Lord, to whom Fortue hath *y*even
Victorie, and as a conquerour to lyven,
Nought greveth us *y*oure glorie and honour;
But we beseken mercy and socour.
Have mercy on our wooe and oure distresse.

Som drope of pitee, thrugh thy gentilnesse,
Uppon us wrecchede wommen lat thou falle.
For Certes, lord, ther nys noon of us alle,
That sche nath ben a duchesse or a queene;
Now be we caytifs, as it is wel seene:
Thanked be Fortune, and hire false wheel,
That noon estat assureth to ben weel.
And certes, lord, to abiden youre presence
Here in the temple of the goddesse Clemence
We han ben waytynge al this fourtenight;
Now help us, Lord, syth it is in thy might.
I wrecche, which that wepe and waylle thus,
Was whilom wyf to kyng Capaneus,
That starf at Thebes, cursed be that day,
And alle we that ben in this array,
And maken al this lamentacioun!
We losten alle our housbondes at that toun,
Whil that the sege ther aboute lay.
And yet the olde Creon, welaway!
That lord is now of Thebes the citee,
Fulfild of ire and of iniquité,
He for despyt, and for his tyrannye,
To do the deede bodyes vileinye,
Of alle oure lordes, whiche that ben i-slawe,
Hath all the bodies on an heep y-drawe,
And wol not suffren hem by noon assent
Nother to ben y-buried nor y-brent,
But maketh houndes ete hem in despite.'
And with that word, withoute more respite,
They fillen gruff, and criden pitously,
'Have on us wrecchede wommen som mercy,
And lat our sorwe synken in thyn herte.'
This gentil duk doun from his courser sterte
With herte pitous, when he herde hem speke
Him thoughte that his herte wolde breke,
Whan he seyh hem so pitous and so maat,
That whilom weren of so gret estat.

And in his armes he hem alle up hente,
And hem comforteth in ful good entente ;
And swor his oth, as he was trewe knight,
He wolde don so ferforthly his might
Upon the tyraunt Creon hem to wreke,
That al the people of Grece scholde speke
How Creon was of Theseus y-served,
As he that hadde his deth ful wel deserved.
And right anoon, withoute more abood
His baner he desplayeth, and forth rood
To Thebes-ward, and al his hoost bysyde ;
No neere Athenes wolde he go ne ryde,
Ne take his eese fully half a day,
But onward on his way that nyght he lay ;
And sente anoon Ypolita the queene,
And Emelye hire yonge suster schene,
Unto the toun of Athenes to dwelle ;
And forth he ryt; ther is no more to telle.

 The reede statue of Mars with spere and targe
So schyneth in his white baner large,
That alle the feeldes gliteren up and doun ;
And by his baner born in his pynoun
Of gold ful riche, in which ther was i-bete
The Minatour which that he slough in Crete.
Thus ryt this duk, thus ryt this conquerour,
And in his hoost of chevalrie the flour,
Til that he cam to Thebes, and alighte
Faire in a feeld ther as he thoughte fighte.
But schortly for to speken of this thing,
With Creon, which that was of Thebes kyng,
He faught, and slough him manly as a knight
In pleyn bataille, and putte the folk to flight ;
And by assaut he wan the citié after,
And rente adoun bothe wal, and sparre, and rafter ;
And to the ladies he restorede agayn
The bones of here housbondes that were slayn,
To don obsequies, as was tho the gyse.

But it were al to long for to devyse
The grete clamour and the waymentynge
Which that the ladies made at the brennynge
Of the bodies, and the grete honour
That Theseus the noble conquerour
Doth to the ladyes, when they from him wente.
But schortly for to telle is myn entente.
When that this worthy duk, this Theseus,
Hath Creon slayn, and wonne Thebes thus,
Stille in that feelde he tooke al night his reste,
And dide with al the contré as him leste.
  To ransake in the tas of bodyes dede
Hem for to streepe of herneys and of wede,
The pilours diden businesse and cure,
After the bataille and disconfiture.
And so byfil, that in the tas thei founde,
Thurgh-girt with many a grevous blody wounde,
Two yonge knightes liggyng by and by,
Bothe in oon armes, wroght ful richely;
Of whiche two, Arcite highte that oon,
And that other knight highte Palamon.
Nat fully quyke, ne fully deede they were,
But by here coote-armures, and by here gere,
The heraudes knewe hem best in special,
As they that weren of the blood real
Of Thebes, and of sistren tuo i-born.
Out of the taas the pilours han hem torn,
And han hem caried softe unto the tente
Of Theseus, and he ful sone hem sente
Tathenes, for to dwellen in prisoun
Perpetuelly, he nolde no raunsoun.
And whan this worthy duk hath thus i-doon,
He took his host, and hom he ryt anoon
With laurer crowned as a conquerour;
And there he lyveth in joye and in honour
Terme of his lyf; what nedeth wordes moo?
And in a tour, in angwisch and in woo,

This Palamon, and his felawe Arcite,
For evermore, ther may no gold hem quyte.
　　This passeth yeer by yeer, and day by day,
Til it fel oones in a morwe of May
That Emelie, that fairer was to seene
Than is the lilie on hire stalke grene,
And fresscher than the May with floures newe—
For with the rose colour strof hire hewe,
I not which was the fayrere of hem two—
Er it were day, as was hire wone to do,
Sche was arisen, and al redy dight;
For May wole han no sloggardye anight.
The sesoun priketh every gentil herte,
And maketh him out of his sleep to sterte,
And seith, ' Arys, and do thin observaunce.'
This makede Emelye han remembraunce
To don honour to May, and for to ryse.
I-clothed was sche fresshe for to devyse.
Hire yelwe heer was browded in a tresse,
Byhynde hire bak, a yerde long I gesse.
And in the gardyn at the sonne upriste
Sche walketh up and doun, and as hire liste
Sche gadereth floures, party whyte and reede,
To make a sotil gerland for hire heede,
And as an aungel hevenlyche sche song.
The grete tour, that was so thikke and strong,
Which of the castel was the cheef dongeoun,
(Ther as the knightes weren in prisoun,
Of which I tolde yow, and telle schal)
Was evene joynant to the gardyn wal,
Ther as this Emelye hadde hire pleyynge.
Bright was the sonne, and cleer that morwenynge,
And Palomon, this woful prisoner,
As was his wone, by leve of his gayler
Was risen, and romede in a chambre on heigh,
In which he al the noble cité seigh,
And eek the gardyn, ful of braunches grene,

Ther as this fresshe Emely the scheene
Was in hire walk, and romede up and doun.
This sorweful prisoner, this Palamon,
Gooth in the chambre, romyng to and fro,
And to himself compleynyng of his woo;
That he was born, ful ofte he seyde, alas!
And so byfel, by aventure or cas,
That thurgh a wyndow thikke, of many a barre
Of iren greet, and squar as eny sparre,
He caste his eyen upon Emelya,
And therwithal he bleynte and cryede, a!
As though he stongen were unto the herte.
And with that crye Arcite anon up-sterte,
And seyde, 'Cosyn myn, what eyleth the,
Thou art so pale and deedly on to see?
Why crydestow? who hath the doon offence?
For Goddes love, tak al in pacience
Oure prisoun, for it may non other be;
Fortune hath yeven us this adversité.
Som wikke aspect or disposicioun
Of Saturne, by sum constellacioun,
Hath yeven us this, although we hadde it sworn;
So stood the heven whan that we were born;
We moste endure it: this is the schort and pleyn.'
  This Palamon answerde, and seyde ageyn,
'Cosyn, for sothe of this opynyoun
Thou hast a veyn ymaginacioun.
This prisoun causede me not for to crye.
But I was hurt right now thurghout myn eye
Into myn herte, that wol my bane be.
The fairnesse of that lady that I see
Yond in the gardyn rome to and fro,
Is cause of all my crying and my wo,
I not whether sche be womman or goddesse;
But Venus is it, sothly as I gesse.'
And therwithal on knees adoun he fil,
And seyde: 'Venus, if it be thy wil

Yow in this gardyn thus to transfigure,
Biforn me sorweful wrecche creature,
Out of this prisoun help that we may scape.
And if so be my destiné be schape
By eterne word to deyen in prisoun.
Of oure lynage have sum compassioun,
That is so lowe y-brought by tyrannye.'
And with that word Arcite gan espye
Wher as this lady romede too and fro.
And with that sighte hire beauté hurte him so,
That if that Palamon was wounded sore,
Arcite is hurt as moche as he, or more.
And with a sigh he seyde pitously :
' The fressche beauté sleeth me sodeynly
Of hire that rometh in the yonder place ;
And but I have hire mercy and hire grace,
That I may seen hire atte leste weye,
I nam but deed ; ther nys no more to seye.'
This Palamon, whan he tho wordes herde,
Despitously he lokede, and answerde :
' Whether seistow this in ernest or in pley ? '
' Nay,' quod Arcite, ' in ernest by my fey.
God help me so, me lust ful evele pleye.'
This Palamon gan knytte his browes tweye :
' It nere,' quod he, ' to the no gret honour,
For to be fals, ne for to be traytour
To me, that am thy cosyn and thy brother
I-sworn ful deepe, and ech of us to other,
That nevere for to deyen in the payne,
Til that the deeth departe schal us twayne,
Neyther of us in love to hyndren other,
Ne in non other cas, my leeve brother ;
But that thou schuldest trewely forthren me
In every caas, and I schal forthren the.
This was thyn oth, and myn also certeyn ;
I wot right wel, thou darst it nat withseyn.
Thus art thou of my counseil out of doute.

And now thou woldest fasly ben aboute
To love my lady, whom I love and serve,
And evere schal, til that myn herte sterve.
Now certes, false Arcite, thou schalt not so.
I lovede hire first, and tolde the my woo
As to my counseil, and my brother sworn
To forthre me, as I have told biforn.
For which thou art i-bounden as a knight
To helpe me, if it lay in thi might,
Or elles art thou fals, I dar wel sayn.'
This Arcite ful proudly spak agayn.
' Thou schalt,' quod he, ' be rather fals than I.
But thou art fals, I telle the utterly.
For *par amour* I lovede hire first er thow.
What wolt thou sayn? thou wistest not yit now
Whether sche be a womman or goddesse.
Thyn is affeccioun of holynesse,
And myn is love, as to a creature;
For which I tolde the myn aventure
As to my cosyn, and my brother sworn.
I pose, that thou lovedest hire biforn;
Wost thou nat wel the olde clerkes sawe,
That who schal yeve a lover eny lawe,
Love is a gretter lawe, by my pan,
Then may be yeve to eny erthly man?
Therefor posityf lawe, and such decré,
Is broke alday for love in ech degree.
A man moot needes love maugre his heed.
He may nought flen it, though he shoulde be deed,
Al be sche mayde, or widewe, or elles wyf.
And eek it is nat likly al thy lyf
To stonden in hire grace, no more schal I;
For wel thou wost thyselven verraily,
That thou and I been dampned to prisoun
Perpetuelly, us gayneth no raunsoun.
We stryve, as dide the houndes for the boon,
They foughte al day, and yit here part was noon;

Ther come a kyte, whil that they were so wrothe,
And bar awey the boon bitwixe hem bothe.
And therfore at the kynges court, my brother,
Ech man for himself, there is non other.
Love if the list; for I love and ay schal;
And sothly, leeve brother, this is al.
Here in this prisoun moote we endure,
And everych of us take his aventure.'
Gret was the stryf and long bytwixe hem tweye,
If that I hadde leyser for to seye;
But to theffect.—It happede on a day,
(To telle it yow as schortly as I may)
A worthy duk that highte Perotheus,
That felawe was unto duk Theseus
Syn thilke day that they were children lyte,
Was come to Athenes, his felawe to visite,
And for to pleye, as he was wont to do,
For in this world he lovede no man so:
And he lovede him as tendrely agayn.
So wel they lovede, as olde bookes sayn,
That when that oon was deed, sothly to telle,
His felawe wente and soughte him doun in helle;
But of that story lyst me nought to write.
Duk Perotheus lovede wel Arcite,
And hadde him knowe at Thebes yeer by yeer;
And finally at requeste and prayer
Of Perotheus, withouten any ransoun
Duk Theseus him leet out of prisoun,
Frely to gon, wher that him luste overal,
In such a gyse, as I you telle schal.
This was the forward, playnly for tendite,
Betwixe Theseus and him Arcite:
That if so were, that Arcite were yfounde
Evere in his lyf, by daye or night, o stound
In eny contré of this Theseus,
And he were caught, it was acorded thus,
That with a swerd he scholde lese his heed;

Ther nas noon other remedy ne reed,
But took his leeve, and homward he him spedde;
Let him be war, his nekke lith to wedde.
  How gret a serwe suffreth now Arcite!
The deth he feleth thurgh his herte smyte;
He weepeth, weyleth, cryeth pitously;
To slen himself he wayteth pryvely.
He seyde, 'Allas the day that I was born!
Now is my prisoun werse than biforn;
Now is me schape eternally to dwelle
Nought in purgatorie, but in helle.
Allas! that evere knew I Perotheus!
For elles hadde I dweld with Theseus
I-fetered in his prisoun evere moo.
Than hadde I ben in blisse, and nat in woo.
Oonly the sighte of hire, whom that I serve,
Though that I nevere hire grace may deserve,
Wolde han sufficed right ynough for me.
O dere cosyn Palamon,' quod he,
'Thyn is the vicorie of this aventure,
Ful blisfully in prisoun maistow dure;
In prisoun? certes nay, but in paradys!
Wel hath fortune y-torned the the dys,
That hast the sighte of hire, and I thabsence.
For possible is, syn thou hast hire presence,
And art a knight, a worthi and an able,
That by som cas, syn fortune is chaungeable,
Thou maist to thy desir somtyme atteyne.
But I that am exiled, and bareyne
Of alle grace, and in so gret despeir,
That ther nys erthe, water, fyr, ne eyr,
Ne creature, that of hem maked is,
That may me helpe or doon confort in this.
Wel oughte I sterve in wanhope and distresse;
Farwel my lyf, my lust, and my gladnesse.
Allas, why pleynen folk so in commune
Of purveiaunce of God, or of fortune,

That yeveth him ful ofte in many a gyse
Wel bettre than thei can hemself devyse?
Som man desireth for to han richesse,
That cause is of his morthre or gret seeknesse,
And som man wolde out of his prisoun fayn,
That in his hous is of his meyné slayn.
Infinite harmes ben in this mateere;
We witen nat what thing we prayen heere.
We faren as he that dronke is as a mous.
A dronke man wot wel he hath an hous,
But he not which the righte wey is thider,
And to a dronke man the wey is slider,
And certes in this world so faren we;
We seeken faste after felicité,
But we gon wrong ful ofte trewely.
Thus may we seyen alle, and namelyche I,
That wende and hadde a gret opinioun,
That yif I mighte skape fro prisoun,
Than hadde I ben in joye and perfyt hele,
Ther now I am exiled fro my wele.
Syn that I may not sen yow, Emelye,
I nam but deed; ther nys no remedye.'

   Uppon that other syde Palamon,
Whan that he wiste Arcite was agoon,
Such sorwe he maketh, that the grete tour
Resowneth of his yollyng and clamour.
The pure fettres on his schynes grete
Weren of his bittre salte teres wete.
'Allas!' quod he, 'Arcita, cosyn myn,
Of al oure strif, God woot, the fruyt is thin.
Thow walkest now in Thebes at thi large,
And of my woo thou yevest litel charge.
Thou maist, syn thou hast wysdom and manhede,
Assemblen al the folk of oure kynrede,
And make a werre so scharpe on this cité,
That by som aventure, or some treté,
Thou mayst have hire to lady and to wyf,

For whom that I mot needes leese my lyf.
For as by wey of possibilité,
Syth thou art at thi large of prisoun free,
And art a lord, gret is thin avauntage,
More than is myn, that sterve here in a kage.
For I moot weepe and weyle, whil I lyve,
With al the woo that prisoun may me yyve,
And eek with peyne that love me yeveth also,
That doubleth al my torment and my wo.'
Therwith the fyr of jelousye upsterte
Withinne his breste, and hente him by the herte
So wodly, that he lik was to byholde
The box-tre, or the asschen deede and colde.
Tho seyde he; 'O cruel goddes, that governe
This world with byndyng of youre word eterne,
And writee in the table of athamaunte
Youre parlement, and youre eterne graunte,
What is mankynde more unto yow holde,
Than is the scheep, that rouketh in the folde?
For slayn is man right as another beest,
And dwelleth eek in prisoun and arreest,
And hath seknesse, and greet adversité,
And ofte tymes gilteles, pardé.
What gouvernaunce is in this prescience,
That gilteles tormenteth innocence?
And yet encresceth al this my penaunce,
That man is bounden to his observaunce
For Goddes sake to letten of his wille,
There as a beeste may al his lust fulfille.
And whan a beeste is deed, he hath no peyne;
But man after his deth moot wepe and pleyne,
Though in this world he have care and woo:
Withouten doute it may stonde so.
The answere of this I lete to divinis,
But wel I woot, that in this world gret pyne is.
Allas! I se a serpent or a theef,
That many a trewe man hath done mescheef,

Gon at his large, and wher him lust may turne.
But I moot ben in prisoun thurgh Saturne,
And eek thurgh Juno, jalous and eek wood,
That hath destruyed wel nygh al the blood
Of Thebes, with his waste walles wyde.
And Venus sleeth me on that other syde
For jelousye, and fere of him Arcyte.'
 Now wol I stynte of Palamon a lite,
And lete him in his prisoun stille dwelle,
And of Arcita forth I wol you telle.
The somer passeth, and the nightes longe
Encrescen double wise the peynes stronge
Bothe of the lovere and the prisoner.
I noot which hath the wofullere myster.
For schortly for to seyn, this Palamoun
Perpetuelly is dampned to prisoun,
In cheynes and in fettres to be deed;
And Arcite is exiled upon his heed
For evere mo as out of that contré,
Ne nevere mo he schal his lady see.
 Yow loveres axe I now this questioun,
Who hath the worse, Arcite or Palamoun?
That on may se his lady day by day,
But in prisoun he moste dwelle alway.
That other wher him lust may ryde or go,
But seen his lady schal he nevere mo.
Now deemeth as you luste, ye that can,
For I wol telle forth as I began.
 Whan that Arcite to Thebes comen was,
Ful ofte a day he swelte and seye alas,
For seen his lady schal he never mo.
And schortly to concluden al his wo,
So moche sorwe hadde nevere creature,
That is or schal whil that the world may dure.
His sleep, his mete, his drynk is him byraft,
That lene he wex, and drye as is a schaft.
His eyen holwe, and grisly to biholde;

His hewe falwe, and pale as asschen colde,
And solitarye he was, and evere allone,
And waillyng al the night, making his moone.
And if he herde song or instrument,
Then wolde he wepe, he mighte nought be stent;
So feble eek were his spiritz, and so lowe.
And chaunged so, that no man couthe knowe
His speche nother his vois, though men it herde.
And in his geere, for al the world he ferde
Nought oonly lyke the loveres maladye.
Of Hereos, but rather lik manye
Engendred of humour malencolyk,
Byforen in his selle fanatastyk.
And schortly turned was al up-so-doun
Bothe habyt and eek disposicioun
Of him, this woful lovere daun Arcite.
What schulde I alday of his wo endite?
Whan he endured hadde a yeer or tuo
This cruel torment, and this peyne and woo,
At Thebes, in his contré, as I seyde,
Upon a night in sleep as he him leyde,
Him thoughte how that the wenged god Mercurie
Byforn him stood, and bad him to be murye,
His slepy yerde in hond he bar uprighte;
An hat he werede upon his heres brighte.
Arrayed was this god (as he took keepe)
As he was whan that Argus took his sleepe;
And seyde him thus: 'To Athenes schalt thou wende;
There is the schapen of thy wo an ende.'
And with that word Arcite wook and sterte.
'Now trewely how sore that me smerte.'
Quod he, 'to Athenes right now wol I fare;
Ne for the drede of deth schal I not spare
To see my lady, that I love and serve;
In hire presence I recche nat to sterve.'
And with that word he caughte a gret myrour,

And saugh that chaunged was al his colour,
And saugh his visage al in another kynde.
And right anoon it ran him in his mynde.
That sith his face was so disfigured
Of maladie the which he hadde endured,
He mighte wel, if that he bar him lowe,
Lyve in Athenes evere more unknowe,
And seen his lady wel neih day by day.
And right anon he chaungede his aray,
And cladde him as a poure laborer.
And al allone, save oonly a squyer,
That knew his pryveté and al his cas,
Which was disgysed povrely as he was,
To Athenes is he gon the nexte way.
And to the court he wente upon a day,
And at the yate he profreth his servyse,
To drugge and drawe, what so men wol devyse.
And schortly of this matere for to seyn,
He fel in office with a chamberleyn,
The which that dwellyng was with Emelye.
For he was wys, and couthe sone aspye
Of every servant, which that serveth here.
Wel couthe he hewen woode, and water bere,
For he was yong and mighty for the nones,
And thereto he was strong and bygge of bones
To doon that eny wight can him devyse.
A yeer or two he was in this servise,
Page of the chambre of Emelye the brighte;
And Philostrate he seide that he highte.
And half so wel byloved a man as he
Ne was ther nevere in court of his degree.
He was so gentil of condicioun,
That thurghout al the court was his renoun.
They seyde that it were a charité
That Theseus wolde enhaunse his degree,
And putten him in worschipful servyse,
Ther as he mighte his vertu excercise.

And thus withinne a while his name is spronge
Bothe of his dedes, and his goode tonge,
That Theseus hath taken him so neer
That of his chambre he hath made him squyer,
And yaf him gold to mayntene his degree ;
And eek men broughte him out of his countré
Fro yeer to yeer ful pryvely his rente ;
But honestly and sleighly he it spente,
That no man wondrede how that he it hadde.
And thre yeer in this wise his lyfe he ladde,
And bar him so in pees and eek in warre,
Ther nas no man that Theseus hath deere.
And in this blisse let I now Arcite,
And speke I wole of Palamon a lyte.
 In derknesse and horrible and strong prisoun
This seven yeer hath seten Palamoun,
Forpyned, what for woo and for distresse;
Who feleth double sorwe and hevynesse
But Palamon? that love destreyneth so,
That wood out of his wit he goth for wo ;
And eke therto he is a prisoner
Perpetuelly, nat oonly for a yeer.
Who couthe ryme in Englissch proprely
His martirdam? for sothe it am nat I ;
Therfore I passe as lightly as I may.
Hit fel that in the seventhe yeer in May
The thridde night, (as olde bookes seyn,
That al this storie tellen more pleyn)
Were it by aventure or destiné,
(As, whan a thing is schapen, it schal be,)
That soone after the mydnyght, Palamoun
By helpyng of a freend brak his prisoun,
And fleeth the cité faste as he may goo,
For he hadde yive his gayler drinke soo
Of a clarré, maad of a certeyn wyn,
With nercotykes and opye of Thebes fyn,
That al that night though that men wolde him schake,

The gayler sleep, he mighte nought awake.
And thus he fleeth as faste as evere he may.
The night was schort, and faste by the day,
That needes-cost he moste himselven hyde,
And til a grove faste ther besyde
With dredful foot than stalketh Palamoun.
For schortly this was his opynyoun,
That in that grove he wolde him hyde al day,
And in the night then wolde he take his way
To Thebes-ward, his frendes for to preye
On Theseus to helpe him to werreye;
And schorteliche, or he wolde lese his lyf,
Or wynnen Emelye unto his wyf.
This is theffect and his entente playn.
Now wol I torne unto Arcite agayn,
That litel wiste how nyh that was his care,
Til that fortune hadde brought him in the snare.

  The busy larke, messager of daye,
Salueth in hire song the morwe graye;
And fyry Phebus ryseth up so brighte,
That al the orient laugheth of the lighte,
And with his stremes dryeth in the greves
The silver dropes, hongyng on the leeves.
And Arcite, that is in the court ryal
With Theseus, his squyer principal,
Is risen, and loketh on the merye day.
And for to doon his observaunce to May,
Remembryng on the poynt of his desir,
He on his courser, stertyng as the fir,
Is riden into the feeldes him to pleye,
Out of the court, were it a myle or tweye.
And to the grove, of which that I yow tolde,
By aventure his wey he gan to holde,
To maken him a garland of the greves,
Were it of woodebyne or hawethorn leves,
And lowde he song ayens the sonne scheene:
' May, with alle thy floures and thy greene,

Welcome be thou, wel faire fressche May,
I hope that I som grene gete may.'
And fro his courser, with a lusty herte,
Into the grove ful hastily he sterte,
And in a path he rometh up and doun,
Ther as by aventure this Palamoun
Was in a busche, that no man mighte him see,
For sore afered of his deth was he.
Nothing ne knew he that it was Arcite:
God wot he wolde han trowed it ful lite.
But soth is seyd, goon sithen many yeres,
That feld hath eyen, and the woode hath eeres.
It is ful fair a man to bere him evene,
For al day meteth men at unset stevene.
Ful litel woot Arcite of his felawe,
That was so neih to herknen al his sawe,
For in the busche he sytteth now ful stille.
Whan that Arcite hadde romed al his fille,
And songen al the roundel lustily,
Into a studie he fel al sodeynly,
As don thes loveres in here queynte geeres,
Now in the croppe, now doun in the breres,
Now up, now doun, as boket in a welle.
Right as the Friday, sothly for to telle,
Now it schyneth, now it reyneth faste,
Right so gan gery Venus overcaste
The hertes of hire folk, right as hire day
Is gerful, right so chaungeth sche array.
Selde is the Fryday al the wyke i-like.
Whan that Arcite hadde songe, he gan to sike,
And sette him doun withouten eny more:
'Alas!' quod he, 'that day that I was bore!
How longe Juno, thurgh thy cruelté,
Wiltow werreyen Thebes the citee?
Allas! i-brou*g*ht is to confusioun
The blood royal of Cadme and Amphioun;
Of Cadmus, which that was the firste man

That Thebes bulde, or first the toun bgban,
And of that cité first was crowned kyng,
Of his lynage am I, and his ofspring
By verray lyne, as of the stok ryal :
And now I am so caytyf and so thral,
That he that is my mortal enemy,
I serve him as my squyer povrely.
And yet doth Juno me wel more schame,
For I dar nought byknowe myn owne name,
But ther as I was wont to hote Arcite,
Now highte I Philostrate, nought worth a myte.
Allas ! thou felle Mars, allas ! Juno,
Thus hath youre ire owre kynrede al fordo,
Save oonly me, and wrecched Palamoun,
That Theseus martyreth in prisoun.
And over al this, to sleen me utterly,
Love hath his fyry dart so brennyngly
I-styked thurgh my trewe careful herte,
That schapen was my deth erst than my scherte.
Ye slen me with youre eyen, Emelye ;
Ye ben the cause wherfore that I dye.
Of al the remenant of myn other care
Ne sette I nought the mountaunce of a tare,
So that I couthe don aught to youre plesaunce.'
And with that word he fel doun in a traunce
A long tyme ; and afterward he upsterte
This Palamon, that thoughte that thurgh his herte
He felte a cold swerd sodeynliche glyde ;
For ire he quook, no lenger nolde he byde.
And whan that he had herd Arcites tale,
As he were wood, with face deed and pale,
He sterte him up out of the bussches thikke,
And seyde : 'Arcyte, false traitour wikke,
Now art thou hent, that lovest my lady so,
For whom that I have al this peyne and wo,
And art my blood, and to my counseil sworn,
As I ful ofte have told the heere byforn,

And hast byjaped here duk Theseus,
And falsly chaunged hast thy name thus;
I wol be deed, or elles thou schalt dye.
Thou schalt not love my lady Emelye,
But I wil love hire oonly and no mo;
For I am Palamon thy mortal fo.
And though that I no wepne have in this place,
But out of prisoun am astert by grace,
I drede not that outher thou schalt dye,
Or thou ne schalt not loven Emelye.
Ches which thou wilt, for thou schalt not asterte.'
This Arcite, with ful despitous herte,
Whan he him knew, and hadde his tale herd,
As fers as a lyoun pullede out a swerd,
And seide thus: 'By God that sit above,
Nere it that thou art sik and wood for love,
And eek that thou no wepne hast in this place,
Thou schuldest nevere out of this grove pace,
That thou ne schuldest deyen of myn hond.
For I defye the seurté and the bond
Which that thou seyst that I have maad to the.
What, verray fool, think wel that love is fre!
And I wol love hire mawgre al thy might.
But, for as muche thou art a worthy knight,
And wilnest to derreyne hire by batayle,
Have heer my trouthe, to-morwe I nyl not fayle,
Withouten wityng of eny other wight,
That heer I wol be founden as a knight,
And bryngen harneys right inough for the;
And ches the beste, and lef the worse for me.
And mete and drynke this night wil I brynge
Inough for the, and clothes for thy beddynge.
And if so be that thou my lady wynne,
And sle me in this woode ther I am inne,
Thou maist wel han thy lady as for me.'
This Palamon answerde: 'I graunte it the.'

And thus they ben departed til a-morwe,
When ech of hem hadde leyd his feith to borwe.
  O Cupide, out of alle charité !
O regne, that wolt no felawe han with the !
Ful soth is seyd, that love no lordschipe
Wol not, his thonkes, han no felaweschipe.
Wel fynden that Arcite and Palamoun.
Arcite is riden anon unto the toun,
And on the morwe, or it were dayes light,
Ful prively two harneys hath he dight,
Bothe suffisaunt and mete to darreyne
The bataylle in the feeld betwix hem tweyne.
And on his hors, allone as he was born,
He caryeth al this harnes him byforn;
And in the grove, at tyme and place i-set,
This Arcite and this Palamon ben met.
Tho chaungen gan the colour in here face.
Right as the honter in the regne of Trace
That stondeth at the gappe with a spere,
Whan honted is the lyoun or the bere,
And hereth him come ruschyng in the greves,
And breketh bothe bowes and the leves,
And thinketh, 'Here cometh my mortel enemy,
Withoute faile, he mot be deed or I ;
For eyther I mot sleen him at the gappe,
Or he moot sleen me, if that me myshappe :'
So ferden they, in chaungyng of here hewe,
As fer as everich of hem other knewe.
Ther nas no good day, ne no saluyng ;
But streyt withouten word or rehersyng,
Everych of hem help for to armen other,
As frendly as he were his owne brother ;
And after that with scharpe speres stronge
They foynen ech at other wonder longe.
Thou myghtest wene that this Palamon
In his fightynge were as a wood lyoun,
And as a cruel tygre was Arcite :
As wilde boores gonne they to smyte,

That frothen white as foom for ire wood.
Up to the ancle foughte they in here blood.
And in this wise I lete hem fightyng dwelle ;
And forth I wol of Theseus yow telle.
  The destyné, mynistre general,
That executeth in the world over-al
The purveiauns, that God hath seyn byforn ;
So strong it is, that though the world hadde sworn
The contrarye of a thing by ye or nay,
Yet somtyme it schal falle upon a day
That falleth nought eft withinne a thousand yeere.
For certeynly our appetites heere,
Be it of werre, or pees, or hate, or love,
Al is it reuled by the sighte above.
This mene I now by mighty Theseus,
That for to honten is so desirous,
And namely at the grete hert in May,
That in his bed ther daweth him no day,
That he nys clad, and redy for to ryde
With honte and horn, and houndes him byside.
For in his hontyng hath he such delyt,
That it is al his joye and appetyt
To been himself the grete hertes bane,
For after Mars he serveth now Diane.
  Cleer was the day, as I have told or this,
And Theseus, with alle joye and blys,
With his Ypolita, the fayre queene,
And Emelye, clothed al in greene,
On honting be thay riden ryally.
And to the grove, that stood ful faste by,
In which ther was an hert as men him tolde,
Duk Theseus the streyte wey hath holde.
And to the launde he rydeth him ful righte,
For thider was the hert wont have his flighte,
And over a brook, and so forth in his weye.
This duk wol han a cours at him or tweye
With houndes, swiche as that him lust comaunde.

And whan this duk was come unto the launde,
Under the sonne he loketh, and anon
He was war of Arcite and Palamon,
That foughten breeme, as it were boores tuo ;
The brighte swerdes went to and fro
So hidously, that with the leste strook
It seemede as it wolde felle an ook ;
But what they were, nothing he ne woot.
This duk his courser with his spores smoot,
And at a stert he was betwix hem tuoo,
And pullede out a swerd and cride, ' Hoo !
Nomore, up peyne of leesyng of youre heed.
By mighty Mars, he schal anon be deed,
That smyteth eny strook, that I may seen !
But telleth me what mester men ye been,
That ben so hardy for to fighten heere
Withoute jugge or other officere,
As it were in a lystes really ?'
This Palamon answerde hastily,
And seyde: 'Sire, what nedeth wordes mo ?
We han the deth deserved bothe tuo.
Tuo woful wrecches been we, tuo kaytyves,
That ben encombred of oure owne lyves ;
And as thou art a rightful lord and juge,
Ne yeve us neyther mercy ne refuge.
And sle me first, for seynte charité ;
But sle my felawe eek as wel as me.
Or sle him first ; for, though thou knowe it lyte,
This is thy mortal foe, this is Arcite,
That fro thy lond is banyscht on his heed,
For which he hath deserved to be deed.
For this is he that com unto thi gate
And seyde, that he highte Philostrate.
Thus hath he japed the ful many a yer,
And thou hast maked him thy cheef squyer.
And this is he that loveth Emelye.
For sith the day is come that I schal dye,

I make pleynly my confessioun,
That I am thilke woful Palamoun,
That hath thy prisoun broke wikkedly.
I am thy mortal foo, and it am I
That loveth so hoote Emelye the brighte,
That I wol dye present in hire sighte.
Therfore I aske deeth and my juwyse ;
But slee my felawe in the same wyse,
For both han we deserved to be slayn.'

  This worthy duk answerde anon agayn,
And seide, ' This is a schort conclusioun :
Youre owne mouthe, by youre confessioun,
Hath dampned you, and I wil it recorde.
It nedeth nought to pyne yow with the corde.
Ye schul be deed by mighty Mars the reede !'
The queen anon for verray wommanhede
Gan for to wepe, and so dede Emelye,
And alle the ladies in the compainye.
Gret pité was it, as it thoughte hem alle,
That evere suche a chaunce schulde falle ;
For gentil men thei were, of gret estate,
And nothing but for love was this debate.
And sawe here bloody woundes wyde and sore ;
And alle cryden, bothe lasse and more,
' Have mercy, Lord, upon us wommen alle !'
And on here bare knees adoun they falle,
And wolde han kist his feet ther as he stood,
Til atte laste aslaked was his mood ;
For pité renneth sone in gentil herte.
And though he first for ire quok and sterte,
He hath considerd shortly in a clause,
The trespas of hem bothe, and eek the cause :
And although that his ire here gylt accusede,
Yet in his resoun he hem bothe excusede ;
And thus he thoughte wel that every man
Wol helpe himself in love if that he can,
And eek delyvere himself out of prisoun ;

And eek his herte hadde compassioun
Of wommen, for they wepen evere in oon;
And in his gentil herte he thoughte anoon,
And softe unto himself he seyde : ' Fy
Upon a lord that wol han no mercy,
But ben a lyoun bothe in word and dede,
To hem that ben in repentaunce and drede,
As wel as to a proud despitous man,
That wol maynteyne that he first bigan !
That lord hath litel of discrecioun,
That in such caas can no divisioun ;
But weyeth pride and humblesse after oon.'
And schortly, when his ire is thus agon,
He gan to loken up with eyen lighte,
And spak these same wordes al on highte.
' The god of love, a ! *benedicite*,
How mighty and how gret a lord is he !
Agayns his might ther gayneth no obstacles,
He may be cleped a god for his miracles ;
For he can maken at his owne gyse
Of everych herte, as that him lust devyse.
Lo her this Arcite and this Palamoun,
That quytly weren out of my prisoun,
And mighte han lyved in Thebes ryally,
And witen I am here mortal enemy,
And that here deth lith in my might also,
And *yet* hath love, maugre here ey*gh*en tuo,
I-brought hem hider bothe for to dye.
Now loketh, is nat that an heih folye ?
Who may not ben a fool, if that he love ?
Byhold for Goddes sake that sit above,
Se how they blede ! be they nought wel arrayed ?
Thus hath here lord, the god of loue, y-payed
Here wages and here fees for here servise.
And yet they wenen for to ben ful wise
That serven love, for ought that may bifalle.
But this is *yet* the beste game of alle,

That sche, for whom they han this jolitee,
Can hem therfore as moche thanke as me.
Sche woot no more of al this hoote fare,
By God, than wot a cockow or an hare.
But al moot ben assayed, hoot and cold;
A man moot ben a fool or *yong* or old;
I woot it by myself ful *yore* agon:
For in my tyme a servant was I on.
And therefore, syn I knowe of loves peyne,
And wot how sore it can a man distreyne,
As he that hath ben caught ofte in his laas,
I you for*yeve* al holly this trespaas,
At requeste of the queen that kneleth heere,
And eek of Emelye, my suster deere.
And ye schul bothe anon unto me swere,
That neveremo *ye* schul my corowne dere,
Ne make werre upon me night ne day,
But ben my freendes in al that *ye* may.
I *yow* for*yeve* this trespas every del.'
And they him swore his axyng fayre and wel,
And him of lordschipe and of mercy prayde,
And he hem graunteth grace, and thus he
  sayde:
'To speke of real lynage and richesse,
Though that sche were a queen or a pryncesse,
Ech of *yow* bothe is worthy douteles
To wedden when tyme is, but natheles
I speke as for my suster Emelye,
For whom *ye* han this stryf and jelousye,
Ye wite *youreself* sche may not wedde two
At oonehs, though ye fighten evere mo:
That oon of *yow*, al be him loth or leef,
He mot go pypen in an ivy leef;
This is to sayn, sche may nought now han bothe,
Al be *ye* nevere so jelous, ne so wrothe.
And for-thy I *you* putte in this degré,
That ech of *you* schal have his destyné,

As him is schape, and herkneth in what wyse;
Lo here youre ende of that I schal devyse.
  My wil is this, for plat conclusioun,
Withouten eny repplicacioun,
If that you liketh, tak it for the beste,
That everych of you shal gon wher him leste
Frely withouten raunsoun or daunger;
And this day fyfty wykes, fer ne neer,
Everich of you schal brynge an hundred knightes,
Armed for lystes up at alle rightes,
Al redy to derrayne hire by bataylle.
And this byhote I you withouten faylle
Upon my trouthe, and as I am a knight,
That whether of yow bothe that hath might,
This is to seyn, that whether he or thou
May with his hundred, as I spak of now,
Slen his contrarye, or out of lystes dryve,
Thanne schal I yeven Emelye to wyve,
To whom that fortune yeveth so faire a grace.
The lystes schal I maken in this place,
And God so wisly on my soule rewe,
As I schal evene juge ben and trewe,
Ye schul non other ende with me make,
That oon of yow ne schal be deed or take.
And if you thinketh this is wel i-sayd,
Sayeth youre avys, and holdeth yow apayd.
This is youre ende and youre conclusioun.'
Who loketh lightly now but Palamoun?
Who spryngeth up for joye but Arcite?
Who couthe telle, or who couthe it endite,
The joye that is maked in the place
Whan Theseus hath don so fair a grace?
But down on knees wente every maner wight,
And thanken him with al here herte and miht,
And namely the Thebans ofte sithe.
And thus with good hope and with herte blithe
They take here leve, and hom-ward gonne they ride
To Thebes with his olde walles wyde.

I trowe men wolde deme it necligence,
If I foryete to telle the dispence
Of Theseus, that goth so busily
To maken up the lystes rially;
That such a noble theatre as it was,
I dar wel sayn that in this world ther nas.
The circuit a myle was aboute,
Walled of stoon, and dyched al withoute.
Round was the schap, in manere of compaas,
Ful of degrees, the heighte of sixty paas
That whan a man was set on o degré
He lette nought his felawe for to se.
   Est-ward ther stood a gate of marbel whit,
West-ward right such another in the opposit.
And schortly to conclude, such a place
Was non in erthe as in so litel space;
For in the lond ther nas no crafty man,
That geometrye or arsmetrike can,
Ne portreyour, ne kervere of ymages,
That Theseus ne yaf hem mete and wages
The theatre for to maken and devyse.
And for to don his ryte and sacrifise,
He est-ward hath upon the gate above,
In worschipe of Venus, goddesse of love,
Don make an auter and an oratorye;
And west-ward, in the mynde and in memorye
Of Mars, he hath i-maked such another,
That coste largely of gold a fother.
And north-ward, in a toret on the walle,
Of alabaster whit and reed coralle
An oratorye riche for to see,
In worschipe of Dyane, of chastité.
Hath Theseus doon wrought in noble wise.
But yit hadde I foryeten to devyse
The noble kervyng, and the purtreitures,
The schap, the contenaunce and the figures,
The weren in these oratories thre.

First in the temple of Venus maystow se
Wrought on the wal, ful pitous to byholde,
The broken slepes, and the sykes colde;
The sacred teeres, and the waymentyng;
The fyry strokes of the desiryng,
That loves servauntz in this lyf enduren;
The othes, that here covenantz assuren.
Plesaunce and hope, desyr, fool-hardynesse,
Beauté and youthe, bauderye and richesse,
Charmes and force, lesynges and flaterye,
Dispense, busynesse, and jelousye,
That werede of yelwe guldes a gerland,
And a cokkow sittyng on hire hand;
Festes, instrumentz, caroles, daunces,
Lust and array, and alle the circumstaunces
Of love, whiche that I rekned have and schal,
By ordre weren peynted on the wal.
And mo than I can make of mencioun.
For sothly al the mount of Citheroun,
Ther Venus hath hire principal dwellyng,
Was schewed on the wal in portreying,
With al the gardyn, and the lustynesse.
Nought was foryete the porter Ydelnesse,
Ne Narcisus the fayre of yore agon,
Ne yet the folye of kyng Salamon,
Ne eek the grete strengthe of Hercules,
Thenchauntementz of Medea and Circes,
Ne of Turnus with the hardy fiers corage,
The riche Cresus caytif in servage.
Thus may ye seen that wisdom ne richesse,
Beauté ne sleighte, strengthe, ne hardynesse,
Ne may with Venus holde champartye,
For as hire lust the world than may sche gye,
Lo, alle thise folk i-caught were in hire las,
Til they for wo ful often sayde allas.
Sufficeth heere ensamples oon or tuo,
And though I couthe rekne a thousend mo.

The statue of Venus, glorious for to see,
Was naked fletyng in the large see,
And fro the navele doun al covered was
With wawes grene, and brighte as eny glas.
A citole in hire right hond hadde sche,
And on hire heed, ful semely for to see,
A rose garland fresch and wel smellyng,
Above hire heed hire dowves flikeryng.
Biforn hire stood hire sone Cupido,
Upon his schuldres wynges hadde he two;
And blynd he was, as it is ofte seene;
A bowe he bar and arwes brighte and kene.
Why schulde I nought as wel eek telle you al
The portreiture, that was upon the wal
Withinne the temple of mighty Mars the reede?
Al peynted was the wal in lengthe and breede
Lik to the estres of the grisly place,
That highte the grete temple of Mars in Trace,
In thilke colde frosty regioun,
Ther as Mars hath his sovereyn mancioun.
First on the wal was peynted a forest,
In which ther dwelleth neyther man ne best,
With knotty narry bareyne trees olde
Of stubbes scharpe and hidous to byholde;
In which ther ran a swymbel in a swough,
As though a storm schulde bersten every bough:
And downward on an hil under a bente,
Ther stood the temple of Marz armypotente,
Wrought al of burned steel, of which thentré
Was long and streyt, and gastly for to see.
And therout cam a rage and such a vese,
That it made al the gates for to rese.
The northen light in at the dores schon,
For wyndowe on the wal ne was ther noon,
Thurgh which men mighten any light discerne.
The dores were alle of ademauntz eterne,
I-clenched overthwart and endelong

With iren tough ; and, for to make it strong,
Every piler the temple to susteene
Was tonne greet, of iren bright and schene.
Ther saugh I first the derke ymaginyng
Of felonye, and al the compassyng ;
The cruel ire, as reed as eny gleede ;
The pikepurs, and eek the pale drede ;
The smylere with the knyf under the cloke ;
The schepne brennyng with the blake smoke ;
The tresoun of the murtheryng in the bed ;
The open werre, with woundes al bi-bled ;
Contek with bloody knyf, and scharp manace.
Al ful of chirkyng was that sory place.
The sleere of himself yet saugh I there,
His herte-blood hath bathed al his here ;
The nayl y-dryven in the schode a-nyght ;
The colde deth, with mouth gapyng upright.
Amyddes of the temple sat meschaunce,
With disconfort and sory contenaunce.
Yet saugh I woodnesse laughying in his rage ;
Armed complaint, outhees, and fiers outrage.
The caroigne in the bussh, with throte y-corve :
A thousand slain, and not of qualme y-storve ;
The tiraunt, with the prey by force y-raft ;
The toun destroied, ther was no thyng laft.
Yet sawgh I brent the schippes hoppesteres ;
The hunte strangled with the wilde beres :
The sowe freten the child right in the cradel ;
The cook i-skalded, for al his longe ladel.
Nought was foryeten by the infortune of Marte ;
The cartere over-ryden with his carte,
Under the whel ful lowe he lay adoun.
Ther were also of Martes divisioun,
The barbour, and the bocher ; and the smyth
That forgeth scharpe swerdes on his stith.
And al above depeynted in a tour
Saw I conquest sittyng in gret honour,

With the scharpe swerd over his heed
Hangynge by a sotil twynes threed.
Depeynted was the slaughtre of Julius,
Of grete Nero, and of Anthonius;
Al be that thilke tyme they were unborn,
Yet was here deth depeynted ther byforn,
By manasyng of Mars, right by figure,
So was it schewed in that purtreiture
As is depeynted in the sterres above,
Who schal be slayn or elles deed for love.
Sufficeth oon ensample in stories olde,
I may not rekne hem alle, though I wolde.

   The statue of Mars upon a carte stood,
Armed, and lokede grym as he were wood;
And over his heed ther schynen two figures
Of sterres, that had been cleped in scriptures,
That oon Puella, that other Rubeus.
This god of armes was arrayed thus:—
A wolf ther stood byforn him at his feet
With eyen reede, and of a man he eet;
With sotyl pencel depeynted was this storie,
In redoutyng of Mars and of his glorie.

   Now to the temple of Dyane the chaste
As schortly as I can I wol me haste,
To telle you al the descripcioun.
Depeynted ben the walles up and down,
Of huntyng and of schamefast chastité.
Ther saugh I how woful Calystopé,
Whan that Dyane agreved was with here,
Was turned from a womman to a bere,
And after was sche maad the loode-sterre;
Thus was it peynted, I can say you no ferre;
Hire sone is eek a sterre, as men may see.
Ther sawgh I Dane yturned til a tree,
I mene nought the goddesse Dyane,
But Penneus doughter, which that highte Dane.
Ther saugh I Atheon an hert i-maked,

For vengeaunce that he saugh Dyane al naked;
I saugh how that his houndes han him caught,
And freten him, for that they knewe him naught.
Yit peynted was a litel forthermoor,
How Atthalaunte huntede the wilde boor,
And Meleagre, and many another mo,
For which Dyane wroughte hem care and woo.
Ther saugh I many another wonder storye,
The whiche me list not drawe to memorye.
This goddesse on an hert ful hyhe seet,
With smale houndes al aboute hire feet,
And undernethe hire feet sche hadde a moone,
Wexyng it was, and schulde wane soone.
In gaude greene hire statue clothed was,
With bowe in honde, and arwes in a cas.
Hir eyghen caste sche ful lowe adoun,
Ther Pluto hath his derke regioun.
A womman travailyng was hire biforn,
But, for hire child so longe was unborn,
Ful pitously Lucyna gan sche calle,
And seyde, 'Help, for thou mayst best of alle.'
Wel couthe he peynte lyfly that it wroughte,
With many a floryn he the hewes boughte.

  Now been thise listes maad, and Theseus
That at his grete cost arrayede thus
The temples and the theatre every del,
Whan it was don, hym likede wonder wel.
But stynte I wil of Theseus a lite,
And speke of Palamon and of Arcite.
  The day approcheth of here retournynge,
That everych schulde an hundred knightes brynge,
The bataille to derreyne, as I you tolde;
And til Athenes, here covenant to holde,
Hath everych of hem brought an hundred knightes
Wel armed for the werre at alle rightes.
And sikerly ther trowede many a man
That nevere, siththen that the world bigan,

As for to speke of knighthod of here hond,
As fer as God hath maked see or lond,
Nas, of so fewe, so noble a compainye.
For every wight that lovede chyvalrye,
And wolde, his thankes, han a passant name,
Hath preyed that he mighte ben of that game;
And wel was him, that therto chosen was.
For if ther felle to morwe such a caas,
Ye knowen wel, that every lusty knight,
That loveth paramours, and hath his might,
Were it in Engelond, or elleswhere,
They wolde, here thankes, wilne to be there.
To fighte for a lady; *benedicite!*
It were a lusty sighte for to see.
And right so ferden they with Palamon.
With him ther wente knyghtes many oon;
Som wol ben armed in an habergoun,
In a brest-plat and in a light gypoun;
And somme woln have a peyre plates large;
And somme woln have a Pruce scheld, or a targe;
Somme woln been armed on here legges weel,
And have an ax, and somme a mace of steel.
Ther nys no newe gyse, that it nas old.
Armed were they, as I have you told,
Everich after his opinioun.

 Ther maistow sen comyng with Palamoun
Ligurge himselfe, the grete kyng of Trace;
Blak was his berd, and manly was his face.
The cercles of his eyen in his heed
They gloweden bytwixe yelwe and reed;
And lik a griffoun lokede he aboute,
With kempe heres on his browes stowte;
His lymes greete, his brawnes harde and stronge,
His schuldres broode, his armes rounde and longe.
And as the gyse was in his contré,
Ful heye upon a char of gold stood he,
With foure white boles in the trays.

Instede of cote armure over his harnays,
With nayles yelwe, and brighte as eny gold,
He hadde a beres skyn, col-blak, for-old.
His longe heer was kembd byhynde his bak,
As eny ravenes fether it schon for-blak.
A wrethe of gold arm-gret, of huge wighte,
Upon his heed, set ful of stoones brighte,
Of fyne rubies and of dyamauntz.
Aboute his char ther wenten white alauntz,
Twenty and mo, as grete as eny steer,
To hunten at the lyoun or the deer,
And folwede him, with mosel faste i-bounde,
Colers of golde, and torettz fyled rounde.
An hundred lordes hadde he in his route
Armed ful wel, with hertes sterne and stoute.

    With Arcita, in stories as men fynde,
The grete Emetreus, the kyng of Ynde,
Uppon a steede bay, trapped in steel,
Covered in cloth of gold dyapred wel,
Cam rydyng lyk the god of armes, Mars.
His coote-armure was of cloth of Tars,
Cowched with perles whyte and rounde and grete.
His sadel was of brend gold newe ybete ;
A mantelet upon his schuldre hangynge
Bret-ful of rubies reede, as fir sparklynge.
His crispe heer lik rynges was i-ronne,
And that was yelwe, and gliterede as the sonne.
His nose was heigh, his eyen bright cytryn,
His lippes rounde, his colour was sangwyn,
A fewe fraknes in his face y-spreynd,
Betwixen yelwe and somdel blak y-meynd,
And as a lyoun he is lokyng caste.
Of fyve and twenty yeer his age I caste.
His berd was wel bygonne for to sprynge ;
His voys was as a trumpe thunderynge.
Upon his heed he werede of laurer grene
A garlond fresch and lusty for to sene.

Upon his hond he bar for his deduyt
An egle tame, as eny lylie whyt.
An hundred lordes hadde he with him ther,
Al armed sauf here hedes in here ger,
Ful richely in alle maner thinges.
For trusteth wel, that dukes, erles, kynges,
Were gadred in this noble compainye,
For love, and for encrees of chivalrye.
Aboute this kyng ther ran on every part
Ful many a tame lyoun and lepart.
And in this wise thise lordes alle and some
Been on the Sonday to the cité come
Aboute prime, and in the toun alight.
This Theseus, this duk, this worthy knight,
When he hadde brought hem into his cité,
And ynned hem, everich at his degré
He festeth him, and doth so gret labour
To esen hem, and don hem al honour,
That yit men wene that no mannes wyt
Of non estat ne cowde amenden it.
The mynstralcye, the servyce at the feste,
The grete yiftes to the moste and leste,
The riche array of Theseus paleys,
Ne who sat first ne last upon the deys,
What ladies fayrest ben or best daunsynge,
Or which of hem can daunce best and singe,
Ne who most felyngly speketh of love;
What haukes sitten on the perche above,
What houndes liggen on the floor adoun:
Of al this make I now no mencioun,
But of theffect; that thinketh me the beste;
Now comth the poynt, and herkneth if you leste.
 The Sonday night, or day bigan to springe,
When Palamon the larke herde synge,
Although it nere nought day by houres tuo,
Yit sang the larke, and Palamon also.
With holy herte, and with an heih corage

He roos, to wenden on his pilgrymage
Unto the blisful Citherea benigne,
I mene Venus, honurable and digne.
And in hire hour he walketh forth a paas
Unto the lystes, ther hire temple was,
And doun he kneleth, and, with humble cheere
And herte sore, he seide as ye schul heere.

'Faireste of faire, o lady myn Venus,
Doughter of Jove, and spouse to Vulcanus,
Thou gladere of the mount of Citheroun,
For thilke love thou haddest to Adoun
Have pité of my bittre teeres smerte,
And tak myn humble prayere to thin herte.
Allas! I ne have no langage to telle
Theffectes ne the tormentz of myn helle;
Myn herte may myne harmes nat bewreye;
I am so confus, that I can not seye.
But mercy, lady brighte, that knowest wele
My thought, and seest what harmes that I fele,
Considre al this, and rewe upon my sore,
As wisly as I schal for evermore,
Emforth my might, thi trewe servaunt be,
And holden werre alway with chastité;
That make I myn avow, so ye me helpe.
I kepe nat of armes for to yelpe.
Ne I ne aske nat to-morwe to have victorie,
Ne renoun in this caas, ne veyne glorie
Of pris of armes, blowen up and doun,
But I wolde have fully possessioun
Of Emelye, and dye in thi servise;
Fynd thou the manere how, and in what wyse
I recche nat, but it may better be,
To have victorie of hem, or they of me,
So that I have my lady in myne armes.
For though so be that Mars is god of armes,
Youre vertu is so gret in hevene above,
That if you list I schal wel han my love.

Thy temple wol I worschipe everemo,
And on thin auter, wher I ryde or go,
I wol don sacrifice, and fyres beete.
And if *ye* wol nat so, my lady sweete,
Than praye I the, to-morwe with a spere
That Arcita me thurgh the herte bere.
Thanne rekke I nat, whan I have lost my lyf,
Though that Arcite wynne hire to his wyf.
This is theffect and ende of my prayere,
*Y*if me my love, thou blisful lady deere.'
Whan thorisoun was doon of Palamon,
His sacrifice he dede, and that anoon
Ful pitously, with alle circumstaunces,
Al telle I nat as now his observaunces.
But atte laste the statue of Venus schook,
And made a signe, wherby that he took
That his prayere accepted was that day.
For though the signe schewede a delay,
*Y*et wiste he wel that graunted was his boone;
And with glad herte he wente him hom ful soone.

   The thridde hour inequal that Palamon
Bigan to Venus temple for to goon,
Up roos the sonne, and up roos Emelye,
And to the temple of Diane gan sche hye.
Hire maydens, that sche thider with hire ladde,
Ful redily with hem the fyr they hadde,
Thencens, the clothes, and the remenant al
That to the sacrifice longen schal;
The hornes fulle of meth, as was the gyse;
Ther lakkede nought to don hire sacrifise.
Smokyng the temple, ful of clothes faire,
This Emelye with herte debonaire
Hire body wessch with water of a welle;
But how sche dide hire rite I dar nat telle,
But it be eny thing in general;
And *y*et it were a game to heren al;
To him that meneth wel it were no charge:

But it is good a man ben at his large.
Hire brighte heer was kempt, untressed al;
A coroune of a grene ok cerial
Upon hire heed was set ful faire and meete.
Tuo fyres on the auter gan sche beete,
And dide hire thinges, as men may biholde
In Stace of Thebes, and thise bokes olde.
Whan kyndled was the fyr, with pitous cheere
Unto Dyane sche spak, as ye may heere.
  'O chaste goddesse of the woodes greene,
To whom bothe hevene and erthe and see is seene,
Queen of the regne of Pluto derk and lowe,
Goddesse of maydens, that myn herte hast knowe
Ful many a yeer, and woost what I desire,
As keep me fro thi vengeaunce and thin yre,
That Atheon aboughte trewely:
Chaste goddesse, wel wost thou that I
Desire to ben a mayden al my lyf,
Ne nevere wol I be no love ne wyf.
I am, thou wost, yit of thi compainye,
A mayde, and love huntyng and venerye,
And for to walken in the woodes wylde,
And nought to ben a wyf, and ben with chylde.
Nought wol I knowe the compainye of man.
Now help me, lady, syth ye may and kan,
For tho thre formes that thou hast in the,
And Palamon, that hath such love to me,
And eek Arcite, that loveth me so sore,
This grace I praye the withouten more,
As sende love and pees betwixe hem two;
And fro me torne awey here hertes so,
That al here hoote love, and here desir,
And al here bisy torment, and here fyr
Be queynt, or turned in another place;
And if so be thou wolt do me no grace,
Or if my destyné be schapen so,
That I schal needes have on of hem two,

As sende me him that most desireth me.
Bihold, goddesse of clene chastité,
The bittre teeres that on my cheekes falle.
Syn thou art mayde, and kepere of us alle,
My maydenhode thou kepe and wel conserve,
And whil I lyve a mayde I wil the serve.'
　The fyres brenne upon the auter cleere,
Whil Emelye was thus in hire preyere;
But sodeinly sche saugh a sighte queynte.
For right anon on of the fyres queynte,
And quykede agayn, and after that anon
That other fyr was queynt, and al agon;
And as it queynte, it made a whistelynge,
As doth a wete brond in his brennynge.
And at the brondes ende out-ran anoon
As it were bloody dropes many oon;
For which so sore agast was Emelye,
That sche was wel neih mad, and gan to crie,
For sche ne wiste what it signifyede;
But oonly for the feere thus sche cryede
And wep, that it was pité for to heere.
And therwithal Dyane gan appeere,
With bowe in hond, right as an hunteresse,
And seyde: 'Doughter, stynt thyn hevynesse.
Among the goddes hye it is affermed,
And by eterne word write and confermed,
Thou schalt ben wedded unto oon of tho
That han for the so moche care and wo;
But unto which of hem I may nat telle.
Farwel, for I ne may no lenger dwelle.
The fyres which that on myn auter brenne
Schuln the declaren, or that thou go henne,
Thyn aventure of love, as in this caas.'
And with that word, the arwes in the caas
Of the goddesse clatren faste and rynge,
And forth sche wente, and made a vanysschynge,
For which this Emelye astoned was,

And seide, 'What amounteth this, allas!
I putte me in thy proteccioun,
Dyane, and in thi disposicioun.'
And hoom sche goth anon the nexte waye.
This is theffect, ther nys no more to saye.
   The nexte houre of Mars folwynge this,
Arcite unto the temple walked is
Of fierse Mars, to doon his sacrifise,
With alle the rites of his payen wise.
With pitous herte and heih devocioun,
Right thus to Mars he sayde his orisoun:
'O stronge god, that in the regnes colde
Of Trace honoured art and lord y-holde,
And hast in every regne and every londe
Of armes al the bridel in thyn honde,
And hem fortunest as the lust devyse,
Accept of me my pitous sacrifise.
If so be that my youthe may deserve,
And that my might be worthi for to serve
Thy godhede that I may ben on of thine,
Then praye I the to rewe upon my pyne.
For thilke peyne, and thilke hoote fyre,
In which thou whilom brentest for desyre,
Whan that thou usedest the gret bewté
Of faire freissche Venus, that is so free
And haddest hir in armes at thy wille;
And though the cries on a tyme mystille.
When Vulcanus had caught the in his laas,
And fand the liggyng by his wyf, allaas!
For thilke sorwe that was in thin herte,
Have reuthe as wel upon my peynes smerte.
I am yong and unkonnyng, as thou wost,
And, as I trowe, with love offended most,
That evere was eny lyves creature;
For sche, that doth me al this wo endure,
Ne reccheth nevere wher I synke or fleete.
And wel I woot, or sche me mercy heete,

I moot with strengthe wynne hire in the place;
And wel I wot, withouten help or grace
Of the, ne may my strengthe nought avaylle.
Then help me, lord, to-morwe in my bataylle,
For thilke fyr that whilom brente the,
As wel as thilke fir now brenneth me;
And do that I to-morwe have victorie.
Myn be the travaille, and thin be the glorie.
Thy soverein temple wol I most honouren
Of any place, and alway most labouren
In thy plesaunce and in thy craftes stronge.
And in thy temple I wol my baner honge,
And alle the armes of my compainye;
And everemore, unto that day I dye,
Eterne fyr I wol biforn the fynde.
And eek to this avow I wol me bynde:
My berd, myn heer that hangeth longe adoun,
That nevere yit ne felte offensioun
Of rasour ne of schere, I wol the yive,
And be thy trewe servaunt whil I lyve.
Now lord, have rowthe uppon my sorwes sore,
Yif me the victorie, I aske the no more.'
   The preyere stynte of Arcita the stronge,
The rynges on the temple dore that honge,
And eek the dores, clatereden ful faste,
Of which Arcita somwhat hym agaste.
The fyres brende upon the auter brighte,
That it gan al the temple for to lighte;
And swote smel the ground anon upyaf,
And Arcita anon his hand up-haf,
And more encens into the fyr he caste,
With othre rites mo; and atte laste
The statue of Mars bigan his hauberk rynge.
And with that soun he herde a murmurynge
Ful lowe and dym, that sayde thus, 'Victorie.'
For which he yaf to Mars honour and glorie.
And thus with joye, and hope wel to fare,

Arcite anoon unto his inne is fare,
As fayn as fowel is of the brighte sonne.
And right anon such stryf ther is bygonne
For thilke grauntyng, in the hevene above,
Bitwixe Venus the goddess of love,
And Mars the sterne god armypotente,
That Jupiter was busy it to stente;
Til that the pale Saturnus the colde,
That knew so many of aventures olde,
Fond in his olde experience an art,
That he ful sone hath plesed every part.
As soth is sayd, eelde hath gret avantage,
In eelde is bothe wisdom and usage;
Men may the olde at-renne, but nat at-rede.
Saturne anon, to stynte stryf and drede,
Al be it that it is agayn his kynde,
Of al this stryf he gan remedye fynde.
'My deere doughter Venus,' quod Saturne,
'My cours, that hath so wyde for to turne,
Hath more power than woot eny man.
Myn is the drenchyng in the see so wan;
Myn is the prisoun in the derke cote;
Myn is the stranglyng and hangyng by the throte;
The murmure, and the cherles rebellynge,
The groyning, and the pryvé empoysonynge:
I do vengeance and pleyn correctioun,
Whiles I dwelle in the sign of the lyoun.
Myn is the ruyne of the hihe halles,
The fallyng of the toures and of the walles
Upon the mynour or the carpenter.
I slowh Sampsoun in schakyng the piler
And myne ben the maladies colde,
The derke tresoun, and the castes olde;
Myn lokyng is the fader of pestilence.
Now wep nomore, I schal don diligence
That Palamon, that is thyn owne knight,
Schal have his lady, as thou hast him hight.

Though Mars schal helpe his knight, yet natheles
Bitwixe you ther moot som tyme be pees,
Al be ye nought of oo complexioun,
That causeth al day such divisioun.
I am thin ayel, redy at thy wille;
Wep thou nomore, I wol thi lust fulfille.'
Now wol I stynten of the goddes above,
Of Mars, and of Venus goddesse of love,
And telle you, as pleinly as I can,
The grete effect for which that I bigan.

Grete was the feste in Athenes that day,
And eek the lusty sesoun of that May
Made every wight to ben in such plesaunce,
That al that Monday jousten they and daunce,
And spenden hit in Venus heigh servise.
But by the cause that they schulde arise
Erly for to seen the grete fight,
Unto their reste wente they at nyght.
And on the morwe when that day gan sprynge,
Of hors and herneys noyse and claterynge
Ther was in the hostelryes al aboute;
And to the paleys rood ther many a route
Of lordes, upon steedes and palfreys.
Ther mayst thou seen devysyng of herneys
So uncowth and so riche, and wrought so wel
Of goldsmithrye, of browdyng, and of steel;
The scheldes brighte, testers, and trappures;
Gold-beten helmes, hauberkes, cote-armures;
Lordes in paramentz on here courseres,
Knightes of retenue, and eek squyeres
Naylyng the speres, and helmes bokelynge,
Giggyng of scheeldes, with layners lasynge;
Ther as need is, they were nothing ydel;
The fomy steedes on the golden bridel
Gnawyng, and faste the armurers also
With fyle and hamer prikyng to and fro;
Yemen on foote, and communes many oon

With schorte staves, thikke as they may goon;
Pypes, trompes, nakeres, clariounes,
That in the bataille blowe bloody sownes;
The paleys ful of peples up and doun,
Heer thre, ther ten, holdyng here questioun,
Dyvynyng of thise Thebane knightes two.
Somme seyden thus, somme seyde it schal be so;
Somme heelde with him with the blake berd,
Somme with the balled, somme with the thikke herd;
Somme sayde he lokede grym and he wolde fighte;
He hath a sparth of twenti pound of wighte.
Thus was the halle ful of divynynge,
Longe after that the sonne gan to springe.
The grete Theseus that of his sleep awaked
With menstralcye and noyse that was maked,
Held yit the chambre of his paleys riche,
Til that the Thebane knyghtes bothe i-liche
Honoured weren into the paleys fet.
Duk Theseus was at a wyndow set,
Arrayed right as he were a god in trone.
The peple presseth thider-ward ful sone
Him for to seen, and doon heigh reverence,
And eek to herkne his hest and his sentence.
An heraud on a skaffold made an hoo,
Til al the noyse of the peple was i-do;
The whan he sawh the peple of noyse all stille,
Tho schewede he the mighty dukes wille.
 'The lord hath of his heih discrecioun
Considered, that it were destruccioun
To gentil blood, to fighten in the gyse
Of mortal bataille now in this emprise;
Wherfore to schapen that they schuln not dye,
He wol his firste purpos modifye.
No man therfore, up peyne of los of lyf,
No maner schot, ne pollax, ne schort knyf
Into the lystes sende, or thider brynge;

Ne schort swerd for to stoke, with point bytynge
No man ne drawe, ne bere by his side.
Ne no man schal unto his felawe ryde
But oon cours, with a scharpe ygrounde spere;
Foyne if him lust on foote, himself to were.
And he that is at mischief, schal be take,
And nat slayn, but be brought unto the stake,
That schal ben ordeyned on eyther syde;
But thider he schall by force, and ther abyde.
And if so falle, the cheventein be take
On eyther side, or elles sle his make,
No lenger schal the turneyinge laste.
God spede you; go forth and ley on faste.
With long swerd and with mace fight youre fille.
Goth now youre way; this is the lordes wille.'
   The voice of peple touchede the hevene,
So lowde cride thei with mery stevene:
' God save such a lord that is so good,
He wilneth no destruccioun of blood!'
Up gon the trompes and the melodye.
And to the lystes ryt the compainye
By ordynaunce, thurghout the cité large,
Hanged with cloth of gold, and not with sarge.
Ful like a lord this noble duk gan ryde,
These tuo Thebanes upon eyther side;
And after rood the queen, and Emelye,
And after that another compainye,
Of oon and other after here degré.
And thus they passen thurghout the cité,
And to the lystes come thei by tyme.
It nas not of the day yet fully pryme,
Whan set was Theseus ful riche and hye,
Ypolita the queen and Emelye,
And other ladyes in degrees aboute.
Unto the seetes preseth al the route;
And west-ward, thurgh the yates under Marte,
Arcite, and eek the hundred of his parte,

With banner red ys entred right anoon;
And in that selve moment Palamon
Is under Venus, est-ward in the place,
With baner whyt, and hardy cheere and face.
   In al the world, to seeken up and doun,
So evene withouten variacioun,
Ther nere suche compainyes tweye.
For ther nas noon so wys that cowthe sye,
That any hadde of other avauntage
Of worthinesse, ne of estaat, ne age,
So evene were they chosen for to gesse.
And in two renges faire they hem dresse.
Whan that here names rad were everychon,
That in here nombre gile were ther noon,
Tho were the yates schet, and cried was loude:
' Doth now your devoir, yonge knightes proude!'
The heraudes lafte here prikyng up and doun;
Now ryngen trompes loude and clarioun;
Ther is nomore to sayn, but west and est
In gon the speres ful sadly in arest;
In goth the scharpe spore into the side.
Ther seen men who can juste, and who can ryde;
Ther schyveren schaftes upon scheeldes thykke;
He feeleth thrugh the herte-spon the prikke.
Up springen speres twenty foot on highte;
Out goon the swerdes as the silver brighte.
The helmes thei to-hewen and to-schrede;
Out brest the blood, with sterne stremes reede.
With mighty maces the bones thay to breste.
He thurgh the thikkeste of the throng gan threste.
Ther stomblen steedes stronge, and doun goon alle.
He rolleth under foot as doth a balle.
He foyneth on his feet with his tronchoun,
And him hurtleth with his hors adoun.
He thurgh the body is hurt, and siththen take
Maugre his heed, and brought unto the stake,
As forward was, right ther he moste abyde.

Another lad is on that other syde.
And som tyme doth hem Theseus to reste,
Hem to refreissche, and drinken if hem leste.
Ful ofte a-day han thise Thebanes two
Togidre y-met, and wrought his felawe woo;
Unhorsed hath ech other of hem tweye.
Ther nas no tygre in the vale of Galgopheye,
Whan that hire whelpe is stole, whan it is lite,
So cruel on the hunte, as is Arcite
For jelous herte upon this Palamoun:
Ne in Belmarye ther nis so fel lyoun,
That hunted is, or for his hunger wood,
Ne of his preye desireth so the blood.
As Palamon to slen his foo Arcite.
The jelous strokes on here helmes byte;
Out renneth blood on bothe here sides reede.
Som tyme an ende ther is of every dede;
For er the sonne unto the reste wente,
The stronge kyng Emetreus gan hente
This Palamon, as he faught with Arcite,
And made his swerd depe in his flessch to byte;
And by the force of twenti is he take
Unyolden, and i-drawe unto the stake.
And in the rescous of this Palamon
The stronge kyng Ligurge is born adoun;
And kyng Emetreus for al his strengthe
Is born out of his sadel a swerdes lengthe,
So hitte him Palamon er he were take;
But al for nought, he was brought to the stake.
His hardy herte mighte him helpe nought;
He moste abyde whan that he was caught,
By force, and eek by composicioun.
Who sorweth now but woful Palamoun,
That moot no more gon agayn to fighte?
And whan that Theseus hadde seen this sighte,
Unto the folk that foughten thus echon
He cryde, 'Hoo! no more, for it is doon!

I wol be trewe juge, and nou*gh*t partye.
Arcyte of Thebes schal have Emelye,
That by his fortune hath hire faire i-wonne.'
Anoon ther is a noyse of peple bygonne
For joye of this, so lowde and heye withalle,
It semede that the listes scholde falle.
   What can now fayre Venus doon above?
What seith sche no? what doth this queen of love?
But wepeth so, for wantyng of hire wille,
Til that hire teeres in the lystes fille;
Sche seyde: 'I am aschamed douteles.'
Saturnus seyde: 'Dou*gh*ter hold thy pees.
Mars hath his wille, his knight hath al his boone,
And by myn heed thou schalt ben esed soone.'
   The trompes with the lowde mynstralcye,
The herawdes, that ful lowde *y*olle and crye,
Been in here wele for joye of daun Arcyte.
But herkneth me, and stynteth now a lite,
Which a miracle ther bifel anoon.
This fierse Arcyte hath of his helm ydoon,
And on a courser for to schewe his face,
He priketh endelonge the large place,
Lokyng upward upon his Emelye;
And sche agayn him caste a frendlych ey*gh*e,
(For wommen, as to speken in comune,
Thay folwen al the favour of fortune)
And was al his cheere, as in his herte.
Out of the ground a fyr infernal sterte,
From Pluto sent, at requeste of Saturne,
For which his hors for feere gan to turne,
And leep asyde, and foundrede as he leep;
And or that Arcyte may taken keep,
He pighte him on the pomel of his heed,
That in the place he lay as he were deed,
His brest to-brosten with his sadel-bowe.
As blak he lay as eny col or crowe,
So was the blood y-ronnen in his face.

Anon he was y-born out of the place
With herte soor, to Theseus paleys.
Tho was he corven out of his harneys,
And in a bed y-brought ful faire and blyve,
For he was yit in memorye and on lyve,
And alway crying after Emelye.
   Duk Theseus, with al his compainye,
Is comen hom to Athenes his cité,
With alle blysse and gret solempnité.
Al be it that this aventure was falle,
He nolde nought disconforten hem alle.
Men seyde eek, that Arcita schal nought dye,
He schal ben heled of his maladye.
And of another thing they were as fayn,
That of hem alle was ther noon y-slayn,
Al were they sore hurt, and namely oon,
That with a spere was thirled his brest boor.
To othre woundes, and to broken armes,
Some hadde salves, and some hadde charmes,
Fermacyes of herbes, and eek save
They dronken, for they wolde here lymes have.
For which this noble duk, as he wel can,
Conforteth and honoureth every man,
And made revel al the longe night,
Unto the straunge lordes, as was right.
Ne ther was holden no disconfytynge;
But as a justes or a tourneyinge,
For sothly ther was no disconfiture,
For fallynge nis not but an aventure;
Ne to be lad with fors unto the stake
Unyolden, and with twenty knightes take,
O persone allone, withouten moo,
And haried forth by arme, foot, and too,
And eek his steede dryven forth with staves,
With footmen, bothe yemen and eek knaves,
It nas aretted him no vyleinye,
Ther may no man clepe it no cowardye.

For which anon Duk Theseus leet crie,
To stynten alle rancour and envye,
The gree as wel of o syde as of other,
And either side ylik as otheres brother;
And yaf hem yiftes after here degré,
And fully heeld a feste dayes thre;
And conveyede the kynges worthily
Out of his toun a journee largely.
And hom wente every man the righte way.
There was no more, but 'Farwel, have good day!'
Of this battaylle I wol no more endite,
But speke of Palamon and of Arcyte.

   Swelleth the brest of Arcyte, and the sore
Encresceth at his herte more and more.
The clothred blood, for eny leche-craft,
Corrumpeth, and is in his bouk i-laft,
That nother veyne blood, ne ventusynge,
Ne drinke of herbes may ben his helpynge.
The vertu expulsif, or animal,
Fro thilke vertu cleped natural,
Ne may the venym voyde, ne expelle.
The pypes of his longes gonne to swelle,
And every lacerte in his brest adoun
Is schent with venym and corrupcioun.
Him gayneth nother, for to gete his lyf,
Vomyt upward, ne dounward laxatif;
Al is to-brosten thilke regioun,
Nature hath now no dominacioun.
And certeynly ther nature wil not wirche,
Farwel phisik; go ber the man to chirche.
This al and som, that Arcyta moot dye,
For which he sendeth after Emelye,
And Palamon, that was his cosyn deere.
Than seyde he thus, as ye schul after heere.

   'Naught may the woful spirit in myn herte
Declare o poynt of alle my sorwes smerte
To you, my lady, that I love most;

But I byquethe the service of my gost
To you aboven every creature,
Syn that my lyf ne may no lenger dure.
Allas, the woo! allas, the peynes stronge,
That I for you have suffred, and so longe!
Allas, the deth! allas, myn Emelye!
Allas, departyng of our compainye!
Allas, myn hertes queen! allas, my wyf!
Myn hertes lady, endere of my lyf!
What is this world? what asken men to have?
Now with his love, now in his colde grave
Allone withouten eny compainye!
Farwel, my swete foo! myn Emelye!
And softe tak me in youre armes tweye,
For love of God, and herkneth what I seye.
 I have heer with my cosyn Palamon
Had stryf and rancour many a day a-gon,
For love of yow, and for my jelousie.
And Jupiter so wis my sowle gye,
To speken of a servaunt proprely,
With alle circumstaunces trewely,
That is to seyn, trouthe, honour, and knighthede,
Wysdom, humblesse, estaat, and hey kynrede,
Fredam, and al that longeth to that art,
So Jupiter have of my soule part,
As in this world right now ne knowe I non
So worthy to be loved as Palamon,
That serveth you, and wol don al his lyf.
And if that evere ye schul ben a wyf,
Foryet not Palamon, the gentil man.'
And with that word his speche faille gan;
For fro his feete up to his brest was come
The cold of deth, that hadde him overcome.
And yet, moreover, for in his armes two
The vital strengthe is lost, and al ago.
Only the intellect, withouten more,
That dwellede in his herte sik and sore,

Gan fayllen, when the herte felte deth,
Dusken his eyghen two, and faylleth breth.
But on his lady yit caste he his eye;
His laste word was, 'Mercy, Emelye!'
His spiryt chaungede hous, and wente ther,
As I cam nevere, I can nat tellen wher.
Therfore I stynte, I nam no dyvynistre;
Of soules fynde I not in this registre,
Ne me ne list thilke opynyons to telle.
Of hem, though that thei writen wher they dwelle.
Arcyte is cold, ther Mars his soule gye;
Now wol I speke forth of Emelye.

 Shrighte Emelye, and howleth Palamon,
And Theseus his suster took anon
Swownyng, and bar hire fro the corps away.
What helpeth it to taryen forth the day,
To tellen how sche weep bothe eve and morwe?
For in swich caas wommen can han such
 sorwe,
Whan that here housbonds ben from hem ago,
That for the more part they sorwen so,
Or elles fallen in such maladye,
That atte laste certeynly they dye.

 Infynyte been the sorwes and the teeres
Of olde folk, and folk of tendre yeeres,
In al the toun, for deth of this Theban,
For him ther weepeth bothe child and man;
So gret a wepyng was ther noon certayn,
Whan Ector was i-brought, al fressh i-slayn,
To Troye; allas! the pité that was ther,
Cracchyng of cheekes, rending eek of heer.
'Why woldestow be deed,' thise wommen crye,
'And haddest gold ynowgh, and Emelye?'
No man ne mighte gladen Theseus,
Savyng his olde fader Egeus,
That knew this worldes transmutacioun,
As he hadde seen it tornen up and doun,

Joye after woo, and woo after gladnesse :
And schewede hem ensamples and liknesse.
  'Right as ther deyde nevere man,' quod he,
'That he ne lyvede in earth in som degree,
Right so ther lyvede nevere man,' he seyde,
'In al this world, that som tyme he ne deyde.
This world nys but a thurghfare ful of woo,
And we ben pilgryms, passyng to and fro ;
Deth is an ende of every worldly sore.'
And over al this yit seide he mochel more
To this effect, ful wysly to enhorte
The peple, that they shulde hem reconforte.
  Duk Theseus, with al his busy cure,
Cast now wher that the sepulture
Of good Arcyte may best y-maked be,
And eek most honorable in his degré.
And atte laste he took conclusioun,
That ther as first Arcite and Palamon
Hadden for love the bataille hem betwene,
That in that selve grove, swoote and greene,
Ther as he hadde his amorouse desires,
His compleynte, and for love his hoote fyres,.
He wolde make a fyr, in which thoffice
Of funeral he mighte al accomplice ;
And leet comaunde anon to hakke and hewe
The okes olde, and leye hem on a rewe
In culpons wel arrayed for to brenne,
His officers with swifte feet they renne,
And ryde anon at his comaundement.
And after this, Theseus hath i-sent
After a beer, and it al overspradde
With cloth of gold, the richeste that he hadde.
And of the same suyte he cladde Arcyte ;
Upon his hondes hadde he gloves white ;
Eek on his heed a coroune of laurer grene,
And in his hond a swerd ful bright and kene.
He leyde him bare the visage on the beere,

Therwith he weep that pité was to heere.
And for the peple schulde seen him alle,
Whan it was day he broughte him to the halle,
That roreth of the crying and the soun.
   Tho cam this woful Theban Palamoun,
With flotery berd, and ruggy asshy heeres,
In clothes blake, y-dropped al with teeres;
And, passyng othere of wepyng, Emelye,
The rewfulleste of al the compainye,
In as moche as the service schulde be
The more noble and riche in his degré,
Duk Theseus leet forth thre steedes brynge,
That trapped were in steele al gliterynge,
And covered with the armes of daun Arcyte.
Upon thise steedes, that weren grete and white,
Ther seeten folk, of which oon bar his scheeld,
Another his spere up in his hondes heeld;
The thridde bar with him his bowe Turkeys,
Of brend gold was the caas and eek the herneys;
And riden forth a paas with sorweful cheere
Toward the grove, as ye schul after heere.
The nobleste of the Grekes that ther were
Upon here schuldres carieden the beere,
With slake paas, and eyghen reede and wete,
Thurghout the cité, by the maister streete,
That sprad was al with blak, and wonder hye
Right of the same is al the strete i-wrye.
Upon the right hond wente old Egeus,
And on that other syde duk Theseus,
With vessels in here hand of gold wel fyn,
Al ful of hony, mylk, and blood, and wyn;
Eek Palamon, with ful gret compainye;
And after that com woful Emelye,
With fyr in hond, as was that time the gyse,
To do thoffice of funeral servise.
   Hey*gh* labour, and ful gret apparaillynge
Was at the service and the fyr makynge,

That with his grene top the hevene raughte,
And twenty fadme of brede tharmes straughte;
This is to seyn, the boowes were so brode.
Of stree first ther was leyd ful many a loode.
But how the fyr was maked up on highte,
And eek the names how the trees highte,
As ook, fyrre, birch, asp, alder, holm, popler,
Wilwe, elm, plane, assch, box, chesteyn, lynde,
    laurer,
Maple, thorn, beech, hasel, ew, whyppyltre,
How they weren feld, schal nought be told for me;
Ne how the goddes ronnen up and doun,
Disheryt of here habitacioun,
In which they woneden in reste and pees,
Nymphes, Faunes, and Amadrydes;
Ne how the beestes and the briddes alle
Fledden for feere, whan the woode was falle;
Ne how the ground agast was of the lighte,
That was nought wont to seen the sonne brighte;
Ne how the fyr was couched first with stree,
And thanne with drye stykkes cloven a three,
And thanne with grene woode and spicerie,
And thanne with cloth of gold and with perrye,
And gerlandes hangyng with ful many a flour,
The myrre, thencens with al so greet odour;
Ne how Arcyte lay among al this,
Ne what richesse aboute his body is;
Ne how that Emelye, as was the gyse,
Putte in the fyr of funeral servise;
Ne how she swownede when men made the fyr,
Ne what sche spak, ne what was hire desir;
Ne what jewels men in the fyr tho caste,
Whan that the fyr was gret and brente faste;
Ne how summe caste here scheeld, and summe
    here spere,
And of here vestimentz, whiche that they were,
And cuppes ful of wyn, and mylk, and blood,

Into the fyr, that brente as it were wood;
Ne how the Grekes with an huge route
Thre tymes ryden al the fyr aboute
Upon the lefte hond, with an heigh schoutyng,
And thries with here speres clateryng;
And thries how the ladyes gonne crye;
Ne how that lad was hom-ward Emelye;
Ne how Arcyte is brent to aschen colde;
Ne how that liche-wake was y-holde
Al thilke night, ne how the Grekes pleye
The wake-pleyes, ne kepe I nat to seye;
Who wrastleth best naked, with oylle enoynt,
Ne who that bar him best in no disjoynt.
I wol not tellen eek how that they goon
Hom til Athenes whan the pley is doon.
But schortly to the poynt than wol I wende,
And maken of my longe tale an ende.

 By processe and by lengthe of certeyn yeres
Al stynted is the moornyng and the teeres
Of Grekes, by oon general assent.
Than semede me ther was a parlement
At Athenes, upon certeyn poyntz and cas;
Among the whiche poyntes yspoken was
To han with certeyn contrees alliaunce,
And han fully of Thebans obeissaunce.
For which this noble Theseus anon
Let senden after gentil Palamon,
Unwist of him what was the cause and why;
But in his blake clothes sorwefully
He cam at his comaundement in hye.
Tho sente Theseus for Emelye.
Whan they were set, and hust was al the place,
And Theseus abyden hadde a space
Or eny word cam fro his wyse brest,
His eyen sette he ther as was his lest,
And with a sad visage he sykede stille,
And after that right thus he seide his wille.

'The firste moevere of the cause above,
Whan he first made the fayre cheyne of love,
Gret was theffect, and heigh was his entente;
Wel wiste he why, and what therof he mente;
For with that faire cheyne of love he bond
The fyr, the eyr, the water, and the loud
In certeyn boundes, that they may not flee;
That same prynce and moevere eek,' quod he,
'Hath stabled, in this wrecched world adoun,
Certeyne days and duracioun
To all that ben engenred in this place,
Over the whiche day they may nat pace,
Al mowe they yit tho dayes wel abregge;
Ther needeth non auctorité tallegge;
For it is preved by experience,
But that me lust declare my sentence.
Than many men by this ordre wel discerne,
That thilke moevere stable is and eterne.
Wel may men knowe, but it be a fool,
That every part deryveth from his hool.
For nature hath nat take his bygynnyng
Of no partye ne cantel of a thing,
But of a thing that parfyt is and stable,
Descendyng so, til it be corumpable.
And therfore of his wyse purveiaunce
He hath so wel biset his ordinaunce,
That spices of thinges and progressiouns
Schullen endure by successiouns,
And nat eterne be withoute lye:
This maistow understande and sen at eye.

'Lo the ook, that hath so long a norisschynge
Fro tyme that it gynneth first to springe,
And hath so long a lyf, as we may see,
Yet atte laste wasted is the tree.

'Considereth eek, how that the harde stoon
Under oure feet, on which we trede and goon,
Yit wasteth it, as it lith by the weye.

The brode ryver somtyme wexeth dreye.
The grete townes seen we wane and wende.
Then may ye see that al this thing hath ende.
　'Of man and womman sen we wel also,
That nedeth in oon of thise termes two,
This is to seyn, in youthe or elles age,
He moot ben deed, the kyng as schal a page:
Som in his bed, som in the deepe see,
Som in the large feeld, as men may se,
Ther helpeth naught, al goth that ilke weye.
Thanne may I seyn that al this thing moot deye.
What maketh this but Jupiter the kyng?
The which is prynce and cause of alle thing,
Convertyng al unto his propre welle,
From which it is deryved, soth to telle.
And here agayns no creature on lyve
Of no degré avaylleth for to stryve.
　'Than is it wisdom, as it thinketh me,
To maken vertu of necessité,
And take it wel, that we may nat eschue,
And namelyche that to us alle is due.
And who so gruccheth aught, he doth folye,
And rebel is to him that al may gye.
And certeynly a man hath most honour
To deyen in his excellence and flour,
Whan he is siker of his goode name.
Than hath he doon his freend, ne him, no schame,
And gladder oughte his freend ben of his deth,
Whan with honour up-yolden is his breth,
Thanne whan is name appalled is for age;
For al forgeten is his vasselage.
Thanne is it best, as for a worthi fame.
To dyen whan a man is best of name.
The contrarye of al this wilfulnesse.
Why grucchen we? why have we hevynesse,
That good Arcyte, of chyvalrye the flour,
Departed is, with dueté and honour

Out of this foule prisoun of this lyf?
Why grucchen heer his cosyn and his wyf
Of his welfare that lovede hem so wel?
Can he hem thank? nay, God woot, never a del,
That bothe his soule and eek hemself offende,
And yet they mowe here lustes nat amende.
  'What may I conclude of this long serye,
But after wo I rede us to be merye,
And thanke Jupiter of all his grace?
And or that we departe fro this place,
I rede that we make, of sorwes two,
O parfyt joye lastyng evere mo:
And loketh now wher most sorowe is her-inne,
Ther wol we first amenden and bygynne.
  'Suster,' quod he, 'this is my fulle assent,
With al thavys heer of my parlement,
That gentil Palamon, youre owne knight,
That serveth yow with herte, wille, and might,
And evere hath doon, syn that ye fyrst him knewe,
That ye schul of youre grace upon him rewe,
And take him for youre housbond and for lord:
Leen me youre hand, for this is oure acord.
Let see now of youre wommanly pité.
He is a kynges brother sone, pardee;
And though he were a poure bacheler,
Syn he hath served you so many a yeer,
And had for you so gret adversité,
It moste be considered, leeveth me.
For gentil mercy aughte to passe right.'
Than seyde he thus to Palamon the knight;
' I trowe ther needeth litle sermonyng
To maken you assente to this thing.
Com neer, and tak youre lady by the hond.'
Bitwixen hem was i-maad anon the bond,
That highte matrimoyne or mariage,
By al the counseil and the baronage.
And thus with alle blysse and melodye

Hath Palamon i-wedded Emelye.
And God, that al this wyde world hath wrought,
Sende him his love, that hath it deere a-bought.
For now is Palamon in alle wele,
Lyvynge in blisse, in richesse, and in hele,
And Emelye him loveth so tendrely,
And he hire serveth al so gentilly,
That nevere was ther no word hem bitweene
Of jelousye, or any other teene.
Thus endeth Palamon and Emelye;
And God save al this fayre compainye!

PERICLES, PRINCE OF TYRE.

It appears to be an accredited opinion, that in "Pericles" we have, out of five acts, three, viz., the third, fourth, and fifth, written by Shakespeare, and the remaining two from another pen. But I confess that I agree rather with Dyce, who observes: "The greater part of 'Pericles' is undoubtedly by some very inferior dramatist; but here and there, more particularly towards the close, the hand of Shakespeare is plainly seen, and the scenes and shorter passages, in which we trace him, belong to his latest style of composition."

It deserves to be pointed out that the Dutch play of "Alexander and Lodwick," published at Amsterdam in 1618, is conjectured to be a sort of adaptation of a lost drama on the subject by Martin Slaughter, performed at Henslowe's theatre in 1597-8, and of which Shakespeare, or whoever wrote "Pericles," may have made a certain use. In "Green's Tu Quoque," by John Cooke, 1614 (Hazlitt's "Dodsley," xi. 239), occurs the following allusion (presumably to Slaughter's piece): "O you pretty sweet-faced rogues! that for your countenances might be Alexander and Lodwick."

Douce sensibly oberves ("Illustr." ii. 144): "However unworthy of Shakespeare's pen this drama, *as an entire composition*, may be considered, many will be of opinion that it contains more *that he might have written* than either "Love's Labour's Lost," or "All's well that ends well."

"Pericles" is quoted by Randolph in his "Oratio Prevaricatoria," 1632, and again in his "Hey for Honesty," 1651 (written before 1635); and in the latter piece of humorous writing there is a playful allusion to Shakespeare's eye for the practical side of authorship.

Randolph mentions the character of the hero himself, in such a way as if he had seen the drama on the stage, and witnessed the performance of the part of the Prince of Tyre by some Roscius of the day "in spangled hose."

1. *The Story of Apollonius of Tyre.*

—o—

[*From Gower's " Confessio Amantis," lib.* 8, *edit.*
1857.]

Omnibus est communis amor, sed et immoderatos
  Qui facit excessus, non reputatur amans.
Sors tamen unde Venus attractat corda videre,
  Que rationis erunt, non ratione finit.

OF a cronique in daies gon,
    The which is cleped Panteon,
In loves cause I rede thus,
How that the great Antiochus,
Of whom that Antioche toke
His firste name, as saith the boke,
Was coupled to a noble quene,
And had a doughter hem betwene.
But such fortune cam to honde,
That deth, which no kind may withstonde,
But every life it mote obey,
This worthy quene toke awey.
The king, which made mochel mone,
Tho stood as who saith all him one
Withoute wife, but netheles
His doughter, which was pereles

Hic loquitur
adhuc contra
incestuosos
amantum coit-
us, et narrat
mirabile exem-
plum de magno
rege Antiocho,
qui uxore mor-
tua propriam
filiam violavit,
et quia filie ma-
trimonium pen-
es alios impe-
dire voluit, tale
ab eo exit
edictum, quod
si quis eam in
uxorem pete-
ret, nisi quod-
dam problema
questionis,
quam ipse rex
proposuerat,
veraciter sol-
veret, capitali
sentencia puni-
retur, super
quo veniens
tandem discre-
tus juvenis

> princeps Tyri
> Appollinus
> questionem
> solvit. Nec
> tamen filiam
> habere potuit,
> sed rex indig-
> natus ipsum
> propter hoc in
> mortis odium
> recollegit, unde
> Appollinus a
> facie regis fu-
> giens quam
> plura, prout in-
> ferius intitu-
> lantur, propter
> amorem peri-
> cula passus est.

Of beaute, dwelt about him stille.
But whan a man hath welth at wille,
The flesshe is frele and falleth ofte,
And that this maide tendre and softe,
Whiche in her faders chambre dwelte,
Within a time wist and felte,
For liking of concupiscence
Without insight of conscience
The fader so with lustes blente,
That he cast al his hole entente
His owne doughter for to spille.
The king hath leiser at his wille,
With strengthe and whan he time sigh,
The younge maiden he forleie.
And she was tendre and full of drede,
She couthe nought her maidenhede
Defende, and thus she hath forlore
The floure, which she hath longe bore.
It helpeth not all though she wepe,
For they that shulde her body kepe
Of women were absent as than.
And thus this maiden goth to man.
The wilde fader thus devoureth
His owne flessh, which none socoureth,
And that was cause of mochel care.
But after his unkinde fare
Out of the chambre goth the king.
And she lay still and of this thing
Within her self such sorwe made,
There was no wight, that might her glade,
For fere of thilke horrible vice.
With that came inne the norice,
Which fro childhode her hadde kepte
And axeth, if she hadde slepte,
And why her chere was unglad.
But she, which hath ben overlad
Of that she mighte nought be wreke,

For shame couth unethes speke.
And netheles mercy she praide
With weping eye and thus she saide:
Helas, my suster, wailoway,
That ever I sigh this ilke day.
Thing, which my body first begate
Into this worlde, only that
My worldes worship hath berefte.
With that she swouneth now and efte
And ever wisheth after death,
So that welnigh her lacketh breth.
   That other, which her wordes herde,
In comforting of her answerde,
To let her faders foul desire,
She wiste no recoverire,
Whan thing is do, there is no bote.
So suffren they that suffren mote.
There was none other, which it wist.
Thus hath this king all that him list
Of his liking and his plesaunce,
And last in such a continuaunce,
And such delite he toke there in,
Him thoughte that it was no sin.
And she durst him no thing withsay.
But fame, which goth every way,
To sondry regnes all aboute
The great beaute telleth oute
Of such a maide of high parage.
So that for love of mariage
The worthy princes come and sende,
As they, the which all honour wende
And knew no thing, how that it stode.
The fader whan he understode,
That they his doughter thus besought,
With all his wit he cast and sought,
How that he mighte finde a lette,
And such a statue than he sette

And in this wise his lawe taxeth,
That what man that his doughter axeth,
But if he couthe his question
Assoile upon suggestion
Of certein thinges, that befelle,
The which he wolde unto him telle,
He shulde in certein lese his hede.
And thus there were many dede,
Her hedes stonding on the gate,
Till ate laste long and late
For lacke of answere in this wise
The remenaunt, that weren wise,
Escheueden to make assay.

<small>De adventu Appollini in Antiochiam, ubi ipse filiam regis Antiochi in uxorem postulavit.</small>

Till it befell upon a day
Appollinus the prince of Tire,
Which hath to love a great desire,
As he, which in his highe mode,
Was liking of his hote blode,
A yonge, a fresh, a lusty knight,
As he lay musing on a night
Of the tidinges, which he herde,
He thought assay how that it ferde.
He was with worthy compaignie
Arraied and with good navie,
To ship he goth, the winde him driveth,
And saileth, till that he ariveth
Sauf in the porte of Antioche.
He londeth and goth to approche
The kinges court and his presence.
Of every natural science,
Whiche any clerke couth him teche,
He couth inough and in his speche
Of wordes he was eloquent.
And whan he sigh the king present,
He praieth, he mote his doughter have.
The king ayein began to crave
And tolde him the condicion,

How first unto his question
He mote answere and faile nought,
Or with his heved it shall be bought.
And he him axeth, what it was.
   The king delareth him the cas
With sterne loke and stordy chere,   *Questio regis Antiochi: scelere vehor, materna carne vescor, quero patrem meum, matris mee virum, uxoris mee filium.*
To him and said in this manere:
With felony I am upbore,
Ete and have it nought forlore
My moders flesh, whose husbonde
My fader for to seche I fonde,
Which is the sone eke of my wife,
Herof I am inquisitife.
And who that can my tale save
Al quite he shall my doughter have.
Of his answere and if he faile,
He shall be dede withoute faile.
Forthy my sone, quod the king,
Be wel avised of this thing,
Which hath thy life in jeopartie.
Appollinus for his partie   *Responsio pollini.*
Whan he that question had herde,
Unto the king he hath answerde
And hath reherced one and one
The points and saide therupon:
   The question, which thou hast spoke,
If thou wolt, that it be unloke,
It toucheth all the privete
Betwene thin owne child and the
And stant all hole upon you two.
The king was wonder sory tho   *Indignacio regis Antiochi super responsione Appollini.*
And thought, if that he said it out,
Than were he shamed all about.
With slighe wordes and with felle
He saith: My sone, I shall the telle,
Though that thou be of litel wit,
It is no great merveile as yit,

Thin age may it nought suffise.
But loke wel thou nought despise
Thin owne life, for of my grace
Of thritty daies full a space
I graunte the, to ben avised.

De recessu Appollini ab Antiochia.

And thus with leve and time assised
This yonge prince forth he wente
And understode wel what it mente.
Within his herte as he was lered,
That for to make him afered,
The kinge his time hath so delaied,
Wherof he drad and was amaied
Of treson that he deie sholde,
For he the king his sothe tolde.
And sodeinly the nightes tide,
That more wolde he nought abide,
Al prively his barge he hente
And home ayein to Tire he wente.
And in his owne wit he saide,
For drede if he the king bewraide,
He knew so wel the kinges herte,
That deth ne shulde he nought asterte,
The king him wolde so pursue.
But he that wolde his death escheue
And knewe all this to-fore the honde,
Forsake he thought his owne londe,
That there wolde he nought abide.
For wel he knew that on some side
This tiraunt of his felonie
By some manere of trecherie
To greve his body woll nought leve.

De fuga Appollini per mare a regno suo

Forthy withouten taking leve
As privelich as ever he might
He goth him to the see by night,
Her shippes that ben with whete laden,
Her takil redy tho they maden
And haleth sail and forth they fare.

But for to telle of the care,
That they of Tire began tho,
Whan that they wist he was ago,
It is a pite for to here.
They losten lust, they losten chere,
They toke upon hem such penaunce,
There was no song, there was no daunce,
But every merthe and melody
To hem was than a malady,
For unlust of that aventure
There was no man which toke tonsure.
In dolfull clothes they hem clothe.
The bathes and the stewes bothe
They shetten in by every wey.
There was no life which liste pley
Ne take of any joie kepe,
But for her lege lord to wepe,
And every wight said as he couth :
Helas, the lusty floure of youth,
Our prince, our heved, our governour,
Through whom we stonden in honour,
Withoute the comune assent,
That sodeinly is fro us went.
Such was the clamour of hem alle.

   But se we now what is befalle
Upon the firste tale pleine
And torne we therto ayeine.

   Antiochus the grete sire,
Which full of rancour and of ire
His herte bereth so as ye herde,
Of that this prince of Tire answerde,
He hath a felow bacheler,
Which was his prive counseiler
And Taliart by name he hight.
The king a strong poison him dight
Within a buist and gold thereto,
In alle haste and bad him go

Nota, qualiter Thaliartus miles, ut Appollinum veneno intoxicaret, ab Antiocho in Tyrum missus ipso ibidem non invento Antiochiam rediit.

Straught unto Tire and for no cost
Ne spare, till he hadde lost
The prince, which he wolde spill.
And whan the king hath said his will,
This Taliart in a galey
With all the haste he toke his wey.
The wind was good, they saileth blive,
Till he toke lond upon the rive
Of Tire and forth with all anone
Into the burgh he gan to gone
And toke his inne and bode a throwe.
But for he wolde nought be knowe,
Desguised than he goth him out.
He sigh the weping all about
And axeth, what the cause was.
And they him tolde all the cas,
How sodeinly the prince is go.
And whan he sigh, that it was so
And that his labour was in veine,
Anone he torneth home ayeine,
And to the king whan he cam nigh,
He tolde of that he herde and sigh,
How that the prince of Tire is fled.
So was he come ayein unsped.
The king was sory for a while,
But whan he sigh, that with no wile
He might acheve his cruelte,
He stint his wrath, and let him be.

Qualiter Appollinus in portu Tharsis applicuit, ubi in hospicio cuiusdam magni viri nomine Strangulionis hospitatus est.

But over this now for to telle
Of adventures that befelle
Unto this prince, of which I tolde,
He hath his righte cours forth holde
By stone and nedel, till he cam
To Tharse, and ther his londe he nam.
A bourgeis riche of golde and fee
Was thilke time in that citee,
Which cleped was Strangulio,

His wife was Dionise also.
This yonge prince, as saith the boke,
With him his herbergage toke.
And it befel that citee so
Before time and than also,
Through stronge famin, whiche hem lad,
Was none, that any whete had.
Appollinus, whan that he herde
The mischefe, how the citee ferde,
All frelich of his owne yifte
His whete among hem for to shifte,
The which by ship he hadde brought,
He yave and toke of hem right nought.
But sithen first this world began,
Was never yet to such a man
More joie made, than they him made.
For they were all of him so glade,
That they for ever in remembraunce
Made a figure in resemblaunce
Of him and in a comun place
They set it up, so that his face
Might every maner man beholde,
So as the citee was beholde,
It was of laton over gilt.
Thus hath he nought his yifte spilt.

   Upon a time with a route
This lord to pleie goth him oute
And in his way of Tire he mette
A man, which on his knees him grette,
And Hellican by name he hight,
Which praide his lord to have insight
Upon him self and said him thus,
How that the great Antiochus
Awaiteth, if he might him spille.
That other thought and helde him stille
And thonked him of his warning
And bad him telle no tiding,

Qualiter Hellicanus civis Tyri Tharsim veniens Appollinum de insidiis Antiochi premunivit.

Whan he to Tire cam home ayeine,
That he to Tharse him hadde seine.
  Fortune hath ever be muable
And may no while stonde stable.
For now it higheth, now it loweth,
Now stant upright, now overthroweth,
Now full of bliss and now of bale,
As in the telling of my tale
Here afterward a man may lere,
Which is a great routhe for to here.
  This lord, which wolde done his best,
Within himself hath litel rest
And thought he wolde his place chaunge
And seke a contre more straunge.
Of Tharsiens his leve anone
He toke and is to shippe gone.
His cours he nam with saile updrawe,
Where as fortune doth the lawe
And sheweth, as I shall reherce,
How she was to this lord diverse,
The which upon the see she ferketh.
The winde aros, the wether derketh,
It blew and made such tempest,
None anker may the ship arest,
Which hath to-broken all his gere.
The shipmen stood in such a fere,
Was none that might him self bestere,
But ever awaite upon the lere,
Whan that they sholden drenche at ones.
There was inough within the wones
Of weping and of sorwe tho.
The yonge king maketh mochel wo
So for to se the ship travaile.
But all that might him nought availe.
The mast to-brake, the sail to-rofe,
The ship upon the waves drofe,
Till that they se the londes coste.

Qualiter Appollinus portum Tharsis relinquens, cum ipse per mare navigio securiorem quesivit, superveniente tempestate navis cum omnibus preter ipsum solum in eadem contentis juxta Pentapolim periclitabatur.

Tho made a vow the leste and moste,
But so they mighten come a londe.
But he, which hath the se on honde,
Neptunus wolde nought accorde,
But all to-brake cable and corde,
Er they to londe mighte approche.
The ship to-clef upon a roche
And all goth down into the depe.
But he, that alle thing may kepe,
Unto this lord was merciable
And brought him sauf upon a table,
Which to the londe him hath upbore,
The remenaunt was all forlore. ..
Herof he made mochel mone.

   Thus was this yonge lorde alone
All naked in a pouer plite.
His colour, which was whilom white,
Was than of water fade and pale,
And eke he was so sore a cale,
That he wist of him self no bote,
It helpe him no thing for to mote
To gete ayein that he hath lore.
But she, which hath his deth forbore,
Fortune, though she woll nought yelpe,
All sodeinly hath sent him helpe,
Whan him thought alle grace awey.
There came a fissher in the wey
And sigh a man there naked stonde.
And whan that he hath understonde
The cause, he hath of him great routh
And onlich of his pouer trouth
Of suche clothes as he hadde
With great pite this lord he cladde.
And he him thonketh as he sholde
And saith him, that it shall be yolde,
If ever he gete his state ayein,
And praieth, that he wolde him sain,

Qualiter Appollinus nudus super litus jactabatur, obi quidam piscator ipsum suo colloblo vestiens ad urbem Pentapolim direxit.

If nigh were any town for him.
He saide: Ye, Pentopolim,
Where bothe king and quene dwellen.
Whan he this tale herde tellen,
He gladdeth him that gan beseche,
That he the wey him wolde teche.
And he him taught. And forth he went
And praide god with good entent
To sende him joy after his sorwe.
It was naught passed yet midmorwe,

<small>Qualiter Appollino Pentapolim advenienté ludus gignasii per urbem publice proclamatus est.</small>

Than thiderward his wey he nam,
Where sone upon the none he cam.
He ete such as he might gete,
And forth anone whan he had ete,
He goth to se the town about,
And cam there as he found a rout
Of yonge lusty men withal.
And as it shulde tho befall,
That day was set of such assise,
That they should in the londes gise
As he herde of the people say
Her comun game thanne pley.
And cried was, that they shuld come
Unto the game all and some
Of hem that ben deliver and wight
To do such maistry as they might.
They made hem naked as they sholde,
For so that ilke game wolde,
And it was tho custume and use,
Amonges hem was no refuse.
The floure of all the town was there
And of the court also there were,
And that was in a large place
Right even before the kinges face,
Whiche Artestrates thanne hight.
The pley was pleied right in his sight.
And who most worthy was of dede

Receive he shude a certain mede
And in the citee bere a price.
Appollinus, which ware and wise
Of every game couth an ende,
He thought assay, how so it wende.
    And fell among them into game,
And there he wanne him such a name,
So as the king him self accompteth,
That he all other men surmounteth
And bare the prise above hem alle.
The king bad, that into his halle
At souper time he shall be brought.
And he cam than and lefte it nought
Withoute compaigny alone.
Was none so semelich of persone,
Of visage and of limmes bothe,
If that he hadde what to clothe.
At souper time netheles
The king amiddes all the pres
Let clepe him up amonge hem alle
And bad his mareshall of his halle
To setten him in such degre,
That he upon him mighte se.
The king was sone sette and served,
And he, which had his prise deserved
After the kinges owne worde,
Was made begin a middel borde,
That bothe king and quene him sigh.
He sette and cast about his eye,
And sigh the lordes in estate
And with him self wax in debate
Thenkend what he hadde lore,
And such a sorwe he toke therfore,
That he sat ever still and thought,
As he, which of no mete rought.
    The king behelde his hevinesse
And of his grete gentilesse

Qualiter Appollinus ludum gignasii vincens in aula regis ad cenam honorifice coeptus est.

Qualiter Appollinus in cena recumbens

<small>nichil comedit, sed doloroso vultu, submisso capite, maxime ingemescebat, qui tandem a filia regis confortatus citharam plectens cunctis audientibus citharizando ultra modum complacuit.</small>

His doughter, which was faire and good
And ate bord before him stood,
As it was thilke time usage,
He bad to go on his message
And founde for to make him glad.
And she did as her fader bad
And goth to him the softe pas
And axeth whenne and what he was,
And praith he shulde his thoughtes leve.
 He saith: Madame, by your leve.
My name is hote Appollinus,
And of my richesse it is thus,
Upon the see I have it lore.
The contre, where as I was bore,
Where that my lond is and my rente,
I lefte at Tire, whan that I wente,
The worship there, of which I ought,
Unto the god I there bethought.
And thus to-gider as they two speke,
The teres ran down by his cheke.
The king, which therof toke good kepe,
Had great pite to se him wepe
And for his doughter send ayein
And praid her faire and gan to sain,
That she no lenger wolde drecche,
But that she wolde anone forth fecche
Her harpe and done all that she can
To gladde with that sory man.
And she to done her faders hest
Her harpe fet and in the feste
Upon a chare, which they fette,
Her self next to this man she sette.
With harpe both and eke with mouthe
To him she did, all that she couthe
To make him chere, and ever he siketh,
And she him axeth, how him liketh.
 Madame, certes well, he saide,

But if ye the mesure plaide,
Which, if you list, I shall you lere,
It were a glad thing for to here.
Ha, leve sire, tho quod she,
Now take the harpe and let me se,
Of what mesure that ye mene.
  Tho praith the king, tho praith the quene,
Forth with the lordes all arewe,
That he some merthe wolde shewe.
He taketh the harpe and in his wise
He tempreth and of suche assise
Singend he harpeth forth with all,
That as a vois celestiall
Hem thought it souned in her ere,
As though that he an aungel were.
They gladen of his melody,
But most of all the company
The kinges doughter, which it herde,
And thought eke of that he answerde,
Whan that it was of her apposed,
Within her hert hath well supposed,
That he is of great gentilesse.
His dedes ben therof witnesse
Forth with the wisdome of his lore,
It nedeth nought to seche more.
He might nought have such manere,
Of gentil blood but if he were.
When he had harped all his fill
The kinges heste to fulfill,
Away goth dish, away goth cup,
Down goth the bord, the cloth was up,
They risen and gone out of halle.
  The king his chamberlein let calle
And bad, that he by alle wey
A chambre for this man purvey,
Which nigh his owne chambre be.
It shall be do, my lord, quod he.

Qualiter Appollinus cum rege pro filia sua erudienda retentus est.

Appollinus, of whom I mene,
Tho toke his leve of king and quene
And of the worthy maide also,
Which praid unto her fader tho,
That she might of the yonge man
Of tho sciences, which he can,
His lore have. And in this wise
The king her graunteth his apprise,
So that him self therto assent.
Thus was accorded er they went,
That he with all that ever he may
This yonge faire freshe may
Of that he couthe shulde enforme.
And ful assented in this forme
They token leve as for that night.

<small>Qualiter filia regis Appollinum ornato apparatu vestiri fecit, et ipse ad puelle doctrinam, in quam pluribus familiariter intendebat, unde placata puella in amorem Appollini exardescens infirmabatur.</small>
And whan it was on morwe right,
Unto this yonge man of Tire
Of clothes, and of good attire
With gold and silver to despende
This worthy yonge lady sende.
And thus she made him well at ese,
And he with all that he can plese
Her serveth well and faire ayeine.
He taught her, till she was certeine
Of harpe, citole and of riote
With many a tune and many a note,
Upon musique, upon mesure,
And of her harpe the temprure
He taught her eke, as he well couth.
But as men sain, that frele is youth
With leiser and continuaunce,
This maide fell upon a chaunce,
That love hath made him a quarele
Ayeine her youthe fresh and frele,
That malgre where she wold or nought,
She mot with all her hertes thought
To love and to his lawe obey.

And that she shall full sore obey,
For she wot never what it is.
But ever among she feleth this,
Thenkend upon this man of Tire,
Her herte is hote as any fire,
And otherwise it is a cale.
Now is she red, now is she pale
Right after the condition
Of her ymagination.
But ever among her thoughtes alle,
She thoughte, what so many befalle,
Or that she laugh, or that she wepe,
She wolde her gode name kepe
For fere of womanisshe shame.
But what in ernest, what in game
She stant for love in such a plite,
That she hath lost all appetite
Of mete and drinke, of nightes rest,
As she that not what is the best.
But for to thenken all her fille
She helde her ofte times stille
Within her chambre, and goth nought out.
The king was of her life in doubt,
Which wiste nothing what it ment.

   But fell a time, as he out went
To walke, of princes sones thre
There came and felle to his knee,
And eche of them in sondry wise
Besought and profreth his service,
So that he might his doughter have.
The king, which wold her honour save,
Saith, she is sike, and of that speche
Tho was no time to beseche,
But eche of hem to make a bille
He bad and write his owne wille,
His name, his fader and his good.
And whan she wist, how that it stood,

Qualiter tres filii principum filiam regis singillatim in uxorem suis supplicacionibus postularunt.

And had her billes oversein,
They shulden have answere ayein.
Of this counseil they weren glad
And writen, as the king hem bad,
And every man his owne boke
Into the kinges hond betoke.
And he it to his doughter sende
And praide her for to make an ende
And write ayein her owne honde,
Right as she in her herte fonde.

Qualiter filia regis omnibus aliis relictis Appollinum in maritum preelegit.

The billes weren well received,
But she hath all her loves weived
And thoughte tho was time and space
To put her in her faders grace
And wrote ayein and thus she saide :
 The shame, which is in a maide,
With speche dare nought be unloke,
But in writing it may be spoke.
So write I to you, fader, thus,
But if I have Appollinus,
Of all this world what so betide,
I woll non other man abide.
And certes if I of him faile,
I wot right well withoute faile,
Ye shull for me be doughterles.
This letter came, and there was pres
To-fore the king, there as he stode.
And whan that he it understode,
He yave hem answere by and by.
But that was done so prively,
That none of others counseil wiste.
They toke her leve, and where hem liste,
They wente forth upon her wey.

Qualiter rex et regina in maritagium filie sue cum Appollino consencierunt.

The king ne wolde nought bewrey.
The counseil for no maner high,
But suffreth till he time sigh.
And whan that he to chambre is come,

He hath unto his counseil nome
This man of Tire and lete him se
The letter, and all the privete,
The which his doughter to him sente.
And he his kne to grounde bente
And thonketh him and her also.
And er they wenten than a two
With good herte and with good corage
Of full love and full mariage
The kinge and he ben hole accorded.
And after, whan it was recorded
Unto the doughter, how it stood,
The yifte of all this worldes good
Ne shuld have made her half so blithe.
And forth with all the kinge als swithe,
For he woll have her good assent,
Hath for the quene her moder sent.
The quene is come, and whan she herde
Of this matere how that it ferde,
She sigh debate, she sigh disese,
But if she wolde her doughter plese,
And is therto assented ful,
Which is a dede wonderful.
For no man knew the sothe cas,
But he him self, what man he was.
And netheles so es hem thought
His dedes to the sothe wrought,
That he was come of gentil blood,
Him lacketh nought but worldes good.
And as therof is no despeire,
For she shall be her faders heire,
And he was able to governe,
Thus woll they nought the love werne
Of him and her in no wise,
But all accorded they devise
The day and time of mariage,
Where love is lorde of the corage.

Him thenketh longe, er that he spede,
But ate laste unto the dede.

<small>Qualiter Appollinus filie regis nupsit, et prima nocte cum ea concubiens ipsam impregnavit.</small>

The time is come, and in her wise
With great offrend and sacrifice
They wedde and make a riche fest,
And every thing was right honest
Withinne hous, and eke without.
It was so done, that all about
Of great worship and great noblesse
There cried many a man largesse
Unto the lordes high and loude.
The knightes, that ben yonge and proude,
They jeste first and after daunce.
The day is go, the nightes chaunce
Hath derked all the brighte sonne.
This lord, which hath his love wonne,
Is go to bedde with his wife,
Where as they lede a lusty life,
And that was after somdele sene,
For as they pleiden hem betwene,
They gete a child betwene hem two,
To whom fell after mochel wo.

<small>Qualiter ambassiatores a Tyro in quadam navi Pentapolim venientes mortem regis Antiochi Appollino nunciaverunt.</small>

Now have I tolde of the spousailes.
But for to speke of the merveiles,
Which afterward to hem befelle,
It is a wonder for to telle.
It fell a day they riden out
The kinge and quene and all the rout
To pleien hem upon the stronde,
Where as they seen toward the londe
A ship sailend of great array.
To knowe what it mene may,
Till it be come they abide.
Then see they stonde on every side
Endlong the shippes bord to shewe
Of penouncels a rich rewe.
They axen, whenne the ship is come.

Fro Tire, anone answerde some.
And over this they saiden more,
The cause why they comen fore
Was for to seche and for to finde
Appollinus, which is of kinde
Her lege lord. And he appereth
And of the tale whiche he hereth
He was right glad, for they him tolde,
That for vengeaunce, as god it wolde,
Antiochus as men may wite
With thunder and lightning is forsmite.
His dochter hath the same chaunce.
So be they both in o balaunce.
Forthy, our lege lord, we say
In name of all the lond and pray,
That lefte all other thing to done,
It like you to come sone
And se your owne lege men
With other, that ben of your ken,
That live in longing and desire,
Till ye be come ayein to Tire.
This tale after the king it had
Pentapolim all oversprad.
There was no joie for to seche,
For every man it had in speche
And saiden all of one accorde :
A worthy king shall ben our lorde,
That thought us first an hevinesse,
Is shape us now to great gladnesse.
Thus goth the tiding over all.
 But nede he mot, that nede shall.
Appollinus his leve toke,
To god and all the lond betoke
With all the people longe and brode,
That he no lenger there abode.
 The king and quene sorwe made,
But yet somdele they weren glade

Qualiter Appollino cum uxore sua impregnata a Pentapoli versus Tyrum navigantibus contigit uxorem, mortis articulo angustiatam, in navi filiam, que postea Thaisis vocabatur, parere.

Of such thing, as they herden tho.
And thus betwene the wele and wo
To ship he goth his wife with childe,
The which was ever meke and milde
And wolde nought departe him fro,
Such love was betwene hem two.
Lichorida for her office
Was take, which was a norice,
To wende with this yonge wife,
To whom was shape a wofull life.
Within a time, as it betid,
Whan they were in the see amid,
Out of the north they sigh a cloude,
The storme aros, the windes loude
They blewen many a dredefull blast,
The welken was all overcast.
The derke night the sonne hath under,
There was a great tempest of thunder.
The mone and eek the sterres bothe
In blacke cloudes they hem clothe,
Wherof her brighte loke they hide.
This yonge lady wept and cride,
To whom no comfort might availe,
Of childe she began travaile,
Where she lay in a caban close.
Her wofull lord fro her arose,
And that was long er any morwe,
So that in anguish and sorwe
She was delivered all by night
And deiede in every mannes sight.

Qualiter Appollinus mortem uxoris sue planxit.

But netheles for all this wo
A maide child was bore tho.
Appollinus whan he this knewe,
For sorwe a swoune he overthrewe,
That no man wist in him no life.
And whan he woke, he saide : Ha, wife,
My joy, my lust and my desire,

My welth and my recoverire,
Why shall I live, and thou shalt deie?
Ha, thou fortune, I the defie,
Now hast thou do to me thy werst.
Ha, herte, why ne wolt thou berst,
That forth with her I mighte passe?
My paines were well the lasse.
In such weping and suche crie
His dede wife, which lay him by,
A thousand sithes he her kiste,
Was never man, that sigh ne wiste
A sorwe to his sorwe liche,
Was ever among upon the liche.
He fell swounende as he, that thought
His owne deth, which he besought
Unto the goddes all above
With many a pitous word of love.
But suche words as tho were,
Yet herde never mannes ere,
But only thilke, which he saide.
The maister shipman came and praide
With other such, as ben therinne,
And sain, that he may nothing winne
Ayein the deth, but they him rede,
He be well ware and take hede,
The see by wey of his nature
Receive may no creature
Within him self as for to holde,
The which is dede. Forthy they wolde,
As they counseilen all about,
The dede body casten out.
For better it is, they saiden all,
That it of here so befall,
Than if they shulden alle spille.
    The king, which understode her will
And knew her counseil that was trewe,
Began ayein his sorwe newe

Qualiter suadentibus nautis corpus uxoris sue

With pitous hert and thus to say:
It is all reson that ye pray.
I am, quod he, but one alone,
So wolde I nought for my persone,
There felle such adversite.
But whan it may no better be,
Doth thanne thus upon my worde,
Let make a coffre stronge of borde,
That it be firm with led and piche.
Anone was made a coffre suche
All redy brought unto his honde.
And whan he sighe and redy fonde
This coffre made and well englued,
The dede body was besewed
In cloth of gold and laid therinne.
And for he wolde unto her winne
Upon some coste a sepulture,
Under her heved in adventure
Of gold he laide sommes great
And of juels a strong beyete
Forth with a letter, and said thus:
 I, king of Tire, Appollinus
Doth alle maner men for to wite,
That here and se this letter write,
That helpeles withoute rede
Here lith a kinges doughter dede,
And who that hapneth her to finde
For charite take in his minde
And do so, that she be begrave
With this tresor, which he shal have.
 Thus whan the letter was full spoke,
They have anone the coffre stoke
And bounden it with iron faste,
That it may with the wawes laste,
And stoppen it by such a wey,
That it shall be withinne drey,
So that no water might it greve.

mortue in quadam cista plumbo et ferro obtusaque circumligata Appollinus cum magno thesauro una cum quadam littera sub eius capite scripta recludi et in mare proici fecit.

Copia littere Appollini capiti uxoris ue supposite.

And thus in hope and good beleve,
Of that the corps shall well arrive,
They cast it over borde as blive.
   The ship forth on the wawes went.
The prince hath chaunged his entent
And saith, he woll nought come at Tire
As thanne, but all his desire
Is first to sailen unto Tharse.
The windy storm began to scarse,
The sonne arist, the weder clereth,
The shipman, which behinde stereth,
Whan that he sigh the windes saught,
Towardes Tharse his cours he straught.
   But now to my matere ayein,
To telle as olde bokes sain,
This dede corps, of whiche ye knowe,
With winde and water was forth throwe,
Now here, now there, till ate last
At Ephesim the see upcast
The coffre and all that was therinne.
Of great merveile now beginne
May here, who that sitteth still.
That god woll save may nought spill.
Right as the corps was throwe a londe,
There cam walkend upon the stronde
A worthy clerke and surgien
And eke a great phisicien,
Of all that lond the wisest one,
Which highte maister Cerimon.
There were of his disciples some.
This maister is to the coffre come,
He peiseth there was somwhat in
And bad hem bere it to his inne,
And goth him selve forth with all.
All that shall falle, falle shall.
   They comen home and tarie nought.
This coffre into his chambre is brought,

Qualiter Apollinus, uxoris sue corpore in mare projecto, Tyrum relinquens cursum suum versus Tharsim navigio dolens arripuit.

Qualiter corpus predicte defuncte super litus apud Ephesim quidam medicus nomine Cerimon cum aliquibus suis discipulis invenit, quod in hospicium suum portans et extra cistam ponens, spiraculo vite in ea adhuc invento, ipsam plene sanitati restituit.

Which that they finde fast stoke,
But they with craft it have unloke.
They loken in, where as they founde,
A body dede, which was iwounde
In cloth of gold, as I said ere.
The tresor eke they founden there
Forth with the letter, which they rede.
And tho they token better hede.
Unsowed was the body sone.
As he that knewe, what was to done,
This noble clerk with alle haste
Began the veines for to taste,
And sigh her age was of youthe.
And with the craftes, which he couthe,
He sought and found a signe of life.
With that this worthy kinges wife
Honestely they token out
And maden fires all about.
They laid her on a couche softe,
And with a shete warmed ofte
Her colde brest began to hete,
Her herte also to flacke and bete,
This maister hath her every jointe
With certaine oil and balme anointe,
And put a liquour in her mouthe,
Which is to few clerkes couthe,
So that she covereth ate laste.
And first her eyen up she caste,
And whan she more of strengthe caught,
Her armes bothe forth she straught,
Held up her hond and pitously
She spake and saide : Where am I?
Where is my lord, what world is this?
As she, that wot nought how it is.
But Cerimon that worthy leche
Answerde anone upon her speche
And said : Madame, ye ben here,

Where ye be sauf, as ye shall here
Here afterward, forthy as now
My counseil is, comforteth you.
For tristeth wel withoute faile,
There is no thing, which shall you faile,
That ought of reson to be do.
Thus passen they a day or two.
They speke of nought as for an ende,
Till she began somdele amende,
And wist her selven, what she mente.

 Tho for to knowe her hole entente
This maister axeth all the cas,
How she cam there, and what she was.
How I came here, wote I nought,
Quod she, but wel I am bethought
Of other thinges all about
Fro point to point, and tolde him out
Als ferforthly as she it wiste.
And he her tolde, how in a kiste
The see her threwe upon the londe,
And what tresor with her he fonde,
Which was all redy at her will,
As he, that shope him to fulfill
With al his might, what thing he shuld.
She thonketh him, that he so wolde,
And all her herte she discloseth
And saith him well that she supposeth,
Her lord be dreint, her childe also.
So sigh she nought but alle wo.
Wherof as to the world no more
Ne woll she torne and praieth therfore,
That in some temple of the citee
To kepe and holde her chastete
She might among the women dwelle.
Whan he this tale herde telle,
He was right glad and made her knowen,
That he a doughter of his owen

Qualiter uxor Appollini sanata domum religionis peciit, ubi sacro velamine munita castam omni tempore se vovit.

Hath, which he woll unto her yive
To serve, while they bothe live
In stede of that, which he hath loste,
All only at his owne coste,
She shall be rendred forth with her.
She saith: Graunt mercy, leve sir,
God quite it you, there I ne may.
And thus they drive forth the day,
Till time cam, that she was hole.
And tho they take her couseil hole
To shape upon good ordenaunce
And made a worthy purveaunce
Ayein the day, whan they be veiled.
And thus whan that they were counseiled,
In blacke clothes they hem cloth
This lady and the doughter both
And yolde hem to religion.
The feste and the profession
After the reule of that degre
Was made with great solempnite,
Where as Diane is sanctified.
Thus stant this lady justified,
In ordre where she thenketh to dwelle.

Qualiter Apollinus Tharsim navigans, filium suam Thaisim Stranguilioni et Dionisie uxori sue educandum commendavit et deinde Tyrum adiit, ubi cum inestimabili gaudio a suis receptus est.

But now ayeinward for to telle,
In what plite that her lord stood inne.
He saileth, till that he may winne
The haven of Tharse, as I saide ere.
And whan he was arrived there,
Tho it was through the cite knowe,
Men mighte se within a throwe
As who saith all the towne at ones.
They come ayein him for the nones
To yiven him the reverence,
So glad they were of his presence.
And though he were in his corage
Disesed, yet with glad visage
He made hem chere and to his inne,

Where he whilom sojourned in,
He goth him straught and was received.
And when the press of people is weived,
He taketh his host unto him tho
And saith: My friend Strangulio,
Lo thus, and thus it is befalle.
And thou thy self art one of alle
Forth with thy wife, which I most
    trist,
Forthy if it you bothe list,
My doughter Thaise by your leve
I thenke shall with you beleve
As for a time, and thus I pray,
That she be kept by alle way.
And whan she hath of age more,
That she be set to bokes lore.
And this avow to god I make,
That I shall neuer for her sake
My berde for no liking shave,
Till it befalle, that I have
In covenable time of age
Besette her unto mariage.
    Thus they accorde, and all is well.
And for to resten him somdele,
As for a while he ther sojorneth,
And than he taketh his leve and torneth
To ship and goth him home to Tire,
Where every man with great desire
Awaiteth upon his coming.
But when the ship cam in sailing
And they perceiven it is he,
Was never yet in no citee
Such joie made, as they tho made.
His herte also began to glade
Of that he seeth his people glad.
Lo, thus fortune his hap hath lad,
In sondry wise he was travailed.

But how so ever he be assailed,
His latter ende shall be good.

Qualiter Thaisis una cum Philotenna Strangulionis et Dionisie filia omnis sciencie et honestatis doctrina imbuta est, sed et Thaisis Philotennam precellens in odium mortale per invidiam a Dionisia recollecta est.

And for to speke how that it stood
Of Thaise his doughter, wher she dwelleth,
In Tharse as the cronique telleth,
She was well kept, she was well loked,
She was wel taught, she was wel boked,
So well she sped her in her youth,
That she of every wisdom couth,
That for to seche in every londe
So wise an other no man fonde
Ne so well taught at mannes eye.
But wo worth ever false envy.
For it befell that time so,
A doughter hath Strangulio,
The which was cleped Philotenne.
But fame, which woll ever renne,
Came all day to her moders ere
And saith, wher ever her doughter were
With Thaise set in any place,
The commun vois, the commun grace
Was all upon that other maide,
And of her doughter no man saide.
Who was wroth but Dionise than?
Her thought a thousand yere till whan
She might be of Thaise wreke,
Of that she herde folk so speke.
And fell that ilke same tide,
That dede was trewe Lichoride,
Whiche had be servaunt to Thaise,
So that she was the wors at ese.
For she hath thanne no servise
But onely through this Dionise,
Which was her dedlich enemy.
Through pure treson and envy
She, that of alle sorwe can,
Tho spake unto her bondeman,

Which cleped was Theophilus,
And made him swere in counseil thus,
That he such time as she him set
Shall come Thaise for to fet
And lede her out of alle sight,
Where that no man her helpe might,
Upon the stronde nigh the see,
And there he shall this maiden slee.
This cherles hert is in a traunce,
As he, which drad him of vengeaunce,
Whan time comth an other day.
But yet durst he nought saie nay,
But swore and said he shall fulfill
Her hestes at her owne will.

 The treson and the time is shape,
So fell it that this cherles knape
Hath lad this maiden where he wold
Upon the stronde, and what she sholde,
She was adrad, and he out braide
A rusty swerde and to her saide :
Thou shalt be dede. Alas, quod she,
Why shall I so ? Lo thus, quod he,
My lady Dionise hath bede,
Thou shalt be murdred in this stede.
This maiden tho for fere shrighte
And for the love of god allmighte
She praith, that for a litel stounde
She mighte knele upon the grounde
Toward the heven for to crave,
Her wofull soule if she may save.
And with this noise and with this cry,
Out of a barge faste by,
Which hid was there on scomer-fare,
Men sterten out and weren ware
Of this felon, and he to go,
And she began to crie tho :
Ha, mercy, help for goddes sake.

Qualiter Dionisia Thaisim ut occideret Theophilo servo suo tradidit, qui cum noctanter longius ab urbe ipsam prope litus maris interficere proposuerat, pirate ibidem latitantes Thaisim de manu carnificis eripuerunt ipsamque usque civitatem Mitelenam ducentes, cuidam Leonino scortorum ibidem magistro vendiderunt.

Into the barge they her take,
As theves shulde, and forth they went.
Upon the see the wind hem hent
And malgre where they wolde or none
To-fore the weder forth they gone,
There halp no sail, there halp none ore,
Forstormed and forblowen sore
In great peril so forth they drive,
Till ate laste they arrive
At Mitelene the citee.
In haven sauf and whan they be,
The maister shipman made him boune
And goth him out into the towne
And profreth Thaise for to selle.
One Leonin it herde telle,
Which maister of the bordel was,
And bad him gon a redy pas
To fecchen her, and forth he went
And Thaise out of his barge he hent
And to the bordeler her solde.
And he, that by her body wolde
Take avauntage, let do cry,
That what man wolde his lechery
Attempt upon her maidenhede
Lay down the gold, and he shuld spede.
And thus whan he hath cried it out,
In sight of all the people about

Qualiter Leoninus Thaisim ad lupanar destinavit, ubi dei gratia preventa ipsius virginitatem nullus violare potuit.

He ladde her to the bordel tho,
No wonder is though she be wo
Clos in a chambre by her self.
Eche after other ten or twelf
Of yonge men in to her went.
But such a grace god her sent,
That for the sorwe, which she made,
Was none of hem, which power had
To done her any vilainy.
    This Leonin let ever aspy

And waiteth after great beyete,
But all for nought, she was forlete,
That no man wolde there come.
Whan he therof hath hede nome
And knew, that she was yet a maide,
Unto his owne man he saide,
That he with strength ayein her leve
Tho shulde her maidenhede bereve.
This man goth in, but so it ferde,
Whan he her wofull pleintes herde
And he therof hath take kepe,
Him liste better for to wepe
Than don ought elles to the game.
And thus she kepte her self fro shame
And kneled down to therthe and praide
Unto this man and thus she saide :

 If so be, that thy maister wolde,
That I his gold encrese sholde,
It may nought falle by this wey,
But suffre me to go my wey
Out of this hous, where I am in,
And I shall make him for to win
In some place elles of the town,
Be so it be of religion,
Where that honeste women dwelle.
And thus thou might thy maister telle,
That whan I have a chambre there,
Let him do cry ay wide where,
What lord, that hath his doughter dere
And is in will, that she shall lere
Of such a scole that is trewe,
I shall her teche of things newe,
Whiche as none other woman can
In all this londe. And tho this man
Her tale hath herde, he goth ayein
And tolde unto his maister plein,
That she hath saide. And therupon,

Whan that he sigh beyete none
At the bordel because of hire,
He bad his man to gon and spire
A place, where she might abide,
That he may winne upon some side,
By that she can. But ate lest
Thus was she sauf of this tempest.

Qualiter Thaisis a lupanari virgo liberata, inter sacras mulieres hospicium habens, sciencias, quibus edocta fuit, nobiles regni puellas ibidem edocebat.

He hath her fro the bordel take,
But that was nought for goddes sake,
But for the lucre, as she him tolde.
Now comen tho, that comen wolde,
Of women in her lusty youth
To here and se, what thing she couth.
She can the wisdome of a clerke,
She can of any lusty werke,
Which to a gentil woman longeth.
And some of hem she underfongeth
To the citole and to the harpe,
And whom it liketh for to carpe
Proverbes and demaundes sligh,
An other such they never sigh,
Which that science so well taught,
Whereof she grete yiftes caught,
That she to Leonin hath wonne.
And thus her name is so begonne
Of sondry thinges, that she techeth,
That all the londe to her secheth
Of yonge women for to lere.

Qualiter Theophilus ad Dionisiam mane rediens affirmavit se Thaisim occidisse, super quo Dionisia una cum Strangulione marito suo dolorem in publico confingentes, exequias et sepulturam honorifice

Now lette we this maiden here
And speke of Dionise ayeine
And of Theophile the vilaine,
Of which I spake of now to-fore,
Whan Thaise shulde have be forlore.
This false cherle to his lady,
Whan he cam home all prively,
He saith: Madame, slain I have
This maide Thaise, and is begrave

In prive place, as ye me bede.
Forthy, madame, taketh hede
And kepe counseil, how so it stonde.
This fend, which hath this understonde,
Was glad and weneth it be soth.
Now herke, hereafter how she doth.
She wepeth, she sorweth, she compleigneth
And of sickenesse, which she feigneth,
She saith, that Thaise sodeinly
By night is dede, as she and I
To-gider lien nigh my lorde.
She was a women of recorde,
And all is levee, that she saith.
And sor to yive a more feith,
Her husbonde and eke she both
In blacke clothes they hem cloth,
And make a great enterrement.
And for the people shall be blent
Of Thaise as for the remembraunce,
After the real olde usaunce
A tumbe of laton noble and riche
With an ymage unto her liche
Liggend above therupon
They made and set it up anon.
Her epitaphe of good assise
Was write about, and in this wise
It spake: O ye, that this beholde,
Lo, here lieth she, the which was holde
The fairest and the floure of alle,
Whose name Thaisis men calle.
The king of Tire Appollinus
Her fader was, now lieth she thus.
Fourtene yere she was of age,
Whan deth her toke to his viage.

    Thus was this false treson hid,
Which afterward was wide kid,
As by the tale a man shall here.

quantum ad extra subdola conjectacione fieri constituerunt.

Qualiter Appollinus in regno suo apud Tyrum existens parliamentum fieri constituit.

But to declare my matere
To Tire I thenke torne ayein
And telle, as the croniques sain.
Whan that the king was comen home
And hath lefte in the salte fome
His wife, which he may nought foryete,
For he some comfort wolde gete,
He let sommone a parlement,
To which the lordes were assent,
And of the time he hath ben out,
He seeth the thinges all about.
And told hem eke, how he hath fare,
While he was out of londe fare,
And praide him alle to abide,
For he wolde at the same tide
Do shape for his wives minde,
As he, that woll nought ben unkinde.
Solempne was that ilke office,
And riche was the sacrifice,
The feste really was holde.
And thereto was he well beholde.
For suche a wife as he had one,
In thilke daies was there none.

<small>Qualiter Appollinus post parliamentum Tharsim pro Thaise filia sua querenda adiit, qua ibidem non inventa abinde navigio recessit.</small>

Whan this was done, than he him thought
Upon his doughter, and besought
Such of his lordes, as he wolde,
That they with him to Tharse sholde
To fet his doughter Thaise there,
And they anone all redy were.
To ship they gone, and forth they went,
Till they the haven of Tharse hent.
They londe and saile of that they seche
By coverture and sleight of speche.
This false man Strangulio
And Dionise his wife also,
That he the better trowe might,
They ladden him to have a sight,

Where that her tombe was arraied,
The lasse yet he was mispaied.
And netheles so as he durst,
He curseth and saith all the worst
Unto fortune, as to the blinde,
Which can no siker weie finde,
For she him neweth ever amonge
And medleth sorwe with his songe.
But sithe it may no better be,
He thonketh god and forth goth he
Sailende toward Tire ayeine.
But sodeinly the winde and reine
Began upon the see debate,
So that he suffre mote algate

   The lawe, which Neptune ordeineth,
Wherof full oft time he pleigneth
And held him wel the more esmaied
Of that he hath to-fore assaied.
So that for pure sorwe and care,
Of that he seeth this world so fare,
The reste he leveth of his caban,
That for the counseil of no man
Ayein therin he nolde come,
But hath beneth his place nome,
Where he wepend allone lay,
There as he sigh no light of day.

   And thus to-fore the wind they drive
Till longe and late they arrive
With great distresse, as it was sene,
Upon this towne of Mitelene,
Which was a noble cite tho.
And happneth thilke time so,
The lordes both and the commune
The highe festes of Neptune
Upon the strond at the rivage,
As it was custume and usage,
Solempneliche they besigh.

Qualiter navis Appollini ventis agitata portum urbis Mitelene in die, quo festa Neptuni celebrare consueverunt, applicuit, sed ipse pre dolore Thaisis fille sue, quam mortuam reputabat, in fundo navis obscuro jacens lumens videre noluit.

Whan they this straunge vessel sigh
Come in and hath his avaled,
The town therof hath spoke and taled.
The lord, which of that cite was,
Whose name is Athenagoras,
Was there and said, he wolde se,
What ship it is, and who they be,
That ben therin. And after sone,
Whan that he sigh it was to done,
His barge was for him arraied,
And he goth forth and hath assaied.
He found the ship of great array.
But what thing it amounte may,
He sigh they maden hevy chere,
But well him thenketh by the manere,
That they be worthy men of blood,
And axeth of hem, how it stood,
And they him tellen all the cas,
How that he lord fordrive was,
And what a sorwe that he made,
Of which there may no man him glade.
He praieth that he her lord may se.
But they him tald it may nought be,
For he lith in so derke a place,
That there may no wight sen his face.
But for all that though hem be loth,
He found the ladder and down he goth
And to him spake, but none answer
Ayein of him ne might he bere,
For ought that he can do or sain.
And thus he goth him up ayein.

Tho was there spoke in many wise
Amonges hem, that weren wise,
Now this, now that, but ate last
The wisdom of the town thus cast,
That yonge Thaise were assent.
For if there be amendement

To glade with this wofull king,
She can so moch of every thing,
That she shall gladen him anone.
   A messager for her is gone.
And she came with her harp on honde
And saide hem, that she wolde fonde
By alle weies, that she can,
To gladde with this sory man.
But what he was, she wiste nought.
But all the ship her hath besought,
That she her wit on him despende,
In aunter if he might amende,
And sain: It shall be well aquite.
When she hath understonden it,
She goth her down, there as he lay,
Where that she harpeth many a lay
And lich an aungel sang with alle.
But he no more than the walle
Toke hede of any thing he herde.
And whan she sigh, that he so ferde,
She falleth with him unto wordes
And telleth him of sondry bordes
And axeth him demaundes straunge,
Whereof she made his herte chaunge,
And to her speche his ere he laide
And hath merveile, of that she saide.
For in proverbe and in probleme
She spake and bad, he shulde deme
In many a subtil question.
But he for no suggestion,
Which toward him she couthe stere,
He wolde nought o word answere,
But as a mad man ate laste,
His heved weping awey he caste
And half in wrath he bad her go.
But yet she wolde nought do so,
And in the derke forth she goth,

Till she him toucheth and he wroth
And after here with his honde
He smote. And thus whan she him fonde
Disesed, courteisly she saide:
Avoy my lorde, I am a maide.
And if ye wiste what I am,
And out of what lignage I cam,
Ye wolde nought be so salvage.
With that he sobreth his corage

<small>Qualiter, sicut deus destinavit patri, filiam inventam recognovit.</small>

And put awey his hevy chere.
But of hem two a man may lere,
What is to be so sibbe of blood.
None wist of other how it stood,
And yet the fader ate last
His herte upon this maide cast,
That he her loveth kindely.
And yet he wiste never why,
But all was knowe er that they went.
For god, which wote her hole entent,
Her hertes both anone descloseth.
This king unto this maide opposeth
And axeth first, what is her name,
And where she lerned all this game,
And of what ken that she was come.
And she, that hath his wordes nome,
Answereth and saith: My name is Thaise,
That was sometime well at ese.
In Tharse I was forthdrawe and fedde,
There lerned I, till I was spedde
Of that I can. My fader eke |
I not, where that I shulde him seke,
He was a king, men tolde me.
My moder dreint was in the see.
Fro point to point all she him tolde,
That she hath longe in herte holde,
And never durste make her mone,
But only to this lord allone,

To whom her herte can nought hele,
Torne it to wo, torne it to wele,
Torne it to good, torne it to harme.
And he tho toke her in his arme.
But such a joy as he tho made
Was never sene, thus be they glade,
That sory hadden be to-forne.
Fro this day forth fortune hath sworne
To set him upward on the whele.
So goth the world, now wo, now wele.

 This king hath founde new grace,   *Qualiter Athe-*
So that out of his derke place   *nagoras Ap-*
He goth him up into the light.   *pollinum de*
And with him cam that swete wight   *navi in hospi-*
His doughter Thaise, and forth anone   *cium honorifice*
They bothe into the caban gone,   *recollegit et*
Which was ordeined for the kinge.   *Thaisim, patre*
And there he did of all his thinge   *consenciente,*
And was arraied really,   *in uxorem*
And out he cam all openly,   *duxit.*
Where Athenagoras he fonde,
The which was lorde of all the londe.
He praieth the king to come and se
His castell bothe and his citee.
And thus they gone forth all in fere,
This king, this lord, this maiden dere.
This lord tho made hem riche feste
With every thing, which was honeste,
To plese with this worthy kinge.
There lacketh hem no maner thinge.
But yet for al his noble array
Wifeles he was unto that day,
As he, that yet was of yonge age.
So fell there into his corage
The lusty wo, the gladde peine
Of love, which no man restreigne
Yet never might as now to-fore.

This lord thenketh all his world forlore,
But if the king woll done him grace.
He waiteth time, he waiteth place,
Him thought his herte woll to-breke,
Till he may to this maide speke
And to her fader eke also
For mariage.   And it fell so,
That all was do, right as he thought,
His purpose to an ende he brought,
She wedded him as for her lorde,
Thus be they alle of one accorde.

Qualiter Appollinus una cum filia et eius marito navim ingredientes a Mitelena usque Tharsim cursum proposuerunt, sed Appollinus in sompnis admonitus versus Ephesim, ut ibidem templo Diane sacrificaret, vela per mare divertit.

Whan al was do right as they wolde,
The kinge unto his sone tolde
Of Tharse thilke treterie,
And said, how in his compaignie
His doughter and him selven eke
Shall go vengeaunce for to seke.
The shippes were redy sone.
And whan they sigh it was to done
Withoute let of any went,
With saile up drawe forth they went
Towardes Tharse upon the tide.
But he, that wot, what shall betide,
The highe god, which wolde him kepe,
Whan that this king was faste a slepe,
By nightes time he hath him bede
To saile unto another stede.
To Ephesim he bad him drawe,
And as it was that time lawe,
He shall do there his sacrifice.
And eke he bad in alle wise,
That in the temple amonges alle
His fortune, as it is befalle,
Touchend his doughter and his wife
He shall beknowe upon his life.
The king of this avision
Hath great ymaginacion,

What thinge it signifie may.
And netheles whan it was day,
He bad cast anker and abode.
And while that he on anker rode,
The wind, which was to-fore straunge,
Upon the point began to chaunge
And torneth thider, as it shulde.
Tho knewe he well, that god it wolde,
And bad the maister make him yare,
To-fore the wind for he wold fare
To Ephesim, and so he dede.
And whan he came into the stede,
Where as he shulde londe, he londeth,
With all the haste he may and fondeth
To sharpen him in suche a wise,
That he may by the morwe arise
And done after the maundement
Of him, which hath him thider sent.
And in the wise, that he thought,
Upon the morwe so he wrought.
His doughter and his sone he nome
And forth unto the temple he come
With a great route in compaigny
His yiftes for to sacrify.
The citezeins tho herden say
Of such a king, that came to pray
Unto Diane the goddesse
And lefte all other besinesse,
They comen thider for to se
The king and the solempnite.

 With worthy knightes environed
The king him self hath abandoned
Into the temple in good entente.
The dore is up, and in he wente,
Where as with great devocion
Of holy contemplacion
Within his herte he made his shrifte.

Qualiter Appolinus Ephesim in templo Diane sacrificans, uxorem suam ibidem velatam invenit, qua secum assumpta in navim versus Tyrum regressus est.

And after that a riche yifte
He offreth with great reverence;
And there in open audience
Of hem, that stoden all about,
He tolde hem and declareth out
His hap, such as him is befalle.
There was no thing foryete of alle.
His wife, as it was goddes grace,
Which was professed in the place,
As she, that was abbesse there,
Unto his tale hath laid her ere,
She knew the vois and the visage,
For pure joy as in a rage
She straught unto him all at ones
And fell a swoune upon the stones,
Wherof the temple flore was paved.
She was anone with water laved,
Till she came to her self ayein.
And thanne she began to sain:
Ha, blessed be the highe sonde,
That I may se min husbonde,
Which whilom he and I were one.
The king with that knewe her anone
And toke her in his arme and kist,
And all the town thus sone it wist.
Tho was there joie manyfold,
For euery man this tale hath told
As for miracle, and were glade.
But never man such joie made
As doth the king, which hath his wife.
And whan men herde, how that her life
Was saved and by whom it was,
They wondren all of suche a cas.
Through all the tonde arose the speche
Of maister Cerimon the leche
And of the cure, which he dede.
The king him self tho hath him bede

And eke this quene forth with him,
That he the the town of Ephesim
Woll leve and go where as they be,
For never man of his degre
Hath do to hem so mochel good.
And he his profite understood
And graunteth with hem for to wende.
And thus they maden there an ende,
And token leave and gone to ship
With al the hole felaship.

   This king, which now hath his desire,   *Qualiter Ap-*
Saith, he woll holde his cours to Tire.   *pollinus una*
They hadden wind at wille tho   *cum uxore et*
With topsail-cole, and forth they go.   *filia sua Tyrum*
And striken never, till they come   *applicut.*
To Tire, wher as they haven nome,
And londen hem with mochel blisse.
There was many a mouth to kisse,
Eche one welcometh other home.
But when the quene to londe come
And Thaise her doughter by her side,
The joy which was thilke tide
There may no mannes tunge telle.
They saiden all : Here cometh the welle
Of all the womanishe grace.
The king hath take his real place,
The quene is into chambre go.
There was great feste arraied tho.
Whan time was they gone to mete,
All olde sorwes ben foryete,
And gladen hem with joies newe.
The descoloured pale hewe
Is now become a ruddy cheke,
There was no merthe for to seke.

   But every man hath what he wolde,   *Qualiter Ap-*
The king as he well couthe and sholde   *pollinus Athen-*
Maketh to his people right good chere.   *agoram cum*
   Thaise. uxore
   sua super
   Tyrum coro-
   nari fecit.

And after sone, as thou shalt here,
A parlement he hath sommoned,
Where he his doughter hath coroned
Forth with the lorde of Mitelene,
That one is king, that other quene.
And thus the faders ordenaunce
This londe hath set in governaunce,
And saide, that he wolde wende
To Tharse for to make an ende
Of that his doughter was betraied,
Wherof were alle men well paied.
And said, how it was for to done.

The shippes weren redy sone.
A strong power with him he toke,
Up to the sky he cast his loke
And sigh the wind was covenable.
They hale up anker with the cable,
They sail on high the stere on honde,
They sailen, till they come a londe
At Tharse nigh to the citee.
And whan they wisten it was he,
The town hath done him reverence.
He telleth hem the violence,
Which the tretour Strangulio
And Dionise him hadde do
Touchende his doughter, as ye herde.
And whan they wiste, how it ferde,
As he, which pees and love sought,
Unto the town this he besought
To done him right in jugement.
Anone they were both assent
With strengthe of men, and comen sone,
And as hem thought it was to done,
Atteint they were by the lawe
And demed for to honge and drawe
And brent and with the wind to-blowe,
That all the world it mighte knowe.

Qualiter Apollinus a Tyro per mare versus Tharsim iter arripiens vindictam contra Strangulionem et Dionisiam uxorem suam pro injuria, quam ipsi Thaisi filie sue intulerunt, judicialiter assecutus est.

And upon this condicion
The dome in execucion
Was put anone withoute faile.
And every man hath great merveile,
Whiche herde tellen of this chaunce,
And thonketh goddes purveaunce,
Which doth mercy forth with justice.
Slain is the mordrer and mordrice
Through verray trouth of rightwisnesse,
And through mercy sauf is simplesse
Of here, whom mercy preserveth.
Thus hath he wel, that wel deserveth.

 Whan all this thing is done and ended,
This king, which loved was and frended,
A letter hath, which came to him
By shippe fro Pentapolim,
In which the lond hath to him write,
That he wolde understonde and wite,
How in good minde and in good pees
Dede is the kinge Artestrates,
Wherof they all of one accorde,
Him praiden, as her lege lorde,
That he the letter wol conceive
And come, his regne to receive,
Which god hath yove him and fortune.
And thus besoughte the commune
Forth with the grete lordes alle.
This king sigh how it was befalle.
Fro Tharse and in prosperite
He toke his leve of that citee
And goth him into ship ayein.
The wind was good, the se was plein,
Hem nedeth nought to a riff to flake,
Till they Pentapolim have take.
The lond, which herde of that tiding,
Was wonder glad of his coming.
He rested him a day or two

Qualiter Artestrate Pentapolim rege mortuo, ipsi de regno epistolas super hoc Appollino direxerunt, unde Appollinus, una cum uxore sua ibidem advenientes ad decus imperii cum magno gaudio coronati sunt.

And toke his counseil to him tho
And set a time of parlement,
Where all the londe of one assent
Forth with his wife have him coroned,
Where alle good him was foisoned.
 Lo, what it is to be well grounded.
For he hath first his love founded
Honestelich as for to wedde,
Honestelich his love he spedde
And hadde children with his wife,
And as him list he lad his life,
And in ensaumple his life was write,
That alle lovers mighten wite,
How ate last it shal be sene
Of love what they wolden mene.
For se now on that other side
Antiochus with all his pride,
Which set his love unkindely,
His ende he hadde sodeinly
Set ayein kinde upon vengeaunce,
And for his lust hath his penaunce.

2. The Patterne of Painefull Adventures.

MR COLLIER'S INTRODUCTION.

It is not our intention to enter at large into the antiquity of the story upon which "Pericles" is founded. Most of the learning on the subject may be seen in Douce's "Illustrations," vol. ii. 135. Our principal object is to speak of it as a narrative of which Shakespeare made use in the composition of the play which has been printed in most of the editions of his works, and in the composition of which few have entertained a doubt that he was importantly concerned.

We have not only internal, but external, evidence that there was an older play upon the same incidents. As to external evidence, the "Memoirs of Edward Alleyn," printed by the Shakespere Society, contain (p. 21) an inventory of apparel belonging to the actor-founder of Dulwich College, including "spangled hose in Pericles;" and though the document is without date, we can have no hesitation in deciding that it was anterior to the beginning of the year 1608, when, we apprehend, "Pericles," as it has come down to us, was first produced on the stage. The internal evidence is derived from a perusal of the play itself, which bears strong marks of two hands in the authorship of it: an older and an inferior style of composition is observable in the commencement of the play; and it is upon the three last acts that we suppose Shakespeare to have been principally engaged. How much of the play, as written by some anterior author, was allowed by our great dramatist to remain, it is impossible with any accuracy to determine. Shakespeare was not the first to give it the title of "Pericles," for it seems to have borne that name when Alleyn acted in it, perhaps some years before the commencement of the seventeenth century.

The hero, at the oldest date at which we hear of him in English, was called "Kynge Appolyn of Thyre;" in 1510, under this title, Wynkyn de Worde printed the romance, as it had been translated from the French by Robert Copland. This was its first appearance in our printed literature. Who was the author of the French version used by Copland we are without information; but it is more than probable that the foundation of it was the narrative in the "Gesta Romanorum" (printed late in the 15th century), to which Belleforest was also to a certain extent indebted in his "Histories," "Tragiques," the publication of which was commenced in 1564. Belleforest, however, claims to have gone to a distinct source, a manuscript having fallen in his way, which purported to be *tiré du Grec:* in fact, it seems to have had its origin in that language, from which it was translated into Latin, and subsequently into French, Spanish, Italian and English. These different versions are enumerated by Mr Douce in the work we have already referred to, but the Anglo-Saxon translation (printed under the learned care of Mr Thorpe) does not seem to have fallen in his way. Latin MSS. of it, as early as the tenth century, appear to be in existence.

The prose romance, which occupies the succeeding pages, was first published [it is supposed] in 1576, [although no copy of so early a date is at present known,] and how soon afterwards it was adapted to the stage in London cannot be decided. It professed originally to be " gathered into English " by Lawrence Twine, and it is singular that Malone, Steevens, and even Douce, fell into the error of attributing the translation to Thomas Twine, " the continuator of Phaer's Virgil." Lawrence Twine was brother to Thomas Twine, and both were sons of John Twine, Lawrence being the eldest, and as Anthony Wood says, "a fellow of All Souls College, Bachelor of Civil Law, and an ingenious poet of his time" (Ath. Oxon. vol. i. 464, Edit. Bliss). He left nothing behind him in verse, as far as we now know, but certain commendatory lines to books by his friends, and the songs and riddles of Tharsia hereafter inserted. How frequently, and at what intervals, Lawrence Twine's " Patterne of Painefull Adventures, containing the most excellent, pleasant, and variable Historie, &c. of Prince Apollonius of Tyre," was reprinted after 1576, we have no exact information; but a new edition of it came out in 1607, the very year before the play of " Pericles," as adapted to the stage by Shakespeare, would seem to have been acted. Our re-publication of the romance is from an edition hitherto unknown, without date, but, as we may judge from the type and other circumstances, published before the opening of the seventeenth century.

The grounds for our opinion, that Shakespeare's " Pericles " (as far as he may lay claim to its authorship) was first acted early in the year 1608, are stated in detail in " Farther Particulars regarding Shakespeare and his Works," 8°, 1839. As only fifty copies of that tract were printed, it may be necessary to add here, that a narrative entitled "The Painfull Adventures of Pericles, Prince of Tyre," was published in 1608, purporting to be " the true History of the Play of Pericles, as it was lately presented by the worthy and ancient Poet John Gower." This " History " is derived directly from the play, as the play had been derived mainly from Twine's translation of " Prince Apollonius, of Tyre ; " and it was printed in consequence of the great success that attended the performance of " Pericles," when it was brought out with Shakespeare's additions and improvements. At the time the " Farther Particulars regarding Shakespeare and his Works" were collected and composed, the author was not aware of the evidence preserved in Dulwich College, and recently inserted in the " Memoirs of Edward Alleyn," of the existence of an earlier drama upon the same story, and under the same title as what we have been accustomed to call Shakespeare's " Pericles." Those who are in possession of the " Farther Particulars," &c., will see that the author traces and compares, in curious detail, the parallel passages in the play and in the " History " founded upon it ; and he may be said to have gone the length of establishing that certain expressions, and even lines, originally recited by the players, have been omitted in the impression of " Pericles," as it has reached us.

The reason why Shakespeare, or his predecessor, introduced " ancient Gower " to open the drama, and to deliver certain interlocutions in the course of it, will be sufficiently obvious to those who are aware that Gower makes the whole story part of his " Confessio Amantis ;" a work full of variety and beauty, to which due justice has, perhaps, never been done, in consequence of the comparison which must be drawn between Gower, as a poet, and his greater contemporary Chaucer. Lidgate has laboured, in a degree, under the same disadvantage ; but the publication of

some of his "Minor Poems," by the Percy Society,
will tend to elevate him in the scale of our early poets.
The "Confessio Amantis" was three times printed
prior to the reign of Elizabeth, viz. by Caxton in
1483, and by Berthelet in 1532 and 1554. We have
appended Gower's versified history of "Appollinus,
the Prince of Tyr" to our reprint of Twine's prose
version of the romance, because it is pretty evident,
from particular expressions, that Shakespeare, or his
dramatic precursor (always supposing two separate
writers to have been engaged on the subject) had reference to it when composing the play of "Pericles."
Malone inferred this fact also from the circumstance
that Pericles is called "*Prince* of Tyre" in the play,
and in Gower's version, whereas, in Copland's translation, he is called "*King* of Tyre;" but the com-
mentator omitted to remark that *Prince de Thyr* are
the words of a French translation by Corozet in 1530;
and the hero is spoken of as "*Prince* Apollonius" in
Twine's "Patterne of Painefull Adventures," which
the play more immediately follows. Our readers will
be enabled to judge from what succeeds of the precise
degree of obligation to the one or to the other.

For our text of Gower's poetical narrative we have
not resorted to either of the three printed copies of
the "Confessio Amantis:" we were anxious to give the
story, with as much fidelity as possible, in the words
of the old poet, and for this reason we have gone to
a fine and nearly contemporary MS. upon vellum
preserved in the British Museum (Harl. 3940),[1] cor-

---

[1] For the following description of this MS. we are indebted
to the kindness of J. Holmes, Esq. :—"At the foot of some of
the pages are emblazoned various Coats of Arms, being those
of Reade, James, Handlo, Borstall, St Amand, De la Pole,
Cottesmore, &c. In all probability, therefore, the MS. belonged to (if indeed it were not written for him) Sir William
Reade of Borstall, Co. Bucks, living *temp.* Henry VII. All the
above were quartered by him." [The text of the story has now
been given from Pauli's edition, 1857.]

rected by another MS. in the same library (Harl. 3869).

It will be found, that the variations between this MS. and the printed copies are chiefly verbal, excepting in one or two instances, where a line has been omitted in the one or in the other: the divisions of the poem, with the Latin headings, are differently arranged. Generally speaking, the MS. has the advantage of the printed copies; but such is not always the case, as where, in the MS., Theophilus is designated " a fals clerke," insteade of " a fals cherle," as it properly stands in the first edition by Berthelet.

We are not aware that it is necessary to say more by way of introduction to what follows, than to add that Gower avowedly adopted his incidents from a metrical version in the " Pantheon" or " Universal Chronicle" of Godfrey of Viterbo, which was compiled at the latter end of the twelfth century, though not printed until 1569.

" Of a cronique in daies done,
The wich is cleped Panteon,
In loves cause I rede thus,"

are Gower's introductory lines; and he subsequently more than once refers to "the booke" to which he was indebted, much in the same way that Ariosto professes his obligations to the narrative by Bishop Turpin, respecting the conquests of Charlemaine and the atchievements of Orlando. On one occasion, when Gower breaks off from one part of his story in order to return to another, he opens a chapter as follows :—

" Bot nowe to my matere ayen,
To telle as olde bokes seyne ; "

as if he had consulted more than one authority; but it is very evident that he had looked no farther than the work, the title of which we have already given, the "Pantheon" of Godfrey of Viterbo.

When[1] I [formerly] wrote upon the subject of the intimate connexion [of the novel by Wilkins] with Shakespeare's "Pericles," I was entirely ignorant[2] of the important fact, that the production was the authorship of George Wilkins, a dramatist of considerable distinction, whose play, called "The Miseries of enforced Marriage" was so popular, that it went through four editions between 1607, when it was first published, and 1637, when the last old impression made its appearance. I did not become acquainted with the circumstance that Wilkins was the writer of the ensuing novel, until I had sent the following communication to the *Athenæum*, which I here beg leave to subjoin, as part of my Introduction.

"The readers of the *Athenæum* may like to hear something more regarding a tract, with which my name was connected, in a paragraph in the *Athenæum* of February 7. It was correctly stated that I formerly printed fifty copies of a small publication devoted principally to an account of that tract, which is certainly, on every ground, the most curious that has fallen under my observation in the course of my life: it is unique in its character, and until recently I never heard of more than one other perfect copy of it, independently of a considerable fragment in my own hands. It now turns out that there is a third perfect copy in a Swiss library, which had once belonged to a foreigner who visited London about

---

[1] [What follows, to the end, was prefixed by Mr Collier to Professor Mommsen's edition of the Novel by G. Wilkins, 8º, Oldenburg, 1857.]

[2] [Owing to both the copies examined by Mr Collier being imperfect.]

the time of Shakespeare's death. I may add, that it is now being reprinted in Germany, and that it well deserves the distinction.

"It is a narrative founded upon Shakespeare's 'Pericles,' which was first acted in 1607 or 1608. Various novels are known of which Shakespeare availed himself in other plays, such as 'The Winter's Tale,' 'As You Like It,' &c.; but the production I am now speaking of differs from all others in this respect—that, instead of having had a drama founded upon it, it was itself founded upon a drama, and that drama 'Pericles.'

"It is now, I believe, generally admitted that, when a play was unusually popular, it was the habit of certain booksellers, in the time of Shakespeare, to employ shorthand writers to take down, in the theatre, as much of the dialogue as they could, and to publish the transcribed notes as the play itself. Such, we may be sure, was the case with 'Hamlet' and 'Romeo and Juliet,' to which the excellent letter of Prof. Mommsen, in the *Athenæum* of February 7, separately applies. Why the same course was not pursued in the case of 'Pericles' does not appear. Perhaps in 1607 or 1608 the trick was becoming somewhat stale, and the bookseller thought that he could make a better thing of a publication in a narrative form, but distinctly stated on the title-page to be derived from a play then daily represented with great applause. Hence the tract I am now directing attention to, which is called, and I quote the terms literally, 'The Painfull Adventures of Pericles Prince of Tyre. Being the true History of the Play of Pericles, at it was lately presented by the worthy and ancient Poet Iohn Gower. At London Printed by T. P. for Nat. Butter, 1608.' It is in quarto, and consists of forty leaves, including the title-page, in the centre of which there is a woodcut of John Gower, with a staff in one hand and a bunch of bays in the other; while before him, upon a table, lies a book, which we may suppose to be a copy of his 'Confessio Amantis,' containing, as is well known, a version of the story of 'Pericles,' under the name of Apollonius of Tyre. His dress, as represented in the woodcut, merits notice, inasmuch as it is, in all probability, such as the actor wore who played the part of Gower, and who spoke the Prologue and interlocutions in Shakespeare's 'Pericles.' It is merely a sort of gown, very plain, opening in front, and reaching just below the knee. In my fifty copies of the small publication relating to this subject, I gave a fac-simile of this interesting dramatic relic.

"Now, to speak a little more particularly of the contents of this literary rarity. It professes, as we have seen by the title-page, to give the 'history of the Play of Pericles' as it had been recently acted on the stage; and, at the end of 'the Argument' prefixed, the reader is entreated to receive the novel 'in the same manner' as the play had been received when 'by the King's Majesties Players it was excellently presented.' The King's Majesty's Players of course consisted of the company to which Shakespeare had been always attached, which performed in the summer at the Globe on the Bankside, and in the winter at the Blackfriars.

"It has always been lamented that in so few old dramas lists of characters are supplied; but here they are furnished as the accompaniment to a mere narration; and, since the names almost entirely accord with those found in Shakespeare's 'Pericles,' though not prefixed to it, it is needless to insert them here. The divisions of the story do not follow the five acts of the play, for the tract is composed of eleven chapters, which include all the incidents, nearly in the course in which they are employed by Shakspeare.

"I am anxious in what follows, and with as much brevity as possible, to establish two points:—1, That the novel before us very much adopts the language of the play; 2, That it not unfrequently supplies portions of the play, as it was acted in 1607 or 1608, which have not come down to us in any of the printed copies of 'Pericles.' The last is infinitely the more important, because we may thereby recover, *pro tanto*, a lost portion of the language of Shakespeare. I proceed to prove, in the first place, that the novel and the play are, in some sort, identical.

"In the novel, when Pericles, undeterred by the warning of Antiochus, insists upon attempting the solution of the enigma, it is said,—

'But Pericles, armed with these noble armours, Faithfulness and Courage, and making himself fit for death, if death proved fit for him, replied, that he was come now to meet death willingly.'

In the play, Pericles tells Antiochus,—

'Like a bold champion I assume the lists,
Nor ask advice of any other thought,
But faithfulness and courage.'—(Act 1, sc. 1.)

"The following is the account Pericles gives of himself—in the third person—in the novel:

'A gentleman of Tyre, his name Pericles, his education been in arts and arms, looking for adventures in the world, was, by the rough and unconstant seas, most unfortunately bereft both of ships and men, and, after shipwreck, thrown upon that shore.'

How does this passage appear in the play? It runs thus in Shakespeare's verse:—

'A gentleman of Tyre (my name Pericles,
My education been in arts and arms),
Who, looking for adventures in the world,
Was, by the rough seas, reft of ships and men,
And, after shipwreck, driven upon this shore.'
(Act 2, sc. 3.)

"I shall pursue this point no farther (though it would be easy to multiply proofs), but proceed to the second point, in order to show, as I think, beyond contradiction, that the novel under consideration contains passages which must have been written by Shakespeare, but which have not come down to us in the play of 'Pericles,' as printed in quarto in 1609, 1619, and 1630, or in folio, in 1664 or 1685. This part of my undertaking is not so easy, because the evidence must necessarily be of a negative character: I have to adduce passages that are like Shakespeare, but that have never yet been imputed to him. In Act 2, sc. 5, of the play, we meet with these lines, put into the mouth of Pericles:—

> 'I came unto your court for honour's cause,
> And not to be a rebel to her state;
> And he that otherwise accounts of me,
> This sword shall prove he's honour's enemy.'

How does this passage, addressed to Antiochus, appear in the novel founded upon the play? Thus:

'That were it any in his court, except himself, durst call him traitor, even in his bosom he could write the lie, affirming that he came into his court in search of honour, and not to be a rebel to his state. His blood was yet untainted, but with the heat got by the wrong the king had offered him, and that he boldly durst and did defy himself, his subjects, and the proudest danger, that either tyranny or treason could inflict upon him.'

"Therefore, for the passage from 'His blood was yet untainted' to the end of the paragraph, there is no parallel in the play; and, omitting only a few unimportant particles, it will be seen in an instant how easily it may be put into blank-verse. Read it thus:—

> 'His blood was yet untainted, but with heat
> Got by the wrong the king had offer'd him;
> And that he boldly durst and did defy him,
> His subjects, and the proudest danger, that
> Or tyranny or treason could inflict.'

Would the above have run so readily into blank-verse if it had not, in fact, been so originally written, and recited by the actor when 'Pericles' was first performed?

"Act 3, sc. 1, of the play, as printed, relates mainly to the birth of Marina at sea during a storm,—and in the prose novel Pericles thus addresses the infant:—

'*Poor inch of nature!* . . . . . thou art as rudely welcome to the world, as ever princess' babe was, and hast as chiding a nativity as fire, air, earth, and water can afford thee.'

"In the play, as printed, we find no corresponding commencement of the apostrophe, 'Poor inch of nature!' which must have come from Shakespeare's pen—no mere hackney scribe could have invented it,—but we meet with the following lines, in other respects nearly identical with what we have above quoted:—

'For thou'rt the rudeliest welcome to this world
That e'er was prince's child. Happy what follows!
Thou hast as chiding a nativity,
As fire, air, water, earth, and heaven can make.'

"Here, 'Poor inch of nature!' is all that is wanting, but, that away, how much of the characteristic beauty of the passage is lost! In Act 4 we have the famous scene in the brothel, where Marina reforms Lysimachus and thus addresses him:—

'Do you know this house to be a place of such resort, and will you come into it? I hear say, you are of honourable parts, and are the Governor of this place.'

This is all she is made to utter in the play at this time, with the exception of the subsequent lines, which come after a short speech of persevering importunity by Lysimachus:

'If you were born to honour, show it now:
If put upon you, make the judgment good,
That thought you worthy of it.'

"Instead of these two passages we read as follows in the prose narrative :—

'If as you say, my lord, you are the governor, let not your authority, which should teach you to rule others, be the means to make you misgovern yourself. If the eminence of your place came unto you by descent, and the royalty of your blood, let not your life prove your birth a bastard : if it were thrown upon you by opinion, make good that opinion was the cause to make you great. What reason is there in your justice, who hath power over all, to undo any? If you take from me mine honour, you are like him that makes a gap into forbidden ground, after whom too many enter, and you are guilty of all their evils. My life is yet unspotted, my chastity unstained in thought: then, if your violence deface this building, the workmanship of heaven, made up for good, and not to be the exercise of sin's intemperance, you do kill your own honour, abuse your own justice, and impoverish me.'

"If these thoughts and this language be not the thoughts and the language of Shakespeare, I am much mistaken, and have read him to little purpose. I might add much more, and furnish many other quotations to the same effect, but I hope soon to receive a few copies of the whole of the tract from Germany, in a reprinted shape, and then such as think with me, as regards the preceding extracts, will be able to gratify themselves to the full. I have here necessarily adverted to some points that I have touched elsewhere; but I dare say that few of the readers of the *Athenæum* have seen my remarks."

. . . . . In the tract we have distinct evidence that Wilkins attended the public performance of Shakespeare's "Pericles" for the purpose of taking notes of the drama as it was delivered from the mouths of the Actors; and being himself a poet of reputation and genius, he afterwards put his memoranda into a narrative which was published by one of the most celebrated booksellers of the day. It is my firm conviction that it supplies many passages, written by

Shakespeare and recited by the performers, which were garbled, mangled, or omitted in the printed Play of "Pericles," as it has come down to us in the quartos of 1609, 1619, and 1630, and in the folios of 1664 and 1685. May not the same course have been pursued with some of the greater works of Shakespeare, with his "Hamlet," "Macbeth," "Lear," "Tempest," or "Othello"?

THE ARGUMENT[1] OF THE WHOLE HISTORIE.

ANTIOCHUS the Great, who was the first founder of Antioch, the most famous Citty in all Syria, hauing one onelie daughter, in the prime and glory of her youth, fell in most vnnaturall loue with her; and what by the power of his perswasions, and feare of his tyranny, he so preuailed with her yeelding heart, that he became maister of his desires; which to continue to himself, his daughter, being for her beauty desired in marriage of many great princes, he made this law, That whoso presumed to desire her in marriage, and could not vnfold the meaning of his questions, for that attempt should loose his life. Fearelesse of this Lawe, many Princes aduentured, and in their rashnesse perished : amongst the number PERICLES the Prince of Tyre, and neighbour to this tyrant King Antiochus, was the last who vndertooke to resolue this Riddle, which he accordingly, through his great wisedome, performed : and finding both the subtiltie and sinne of the Tyrant, for his owne safetie

---

[1] [This Argument, not in Twine, and the list of characters, a most unusual feature in a novel, are given from the tract by Wilkins, and placed between brackets. They are peculiar to his work.]

fled secretly from Antioch backe to Tyre, and there acquainted Helycanus a graue Counsellour of his with the proceedings, as also with his present feare what might succeed, from whose counsell he took aduise, for a space to leaue his kingdome, and betake himselfe to trauell; to which yeelding, Pericles puts to sea, ariues at Tharsus, which he finds (thorow the dearth of corne) in much distresse; he there relieues Cleon and Dyonysa with their distressed City, with the prouision which he brought of purpose; but by his good Counsellour Helycanus hearing newes of Antiochus death, he intends for Tyre, puts againe to Sea, suffers shipwracke, his shippes and men all lost, till (as it were) Fortune tyred with his mis-happes, he is throwne vpon the shoare, releeued by certaine poore Fishermen, and by an Armour of his which they by chaunce dragged vp in their nettes, his misfortunes being a little repaired, Pericles arriues at the Court of good Symonides King of Pentapolis, where through his noblenesse both in Armes and Arts, he winnes the loue of faire Thaysa the kings daughter, and by her fathers consent marries her.

In this absence of his, and, for which absence the Tyrians his subiects muteny, would elect Helycanus (whome Pericles ordained his substitute in his absence) their King, which passion of theirs Helycanus by his graue perswasions subdewed, and wonne them to go in quest of their lost Prince Pericles: In this search he is found, and with his wife Thaysa, who is now with childe, and Lycorida her Nurse; hauing taken leaue of his kingly Father, puts againe for Tyre, but with the terrour of a tempest at Sea, his Queene falles in

trauell, is deliuered of a daughter, whome he names
Marina, in which childe-birth his Queene dies, she is
throwne ouer boorde, at departure of whome Pericles
altereth his course from Tyre, being a shorter cut, to
his hoste Cleon in Tharsus ; hee there leaues his yoong
daughter to be fostered vp, vowing to himselfe a solitary & pensiue life for the loose of his Queene.

 Thaysa thus supposed dead, and in the seas buried,
is the next morning on the shore taken vp at Ephesus
by Cerimon a most skilfull Physition, who by his Arte
practised vpon this Queene, so preuailed, that after
fiue houres intraunced, she is by his skill brought to
able health againe, and by her owne request, by him
placed to liue a Votary in Dianaes Temple at Ephesus.
Marina Pericles sea-borne daughter, is by this growen
to discreete yeares, she is enuied of Dyonysa Cleons
wife, her foster mother, for that Marinaes perfection
exceedeth a daughter of hers, Marina by this enuy of
hers should haue beene murthered, but being rescued
by certaine Pyrates, is as it were reserued to a greater
mishap, for by them she is caried to Metelyne, sold
to the deuils broker a bawd, to have bin trained vp in
that infection, shee is courted of many, and how
wonderfully she preserues her chastitie.

 Pericles returnes from Tyre toward Tharsus, to
visite the hospitable Cleon, Dyonysa, and his yoong
daughter Marina, where by Dyonysaes dissembling
teares, and a Toombe that was erected for her,
Pericles is brought to beleeue, that his Marina lies
there buryed, and that she died of her naturall death,
for whose losse hee teares his haire, throwes off his
garments, forsweares the societie of men, or any other

comfort. In which passion for many moneths continuing, hee at last arriues at Metelyne, when being seene and pittied by Lysimachus the Gouernour, his daughter (though of him vnknowen so) is by the Gouernour sent for, who by her excellent skill in Song, and pleasantnesse in discourse, with relating the story of her owne mishap, shee so winnes againe her fathers lost sences, that he knowes her for his childe, shee him for her father; in which ouer-ioy, as if his sences were now all confounded, Pericles falles asleepe, where in a dreame he is by Diana warned to goe to Ephesus, and there to make his sacrifice. Pericles obayes, and there comes to the knowledge of Thaysa his wife, with their seuerall Ioyes that they three so strangely diuided, are as strangely mette. Lysimachus the Gouernour marrieth Marina, and Pericles leauing his mourning, causeth the bawde to be burned. Of his reuenge to Cleon and Dyonysa, his rewarding of the Fishermen that releeued him, his iustice toward the Pyrats that made sale of his daughter, his returne backe to his kingdome, and of him and his wifes deaths. Onely intreating the Reader to receiue this Historie in the same maner as it was vnder the habite of ancient Gower the famous English Poet, by the Kings Maiesties Players excellently presented.

THE NAMES OF THE PERSONAGES MENTIONED IN THIS HISTORIE.

———o———

JOHN GOWER *the Presenter.*
ANTIOCHUS *that built Antioch*
His daughter.
PERICLES *Prince of Tyre.*
THALYART *a villaine.*
HELYCANUS } *Twoo graue*
ESCHINES } *Counsellors.*
CLEON *Gouernor of Tharsus.*
DYONYSA *his wife.*
Two or three Fishermen.
SYMONIDES *king of Pentapolis.*
THAYSA *his daughter.*

Fiue Princes.
LYCORIDA *a Nurse.*
CERIMON *a Phisition.*
MARINA *Pericles daughter.*
A Murtherer.
Pirates.
A Bawde.
A Leno.
A Pander.
LYSIMACHUS *Gouernour of Meteline.*
DIANA *Goddesse of chastitie.*

The Patterne of
painefull Ad-
uentures:
Containing the most excel-
lent, pleasant and variable Hi-
storie of the strange accidents that be-
fell vnto Prince Apollonius, the
Lady Lucina his wife, and
Tharsia his daughter.
Wherein the vncertaintie of
this world, and the fickle state
of mans life are liue-
ly described.
Gathered into English by
LAVRENCE TVVINE
Gentleman.

Imprinted at London by Va-
lentine Simmes for the
Widow Newman.

To the worshipfull

Master Iohn Donning, Customer and Jurate of the towne of Rie in Sussex.

———o———

BEING diuersely mooued *in mind,* to signifie my good will and hartie loue towardes *you,* gentle *M. Donning,* I could not deuise any meanes more *effectual,* then by presenting the same to you, which *cost me some small* labor and trauel. *Not* seeming therby to *acquite* your *manifold* curtesies, *towards* me diuersly *extended,* but *rather to* discharge me of *the note of* Ingratitude, *which* otherwise *I might seeme to incurre.* Wherefore in steede of *a greater present to counteruaile your* friendlines, *I* am bold in the setting foorth of this simple Pamflet vnder your name, to make *a proffer of my thankful heart to* **you againe.** Wherin though want *of farther abilitie* appeare, yet *is there no let,* but that a wel-willing heart may be exprest, yea *in the smallest gift.* Now if haply the argument hereof appeare vnto you other than you could **much** wish, *or I well afford,* yet haue I no feare of any **great** misliking, considering your natural disposition, *which is to be delighted with honest pleasure, and commendable recreation, and not to lie euermore weltering, as it were, in dolefull dumpishnesse. Which thing did put me in the greater hope, that this worke would be the welcommer vnto you, especially considering the delectable varietie, and the often changes and chances contained in this present historie, which cannot but much stirre vp the mind and sences vnto sundry affections. What euer it be take it I beseech you, in good part, in stead of some better thing which I might well affoord, promising the same when occasion shall serue, not being at this present so well furnished as I could wish of God: to whose good grace I recommend you and yours, both nowe and evermore.*

Your worships to vse,

LAURENCE TWINE.

THE TABLE.

———o———

How *Antiochus* committed incest with his owne daughter, and beheaded such as sued vnto her for marriage, if they coulde not resolue his questions. CHAP. I.

How *Apollonius* arriuing at Antiochia, resolued the King's question; and howe *Taliarchus* was sent to slay him. CHAP. II.

How *Taliarchus*, not finding *Apollonius* at Tyrus, departeth joyfully; and *Apollonius* arriving at Tharsus, relieueth the citie with victuall. CHAP. III.

How *Apollonius* departing frō Tharsus by the perswasion of *Stranguilio* and *Dionisiades* his wife, committed shipwracke, and was relieued by *Altistrates* King of Pentapolis. CHAP. IV.

How *Lucina* king *Altistrates* daughter desirous to heare Apollonius aduentures, fell in love with him. CHAP. V.

How *Apollonius* is made schoolemaster to *Lucina*; and how shee preferreth the love of him aboue all the Nobilitie of Pentapolis. CHAP. VI.

How *Apollonius* was married to the Lady *Lucina*, and hearing of king *Antiochus* death, departeth with his wife towards his own country of Tyrus. CHAP. VII.

How faire *Lucina* died in trauell of childe vpon the sea, and being throwen into the water, was cast on land at Ephesus, and taken home by *Cerimon* a Physicion. CHAP. VIII.

How *Lucina* was restored to life by one of *Cerimon* the Physicions schollers; and how *Cerimon* adopted hir to his daughter, and placed her in the Temple of *Diana*. CHAP. IX.

How *Apollonius* arriuing at Tharsus, deliuereth his yong daughter Tharsia vnto *Stranguilio* and *Dionisiades* to be brought vp; and how the Nurce, lying in her death bed declareth vnto *Tharsia* who were hir parents. CHAP. X.

How after the death of *Ligozides* the Nurce, *Dionisiades*, envying at the beautie of *Tharsia*, conspired her death, which should have been accomplished by a villaine of the countrey. CHAP. XI.

How certain Pirats rescued *Tharisa* when she shuld haue been slaine, and carried hir vnto the citie *Machilenta*, to be sold among other bondslaues. CHAP. XII.

How the Pirats which stole away *Tharsia*, brought her to the citie *Machilenta*, and sold her to a common bawd; and how she preserued her virginitie. CHAP. XIII.

How *Tharsia* withstood a second assault of her virginitie, and by what meanes shee was preserued. CHAP. XIV.

How *Apollonius* comming to Tharsus, and not finding his daughter, lamented her supposed death, and taking ship againe, was driuen to Machilenta where *Tharsia* was. CHAP. XV.

How *Athanagoras* prince of Machilenta seeing the beautie of *Apollonius* ship, went aboord of it, and did the best to comfort him. CHAP. XVI.

How *Athanagoras* sent for *Tharsia*, to make her father *Apollonius* merrie, and how, after long circumstance they came into knowledge one of another. CHAP. XVII.

How *Apollonius* leauing off mourning, came into the citie Machilenta, where he commanded the bawd to be burned, and how *Tharsia* was married vnto Prince *Athanagoras*. CHAP. XVIII.

How *Apollonius*, meaning to saile into his owne Countrey by Tharsus, was commanded by an Angell in the night to goe to Ephesus, and there to declare all his aduentures in the Church, with a loud voice. CHAP. XIX.

How *Apollonius* came to the knowledge of his wife the Ladie *Lucina*; and how they reioyced at the meeting of ech other. CHAP. XX.

How *Apollonius* departed for Ephesus and sailed himselfe, his wife, his sonne and daughter vnto Antiochia, and then to Tyrus, and from thence to Tharsus, where he reuenged himselfe vpon *Stranguilio* and *Dionisiades*. CHAP. XXI.

How *Apollonius* sayled from Tharsus to visite his father in law *Altistrates*, king of Pentapolis, who died not long after *Apollonius* comming thither. CHAP. XXII.

How *Apollonius* rewarded the fishermen that relieued him after he had suffered shipwracke: how he dealt also with old *Calamitus*, and likewise with the Pirates that stole away *Tharsia*. CHAP. XXIII.

How Apollonius had a yong sonne and heire by his wife *Lucina*, likewise of *Apollonus* age, and how hee died: with some other accidents thereunto incident. CHAP. XXIV.

The First Chapter.

Howe Antiochus committed incest with his owne daughter, and beheaded such as sued vnto her for marriage, if they coulde not resolue his questions.

THE most famous and mightie king Antiochus, which builded the goodly citie of Antiochia in Syria, and called it after his own name, as the chiefest seat of all his dominions, and most principal place of his abode, begat vpon his wife one daughter, a most excellent and beautifull yoong Ladie. Who in processe of yeeres growing vp as well in ripenesse of age, as perfection of beautie: many Princes and noble men resorted vnto her for intreaty of marriage, offering inestimable riches in iointure. Howbeit the king her father, euermore requiring deliberation, vpon whom rather than other to bestow his daughter, perceiued eftsoones an vnlawfull concupiscence to boyle within his breast, which he augmented with an outragious flame of crueltie sparkling in his heart, so that he began to burne with the loue of his owne childe more than it was beseeming for a father. Thus being wrapped in the toyle of blind desire, hee sustained within himselfe a fierce conflict, wherein Madnesse put Modestie to flight, & he wholly yeelded himselfe vnto loue. 'Wherefore, not long after, on a certaine day hee came into his daughters chamber, and bidding all that were there for to depart, as though he had had some secret matter to conferre with her: the furious rage of lust pricking him forward thereunto, he violently forced her, though seely maiden she withstood him long to her power, and threwe away all regard of his owne honestie, and vnlosed the knot of her virginitie. Now, when he was departed, and she, being alone, deuised within her self what it were best for her to doe, sodainelie her nurse entred in, and perceiuing her face al be blubbred with teares, What is the matter, deare childe and Madam (quoth she) that you sit thus sorrowfully? O, my beloued nurse, answered the Ladie, euen nowe two noble names were lost within this chamber. Howe so said the nurse? Because (quoth shee) before marriage, through wicked villanie I am most shamefully defiled. And when the nurse had heard these wordes, and looking about more diligently, perceiued indeede what was done, being inraged with sorrowe and anger, and almost distract of her wittes. Alas what wretch or rather infernal feend (quoth she) durst thus presumptuously defile the bed of a Princesse? Ungodlinesse hath done this doede (quoth the Ladie.) Why then doe you not tell it the king your father, saide the nurse? Ah nurse, answered the Ladie, where is my father? For if you well understoode the matter, the name of Father is lost in me, so that I can haue no remedie now but death onely. But the nurse nowe by a few wordes perceiuing the whole tale, and weying that the yong Lady gaue inkling of remedie by death, which she much feared, beganne to assuage her griefe with comfortable wordes, and to withdrawe her minde from that mischievous purpose. Wherein she preuailed so effectually in short time, that she appeased the fresh bleeding of the greene wound, howbeit the scarre continued long time, as deeply stroken within her tender heart, before it could be throughlie cured.

In the meane season, while this wicked father sheweth the countenance of a louing sire abroad in the eies of al his people, notwithstanding, within doores, and in his minde, he reioyceth that he hath played the part of an husband with his daughter: which false resemblance of hateful marriage, to the intent he might alwaies enioy, he inuented a strange deuise of wickednesse, to driue away all suters that should resort vnto her, by propounding certaine questions, the effect and law whereof was thus published in writing: *Who so findeth out the solution of my question, shall haue my daughter to wife, but who so faileth, shal lose his head.*

Now, when Fame had blowen abroade the possibilitie to obtaine this Ladie, such was the singular report of her surpassing beautie, that many kings and men of great nobility repaired thither. And if haply any through skill or learning had found out the solution of the kings question, notwithstanding hee was beheaded as though hee had answered nothing to the purpose: and his head was set vp at the gate to terrifie others that should come, who beholding there the present image of death, might aduise them from assaying anie such danger. These outrages practised Antiochus, to the ende he might continue in filthie incest with his daughter.

The Second Chapter.

How Apollonius arriving at Antiochia resolued the kings question, and how Taliarchus was sent to slay him.

WHILEST Antiochus thus continued in exercising tyrannie at Antiochia, a certaine yong Gentleman of Tyrus, Prince of the country, abounding in wealth, and very well learned, called Apollonius, arriued in the coast, and comming vnto the citie of Antiochia, was brought into the kings presence. And when he had saluted him, the king demanded of him the cause of his coming thither. Then saide the yoong prince, Sir, I require to haue your daughter in marriage. The king hearing that which he was vnwilling to heare, looking fiercely vpon him, saide vnto him: Doest thou know the conditions of the marriage. Yea sir king, said Apollonius, and I see it standing vpon the gate. Then the king being sharply moued, and disdaining at him, said, Heare then the question which thou must resolue, or else die: *I am carried with mischiefe, I eate my mothers fleshe: I seeke my brother my mothers husband and I can not finde him.* Apollonius hauing receiued the question, withdrew himselfe a while out of the kinges presence, and being desirous to vnderstand what it meant, he found out the solution thereof in short space through the help of God, and returned againe to the king, saying; Your grace proposed a question vnto me, I pray you heare the solution thereof. And whereas you said in your probleme, *I am carried with mischiefe:* you haue not lied, for looke vnto your owne selfe. But whereas you say further, *I eate my mothers flesh*, looke vpon your daughter.

Now the king, as soone as he perceiued that Apollonius had resolued his problems, fearing lest his wickednesse should be discovered, he looked vpon him with a wrathful countenance, saying; Thou art farre wide from the solution of my demand, and hast hit no part of the meaning thereof: wherefore thou hast deserued to be beheaded. Howbeit, I will shew thee this courtesie, as to giue thee thirtie daies respite to bethinke thy selfe of this matter. Wherefore returne home into thine owne countrey, and if thou canst find out the solution of my probleme, thou shalt haue my daughter to wife : If not thou shalt be beheaded. Then Apollonius being much troubled and molested in mind, accompanying himself with a sufficient train, tooke shipping, and returned into his owne countrey. But so soone as he was departed, Antiochus called vnto him his steward, named Thaliarchus, to whom he spake in maner following.

Thaliarchus, the only faithfull and trustie minister of my secrets : vnderstand that Apollonius, prince of Tirus, hath found out the solution of my question. Wherefore, take shipping and followe him immediatly, and if thou canst not ouertake him vpon the sea, seeke him out when thou commest to Tirus, and slay him either with sword or poyson ; and when thou returnest I will bountifully reward thee. Taliarchus promised to accomplish his commandement with all diligence, and taking to him his shield, with monie sufficient for the iourney, departed on his way, and shortly after arriued at the coast of Tirus. But Apollonius was come home vnto his owne Pallace long time before, and withdrawing himselfe into his studie, perused all his bookes concerning the kings probleame, finding none other solution than that which he had alreadie told the king. And thus he said within himselfe : Surely, vnlesse I be much deceiued, Antiochus burneth with disordinate loue of his daughter : and discoursing further with himselfe vpon that point : What sayest thou now, or what intendest thou to doe, Apollonius, said he to himselfe ? Thou hast resolued his probleme, and yet not receiued his daughter, and God hath therefore brought thee away that thou shouldest not die. Then brake hee off in the midst of these cogitations, and immediatly commanded his ships to be prepared, and to be laden with an hundred thousand bushels of wheat, and with great plenty of gold, siluer and rich apparell : and taking vnto him a few of his most trustiest servants, about midnight imbarked himself, and hoysing vp his sails, committed himselfe to the wide sea. The day following his subiects the citizens came vnto the Pallace to haue seene their Prince, but when they found him not there, the whole citie was forthwith surprised with wonderfull sorrowe, euerie man lamenting that so worthy a Prince [was] so sodainly gone out of sight and knowledge, no man knew whether. Great was the grief, and wofull was the wayling which they made, lamenting his owne priuate estate and the commonwealths in generall, as it alwaies hapneth at the death or losse of a good Prince, which the inhabitants of Tirus tooke then so heauily, in respect of their great affection, that a long time after no barbers shops were opened, the common shews and plaies surceased, baines and hoat houses were shut vp, tauerns were not frequented, and no man repaired vnto the Churches, al thing was full of sorrowe and heauinesse, what shall I say? there was nothing but heauienesse.

The Third Chapter.

How Taliarchus not finding Apollonius at Tirus, departeth ioyfully, and Apollonius arriuing at Thasus, relieueth the citie with vittell.

In the middes of this sorrowful season Taliarchus commeth to Tirus to execute the cruell commandement of Antiochus; where, finding al-thing shut vp, and a generall shew of mourning, meeting with a boy in the streete Tell me, said he, or I will slay thee, for what cause is al this citie thus drowned in heauines? To whom the child answered: My friend, doest thou not know the cause, that thou askest it of me? This citie mourneth because the Prince thereof Apollonius, returning back from king Antiochus, can no where be found or heard of. Now, so soone as Taliarchus heard these tidings, he returned ioyfully vnto his ships, and tooke his iourney backe to Antiochia, and being landed, he hastened vnto the king, and fell downe on his knees before him, saying: All haile most mightie Prince, reioyce and be glad; for Apollonius being in feare of your grace is departeth no man knoweth whether. Then answered the king: He may well flie away from mee, but he shall neuer escape my handes. And immediatly he made proclamation, that whosoeuer could take that contemner of the king Apollonius prince of Tirus, and bring him aliue vnto the kinges presence, should haue an hundred talents of golde for his labour; and whosoeuer coulde bring his head, should haue fiftie talentes. Which proclamation beeing published, not onely Apollonius ennemies, but also his friendes, made all haste possible to seeke him out, allured thereto with couetouseness of the money. Thus was this poore Prince sought for about by sea and by land, through woodes and wilde deserts, but could not be found. Then the king commanded a great Nauie of ships to be prepared to scoure the seas abroad, if haply they might meet with him; but for that euery thing requireth a time ere it can be done, in the mean season Apollonius arriueth at Tharsus, where walking along by the sea side, he was espied by one of his owne seruauntes, named Elinatus, who landed there not long before, and ouertooke him as he was going; and comming neere vnto him with dutifull obeisance, said vnto him: God saue you prince Apollonius. But he being saluted, did euen so as noble men and princes vse to doe, set light by him. But Elinatus taking that behauiour vnkindly, saluted him againe saying: God saue you Prince Apollonius salute me againe, and despise not pouertie beautified with honestie. And if you knewe that which I know, you would take good heed to your self. Then answered Apollonius: If you thinke good, I pray you tell me. Elinatus answered, you are by proclamation commanded to be slaine. And who said Apollonius, dares commaund by proclamation, the prince of a countrey to be slaine? Antiochus, said Elinatus. Antiochus! For what cause, demanded Apollonius. For that, said Elinatus, thou wouldst be vnto his daughter which he himselfe is. Then demanded Apollonius, For what summe of mony is my life sold by that proclamation? Elinatus answered, whosoeuer can bring you aliue vnto the king shall haue an hundred talents of gold in recompence: but whoso bringeth your head shall haue fiftie talents of gold for his labour, and therefore I aduise you my lord, to flie vnto some place for your defence: and when he had so said he tooke his leaue and departed. But Apollonius called him againe, and said that hee would giue him an hundred talents of gold; for, said he, receiue thus much now of my pouertie, where nothing is now left vnto me but flight, and pining misery. Thou hast deserued the reward, wherefore draw out thy sword, and cut off my head, & present it to the king, as the most ioyfull sight in the world. Thus mayst thou win an hundred talents of gold, and remaine without all blame or note of ingratitude, since I my selfe haue hyred thee in the kinges behalfe to gratefie him with so acceptable a present. Then answered Elinatus: God forbid my lord that by anie such sinister means I should deserue a reward. In all my life I neuer consented to any such matter in my heart. And, my lord, if the deed were good, the loue of vertue were a sufficient force to allure any man thereunto. But since it respecteth your life, to whome in consideration of the cause no man may doe violence without villanie: I commit both you and your matter vnto God, who no

doubt will be your defender: And when he had thus
said, he departed. But Apollonius walked forth along
vpon the shoare, where he had gone not farre, but he
descried a man afarre off comming towardes him with
heauie cheere and a sorrowfull countenance; and this
was Stranguilio a Tharsian borne, and of good reputation in the citie. To whom saide Apollonius, God
saue you Stranguilio: and he likewise resaluted him
saying, And you likewise my good lord Apollonius:
I pray you tel me what is the cause that you walk in
this place thus troubled within your minde? Apollonius answered: because, being promised to haue
king Antiochus daughter to my wife, if I told him the
true meaning of his question, nowe that I haue so done,
I am notwithstanding restrained from her. Wherefore
I request you it may so be, that I may liue secretly in
your citie; for why, I stand moreouer in some doubt
of the kinges farther displeasure. Stranguilio answered: My lord Apollonius, our citie at this present
is verie poore, and not able to sustaine the greatnesse of your dignitie: and euen now we suffer great
penurie and want of vittell, insomuch that there remaineth small hope of comfort vnto our citizens, but
that we shall perish by extreme famine: and now certes
there resteth nothing but the fearefull image of gastly
death before our eies. When Apollonius heard these
wordes, he said vnto him: Then giue thankes vnto
God, who in my flight hath brought me a land into
your costes. For I have brought great store of prouision with me, and will presently giue vnto your
citie an hundreth thousand bushels of wheate, if you
will only conceale my comming hither. At these
wordes Stranguilio being strooken, as it were, into a
sodaine amazednesse, as it happeneth when a man is
ouerioyed with some glad tidinges, fell downe prostrate before prince Apollonius feete, and saide: My
lord Apollonius, if you coulde, and also if it might

please of your great goodnesse, in such sort as you
say, to succour this afflicted and famished citie, we
wil not onely receiue you gladly, and conceale your
abode: but also, if neede so require, willingly spend
our liues in your quarrell. Which promise of mine,
to the intent you may heare to be confirmed by the
full consent of the citizens, might please your Grace
to enter into the citie, aud I most willingly will attend
vpon you. Apollonius agreed thereto, and when
they came into the citie, he mounted vp into the place
of iudgment, to the intent he might the better be
heard, and, gathering al the people together: thus
hee spake vnto the whole multitude. Ye citizens of
Tharsus, whom penurie of vittell pincheth at this
present vnderstand ye, that I Apollonius prince of
Tirus, am determined presently to relieue you: In
respect of which benefite I trust ye will be so thank-
full as to conceale mine arriuing hither. And know
ye moreouer, that not as being driuen away through
the malice of king Antiochus, but sayling along by
the Seas I am happily fallen into your hauen. Wherefore I meane to vtter vnto you an hundred thousand
bushels of wheate, paying no more than I bought it
for in mine own countrey, that is to say, eight peeces
of brasse for euery bushell. When the citizens heard
this, they gaue a shout for ioy, crying, God saue my
Lord Apollonius, promising to liue and die in his
quarrell, and they gaue him wonderfull thankes, and
the whole citie was replenished with ioy, and they
went forthwith vnto the ships, and bought the corne.
But Apollonius, doubting lest by this deede, he should
seeme to put off the dignitie of a prince, and put on
the countenance of a merchant rather than a giuer,
when he had receiued the price of the wheate, he
restored it backe againe to the vse and commoditie
of the same citie. And when the citizens perceiued
the great benefites which he had bestowed vpon their

citie, they erected in the marked place a monument in the memoriall of him, his stature[1] made of brasse standing in a charret, holding corne in his right hand, and spurning it with his left foot : and on the baser foot of the pillar whereon it stoode, was ingrauen in great letters this superscription : Apollonius prince of Tirus gaue a gift vnto the citie of Tharsus whereby hee deliuered it from a cruel death.

The Fourth Chapter.

How Apollonius departing from Tharsus by the perswasion of Stranguilio and Dionisiades his wife, committed shipwracke, and was relieued by Altistrates king of Pentapolis.

Thus had not Apollonius aboden many daies in the citie of Tharsus but Stranguilio & Dionisiades his wife, earnestly exhorted him, as seeming very carefull and tender of his welfare, rather to addresse himselfe vnto Pentapolis or among the Tirenians, as a place most fit for his securitie, where he might lie and hide himselfe in greatest assurance & tranquilitie. Wherefore hereunto, he resolved himselfe, and with conuenient expedition prepared al things necessarie for the iourney. And when the day of his departure was come, he was brought with great honour by the citizens vnto his ships, where with a courteous farewell on ech side giuen, the marriners weighed anker, hoysed sailes, and away they goe, committing themselues to

---

[1] [Shakespeare wrote *statue* for *statute*, probably as a joke at the expense of the ignorant folks *temp.* Elizabeth ; but in the " Gesta Romanorum," ed. Madden, p. 25, we have *statute* for *statue*, and it is to be suspected that the word in the text should properly be *statute*.]

the wind and water. Thus sailed they forth along in their course, three days and three nights with prosperous winde and weather, vntill sodainly the whole face of heauen and sea began to change; for the skie looked blacke and the Northerne wind arose, and the tempest increased more and more, insomuch that prince Apollonius and the Tyrians that were with him were much apalled, and began to doubt of their liues. But, loe, immediatly, the wide blew fiercely from the South-west, and the North came singing on the other side, the rain powred down over their heads, and the sea yeelded forth waues as it had beene mountanes of water, that the ships could no longer wrestle with the tempest, and especially the admirall, wherein the good prince himselfe fared, but needs must they yeeld vnto the present calamitie. There[1] might you haue heard the winds whistling, the raine dashing, the sea roaring, the cables cracking, ye tacklings breaking, the shippe tearing, the men miserable shouting out for their liues. There might you haue seene the sea searching the shippe, the bordes fleeting, the goods swimming, the treasure sincking, the men shifting to saue themselues, where, partly through violence of the tempest, and partly through darcknes of the night which then was come vpon them, they were all drowned, onely Apollonius excepted, who by the grace of God, and the helpe of a simple boord, was driuen vpon the shoare of the Pentapolitanes. And when he had recouered to land, wearie as he was, he stoode vpon the shoare, and looked vpon the calme sea, saying: O most false and vntrustie sea! I will choose rather to fall into the handes of the most cruell king Antiochus, than venture to returne againe by thee

---

[1] [It is mentioned in the forewords attached to the "Tempest," that this passage was not improbably seen and used by Shakespeare.]

into mine owne Countrey: thou hast shewed thy spite vpon me, and deuoured my trustie friendes and companions, by meanes whereof I am nowe left alone, and it is the prouidence of almightie God that I haue escaped thy greedie iawes. Where shall I now finde comfort? or who will succour him in a strange place that is not knowen? And whilest he spake these wordes, hee sawe a man coming towardes him, and he was a rough fisherman, with an hoode upon his head, and a filthie leatherne pelt vpon his backe, vnseemely clad, and homely to beholde. When hee drewe neare, Apollonius, the present necessitie constraining him thereto, fell down prostrate at his feet, and powring forth a floud of teares he said unto him: whosoeuer thou art, take pitie vpon a poore sea-wracked man, cast up nowe naked, and in simple state, yet borne of no base degree, but sprung foorth of noble parentage. And that thou maiest in helping me knowe whome thou succourest: I am that Apollonius prince of Tyrus, whome most part of the worlde knoweth, and I beseech thee to preserue my life by shewing mee thy friendly reliefe. When the fisherman beheld the comlinesse and beautie of the yoong Gentleman, hee was moued with compassion towardes him, and lifted him vp from the ground, and lead him into his house and feasted him with such fare as he presently had, and the more amplie to expresse his great affection towardes him, he disrobed himselfe of his poore and simple cloke, and diuiding it into two parts, gaue the one halfe thereof vnto Apollonius, saying: Take here at my handes such poore entertainment and furniture as I haue, and goe into the citie, where perhappes thou shalt finde some of better abilitie, that will rue thine estate: and if thou doe not, returne then againe hither vnto mee, and thou shalt not want what may be perfoormed by the pouertie of a poore fisherman. And in the meane time of this one thing onelie I put thee in mind, that when thou shalt be restored to thy former dignitie, thou doe not despise to thinke on the basenesse of the poor peece of garment. To which Apollonius answered: If I remember not thee and it, I wish nothing else but that I may sustaine the like shipwracke. And when hee had saide so, he departed on the way which was taught him, and came vnto the citie gates, whereinto he entred. And while he was thinking with himselfe which waie to seeke succor to sustaine his life, he saw a boy running naked through the streete, girded only with a tuell about his middle, and his head annointed with oyle, crying aloude, and saying: Hearken all, as well citizens as strangers and seruants, hearken: Whosoeuer will be washed, let him come to the place of exercise. When Apollonius heard this, he followed the boy, and comming vnto the place cast off his cloake, and stripped himselfe, and entred into the Baine, and bathed himselfe with the liquor. And looking about for some companion with whome he might exercise himself, according vnto the manner of the place and countrey, and finding none: sodainelie vnlooked for entred in Altistrates king of the whole land, accompanied with a great troupe of seruitours. Anone he beganne to exercise himselfe at tennis with his men, which when Apollonius espied, he intruded himselfe amongst them into the kings presence, and stroke back the ball to the king, and serued him in play with great swiftnes. But whē the king perceiued the great nimblenesse and cunning which was in him, surpassing the residue: stand aside (quoth he) vnto his men, for me thinkes this yong man is more cunning than I. When Apollonius heard himselfe commended, hee stept foorth boldly into the middes of the tennis court, and, taking vp a racket in his hand, he tossed the ball skilfully, and with wonderful agilitie. After play, he also washed the king very reuerently in

the Baine: and when all was done, hee tooke his leaue
duetifully, & so departed. When Apollonius was gone,
the king said vnto them that were about him: I sweare
vnto you of truth as I am a Prince, I was neuer exercised nor washed better then this day, and that by the
diligence of a yong man I know not what he is. And
turning back, Go, said he vnto one of his seruants,
and know what that yong man is that hath with
such duty & diligence taken pains with me. The
seruant going after Apollonius, and seeing him clad
in a filthy fishers cloke, returned againe to the king,
saying: If it like your grace, the yong man is a sea-
wracked man. How knowest thou that said the king?
The seruāt answered: Though he told me not so
himselfe, yet his apparel bewraieth his state. Then
said the king to his seruant: Go apace after him, &
say vnto him, that the king desireth him to sup with
him this night. Then the seruāt made haste after
Apollonius, & did the kings message to him, which so
soone as he heard, he granted thereto, much thanking,
the kinges maiestie, & came back with the seruant.
When they were come to the gate, the seruant went
in first vnto the king, saying: The sea-wracked man,
for whom your grace sent me, is come, but is ashamed
to come into your presence, by reason of his base
aray: whome the king commaunded immediatly to
be clothed in seemely apparell, and to be brought in
to supper, and placed him at the table with him, right
oueragainst himselfe. Immediately the boord was
furnished with all kinde of princelie fare, the guests
fed apace, euery man on that which he liked, onelie
Apollonius sate still and eate nothing, but earnestlie
beholding the golde, siluer, and other kingly furniture,
whereof there was great plentie, hee could not refraine
from teares. Then said one of the guests that sate at
the table, vnto the king: This yoong man, I suppose,
enuieth at your graces prosperitie. No, not so, an-

swered the king, you suppose amisse; but he is sorie to remember that he hath lost more wealth then this is: and looking vpon Apollonius with a smiling countenance, Be mery yong man, quoth he, and eate thy meate with vs, and trust in GOD, who doubtlesse will send thee better fortune.

The Fifth Chapter.

How Lucina King Altistrates daughter desirous to heare Apollonius aduentures, fel in loue with him.

Now while they sate at meate, discoursing of this and such like matters at the boord, suddenlie came in the kings daughter and onelie child named Lucina, a singular beautifull ladie, and a maiden now of ripe yeeres for marriage: and she approched nigh, and kissed the king her father, and al the guests that sate with him at the table. And when she had so done, she returned vnto her father, and saide, Good father, I pray you, what yong man is this which sitteth in so honourable a place ouer against you, so sorrowfull and heauie? O sweete daughter, answered the king, this yong man is a sea-wracked man, and hath done me great honour to day at the baines and place of exercise, for which cause I sent for him to sup with me; but I knowe not neither what, neither whence he is. If you be desirous to know these things, demaund of him, for you may vnderstand all things; and peraduenture when you shall knowe, you will be mooued with compassion towardes him. Nowe when the lady perceiued hir fathers mind, she turned about vnto Apollonius, and saide: Gentleman, whose grace and cominesse sufficiently bewraieth the nobilitie of your birth, if it be not grieuous unto you, shew me your

name I beseech you, and your aduentures. Then
answered Apollonius: Madam, if you aske my name,
I have lost it in the sea : if you enquire of my nobilite,
I haue left that at Tyrus. Sir, I beseech you then
said the Lady Lucina, tel me this more plainly, that
I may vnderstand. Then Apollonius, crauing silence
to speake, declared his name, his birth and nobilitie,
and vnripped the whole tragedie of his aduentures, in
order as is before rehearsed ; and when he had made
an end of speaking, he burst foorth into most plenti-
full teares. Which when the king beheld, he saide
vnto Lucina : deere daughter, you haue done euill in
requiring to know the yong mans name, and his aduentures, wherein you haue renued his forepassed
griefes. But since nowe you haue vnderstoode all the
trueth of him, it is meete, as it becommeth the daughter of a king, you likewise extend your liberalitie
towards him, and whatsoever you giue him I will see
it be perfourmed. Then Lucina hauing already in
hir heart professed to doe him good, and nowe perceiuing very luckily her fathers mind to be inclined to
the desired purpose, she cast a friendly looke vpon
him, saying: Apollonius, nowe lay sorrowe aside, for
my father is determined to inrich you : and Apollonius, according to the curtesie that was in him, with
sighes and sobbes at remembrance of that whereof he
had so lately spoken, yeelded great thankes vnto the
faire ladie Lucina.

Then saide the king unto his daughter : Madame I
pray you take your harpe into your handes, and play
vs some musike to refresh our guests withall, for we
haue all too long hearkened vnto sorrowfull matters :
and when she had called for her harpe, she beganne to
play so sweetely, that all that were in companie highly
commended her, saying that in all their liues they
neuer heard pleasanter harmonie. Thus, whilest the
guests, euery man for his part much commended the

ladies cunning, onely Apollonius spake nothing. Then saide the king vnto him: You are too blame Apollonius, since all praise my daughter for her excellencie in musike, and you commend not her, or rather dispraise her by holding your peace. Apollonius answered: My soueraine and good lord, might it please you to pardon me, & I will say what I think: The lady Lucina your daughter is pretily entred, but she is not yet come to perfection in musike. For proofe whereof, if it please your Grace to command the harp to be deliuered vnto me, she shal well perceiue, that she shal heare that which she doth not yet know. The king answered: I see well Apollonius you haue skill in all things, and is nothing to be wished in a gentleman, but you haue perfectly learned it, wherfore, hold, I pray you take the harpe, and let vs heare some part of your cunning. When Apollonius had receiued the harp, he went forth, and put a garland of flowers vpon his head, and fastned his raiment in comly maner about him, and entred into the parlour againe, playing before the king, and the residue with such cunning and sweetnes, that he seemed rather to be Apollo then Apollonius, and the kings guests confessed that in al their liues they neuer heard the like before. But whē Lucina had heard and seene what was done, she felt hir selfe sodainely mooued within, and was sharpelie surprised with the loue of Apollonius, and, turning to her father: Nowe suffer me good father, saide she, to giue vnto this yoong gentleman some reward, according as I shall think conuenient. I giue you leaue to do so faire daughter, saide the king. Then she, looking towards Apollonius, My lord Apollonius, said she, receiue heere of my fathers liberalitie two hundred talents of gold, foure hundred poundes of siluer, store of raiment, twentie men seruants, and tenne handmaidens. Nowe therefore, said she vnto the officers that stood by, bring hither all these things which I haue here promised, and lay them downe in the parlour, in the presence of our friends. And immediatly they were all brought into their sight as she had commaunded. When this was done, the guests arose from the table, and giuing thankes vnto the king and ladie Lucina, tooke their leaue and departed. And Apollonius, thinking it likewise time for him to be gone, Most gratious king Altistrates (quoth he) thou which art a comforter of such as are in miserie; and thou also renowmed princesse, a fauourer of philosophie, and louer of all good studies, I bid you now most heartily farewell, as for your great deserts toward me, I leaue them to GOD to requite you with deserued recompence: and looking vnto his seruants which the ladie Lucina had given him, Sirs, take up this geere, quoth hee, which is giuen me, and bring it away, and let vs go seeke some lodgings.

When Lucina heard those words she was sodainlie stroken into a dump, fearing that she shoulde haue lost her newe louer, before she had euer reaped anie fruit of his companie, and therefore turning to her father, said: I beseech you good father and gratious king, forasmuch as it has pleased you this day to inrich Apolonius with many great gifts, you would not suffer him now to depart so late, lest he be by some naughtie persons spoiled of the things which you haue giuen him. The king willingly granted the ladies request, and commanded forthwith that there should be a faire lodging prepared for him and his, where he might lie honourably, and when he sawe conuenient time he went to bed, and tooke his rest.

The Sixth Chapter.

How Apollonius is made Schoolemaster to Lucina, and how she preferreth the loue of him, aboue all the nobilitie of Pentapolis.

WHEN night was come, and euery one was at rest, Lucinia laie unquietly tumbling in her bed, alwaies thinking upon Apollonius, and could not sleep. Wherefore, in the morning she rose very early, & came in to the king her fathers chamber. Whom when her father saw, what is ye matter, daughter Lucina, (quoth he) that contrary to custome you be stirring so earleie this morning? Deere father quoth Lucina, I could take no rest al this night, for the desire I haue to learn musicke of Apollonius; and therefore I pray you good father, to put me unto him to be instructed in the Art of Musicke, and other good qualities, wherein hee is skilfull. When Altistrates heard his daughters talke, he smiled within himselfe, when hee perceiued the warmed affection kindled within her breast, which with so seemely a pretence she had couered, as the desire to learne, and determined in part presently to satisfie her request: and when time serued, he sent a messenger for Apollonius. And when he was come, he said unto him: Apollonius my daughter much desireth to be your scholler, and therefore I pray you take her to your gouernement, and instruct her the best you can, and I will reward you to your contentation. Apollonius answered, gracious prince, I am moste willing to obey your commaundement. So hee tooke the ladie, and instructed her in the best maner he coulde, euen as himselfe had learned: wherein she profited so well, that in short time she matched, or rather surpassed her maister. Thus increased shee not onely in learning, but grew also daily in more feruent loue of Apollonius, as, whether stāding in doubt of her fathers resolute good wil if he were moued concerning marriage, or fearing the time woulde be deferred in respect whereof she was presently ready, in so much that she fell sicke and became weaker euerie day than other. When the king perceiued his daughters infirmitie to increase, hee sent immediatlie throughout all the dominions for the learnedst phisitions to search out her griefe and to cure it, who examining her vrine, and feeling her pulse, coulde finde out no manifest cause or substance of her disease. After a few dayes that this happened, three noble yong men of the same countrey, which had been suters a long time vnto Lucina for marriage, came vnto the Court, and being brought into the kinges presence saluted him dutifully. To whom the king said, Gentlemen, what is the cause of your comming? They answered, your Grace had oftentimes promised to bestow your daughter in marriage, vpon one of vs, and this is the cause of our comming at this time. Wee are your subiectes, wealthie, and descended of noble families, might it therefore please your Grace to choose one among vs three, to be your sonne in law. Then answered the king you are come vnto me at an vnseasonable time, for my daughter now applieth her studie, and lieth sicke for the desire of learning, and the time is much vnmeet for marriage. But to the intent you shall not altogether loose your labour, nor that I will not seeme to deferre you too long, write your names euery one seuerally in a peece of paper, and what ioynter you will make, and I will send the writinges to my daughter, that she may choose him whom she best liketh of. They did forthwith as the king had counselled them, and deliuered the writings vnto the king, which hee read, and signed them, and deliuered them vnto Apollonius, saying: Take here these billes, and deliuer them to your scholler, which Apollonius receiued, and tooke them immediatly vnto the ladie Lucina. Now when she sawe her schoolemaister whom she loued so entirely, she said vnto him : Maister, what is the cause that you come alone into my chamber? Apollonius answered : Madame, I haue brought writings from the king your father, which he willeth you to reade. Lucina then receiued the writinges, and brake them vp, and when she had reade the names of the three noblemen her suters, shee threw away the billes, and looking vpon Apollonius, she said vnto him: My welbeloued Schoolemaister Apollonius, doth it not greeue you that I shall be married vnto another? Apollonius answered, No madame it greeueth not me, for whatsoeuer shall be for your honour, shall be vnto me profitable. Then said Lucina, Maister, if you loued me you woulde be sorie, and therewithall she called for inke and paper, and wrote an answere vnto her father in forme following. Gracious king and deare father, forasmuch as of your goodnesse you have giuen me free choice, and libertie to write my minde : these are to let you vnderstand, that I would marry with the Sea-wrecked man, and with none other: your humble daughter, Lucina. And when she had sealed it, she deliuered it vnto Apollonius to be carried vnto the king. When the king had receiued the letters, he perused them, wherein he perceiued his daughters minde, not knowing whom she meant by the sea-wrecked man : and therefore turning himselfe towardes the three Noblemen, hee demaunded of them which of them had suffered shipwracke? Then one of them named Ardonius, answered, If it like your Grace, I haue suffred shipwrack? The other twaine named Munditius, and Carnillus, when they heard him say so, waxed wroth, and fel into termes of outrage against him, saying : sicknesse, and the fiends of hell consume thee, for thy foule & impudent lie: doe not we, who are thy equals both of birth and age, know right well that thou neuer wentest almost out of this citie gates? And how couldest thou then suffer shipwracke? Nowe when the king Altistrates could not finde out which of them had suffered shipwrack, he looked towards Apollonius, saying: Take these letters and read them, for it may be that I doe not knowe him whom thou knowest, who was present. Apollonius receiuing the letters, perused them quickly, and perceiuing himselfe to be loued, blushed wonderfully. Then said the king to Apollonius, hast thou found the sea-wrecked man? But Apollonius answered litle or nothing, wherein his wisedome the rather appeared according to the saying of the wise man: *in many words there wanteth discretion;* where as cōtrariwise, many an vndiscreet person might be accounted wise if hee had but this one point of wisdom, to hold his tongue. Wherin indeed consisteth the whole triall or rather insight of a man, as signified the most wise Philosopher Socrates.

The Seventh Chapter.

How Apollonius was married to the ladie Lucina, and hearing of king Antiochus death, departeth with his wife towards his owne countrey of Tyrus.

But to returne againe to my storie from which I haue digressed: when king Altistrates perceiued that Apollonius was the man whom his daughter Lucina disposed in her heart to preferre in loue before anie of the other three noble men, hee found meanes to put them off for that present, saying that he would talke with them farther concerning that matter another time: who taking their leaue, immediatly departed, but the king withdrew himself into the chamber where his daughter lay sicke, and sayd vnto her: whom haue you chosen to be your husband? To whom Lucina humbling her selfe, and with trickling teares, answered: Gratious Prince and deare father, I haue chosen in my heart the Sea-wrecked man, my schoolemaister Apollonius, for whom I most duetifully desire your fatherly goodwil: when the king saw her teares, his heart bled inwardly with compassion toward his childe whom hee loued tenderly, and he kissed her, and saide vnto her: My sweete Lucina be of good cheere, and take not thought for anie thing, and assure thy selfe thou hast chosen the man that I liked of assoone as I first sawe him: whom I loue no lesse then thee: that is to say, than if hee were my naturall childe. And therefore since the matter is nowe thus fallen out, I meane forthwith to appoint a day for your marriage, after that I haue broken the matter vnto Apollonius. And when he had said that, Lucina with blushing cheekes thanked her Father much, and he departed. Nowe would I demand of louers, whether Lucina reioyced or not? or whether there were anie better tidings in the worlde coulde chance to a man or woman? I am sure they would answer no. For such is the nature of this affection, that it preferreth the beloued person aboue all earthly thinges, yea and heauenly too, vnlesse it be brideled with reason: as the same likewise though moderately, and within the boundes of modest womanhoode, working the woonted effect in the ladie Lucina, reuiued her so presently, that shee forsooke her bed, and cast away her mourning apparrell, and appeared as it had been a newe woman restored from death to life, and that almost in a moment. The king being alone in the parlour called for Apollonius, and when he was come, he said thus vnto him: Apollonius, the vertue which I haue seene in thee, I haue testified by my liberalitie towards thee, and thy trustinesse is prooued by committing mine onelie childe and daughter to thine instruction. As these haue caused mee to preferre thee, so haue they made my daughter to loue thee, so that I am as well contented with the one as I am well pleased with the other. And for thy part, likewise I hope Apollonius, that as thou hast been glad to be my client, thou wilt reioyce as much to be my sonne in law. Tell me thy minde out of hand, for I attend thine answere. Then Apollonius much abashed at the kinges talke, falling downe vpon his knees, answered: Most gratious soueraigne, your wordes sound so strangely in mine eares, that I scarcely know how to giue answer, & your goodnesse hath been so great towardes me, that I can wish for no more. But since it is your Graces pleasure that I should not be indebted to many, but owe all thing vnto you, as life, and wife, honour, and goods, and all: you shall not find me vnthankful, howsoeuer God or fickle fortune deale with me, to remaine both loyall and constant to you, and your daughter, whom aboue all creatures, both for birth and beauty and good qualities, I loue and honour most intirely. Altistrates reioiced much to heare so wise and conformable an answere, and embracing Apollonius, called him by the name of deare beloued sonne. The next day morning the king addressed his messengers & purseuants, to assemble the nobliest of his subiects and frends out of the confederat cities, and countries, and to shew them that he had certaine affaires to communicat vnto them: and when they were come altogither vnto Pentapolis, after due greeting, and accustomable intertainments shewed as in the maner of great estates, he said thus vnto them. My loving friends, and faithfull subiects, my meaning was to let you vnderstand, that my daughter is desirous to marrie with her schoolemaster Apollonius, and I am wel pleased therwith. Wherfore, I beseech you all to reioyce thereat, and be glad for my daughter shalbe matched to a wise man. And know you moreouer, that I appoint this day six weekes for the solemnization day of the marriage, at what time I desire you all to be here present, that like friends we may reioyce, and make merry togither: and when he had all said, he dismissed the assembly. Now as the time wore away, so the wedding day drue neere, and there was great preparation made aswell for the feast, as for iewels, and rich clothes to furnish the bridegroome, and bride withall, as althing els that appertaine[d] to the beautifying of so great a wedding. And when the day was come, the king apparrelled in his princely robes with a diadem of great price vpon his head, accompanied his daughter Lucina and Apollonius vnto the Church, whom thousands of lordes and ladies followed after, all cloathed in rich attire, and marshalled in comely order. The bride woare on a gowne of cloth of gold cut, & drawen out with cloth of siluer, and a kirtle of crimsin veluet imbrodered with pure golde, and thickly beset with orientall pearles. Her haire hung downe in tresses fairely broided with a lace of gold, and a Coronet vpon her head set with pretious stones of inestimable value. Her necke was bare, whereby her naked skinne appeared whiter than the driuen snowe, curiously bedecked with chaines of golde, and euery other lincke enameled with blacke amell. Great baudrickes of perfect goldsmithes worke vppon eche arme to fasten the sleeues of her garment from sliding vp at the wreast. Lastly, a massie collar of fine golde, made esse wise vppon her shoulders, hanging downe behinde and before, with a Diamond reaching downe vnto her middle, esteemed in value at threescore thousand pound, which the king her father had

sent vnto her for a present, that morning while she
was apparrelling. The bridegrome wore on a dublet
and hosen of costly cloth of siluer, garded with Goldsmithes worke of the same colour, and a gowne of
purple Satten, embroidred with golde, and beset with
rich stones. His cap was of fine blacke Veluet, all
ouer bespangled with Rubies, set in gold and fastned
on by loopes: the hand of massie golde, beset with
courses of stones in order, first a Rubie, then a
Turkeis, then a Diamond, and so beginning againe
with a Rubie. This was their raiment, and thus
went they forth togither, hand in hand, after whom,
as is already declared, the lordes and ladies followed by three and three in a ranke. When the
solemnities were done at the Church, and the wordes
spoken, and the Princes ioyned in marriage, they returned home and went to dinner. What shall I nowe
speake of the noble cheare and Princely prouision
for this feast? And after dinner of the exquisite
Musicke, fine dauncing, heauenly singing, sweete deuising, and pleasant communication among the
estates? I may not discourse at large of the liberall
challenges made and proclaimed at the tilt, barriers,
running at the ring, ioco di can, managing fierce
horses, running a foote and daunsing in armour: And
at night of the gorgeous plaies, shewes, disguised
speeches, masks and mummeries, with continuall harmony of all kindes of musicke, and banqueting in
all delicacie : All these things I leaue to the consideration of them which haue seene the like in the Courts,
and at the weddinges of Princes, where they haue
seene more than my simple pen is able to describe,
or may be comprehended within the recital of so short
an historie. When night was come, and reuels were
ended, the bride was brought to bed, and Apollonius
tarried not long from her, where hee accomplished the
duties of marriage, and faire Lucina conceiued childe

the same night. The next daie, every man arose to feasting and iollitie, for the wedding triumphes continued an whole moneth. This while Lucinas bellie began to grow, and as it fortuned that the lord Apollonius and his ladie on a day walked along the sea side for their disporte, hee sawe a faire shippe fleeting vnder saile, which hee knew well to be of his countrey, and he hallowed vnto the maister, whose name was Calamitus and asked of him of whence his ship was? The maister answered of Tyrus. Thou hast named my coūtry said Apollonius: Art thou then of Tyrus, said the maister? Yea, answered Apollonius. Then said the maister, knowest thou one Apollonius prince of that countrey? If thou doe, or shalt heare of him hereafter, bid him now be glad and reioyce, for king Antiochus and his daughter are strooken dead with lightning from heauen. And the Citie of Antiochia with all the riches, and the whole kingdome are reserued for Apollonius.

With these words the ship being vnder saile, departed, & Apollonius being filled with gladnes, immediatly began to breake with his ladie to giue him leaue to go and receiue his kingdom. But when faire Lucina heard him beginne to mooue words of departing, she burst out into teares, saying: My Lorde, if you were nowe in some farre countrie, and heard say that I were neere my time to be deliuered, you ought to make haste home vnto me. But since you be nowe with me, and know in what case I am me thinks you should not now desire to depart from me. Howbeit, if your pleasure be so, and tarriance breede danger, and kingdomes want not heirs long, as I would not perswade you to tarry, so doe I request you to take me with you. This discreete answere pleased Apollonius well; wherefore he kissed his lady, and they agreed it should be so. And when they were returned from walking, Lucina reioycing, came vnto the king her father, saying, deare father, reioice I beseech you, and be glad with my lord Apollonius and me, for the most c[r]uell tyrant Antiochus and his daughter are by the iust iudgement of God destroied with lightning from heauen; and the kingdome and riches are reserued for us to inherite: moreouer, I pray you good father, let me haue your goodwil to trauel thither with my husband. The king reioyced much at this tidings, and graunted her reasonable request, and also commaunded all things to be prouided immediatly that were necessary for the iourney. The shippes were strongly appointed and brought vnto the shoare, and fraught with al things conuenient, as golde, siluer, apparell, bedding, vittells and armour. Moreouer, whatsoeuer fortune might befal, the king prepared to sail with them Ligozides the nurse, and a midwife, and all things meet for the childe whensoeuer Lucina shoulde neede them: and with great honour himselfe accompanieth them vnto the sea side, when the time appointed for their departure was come; where with many teares, and great fatherly affection hee kissed his daughter, and embraced his sonne in law, and recommended them vnto GOD, in whome hee did wish unto them a most prosperous iourney, and so returned vnto his pallace.

THE EIGHTH CHAPTER.

How faire Lucina died in trauell of child vpon the sea; and being throwen into the water, was cast on land at Ephesus, and taken home by Cerimon a Phisition.

THE marriners immediatly merrily hoissed saile and departed; & when they had sailed two dayes, the master of the shippe warned Apollonius of a tempest approching, which nowe came on, and increased so fast, that all the companie was amazed, and Lucina, what with sea-sicknes & feare of dāger, fel in labor of child, wherewith she was weakened, that there was no hope of recouerie, but she must now die: yet being first deliuered of a faire daughter, insomuch that now all tokens of life were gone, and she appeared none other but to be dead. When Apollonins beheld this heauie spectacle, no heart was able to conceiue his bitter grief, for like a mad man distracted he tore his cloths, and rent his haire, and laying himselfe upon the carkas, he vttered these wordes with great affection: O my deare lady and wife, the daughter of king Altistrates, what shall I now answer to thy father for thee: would God thou haddest remained with him at home; & if it had pleased God to haue wrought this his pleasure in thee, it had rather chanced with thy loving father in his quiet land, than with me thy woful husband vpon the wild seas. The whole company also made great lamentation for her, bewailing the death of so noble and beautifull a ladie, and so curteous a gentlewoman. Howbeit in the hotest of the sorrowe the gouernour of the ship came vnto Apollonius, saying, My lord, plucke vp your heart, and be of goode cheere, and consider I pray you that the ship may not abide to carie the dead carkas, and therefore command it to be cast into the sea, that we may the better escape. Then answered Apollonius: What saiest thou varlet! wouldest thou haue me cast this bodie into the sea, which receiued me into house and fauour, when I was in miserie, and drenched in the water, wherein I lost ship, goods & all? But taking further consultation, and aduising himselfe what were best to do, he called certaine of his men vnto him, & thus he deuised with them. My trusty seruants, whome this common mischance grieueth as wel as me, since sorrowing wil not help that which is chanced, assist me, good sirs, to prouide for the present necessity. Let vs make forthwith a large chest, and bore the lid full of small holes, and we will seare it all ouer within with pitch and rosen molten together, whereinto we will put cunningly a sheete of lead, and in the same we will inclose the tender corps of the wife of me, of all other a most vnfortunate husband. This was no sooner said, but it was almost likewise done with sembable celeritie. Then tooke they the body of the fair lady Lucina, and arraied her in princely apparel, and layd her into the chest, and Apollonius placed a great summe of golde at her head, and a great treasure of siluer at her feet, & he kissed her, letting fall a flood of salt teares on hir face, and he wrote a bill, and put in it also, the tenor whereof was in forme as foloweth: Whoseuer shal find this chest, I pray him to take ten pieces of gold for his paines, and to bestowe tenne pieces more vpon the buriall of the corpes; for it hath left many teares to the parents and friends, with dolefull heaps of sorow and heauines. But whosoeuer shall doe otherwise than the present griefe requireth, let him die a shamefull death, and let there be none to bury his body. And then closing all vp verie safe, commaunded the chest to be lifted ouerboorde into the sea: and willed the child to be nursed with all diligence, that if euer fortune should so fall, he might present vnto good king Altistrates a neece in steede of a daughter.

Now fleeted away the ship fast with the wind, and the coffin tumbled backeward with the tide, and Apollonius could not keep his eie from the bodie whereon his heart rested, vntil kenning failed, and the sea rose vp with a banke between. There were two days passed, and the night was now at hand, when the next day morning the waues rolled foorth this chest to the land, and cast it ashore on the coast of Ephesus. Not farre from that place there dwelt a physition whose name was Cerimon, who by chaunce walking abroad vpon the shore that day with his schollers, found the chest which the sea had cast up, & willed his seruants to take it vp, & diligently to cary it to the next towne, where hee dwelt, and they did so. When Cerimon came home he opened the chest, marueling what shuld be therein, and found a lady arrayed in princely apparell and ornaments, very faire and beautifull to beholde. Whose excellencie in that respect as many as beheld, were strangely affectioned thereat, perceiuing such an incomparable gleame of beautie to be resident in her face, wherein nature had not committed the least errour that might be deuised, sauing that shee made her not immortall. The haire of her head was naturally as white as snowe, vnder which appeared her goodly forehead, faire and large, wherein was neither blemish nor wrinkle. Her eies were like two starres turning about in their naturall course, not wantonly roving here and there, but modestly moouing as gouerned by reason, repre-senting the stabilitie of a setled mind. Her eie brows decently commending the residue of her countenance. Her nose straight, as in were drawen with a line, comely diuiding her cherry cheeks asunder, not reach-ing foorth too long, nor cut off too short, but of a commendable proportion. Hir necke was like the white alabaster shining like the bright sunne beames, woonderfully delighting the mindes of the beholders. Her bodie of comely stature, neither too high nor too lowe, not scregged with leanenesse, nor vndecently corpulent, but in such equality consisting that no man woulde wish it otherwise. From her shoulders sprang foorth her armes, representing two branches growing out of a tree, beautified with a white hand, and fingers long and slender, surpassing to behold. To be short,

such was the excellencie of her beutie in each respect,
that it could suffer no deformitie to accompany it,
whereby also may be discerned a singular perfection
of her minde, created by God and infused into her
bodie, whereby it was mooued, and those good qualities of hers expressed in operation: so that all outward beautie of the bodie proceedeth from the inward
beuty of the minde, from whence sprang up the olde
and true saying of the wisest Philosophers, that the
sundry nature of the forme or soule, diuersely disposeth the matter according vnto it[s] owne qualitie:
as it expresly appeared in the beutiful countenaunce
and stature of this Ladies bodie, whereof Cerimon
stoode amazedly taking the view.

The Ninth Chapter.

*How Lucina was restored to life by one of Cerimon the
Phisitions schollers; and howe Cerimon adopted
her to his daughter, and placed her in the temple of
Diana.*

The surpassing beauty of faire Lucina, being such as
is before recited, no woonder it was though Cerimon
were maruellously rauished at ye sight, whereby his
affection inforced him to breake out into these words:
Alas good beautiful gentlewoman, what vnhappy and
cruell chance hath thus made thee away, and caused
thee to be so wofully forsaken? And as he spake
those wordes, hee perceiued the golde that lay at her
head, and the siluer that lay at her feet, with a scroll
of paper written, the which hee tooke vp and read,
the tenor whereof was this: Whosoeuer shal finde
this chest, I pray him for to take ten pieces of golde for
his paines, and to bestowe ten peeces more on the

buriall of the corps; for it hath left many teares to the parents and friends, with dolefull heapes of sorrowe and heauinesse. But whosoeuer shall doe otherwise than the present griefe requireth, let him die a shamefull death, and let there be none to burie his bodie. And as soone as he had read ouer the writing, he said vnto his servants: now let vs perfourme vnto the bodie that which the sorrowe requireth; and I sweare to you, by the hope which I haue to liue, that I will bestow more money vpon the accomplishing of the same, than the sorrowful scedul requireth. Wherfore, according to the maner of the buriall which was at that time to burn the bodies of the dead, and to burie the ashes, gathered vp and put into pottes, he commaunded a pile of wood to be erected, and vpon the top thereof he caused the body to be layed.

Nowe Cerimon had a scholler in Physicke, whose name was Machaon very towardly in his profession, of yeres but yong, but antient in wit and experience, who comming in while these things were doing, and beholding so beautifull a corps layd vpon the pile, hee stoode still and wondered at it. Which thing Cerimon perceiuing, Thou art come in good time said he to Machaon, and I looked for thee about this time. Take this flagon of precious ointment, and powre it vppon the corps, being the last ceremonie of the sepulture. Then came Machaon vnto the corps, and pulled the clothes from the ladies bosome, and poured foorth the ointment, and bestowing it abroad with his hãd, perceiued some warmth in her breast, and that there was life in the body. Machaon stoode astonished, and hee felt her pulses, and layde his cheeke to her mouth, and examined all other tokens that he coulde deuise, and he perceiued how death striued with life within her, and that the conflict was daungerous and doubtfull, who should preuaile. Then saide he vnto the seruants: set fire vnto the wood at the foure corners of the pile, and cause it to burne moderatly, and bring me hither a bed that I may take the body out of the chest, and lay it thereon.

This being done, he chafed the body against the fire, vntill the blood, which was congealed with colde, was wholly resolued. Then went Machaon vnto his master Cerimon and saide: The woman whome thou thinkest to be dead, is aliue, and that you may the better beleeue my saying, I will plainely prooue it to be so. And when he had so saide, he tooke the body reuerently in his armes, and bare it into his owne chamber, and layed it vpon his bed groueling vpon the breast. Then tooke he certaine hote and comfortable oyles, and warming them vpon the coales, he dipped faire wooll therein, and fomented all the bodie ouer therewith, vntil such time as the congealed blood and humours were throughly resolued, and the spirits eftsoones recouered their wonted course, the veines waxed warme, the arteries beganne to beate, and the lungs drew in the fresh ayre againe, and she opened her eies and looked about, and being perfectly come to herselfe, what art thou, said shee vnto Machaon? see thou touch me not otherwise than thou oughtest to do, for I am a Kings daughter, and the wife of a King. When Machaon heard her speak these words, he was exceeding glad, and he ran vnto his master and saide: Sir, the woman liueth, and speaketh perfectly. Then answered Cerimon: My welbeloued schollar Machaon, I am glad of this fortunate chaunce, and I much commende thy wisedome, and praise thy learning, and cannot but extoll thy diligence. Wherefore be not vnthankfull to thy knowledge, but receiue here the reward which is due vnto thee, namely, that which by the writing was appointed to be bestowed vpon her buriall for thou hast restored her vnto life, and shee hath brought with her great summes of mony. When he had so saide, they came vnto her and saluted her, and caused her to be apparelled with wholsome and comfortable clothes, & to be refreshed with good meats. A few daies after, when she had fully recouered strēgth, and Cerimon by communication knew that she came of the stocke of a king, he sent for many of his friends to come vnto him, and he adopted her for his owne daughter : and she with many tears requiring that she might not be touched by any man, for that intent her placed in the Temple of Diana, which was there at Ephesus, to be preserued there inuiolably among the religious women.

The Tenth Chapter.

How Apollonius arriuing at Tharsus, deliuereth his yong daughter Tharsia vnto Stranguilio and Dionisiades to be brought vp ; and how the nurce lying in her death-bed declareth vnto Tharsia who were her parents.

LET vs leaue now a while the lady Lucina among the holy nunnes in the Temple of Diana at Ephesus, and let vs looke backe vnto sorrowful Apollonius, whose ship with fortunate winde, and the good prouidence of God directing the same, arriued at the shoare of Tharsus, where hee immediatly came forth of the ship, and entred into the house of Stranguilio and Dionisiades, whom he saluted, and told thē the heauy chances that had befallen him, both of the great stormes and tempests on the sea, which hee had endured, as also of the death of the good lady Lucina his wife : howbeit said he, God be thanked, my daughter remaineth aliue, for the which I am very glad : wherfore, deare friends Stranguilio and Dionisiades, according to the trust which I haue in you, I mean in some things to vse your friendship, while I go about to recouer the kingdome which is reserued for me. For I will not returne backe againe vnto king Altistrates my father-in-law, whose daughter, alas I haue lost in the sea; but meaning rather to exercise the trade of merchandize, I commit my daughter vnto you, to bee nourished and brought vp with your yoong daughter Philomacia, and I will that my daughter be called Tharsia. Moreouer I wil leaue my deare wife Lucinas nurse here also, called Ligozides, to tend the child, that she may be lesse troublesome vnto you. And when hee had made an end of talking, he deliuered the infant and the nurse vnto Stranguilio, and therewithal great store of gold, siluer, and raiment; and hee sware a solemne othe, that he would not poule his head, clip his beard, nor pare his nailes, vntill hee had married his daughter at ripe yeares. They wondred much at so strange an othe, promising faithfully to bring up his daughter with all diligence. When these things were ended according to his mind, Apollonius tooke his leaue, departed vnto his ship, and sailed into far countries, and vnto the uppermost parts of Egypt. Therewhile the yoong maiden, Tharsia sprang vp in yeeres, and when she was about fiue yeares olde, being free borne she was set to schoole with other free children, alwaies jointly accompanied with Philomacia, being of the same age that she was of. The time passed forth a pace, & Tharsia grew vp so wel in learning as in yeers vntil comming to the age of fourteene yeeres, one day when she returned from schoole, she found Ligozides her nurse sodainly falne sicke, and sitting beside her vpon the bed, demanded of her the cause, and maner of her sickenesse. Then said the nurce vnto her, hearken vnto my wordes deare daughter Tharsia, and lay them vp in thine heart. Whom thinkest thou to be thy father, and thy mother, and in what countrey supposest thou wast thou borne? Tharsia answered, why, nurce, why aske you me this question? Stranguilio is my father, Dionisiades my mother, and I was borne in Tharsus. Then sighed the nurce, and saide: No, sweete Tharsia, no, thou art deceiued. But hearken vnto me, and I will declare vnto thee the beginning of thy birth, to the intent thou mayst know how to guide thy selfe after my death. Apollonius ye prince of Tyrus is thy father, and Lucina king Altistrates daughter was thy mother, who being in trauell with thee, died after thou wast borne, and thy father, Appollonius, inclosed her bodie in a chest with princely ornaments, laying twenty talents of gold at her head, and as much at her feete in siluer, with a scedule written, that whether soeuer it were driuen, it might suffice to burie her, according to her estate. Thus wast thou born vpon the Sea; and thy fathers ship with much wrestling of contrarie windes, and with his vnspeakeable griefe of minde arriued at this shoare, and brought thee in thy swading clothes vnto this citie, where hee with great care deliuered thee vnto this thine hoste Stranguilio and Dionisiades his wife to be fostered vp diligently, and left me heere also to attend vpon thee. Moreouer he sware an othe, that he would not poule his head, clip his beard, nor pare his nayles, vntill he had married thee vnto some man at ripe yeares. Wherefore now I admonishe thee, that if after my death thine hoste or thine hostesse, whom thou callest thy parents, shall haply offer thee any iniurie, then runne thou into the market place, where thou shalt find the stature of thy father standing; and take hold of it, and cry aloud saying: O Citizens of Tharsus, I am his daughter, whose image this is: and the citizens being mindfull of thy fathers benefites, will doubtlesse reuenge thine iniurie. Then answered Tharsia: Deare nurce Ligozides, I take God to witnesse, if you had not told me thus

much, I should utterly have been ignorant from
whence I had come. And therefore now, good
nurce, I thank thee with all my heart, and if euer
need so require, thy counsel shal be followed: and
while they were debating these matters betweene
them, Ligozides being verie sicke and weake, gaue
up the ghost, and by the death of this present bodie,
passed into the state of live euerlasting.

THE ELEVENTH CHAPTER.

*How after the death of Ligozides the nurce Dionisiades
enuying at the beautie of Tharsia, conspired her
death, which should haue been accomplished by a
villaine of the countrey.*

THARSIA much lamented the death of Ligozides her
nurce, and caused her bodie to be solemnly buried
not farre of, in a field without the walles of the citie,
and mourned for her an whole yeere following. But
when the yeare was expired, she put off her mourning
attire, and put on her other apparel, and frequented
the schooles, and the studie of liberall Sciences as
before. And whensoeuer she returned from schoole,
she would receiue no meate before she had visited
her nurces sepulchre, which she did daily, entring
thereinto, and carrying a flagon of wine with her,
where she used to abide a space, and to call vppon
her father and mother. Now on a day it fortuned,
that as she passed through the street with Dionisiades,
and her companion Philomacia, the people beholding
the beautie and comlinesse of Tharsia, said: Happy
is that father that hath Tharsia to his daughter, but
her companion that goeth with her, is foule and euill
fauoured. When Dionisiades heard Tharsia commended, and her owne daughter Philomacia so dis-

praised, shee returned home wonderfull wroth, and withdrawing her self into a solitary place, began thus secretly to discourse of ye matter. It is now fourteen yeares since Apollonius this foolish girles father departed from hence, and he neuer sendeth letters for her, nor any remembrance vnto her, whereby I coniecture that he is dead. Ligozides her nurse is departed, and there is no bodie now of whom I should stande in feare, and therefore I will now slay her, and dress vp mine owne daughter in her apparell and iewels. When shee had thus resolved her selfe uppon this wicked purpose, in the mean while there came home one of their countrey villaines called Theophilus, whom shee called, and said thus vnto him: Theophilus, my trustie friend, if euer thou looke for libertie, or that I shoulde doe thee pleasure, doe so much for me as to slay Tharsia. Then said Theophilus: Alas mistresse, wherein hath that innocent maiden offended, that she should be slaine? Dionisiades answered, Shee innocent! nay she is a wicked wretch, and therefore thou shalt not denie to fulfill my request, but doe as I commaund thee, or els I sweare by God thou shalt dearely repent it. But how shall I best doe it, Mistres, said the villaine? Shee answered: shee hath a custome, as soone as shee returneth home from Schoole, not to eate meat before that she haue gone into her Nurces sepulchre, where I would haue thee stand readie, with a dagger drawn in thine hand; and when she is come in, gripe her by the haire of the head, and so slay her: then take her bodie and cast it into the Sea, and when thou hast so done, I will make thee free, and besides reward thee liberally. Then tooke the villaine a dagger, and girded himselfe therewith, and with an heauy heart and weeping eies went forth towards the graue, saying within himselfe, Alas poore wretch that I am, alas poore Theophilus that canst not deserue thy libertie but by shedding of innocent bloud: and with that hee went into the graue and drue his dagger, and made him readie for the deede. Tharsia was now come from schoole, and made haste vnto the grave with a flagon of wine as shee was wont to doe, and entred within the vault. Then the villaine rushed violently vpon her, and caught her by the haire of the head, and threw her to the ground. And while he was now readie to stab her with the dagger, poore silly Tharsia all amazed casting her eies vpon him, knew the villain, and holding vp her handes, said thus vnto him: O, Theophilus against whom haue I so greeuously offended, that I must die therefore? The villaine answered, Thou hast not offended, but thy father hath, which left thee behind him in Stranguilios house with so great a treasure in mony, and princely ornaments. O, said the mayden, would to God he had not done so: but I pray thee Theophilus, since there is no hope for me to escape with life, giue mee licence to say my praiers before I die. I giue thee licence said the villaine, and I take God to record that I am constrained to murther thee against my will.

The Twelfth Chapter.

How certaine Pyrats rescued Tharsia when she should haue been slaine, and carried her vnto the citie Machilenta to be sold among other bondslaues.

As fortune, or rather the prouidence of God serued, while Tharsia was deuoutly making her praiers, certaine pyrats which were come aland, and stood vnder the side of an hill watching for some prey, beholding an armed man offering violence vnto a mayden, cried vnto him, and said: Thou cruel tyrant! that maiden is our prey and not thy victorie; and therfore hold thine hands from her, as thou louest thy life. When the villain heard that, he ran away as fast as he could, and hid himselfe behind the sepulchre. Then came the pyrats and rescued Tharsia, and caried her away to their ships, and hoysed saile, and departed. And the villaine returned home to his mistres, and saide vnto her: that which you commaunded me to doe is dispatched, and therefore now I thinke it good that you put on a mourning garment, and I also, and let vs counterfeit great sorrowe and heauinesse in the sight of all the people, and say that shee died of some greeuous disease. But Stranguilio himselfe consented not to this treason, but so soone as hee heard of the foule mischaunce, beeing as it were a mopte, and mated with heauinesse and griefe, he clad himselfe in mourning aray, and lamented that wofull case, saying: Alas in what a mischiefe am I wrapped? what might I doe, or say herein? The father of this mayden deliuered this citie from the peril of death; for this cities sake he suffered shipwracke, lost his goodes and endured penury, and now he is requited with euil for good. His daughter which he committed vnto me to be brought vp, is now deuoured by a most cruell Lionesse: thus I am depriued as it were of mine owne eies, & forced to bewaile the death of an innocent, and am vtterly spoiled through the fierce biting of a moste venemous serpent.[1] Then casting his eies vp towards heauen, O God said hee, thou knowest that I am innocent from the bloud of silly Tharsia, which thou hast to require at Dionisiades handes: and therewithall he looked towards his wife, saying: Thou wicked woman, tell me, how hast thou made

---

[1] [" The serpent that did sting thy father's life,
Now wears his crown ———"
— HAMLET, i. 5.]

away prince Apollonius daughter? thou that liuest both to the slaunder of God, and man? Dionisiades answered in manie wordes euermore excusing herselfe, and, moderating the wrath of Stranguilio, shee counterfeited a fained sorrowe by attiring her selfe and her daughter in mourning apparell, and in dissembling teares before the people of the citie, to whom shee saide: Dearly beloued friendes and Citizens of Tharsus, for this cause we doe weepe and mourne in your sight, because the ioy of our eyes and staffe of our olde age, the Mayden Tharsia is dead, leauing vnto vs bitter teares, and sorrowfull heartes. Yet haue we alreadie taken order for her funerals, and buried her according to her degree. These wordes were right greeuous vnto the people, and there was almost none that let not fall some teares for sorrowe. And they went with one accord vnto the market place, whereas her fathers image stood, made of brasse, and erected also another vnto her there with this inscription: *Vnto the virgin Tharsia in liew of her fathers benefites, the Citizens of Tharsus haue erected this monument.*

The Thirteenth Chapter.

How the Pirats which stole away Tharsia brought her to the citie Machilenta, and sold her to a common bawd, and how she preserued her virginitie.

THE meane time while these troubles were at Tharsus, the Pirats being in their course vpon the Sea, by benefite of happie winde arriued at Machilenta, and came into the citie. Nowe had they taken manie mo men and women besides Tharsia, whom all they brought a shoare, and set them to sell as slaues for money. Then came there sundrie to buy such as they lacked for their purposes, amongst whom a moste vile man-bawd, beholding the beautie and tender yeeres of Tharsia, offered money largely for her. Howbeit Athanagoras, who was Prince of the same Citie, beholding likewise the noble countenance, and regarding the great discretion of the mayden in communication, out-bid the bawd, and offered for her ten sestercies of gold. But ye bawd, being loth to loose so commodious a prey, offered twenty. And I wil giue thirty said Athanagoras. Nay I wil giue forty said the bawd: and I fiftie quoth Athanagoras, and so they continued in outbidding one an other vntill the bawd offered an hundred sestercies of gold to be payed ready downe, and whosoeuer wil giue more, saide he, I will yet giue ten sestercies more than he. Then prince Athanagoras thus bethought him secretly in his minde: if I should contend with the bawd to buy her at so hie a price, I must needes sell other slaues to pay for her, which were both losse and shame vnto me. Wherefore I will suffer him to buy her; and when he setteth her to hire, I will be the first man that shall come vnto her, and I will gather the floure of her virginitie, which shall stand mee in as great steade as if I had bought her. Then the bawd payed the money, and tooke the maiden and departed home; and when he came into his house, hee brought her into a certaine chappel where stoode the idoll of Priapus made of gold, and garnished with pearls and pretious stones. This idoll was made after the shape of a man, with a mighty member vnproportionable to the body, alwayes erected, whome bawds and leachers doe adore, making him their god, and worshipping him. Before this filthy idoll he commaunded Tharsia to fall downe. But she answered, God forbid master, that I should worship such an idoll. But (sir) said she, are you a Lapsatenian? Why askest thou said the bawd? I aske, quoth she, because the Lapsatenians doe worship Priapus: this spake she of simplicitie, not knowing what she was. Ah wretch answered he, knowest thou not that thou arte come into the house of a couetous bawd? When Tharsia heard that, she fell downe at his feet and wept, saying: O master, take compassion vpon my virginity, and do not hire out my body for so vile a gaine. The bawd answered, knowest thou not, that neither bawd nor hangman do regard teares or prayers? Then called he vnto him a certaine villaine which was gouernour ouer his maids, and said vnto him: Let this maiden be decked in virgins apparell, pretious and costly, and write vpon her: whoseeuer defloureth Tharsia shal pay ten peeces of golde, and afterward she shall be common vnto the people for one peece at a time. The villaine fulfilled his masters commaundement, and the third day after that she was bought, shee was with great solemnitie conducted through the streete with musicke, the bawd himselfe with a great multitude going before, and so conueyed vnto the brothell house. When shee was come thither, Athanagoras the Prince disguising his head and face because hee woulde not be knowen, came first in vnto her; whome when Tharsia sawe, she threw her selfe downe at his feete, and saide vnto him: For the loue of God, Gentleman, take pitty on me, and by the name of God I adiure and charge you, that you do no violence vnto me, but bridle your lust, and hearken vnto my unhappy estate, and consider diligently from whence I am sprung. My father was poore Apollonius prince of Tyrus, whome force constrained to forsake his owne countrey. My mother was daughter to Altistrates king of Pentapolis, who died in the birth of me, poore wretch, vpon the sea. My father also is dead as was supposed, which caused Dionisiades wife of Stranguilio of Tharsus, to whom my father committed me of special trust to be brought vp being but an infant, enuying mine estate, and thirsting after my wealth, to seeke my death by the handes of a villaine; which had beene accomplished, and I would to God it had before I had seen this day, but that I was suddenly taken away by the pyrates which solde me vnto this filthie bawd. With these or such like wordes declared shee her heauie fortune, eftsoones sobbing and bursting out into streames of tears, that for extreme griefe she could scarsly speake. When she had in this manner vttered her sorow, the good prince being astonied and mooued with compassion, said vnto her: Be of good cheere Tharsia, for surely I rue thy case; and I my selfe haue also a daughter at home, to whome I doubt that the like chances may befall.

And when he had so said, he gaue her twenty peeces of gold, saying: Holde heere a greater price or reward for thy virginitie than thy master appointed: and say as much vnto others that come vnto thee as thou hast done to me, and thou shalt withstand them. Then Tharsia fell on her knees, and weeping saide unto him: Sir, I giue you most hartie thankes for your great compassion and curtesie, and most hartily I beseech you vpon my knees, not to descry vnto any that which I haue said vnto you. No surely, answered Athanagoras, vnlesse I tell it vnto my daughter, that she may take heede when she commeth vnto the like yeares, that she fall not into the like mishappe: and when he had so saide, he let fall a few teares, and departed. Now as he was going he met with an other pilgrime that with like deuotion came for to seeke the same saint, who demaunded of him howe hee liked of the maidens company. Truly, answered Athanagoras neuer of any better. Then the yong man whose name was Aportatus entred into the chamber; and the maiden, after the manner, shut the

doore to, and Athanagoras listned at the windowe.
Then saide Aportatus vnto Tharsia, How much did
the prince giue vnto thee? She answered fortie
peeces of golde. Then said he, receiue here of me
an whole pound weight of golde. The Prince which
heard this talke thought then in his minde, the more
that you do giue her, the more she will weepe, as
thinking that you would looke for recompence, the
which shee meaneth not to perfourme.

The maiden receiued the money, and fell down on
her knees at his feete, and declared vnto him all her
estate with teares, as is before shewed. When Aportatus heard that, he was mooued with compassion,
and he tooke her vp from the ground, saying: Arise
Ladie Tharsia: we are al men, and subiect to the
like chances, & therewithall he departed. And when
he came foorth he found prince Athanagoras before
the doore laughing at him, to whom he said: Is it
wel done, my liege, thus to delude a poore gentleman? Was there none to whom you might beginne
in teares but vnto me only? Then communed they
further of the matter, and sware an othe betweene
themselues, that they would not bewray those words
vnto any; & they withdrew themselues aside into a
secret place, to see the going in and comming foorth
of other, and they sawe many which went in and gaue
their mony, and came foorth againe weeping. Thus
Tharsia through the grace of God, and faire perswation, preserued her body vndefiled.

THE FOURTEENTH CHAPTER.

How Tharsia withstoode a second assault of her virginitie, and by what means she was preserued.

WHEN night was come the master bawd vsed always
to receiue the money which his women had gotten by

the vse of their bodies the day before. And when it
was demaunded of Tharsia, she brought him the
mony, as the price and hire of her virginitie. Then
said the bawd vnto hir: It is wel doone Tharsia: vse
diligence henceforth, and see that you bring mee
thus much mony euery day. When the next day
was past also, and the bawd vnderstoode that she
remained a virgin stil, he was offended, and called
vnto him the villaine that had charge ouer the maides,
and said vnto him: Sirra, how chanceth it that Tharsia
remaineth a virgin still? Take her vnto thee, and
spoile her of her maidenhead, or be sure thou shalt
be whipped. Then said the villaine vnto Tharsia, tel
me, art thou yet a virgin? She answered, I am, and
shalbe as long as God will suffer me. How then,
said he, hast thou gotten all this mony? She
answered, with teares falling downe vpon her knees,
I haue declared mine estate, humbly requesting all
men to take compassion on my virginitie. And nowe
likewise, falling then downe at his feete also, take
pitty on me, good friend, which am a poore captiue,
and the daughter of a king, and doe not defile me.
The villaine answered: Our master the bawd is very
couetous and greedie of money, and therefore I see
no meanes for thee to continue a virgin. Whereunto
Tharsia replied: I am skilful in the liberal sciences,
and well exercised in all studies, and no man singeth
or playeth on instruments better than I, wherefore
bring mee into the market place of the citie that men
may heare my cunning. Or let the people propound
any maner of questions, and I will resolue them: and
I doubt not but by this practise I shall get store of
money daily. When the villaine heard this deuise,
and bewailed the maidens mishappe, he willingly gaue
consent thereto, and brake with the bawd his master
touching that matter, who hearing of her skill, and
hoping for the gaine, was easily perswaded.

Now when she was brought into the market place, all the people came thronging to see and heare so learned a virgin, before whom shee vttered her cunning in musicke, and her eloquence in speaking, and answered manifestly vnto all such questions as were propounded vnto her with such perspicuitie, that all confessed themselues fully satisfied, and she wonne great fame thereby, and gained great summes of money. But as for Prince Athanagoras, he had evermore a speciall regard in the preseruation of her virginitie, none otherwise than if she had been his owne daughter, and rewarded the villaine very liberally for his diligent care over her.

The Fifteenth Chapter.

How Apollonius comming to Tharsus, and not finding his daughter, lamented her supposed death; and taking shippe againe, was driuen by a tempest to Machilenta where Tharsia was.

RETURNE we now againe vnto Prince Apollonius, who whiles these things were doing at Machilenta when the foureteenth yeere was expired, arriued at Tharsus, and came into the citie vnto the house of Stranguilio and Dionisiades, with whome he had left his yong daughter Tharsia. Whome when Stranguilio beheld and knew, he ranne hastily vnto his wife Dionisiades and saide: Thou reportedst that Prince Apollonius was dead, and loe now where he is come to require his daughter. What shall wee now doe, or say vnto him? Then cried she out alas wretched husband and wife that we are! let vs quickely put on our mourning attire, and shead foorth teares, and he wil beleeue us that his daughter died a naturall death. And when they had apparelled themselues, they came foorth vnto Apollonius, who seeing them in mourning attire, said vnto them: My trusty friends, Stranguilio and Dionisiades, why weep ye thus at my comming? & tell me, I pray you (which I rather beleeue) whether these teares be not rather mine than yours. Not so (my lord Apollonius) answered the wicked woman. And I woulde to God some other body, and not mine husband or I, were inforced to tel you these heauie tidings, that your deare daughter Tharsia is dead. When Apollonius heard that word, hee was suddenly cut to the heart, and his flesh trembled, and he coulde scarce stand on his legges, and long time hee stoode amazed with his eies intentiuely fixed on the ground, but at length recouering himselfe and taking fresh breath, he cast vp his eyes vpon her, and saide: O woman, if my daughter be dead, as thou sayest she is, is the money also and apparell perished with her? She answered, some is, and some yet remaineth. And as for your daughter, my Lorde, we were alwaies in good hope, that when you came, you should haue found her aliue and merry. But to the intent that you may the better beleeue vs concerning her death, we haue a sufficient witnes. For our citizens being mindfull of your benefites bestowed vpon them, haue erected vnto her a monument of brasse by yours, which you may go see if you please. And when she had so saide, she brought foorth such money, iewels and apparell which it pleased her to say were remaining of Tharsias store. And Apollonius belieeuing indeede that she was dead, said vnto his servants: take vp this stuffe and beare it away vnto the ships, and I will goe walke vnto my daughters monument: and when he came there, hee read the superscription in manner as is aboue written, and he fell suddenly, as it were into an outragious affection and cursed his owne eies, saying: O most cruell eies, why can you not yeelde foorth sufficient teares, and woorthily bewaile the death of my deare daughter? and with that word, with griefe and extreme sorrowe he fell into a sowne, from which so soone as euer he was once reuiued, immediatelie hee went vnto the shippes vnto his seruauntes, vnto whome hee saide, cast mee, I beseech you, vnto the very bottome of the sea, for I haue no ioy of my life, and my desire is to yeelde vp my Ghost in the water. But his seruants vsed great perswasions with him to assuage his sorrowe, wherein presently they some deale preauiled, as they might in so wofull a case; and partly the time, which is a curer of all cares, continually mittigated some part of the griefe, and hee espying the winde to serue well for their departure, hoised vp saile, and bid the land adue. They had not thus sailed long in their course, but the winde came about to a contrary quarter, and blew so stifly that it troubled both sea and shippes. The raine fell fiercely ouer head, the sea wrought wonderously vnder the ships, and to be short, the tempest was terrible for the time. It was then thought best in that extremitie to strike saile, and let the helme go, and to suffer the shippe to driue with the tide, whither it shoulde please God to direct it. But as ioy euermore followeth heauinesse, so was this sharpe storme occasion of a sweet meeting of the father with the daughter, as in processe heereafter it shall appeare. For while Apollonius shippe runneth thus at random, it striketh vpon the shoare of the Citie Machilenta, where at that present his daughter Tharsia remained.

Nowe it fortuned that this verie day of their arriuall was the birth day of Prince Apollonius, and when as the Marriners sawe themselues so happily come to the land, both for the gladnesse of the one, and ioy of the other, the master of the shippe, and all the whole company gaue a great shout.

When Apollonius, who lay solitarily vnder the hatches, heard such a sodaine voice of mirth, hee called vnto the master, and demaunded what it meant. The master aunswered, we reioyce, and be you glad also with us my lorde, for this day we doe solemnize the feast of your birth. Then Apollonius sighed, and said himselfe: All keepe hollyday saue I onely, and let it suffice vnto my servants that I onely remaine in sorrowe and heauinesse: Howbeit, I giue vnto them ten peeces of goold, to buy what they will to keepe holyday withall. But whosoeuer shall call me vnto the feast, or goe about to prouoke me vnto mirth, I commaund that his thighes shall be broken. So the cater tooke the money, and went aland, and prouided necessaries, and returned againe vnto the ship.

The Sixteenth Chapter.

How Athanagoras prince of Machilenta seeing the beautie of Apollonius ship, went aboord of it, and did the best he could to comfort him.

As fortune thereto serued, and delight to take the fresh aire moued Athanagoras prince of ye Citie, to walk toward the sea side, he sawe Apollonius ships riding at anker: at the view wherof he tooke great pleasure, especially at ye Admirall which was a great ship and a beautiful, wherin Apollonius himself was carried, the like wherof haply he had not seene often before. This was that Anthagoras that loued Tharsia so tenderly, and he haled vnto the Marriners, and asked of whence that faire ship was? The Marriners answered, that she came now from Tharsus. Truly, said Athanagoras, it is a faire shippe, and well ap-

pointed, and of all that I haue seene, I like best of
her. Now when the Marriners heard their shippe so
highly commended, they desired him to come aboord,
whereunto he willingly graunted. And when he
was come abord, he sate downe with them at meat,
and he drue his purse, and laid downe ten peeces of
gold vpon the table, saying you shall not say that you
haue bidden an vnthankfull person, take this small
summe of money at my handes for a reward, and they
thanked him. But when he was set downe, and beheld al that sate at the boord, he demaunded who was
owner of the ship, and where he was? The maister
answered, our owner is sicke, and weake with sorrowe
and taking thought, and needes will die. He lost his
wife vppon the Sea, and his daughter in a strange
land. Athanagoras said vnto one of the servants
called Ardalius: I will giue thee two peeces of gold,
to go down and tell thy master that the prince of this
Citie desireth him to come vp out of darknesse into
light. The seruaunt answered, I cannot buy new
thighes for thy golde, and therefore get some man els
to go on the errand, for he hath said that whosoeuer
troubleth him, his thighes shall be broken. That law
hath he made ouer you, said Athanagoras, and not
ouer mee, and therefore I will go downe vnto him:
but first tell me, I pray you, what you call his name?
They answered, Apollonius. And when he heard that
name, hee remembred in his minde that hee heard
Tharsia call her father so, and he went downe vnto
him where he lay, whom when hee beheld, hauing a
long beard, and rough fligged haire, and long nailes
on his fingers, he was somewhat astonied, and called
vpon him with a soft voice, saying: Apollonius!
When Apollonius heard himselfe named, thinking
it had been some of his men that had called him,
arose vp sodainly with a fierce countenance, and seeing a stranger looking verie comely and honourably

attired, he held his peace. Then spake Athanagoras: Sir, I thinke you doe maruell, that I being a stranger, am so bold as to come to trouble you. You shall vnderstand that I am prince of this citie, and my name is Athanagoras. I walked by chance vnto the Sea side, where beholding thy ships, especially commending this wherin thou art, for beautie and strength: I was by thy men desired to come aboord which I did, and haue eaten with them. Then inquired I for the owner, and they told me thy name, and that thou remainest in great sorrow, and for that cause I am come downe vnto thee to bring thee, if I may, out of darknesse into light, hoping that after this heauinesse God shal restore thee vnto gladnesse. Apollonius lifted vp his eies, saying: I thanke thee, my Lord, whosoeuer thou art, and I beseech thee not to trouble me longer, for I am not worthy to eate meat or make good cheare, & I will liue no longer. Athanagoras much mused at this answere, and wondred at the wilfulnesse of the man, and came vp vppon the decke and saide vnto the seruauntes: I cannot perswade your lord to come vp out of that darke place into the light: what way therefore, were I best to deuise to bring him from his purpose, and to preserue him from an obstinate death? For it were great pitie that a notable gentleman should so consume away in hucker mucker, and die by a dishonourable death.

The Seventeenth Chapter.

How Athanagoras sent for Tharsia to make her father Apollonius merry: and how after long circumstance they came into knowledge one of another.

AND as he was deuising with himselfe, it came into his mind to send for the maidē Tharsia, for which purpose he called vnto him one of his men, and saide vnto him. Go vnto the baud, desire him to send Tharsia hither vnto me, for she hath wisdom, & can moue pleasant talke, and perhaps she may perswade him not to die thus wilfully. The messenger went speedily, & returned immediatly, bringing the maiden Tharsia with him vnto the ship. Whom when Athanagoras beheld, come hither vnto me Tharsia, quoth he, and shew now the vttermost of thy cunning and knowledge, in comforting the owner of the ship, which lieth in darknes and will receiue no comfort, nor come abroad into the light, for the great sorrow that he taketh for his wife and his daughter. Goe vnto him, good Tharsia, and proue if thou canst perswade him to come into the light: for it may be that God hath appointed by thy meanes, to bring him from sorrowe into gladnesse. Which thing if thou canst bring to passe, as I am a gentleman, I will giue thee thirtie sestercies of gold, and as many of siluer, and I will redeeme thee from the bawd for thirtie dayes. When Tharsia heard this, she went boldly downe into the cabin vnto him, and with a milde voice saluted him, saying: God saue you sir whosoeuer you be, and be of good comfort, for an innocent virgin, whose life has been distressed by shipwracke, and her chastitie by dishonestie, and yet hath both preserued, saluteth thee. Then began she to record in verses, and therewithall to sing so sweetly, that Apollonius, notwithstanding his great sorrow, wondred at her. And these were the verses which she soong so pleasantly vnto the instrument:

>   *Amongst the harlots foule I walke,*
>   *yet harlot none am I:*
>   *The Rose amongst the Thorns grows,*
>   *and is not hurt thereby.*
>   *The thiefe that stole me, sure I thinke,*
>   *is slaine before this time,*

A bawd me bought, yet am I not
 defilde by fleshly crime.
Were nothing pleasanter to me,
 than parents mine to know:
I am the issue of a king,
 my bloud from kings doth flow.
I hope that God will mend my state,
 and send a better day.
Leaue off your teares, plucke vp your heart,
 and banish care away.
Shew gladnesse in your countenance,
 cast vp your cheerfull eyes:
That God remaines that once of nought
 created earth and skies.
He will not let in care and thought
 you still to liue, and all for nought.

When Apollonius heard her sing these verses, lifting vp his eyes, and sighing he said: Alas poore wretch as I am, how long shall I striue with life, and abide this greeuous conflict? Good maiden, I giue hearty thanks both to your wisedome and nobilitie: requiting you with this one thing, that whensoeuer, if euer such occasion doe chance, I shall haue desire to be merrie I will then thinke on you, or if euer I be restored vnto my kingdome. And perhaps, as you say, you are descended of the race of kings, and indeed you doe well represent the nobilitie of your parentage. But nowe I pray you receiue this reward at my handes, an hundred peeces of golde, and depart from me and trouble me no longer, for my present griefe is renued by your lamentable recitall, and I consume with continuall sorrowe. When the maid had receiued the reward, shee was about to depart. Then spake Athanagoras, whither goest thou Tharsia, quoth hee? hast thou taken paine without profite, and canst thou not worke a deed of charitie, and relieue

the man that wil consume his life with mourning?
Tharsia answered: I haue done all that I may, and
he hath giuen me an hundred peeces of gold, and
desired me to depart. I wil giue thee two hundred,
said Athanagoras, and goe downe vnto him againe,
and giue him his money, and say vnto him, I seeke
thy health and not thy money. Then went Tharsia
downe againe, and set her selfe downe by him, and
saide vnto him: Sir, if you bee determined to continue alwaies in this heauinesse, giue mee leaue, I
pray you, to reason a little with you. And I meane
to propose certaine parables vnto you, which if you
can resolue, I will then depart, and restore your
money. But Apollonius, not willing to receiue the
money againe, but thankefully to accept whatsoeuer
shee should vtter, without discouraging of her: albeit
in my troubles quoth he, I haue none other felicitie
but to weepe and lament, yet because I will not want the
ornamentes of your wisedome, demaund of me whatsoeuer shall be your pleasure, and while I am aunswer-
ing you, pardon me I pray you, if sometime I giue
libertie vnto my teares, and shall not be able to
speake for sobbing. Sir, I will beare with you somewhat in that respect said Tharsia, and nowe if it
please you I will begin:

> *A certaine house on earth there is,*
>   *that roomths hath large and wide:*
> *The house makes noise, the guests make none,*
>   *that therein doth abide;*
> *But house and guest continually,*
>   *togither forth doe slide.*

Now if indeed you be a Prince, as your men say
you are, it behooueth you to be wiser than a simple
maiden, and to resolue my probleme. Apollonius
answered: Maiden, to the intent you may not thinke

you were tolde a lie, hearken now to the resolution.

The house on the earth is the Sea or euery great water, the fish is the dumbe guest, which followeth the water whither soeuer it runne. Sir, you haue answered truely said Tharsia; and now I assaile you the second time:

> *In length forth long I runne,*
> *faire daughter of the wood,*
> *Accompanied with many a one,*
> *of foote and force as good,*
> *Through many waies I walke,*
> *but steps appeare none where I stood.*

Apollonius answered: If I might be so bold, and opportunitie serued thereto, I could declare vnto you many things that you doe not knowe, faire maiden, but not interrupting your questions whereunto I haue to answere, wherein I much wonder at your yoong yeares, so plentifully fraught with excellent knowledge. But to come to the purpose: The daughter of the wood, is the tree whereof is made the long ship, which is accompanied with many companions, and walketh vppon the seas many wayes leauing no print, or footsteppes behinde. You have guessed right said Tharsia, and therefore nowe I propose my third parable:

> *There is an house through which the fire*
> *doth passe, and doth no harme:*
> *Therein is heat, which none may mooue;*
> *from thence, it is so warme.*
> *A naked house, and in that house*
> *guests naked doe desire*
> *To dwell, from whence if boords you draw,*
> *then fall you in the fire.*

Apollonius answered: Maiden, this that you meane, were a meet place for men that liue in delight and pleasure. And the time hath been, when I haue also delighted in the bath and hoat-house, where the heate entreth through the creuises of the boordes and chinkes of the stones, and where by reason of sweating, it behooueth a man to be naked. When he had done speaking, Tharsia wondering at his wisedome, and the rather lamenting his discomfortablenesse, threw her selfe vppon him, and with clasped armes embraced him, saying, O good gentleman, hearken vnto the voice of her that beseecheth thee, and haue respect to the suite of a virgin, that thinking it a far vnworthy thing that so wise a man should languish in griefe, and die with sorrow. But if God of his goodnesse would restore vnto thee thy wife safe, whom thou so much lamentest: Or if thou shouldst find thy daughter in good case, whom thou supposest to be dead, then wouldest thou desire to liue for ioy. Then Apollonius fell in a rage, and forgetting all courtesie, his unbridled affection stirring him thereunto, rose vp sodainly, and stroke the maiden on the face with his foote, so that shee fell to the ground, and the bloud gushed plentifully out of her cheekes. And like it is that shee was in a swoone, for so soone as shee came to her selfe, shee beganne to weepe, saying, O immortall God, which madest heauen and earth, looke vppon my afflictions, and take compassion vppon mee. I was borne among the waues and troublesome tempests of the sea. My mother died in pangues and paines of childbed, and buriall was denied her vpon the earth, whom my father adorned with iewels, and laid twentie sestercies of gold at her head, and as much in siluer at her feete, and inclosed her in a chest, and committed her to the Sea. As for mee vnfortunate wretch, I was at Tharsus committed to Stranguilio and wicked Dionisiades his wife, whom my father put in trust with me, with mony & princely furniture, and their seruants were commāded to slay me. And when I desired time to pray, which was grāted me, there came pyrates in the meane while, and carried mee away, and brought me vnto this wofull city, where I was solde to a most cruell bawd, and with much adoe haue preserued my virginitie, and I see nothing ensuing but continuall sorrowe, whereof I feele both now and euery day some part, and shall doe euer more and more, vntil it please God to restore me vnto my father Apollonius. Apollonius gaue good eare vnto her words, and was strangely moued within himselfe, knowing that all these signes and tokens were most certaine that she was his daughter, and hee cried out with a mighty voice and saide: O mercifull God, which beholdest, heauen, earth and hell, and discouerest all the secretes therein, blessed bee thy most holy name for euer: and when he had said those words, he fell vpon his daughter Tharsias necke, and kissed her, and for extreame ioy wept bitterly, saying: O most sweete and onely daughter, the halfe part of my life, for the loue of thee I lust not nowe to die, for I haue found thee for whome I had desire to die onely. And therewithall he cryed out aloude, saying: Come hither my servants and frends, come ye al hither, and see now the end of all my sorrow, for I have found my deare daughter and onelie childe which I had lost. When the seruants heard the noise, they came hastily togither, and with them prince Athanagoras; & when they came downe vnder the hatches, they found Apollonius weeping for ioy, and leaning vpon his daughters shoulders, and he said unto them: Behold here my daughter, for whome I have mourned, beholde the one halfe of my life, and for whose sake I nowe desire to liue. And they al reioyced and wept with him for company, and thanked God for that happy day.

The Eighteenth Chapter.

Howe Apollonius leauing off mourning, came into the citie Machilenta, where he commaunded the bawd to be burned, and how Tharsia was married vnto prince Athanagoras.

THARSIA hearing her fathers words, fell down at his feet and kissed him, saying: O father, blessed be God that hath giuen me the grace to see you, & that I may die with you. But Apollonius lifted vp his heart, and cast away his mourning apparell, and put on other sweete and cleane raiment. And when Athanagoras and the seruants looked earnestly vpon him, and vpon his daughter, they wondred, saying, O my lord Apollonius, how like in countenance is your daughter Tharsia vnto you? that if you had no other argument, this were sufficient proofe to shewe that she is your childe. Apollonius thanked them, saying, that now he stoode not in any doubt thereof. Then Tharsia beganne to discourse vnto her father, howe she was sold vnto the bawd, and howe hee thrust her into the common brothell, and by what meanes she alwayes preserved her chastitie, and howe much she was bounden vnto good prince Athanagoras there present. Now Athanagoras was a widower, and a lusty yoong gentleman, and prince of the citie, as it is declared, who fearing lest Tharsia should be bestowed in marriage vpon some other man, and using the benefite of the time, cast him selfe downe at Apollonius feete, and besought him for her, saying, Most noble Prince, I beseech you for the liuing Gods sake, which hath thus myraculously restored the father vnto his daughter, bestowe not your daughter vpon any other in marriage then me onely. I am prince of this citie, and through my meanes she hath continued a virgin, and by my procurement she is nowe come vnto the knowledge of thee her father. Apollonius courteously embracing him answered: I thanke you most heartily, good Prince Athanagoras, for your friendly offer, which I may in no wise gainsay both in respect of your owne woorthinesse, and for the pleasure which you have shewed my daughter, and, therfore you haue my goodwill to be her husband. Then, turning his face towards Tharsia, how say you my deare daughter, said he, are you contented to bee wife vnto Athanagoras? Tharsia with blushing cheeks answered: Yea forsooth father; for since I came from Stranguilioes house, I neuer found rest nor pleasure sauing through his alonely curtesie. Nowe whether Athanagoras reioyced at this answere or not, I referre me to the iudgement of those, who, being passionate with the same affection, would be well pleased with a ioyntly grant of the like goodwil. When these matters were thus concluded, Apollonius mooued Athanagoras concerning reuenge to be executed vppon the bawd. Then Athanagoras took his leaue for a while of Apollonius and departeth vnto the citie, and, calling al the citizens togither to the market place, he spake thus vnto them: My friends and welbeloued citizens, vnderstand ye that Apollonius, prince of Tyrus and father vnto Tharsia, is arriued in our coast with a great fleete of ships, wherein hee hath brought a mighty army of men to destroy our city for ye bawds sake, who placed his daughter in a common brothell, to hire out the vse of her body for monie. Wherefore looke vnto your selues, and aduise your selues what you were best to doe, for it were pittie that the whole citie should perish for one wicked mans sake.

When as hee made an ende of this speech, the whole multitude trembled and was sore afraide, and foorthwith determined that they would all, as well

men, women and children, goe foorth to see prince
Apollonius, and to craue pardon of him. Not so,
said Athanagoras, but we will desire him to come
peaceablie into our citie, and what he list to commaund shall be fulfilled. The people liked well of
that counsel, and committed the matter vnto his discretion wholly to prouide for their safetie. Then
went he foorth vnto Apollonius, and desired him in
the peoples name to come into the citie, where he
should be most heartily welcome. Apollonius refused
not that friendly offer, but immediately prepared himselfe to goe with him, and caused his head to be
polled, and his beard to be trimmed, and his nailes
to be pared, and put on a princely robe vpon his
backe, and a crowne of golde vpon his head, and so
passed foorth togither vpon the way. And when they
were come into the citie, the citizens saluted Apollonius, and hee was placed in the highest seate whence
the prince was woont to giue iudgement, and his
daughter Tharsia by his side, and he spake vnto the
people in this manner following: Good people of the
city of Machilenta, you see the virgine Tharsia, whome
I her father haue found out this present day: hir hath
the most filthie bawd, as much as in him lay, constrained to dishonest her body, to her vtter destruction. From which his deuillish purpose no intreatie
could persuade him, no price could allure him. Wherfore my request vnto you (good people) is, that I may
haue due revenge on him for the iniury done vnto my
daughter. When the people heard his reasonable
demaund, they cried out with one accord, saying:
My lorde Apollonius, we iudge that he be burned
aliue, and his goods be given vnto the maiden Tharsia. The reuenge pleased Apollonius well, and foorthwith they apprehended the bawd, and bound him
hand and foot; and they made a great fire, and at
Apollonius commaundement cast him aliue into it,

and burnt him to ashes. Then called Tharsia for the villaine, and saide vnto him: Because by thy meanes, and all the citizens, I haue hitherto remained a virgine euen vntill my fathers comming, my will is that thou be free; and moreouer, I heere giue vnto thee two hundred peeces of gold for a reward. Secondly, she called for all the women that were in the bawdes brothell, and saide vnto them: good women, whose chances, perhaps, hath beene as greeuous vnto you as mine was vnto me, I set you al at liberty, and whereas heretofore you haue gained money by hiring foorth the vse of your bodies, receiue of mee here this rewarde, that you may liue hereafter more in the feare of God, and practise some more commendable way to sustaine necessitie, and therewithall she gaue to euerie one of them a rewarde, and so dismissed them. And when all these things were ended, Apollonius minding to depart, spake vnto the people saying: Noble Prince Athanagoras, and beloued citizens of Machilenta, I acknowledge my selfe much bounden to you, and I yeeld you hearty thanks for all your benefites bestowed vppon me and my daughter. And now in recompence thereof I giue vnto you fifty poundes weight of golde to be diuided amongest you, that when I am gone from you, you may be mindefull of me. The citizens thanked him, and bowed their heads in token of reuerence; and they agreed together, and they erected two statues of brasse one vnto him, another to his daughter in the market place of the citie with these superscriptions written in their bases: *Vnto Apollonius prince of Tyrus, the preseruer of our houses; and vnto his vertuous daughter Tharsia, a virgin, the mindefull citizens of Machilenta haue erected those monuments.* But Apollonius remembring the great curtesie of Athanagoras, and his promise made vnto him concerning Tharsia, appointed a short time for their mariage, against which there was great prouision as might be at so smal warning, the solemnities, riches, brauerie, cost, feasts, reuelles, intertainement, and all things else appertaining thereunto, and requisite for so great personages, I shall not here neede particularly to set downe, since euery man may iudge what belongeth to such a matter, and none can precisely describe this vnlesse he had beene there present. Of this thing sure I am, that this mariage brought great pleasure to the father, contentment to the parties, and ioy to all the people.

The Nineteenth Chapter.

How Apollonius meaning to saile into his owne countrey by Tharsus, was commaunded by an Angel in the night to go to Ephesus, and there to declare all his aduentures in the Church, with a loude voice.

The solemnities of the wedding being finished, Apollonius made haste to depart; and all things being in a readinesse, he tooke shipping with his sonne in lawe and his daughter, and weyghed anchor, and committed the sailes vnto the winde, and went their way, directing their course euermore towarde Tharsus, by which Apollonius purposed to passe unto his owne countrie Tyrus. And when they had sailed one whole day, and night was come, that Apollonius laide him downe to rest there appeared an Angell in his sleepe, commaunding him to leaue his course toward Tharsus, and to saile vnto Ephesus, and to go into the Temple of Diana, accompanied with his sonne in lawe and his daughter, and there with a loude voyce to declare all his aduentures, whatsoeuer had befallen him from his youth vnto that present day.

When Apollonius awoke in the morning, he won-

dered at the vision, and called for Athanagoras
his sonne in lawe and his daughter Tharsia, and
declared it to them in order as is before recited.
Thus saide he vnto them, what counsell do you giue
me in this matter? They answered, whatsoever it
pleaseth to you to doe that we shall like well of.
Then Apollonius called vnto him the Master of the
shippe, and commaunded him to winde saile and
coast towards Ephesus, which he did; and immediately the winde serued them so prosperously, that
in fewe days they safely arriued there. Apollonius
and his companie foorthwith forsooke their shippes,
and came aland, and according to the commaundement of the Angell, tooke his iourney to the Temple
of Diana, whereas it is before mentioned, his long
lamented wife lady Lucina, remained in vertuous life
and holy contemplation among the religious Nunnes.
And when he was come thither, he besought one of
the Nunnes that had the keeping of the Temple that
he might haue licence to go in, and she willingly
granted his request, and opened the doore vnto him.
By this time report was blowen abroad, that a certaine strange Prince was lately landed with his sonne
in lawe and his daughter in very costly and rich ornaments, and gone into the Temple: and the ladie
Lucina as desirous as the rest to see the strangers,
decked her head with rich attire, and put on a purple
robe, and, with conuenient retinue attending vpon her,
came into the Temple.

Now Lucina was passing beautifull, and for the
great loue which she bare vnto chastitie all men reue-
renced her, and there was no virgin in al the number
in like estimation vnto her. Whom when Apollonius
beheld, although he knew not what she was, yet such
was the exceeding brightnes and maiestie of her
countenance, that he fel down at her feet, with his
sonne in law likewise and his daughter, for hee

thought shee glittered like a diademe, and exceeded
the brightest starres in beautie. But Lucina curteously lifted them vp from the ground, and bid them
welcome, and afterward went to bestow the plate and
ornaments of the temple in decent order, which
thing was part of the Nunnes duety. Then Apollonius setled himselfe to doe as the Angell had commaunded him in the vision, and thus he beganne to
say: I being borne Prince of Tyrus, was called Apollonius, and when in youth I had attained vnto all
kinde of knowledge, I resolued the cruel king Antiochus parable, to the intent to have married with his
daughter, whome he most shamefully defiled, and
kept her from all men to serue his owne filthie lust,
and sought meanes to slay me. Then I fled away,
and lost all my goodes in the sea, hardly escaping my
selfe with life, and in my greatest extremitie I was
courteously intertained by Altistrates king of Pentapolis; and so highly receiued into fauor, that he
left no kindes of fauor on me vntried, insomuch that
hee bestowed vpon mee his faire daughter and only
childe Lucina to be my wife. But when Antiochus
and his daughter by the iust iudgement of God, were
stroken dead by lightning from heauen, I carried my
wife with me to receiue my kingdome, and she was
deliuered of this my daughter and hers vpon the sea,
and died in the trauell, whome I enclosed in a chest,
and threwe into the sea, laying twenty sestercies of
golde at her head, and as much in siluer at her feete,
to the intent that they that should find her might
haue wherewithall to bury her honorably, leauing also
a superscription that they might perceiue with what
griefe of her friends she died, and of what princelie
parentage shee descended. Afterwardes I arriued at
the citie of Tharsus, where I put in trust my yoong
daughter to be brought vp vnto certain wicked persons, and from thence I departed vnto the higher

partes of Egypt. But when from that time fourteene yeeres were expired, and I returned thither to fetch my daughter, they told me that shee was dead, which I beleeving to be true, put on mourning attire, and desired nothing so much as to die, and while I was in that extremitie of sorrowe, and determined to haue sayled vnto Tyrus, while I was on my way vpon the sea the winde turned, and there arose a tempest, and draue me vnto the citie Machilenta, where my daughter was restored vnto me. Then went I with my sonne in law, and my daughter once againe, to haue sailed vnto Tyrus by Tharsus; and as I was now in the iourney, I was admonished in my sleepe by an Angell to turne my course vnto Ephesus, and there in the temple to declare aloud al my aduentures that had befallen me since my youth vnto this present day, which hath hither to guided me in all my troubles, will nowe send an happy end vnto all mine afflictions.

The Twentieth Chapter.

How Apollonius came to the knowledge of his wife the ladie Lucina, and how they reioyced at the meeting of ech other.

The ladie Lucina was not so busie in executing her office in the Church, but that she gaue also attentiue eare vnto her lord Apollonius talke, whom at first she knew not. But when shee heard the long discourse, whereby she knewe by all signes that hee was her husband, and shee was his wife, her heart burned within her, and she could scarce temper her affections vntil hee had done talking. Yet measuring her loue with modestie, as nowe of long time hauing learned the true trade of pacience, shee gaue him libertie to make an end: which done, shee ran hastily vnto him and embraced him hard in her armes, and woulde haue kissed him. Which thing, when Apollonius sawe, hee was mooued with disdaine, and thrust her from him, as misliking such lightnesse in her whose modestie and good grace hee had so lately before commended in his heart, and nothing at all suspecting that she had been his wife. Then shee pouring foorth teares aboundantly, O my lord Apollonius, said she, the one halfe of my life, why deal you thus vngently with me? I am your wife, daughter vnto Altistrates, king of Pentapolis, and my name is Lucina. And you are Apollonius, prince of Tyrus, my lord and deare husband, and you are my schoolemaister, which taught mee musicke: and moreouer you are the sea-wrecked man whom I especially loued aboue many, not for concupiscence sake, but for desire of wisedome. When Apollonius heard those words, he was sodainly astonied; and as the strangenes of the chance appalled him much: so the great ioy reuiued his spirites againe, and he cast his eies earnestly vppon her, and immediatly called her to remembrance, and knew perfitly that it was shee indeede, and he went vnto her, and fell vppon her necke, and for exceeding ioy brast out into teares, and then lifting vp his handes and eyes to heauen, hee saide: Blessed be the moste mightie God of heauen, which sitteth aboue and beholdeth the state of men on earth, and dealeth with them according to his great mercie: who nowe also of his vnspeakeable goodnesse, hath restored vnto mee my wife and my daughter. Then did hee most louingly embrace and kisse his ladie, whom he supposed long before to be dead: and shee likewise requited him with the like fruites of good will and courtesie, whom she surely thought she should neuer haue seene againe. And when they had continued a good space in intertaining the one another: O my moste deare lord Apollonius, saide the lady Lucina, where is my childe, whereof I was deliuered? Apollonius aunswered: My best beloued ladie, it was a daughter, and she was named Tharsia, and this is she, and therewithal he shewed her Tharsia. Then kissed and embraced she her daughter, and likewise her sonne in law Athanagoras, and they greatly reioyced one in another.

And when report heereof was spread abroad, there was great ioy throughout all the Citie of Ephesus, and the report has blowen about in euerie place how prince Apollonius had found out his ladie and wife among the Nunnes in the Temple. Then Lucina discoursed vnto her lord and husband Apollonius, of all the strange accidents that happened vnto her after his casting her forth into the Sea. Namely, howe her chest was cast on land at the coast of Ephesus, and taken vp by a Phisition; and how she was reuiued and by him adopted, and for preseruation of her honestie, placed among the Nunnes in the Temple of Diana, where hee there found her, accordingly as it appeareth before in the historie, wherefore they blessed the name of God, and yeelded most heartie thankes vnto him, that hee had preserued them hitherto, and graunted them so ioyfull a meeting.

The Twenty-First Chapter.

How Apollonius departed from Ephesus, and sailed himselfe, his wife, his sonne, and daughter vnto Antiochia, and then to Tyrus, and from thence to Tharsus, where he revenged himselfe vpon Stranguilio, and Dionisiades.

APOLLONIUS and Lucina his wife, and the residue of their traine, hauing rested themselues and made merrie

sufficient time at Ephesus, when the winde serued,
tooke leaue of their friendes and went aboord of their
ships, and lanched from the shore and departed vnto
Antiochia; where according as Calamitus the maister
of the ship of Tyrus had tolde him before, the kingdome was reserued for him since the death of Antiochus. But when the citizens heard that he was
arriued, they were all exceeding glad, and put on their
brauest apparell, and garlandes of bayes vpon their
heads, and went forth in procession to meet him, and
brought him in triumph into the Citie, and crowned
him king with all ioy and gladnesse. And when all
the solemnities of the coronation, the feastes, triumphes, largesses, and pardons were finished, hee
abode with them certaine daies to dispose some matters in order that required redresse, and to establish
certaine lawes for the due administration of iustice.
Which being all accomplished according to his desire,
he tooke his leaue of the Citizens, and with his wife,
sonne, and daughter, departed to the sea, and sayled
vnto Tyrus his owne natiue country, where he was
ioyfully received of his subiects, and found his kingdome gouerned in good order. There placed he for
his lieuetenant his sonne in lawe Athanagoras, which
had married his daughter Tharsia, to rule the countrey
in his absence, and when he had aboden a conuenient
time amongst them to make merrie, and to prouide
necessaries for his farther affaires, he leuied in shorter
space a mightie armie of the best approoued soul-
diours, with sufficient store of money and munition,
and taking with him moreouer his lady, and his daughter Tharsia, tooke shipping in the hauen, and had so
prosperous winde, that in few dayes they landed in
the coast of Tharsus. And when they were come all
ashoare, they marched forward in battell aray, and
came into the Citie to the great terrour of al the inhabitants. When he was come into the market place,

he commaunded that Stranguilio and Dionisiades should be brought before him, which being done, he thus spake vnto the people. Ye Citizens of Tharsus, I am come hither in armes as you see, not moued by my will, but constrained by iniurie. Wherfore tell me, was I euer vnthankfull vnto your Citie in generall, or vnto any of you al in particular? They all answered with one voice no my lord, and therfore wee are ready all to spend our liues in thy quarrell: and as thou knowest well wee haue erected heere, in perpetuall memorie of thee, a statue of brasse, because thou preseruedst vs from death, and our citie from vtter destruction. Then said Apollonius, vnderstand then this much my friends, that when I departed last from this citie, I committed my daughter in trust vnto Stranguilio and his wife Dionisiades; and when I came to require her they would not deliuer her vnto me, nor tell me the trueth what is become of her. Immediatly they were both called forth to answere vnto these matters before Apollonius, where falling downe on their knees before him, Dionisiades answered in this manner: My lord, I beseech you stand favourable vnto my poore husband and mee, and not to beleeue any other thing concerning your daughter, then that shee is departed this life. And as for hir graue, you haue seene it, and also the monument of brasse erected by the whole citie in the memoriall of her, and moreouer you haue read the superscription. Then Apollonius commaunded his daughter to stand foorth in the presence of them all, and shee saide vnto Dionisiades: beholde thou wicked woman, dead Tharsia is come to greete thee, who as thou diddest well hope, shoulde neuer haue been forth comming to haue bewrayed thy wickednesse. But when the miserable woman beheld Tharsia, her heart quaked for feare, and shee fell to the ground in a swoond: and when shee recouered againe, shee cried out vpon the just iudgment of God,

and cursed the time that shee was borne. And all
the people ranne thronging about Tharsia, and
wondered at her, thinking howe greatly they had been
of long time abused by Stranguilio, and Dionisiades;
and they reioyced much in her safetie, and all knewe
by her countenance that it was shee, and none other.
O now, who were able to declare the bitter griefe and
intolerable care which eftsoones assaied the wearisome
consciences of these twaine, the husband and the
wife when they sawe her liuing and in good liking
before their faces, whose death they had so traiterously
conspired. Euen hell it selfe is not comparable vnto
so heauie a burden, the vnspeakable weight whereof
all men ought to feare, and none can sufficiently
describe vnlesse hee haue been semblably plunged
in the like gulfe of horrible desperation. Then
Tharsia called for Theophilus Stranguilios villaine,
and when he was come into her presence, shee saide
vnto him: Theophilus, aunswere mee aloud that all
the people may heare, who sent thee forth to slay me?
Hee aunswered, Dionisiades my Mistresse. What
mooued her thereunto saide Tharsia? None other
thing, I suppose, saide the villaine, but to enioy the
money and ornamentes, and also because thy beautie
and comelinesse were commended aboue Philomacias
her daughters. Nowe when the people heard this,
they ranne vppon Stranguilio, and Dionisiades, and
tooke them violently, and bound them, and drew
them out of the citie, and stoned them to death; and
would likewise have slaine Theophilus the villaine,
for that at his mistress commandement he would haue
murdered the innocent maiden. But Tharsia intreated
for him, saying, Not so my deare friends. I pray you
let me obtaine pardone for him at your handes; for
vnlesse he had giuen me respite to say my praiers, I
had not been heere now to haue spoken for him:
and when she had said so, the furious multitude was

appeased. And Apollonius gaue many exceeding rich giftes vnto the citie, and repared it strongly in many places where it was decaied, and abode there with them the space of three monthes in feasting and making merry before he departed.

The Twenty-Second Chapter.

How Apollonius sailed from Tharsus to visite his father-in-law Altistrates king of Pentapolis, who died not long after Apollonius comming thither.

THE terme of three monethes, that Apollonius purposed for his delight to remaine at Tharsus, was almost expired, and he cōmanded all things to be prepared for the iourney; and when the day was come, hee made generall proclamation vppon paine of death euery man to ship. And when the whole army was imbarked, he took ship himselfe with his wife and his daughter, being honourably accompanied by the citizens vnto the water side; and after due courtesie on both sides done and receiued, he hoysed sayle and departed towardes Pentapolis king Altistrates Citie. And when they had sailed with prosperous winde ten dayes vppon the Sea, they discouered a farre off the Steeples and Towres of Pentapolis, and the Souldiers reioyced and gaue a shout for gladnesse that they were so neere to their wished land. Then they cast about and cut towards the hauen, and cast anker, and landed all safe, and Apollonius with his wife and daughter after hee had taken order for the companie, rode vnto the court vnto king Altistrates, whom they found in good health, and merry. And when Altistrates saw his sonne-in-lawe, his daughter and his neece Tharsia, hee bid them welcome, and reioyced exceedingly, and sent for the Nobles of his land to keepe them companie, and gaue them the best entertainement that hee could deuise, and they soiourned with him an whole yeare in pleasure and pastime, whereof the king tooke as great comfort as was possible for a man to doe in any worldly felicitie. But as there was neuer yet any thing certaine or permanent in this mortall life, but alwaies we be requited with sowre sauce to our sweete meate, and when wee thinke ourselues surest in the top of ioy, then tilt wee downe soonest into the bottome of sorrow, so fared it now vnto those personages in the midst of their jollitie. For the good old king Altistrates fell sodainly sick which much appalled them all, and grew euerie day weaker than other. Then were the Phisitions sent for in haste, who left nothing vntried that appertained vnto Art and experience to doe; and aboue all Apollonius and Lucina his wife plaied the parts of duetifull children, in tending their aged and weake father with all care and diligence possible. But alas olde age which of it selfe is an vncurable sickenesse, and had beene growing nowe well nigh an hundred yeares lacking seuen vpon him, accompanied with the intollerable paine of the gowt, and the stone of the bladder, had consumed naturall moisture, so that his force gaue ouer to the disease, and shortely after changed this transitorie life for a better. When report was spread abroad of the kings death, there was great sorrowe and lamentation made in all places, neither was there any that tooke not grieuously the losse of so good a Prince. But to describe the inward affliction of Apollonius, and the teares of Lucina and Tharsia her daughter, woulde make any heart of flint to bleede, considering the tender affections of women aboue men, and howe prone they bee that way, yea, sometime (God knowes) in smaller cases than at the death of husband, father, or mother. But as al things haue their time, so haue sorrowe and teares also, which are best dried vp with the towell of continuaunce; which gaue nowe iust occasion vnto Apollonius to cast off drowsie sorrowe, and to prouide for the funeralles of his father in lawe, which he accomplished with so seasonable expedition, and in so honourable a sort, as was seemely for so mighty a king, and so vertuous a prince, whome hee buried among the auntient race of kings his auncestours in the Temple within the citie of Pentapolis. Which beeing all finished, as it is also a worke of charitie to fulfill the will of the dead, he applied himselfe to execute his fathers testament, wherin he had giuen halfe his kingdome vnto Apollonius, and the other halfe to Tharsia his neece, to haue and to holde to them and to their heires for euer.

The Twenty-Third Chapter.

How Apollonius rewarded the fisherman that releeued him after he had suffered shipwracke: howe hee dealt also with olde Calamitus, and likewise with the Pyrates that stole away Tharsia.

By this time, when all cares were banished, and Apollonius inioyed his kingdome in quiet possession, he gaue himselfe sometimes to delight as other Princes are wont to do. And it fortuned that on a day when he had dined, he walked foorth for recreation vnto the sea side, with his wife and a fewe seruants. And when hee came there, he sawe a small fisher boat fleeting vnder saile, which hee thought by all signes he should knowe well, for hee supposed it to be the fishermans boat which succoured him, when he had suffered shipwracke in sailing from Tharsus towardes Pentapolis.

Wherefore hee commaunded some of his seruantes, to take another shippe which rode at anchor there on the shore, to go after and take him, and to bring the fisherman vnto him vnto the Coort. When the poore man saw himselfe boorded of so many and so gay a multitude, hee feared they had beene pyrates, and that they woulde haue slaine him; and he fell downe on his knees, and besought them to haue compassion vpon him: he was but a poore fisherman, and had not that which they sought for: it were others that were more fit for their purpose to meete withall, such as ventured further in greater vessells, carrying foorth great summes of money, and bringing home plenty of costly merchandize: As for him, they should not only find miserable pouertie in ransacking his boat, but if they were also determined to take away his life from him, they should likewise with the same stroke bereaue the liues of his poore wife, and many small Children, which were maintained by his hand onely. These or the like words vttered then the poore fisherman. But they smiling in their conceits, and mindefull of their Princes commaundement, bade him not feare that they would robbe him, but saide that he must goe with them, and brought him away vnto the court. And when he was come into the kings presence, Apollonius knewe him well, and saide vnto the Queene and the Nobles that were about him: Beholde, this is the man that receiued me into his house, and succoured mee when I suffered shipwracke, and shewed me the way into the Citie, by which meanes I came acquainted with good king Altistrates. And he rose out of his seate, and embraced him and said: I am Apollonius Prince of Tyrus whome thou diddest succour, and therefore bee of good cheere, for thou shalt be rewarded. And the poore fisherman wept exceedingly for ioy. And Apollonius commaunded two hundred sestercies of gold to be giuen vnto him, and thirty seruants, and twenty handmaides, and fortie horses, and fiftie sutes of apparell, and a faire pallace to dwel in, and made him an earle, and vsed no man so familiarly as he did him all the dayes of his life. Nowe it was not long after that these things were done, but one called Calamitus the master of the ship of Tyrus, an olde man, who, as we haue before declared, shewed vnto Apollonius as hee was walking by the sea side with Lucina, that Antiochus and his daughter were dead, and the kingdome was reserued for him, came before Apollonius, and, falling downe on his knees : Remember me, my most gratious Lorde Apollonius saide hee, since the time I tolde your grace the good tidings of king Antiochus death.

Then king Apollonius tooke him vp by the hand, and caused him to sit downe by him, and talked familiarly with him, and gaue him great thankes, and made him a great lord in his countrey. Thus Apollonius busied himselfe, not onely in bestowing himselfe curteously at home, but he also prouided as well for the quiet gouernement of the state abroad, as it appeared by the diligence of his officers, who hauing lately taken certaine pyrates vpon the sea, brought them to Pentapolis, where Apollonius then remained, to haue iustice executed vpon them. When they were arriued, they were found guilty of the facte of which they were accused, and the next day being appointed for them to suffer, when they came vnto the gallowes, they confessed many robberies, and among store, how once at Tharsus they rescued a maide named Tharsia from a villaine that woulde haue slaine her, and brought her to Machilenta, where they solde her to him that offered most money, and hee which bought her (as they thought) was a bawd. When the citizens, who were none of them ignorant of the Ladie Tharsias aduentures, heard this, they stayed execution, and sent word vnto king Apollonius, saying: May it please your grace to vnderstand that we haue certaine pyrates at the gallowes ready to be executed, and it appeareth that they be those that stole away the lady Tharsia your daughter from Tharsus, and sold her to the bawd at Machilenta. Which when we perceiued, we thought it good to know your graces pleasure what shall be doone with them. Apollonius thanked them, and willed the pirats to be brought before him, & examined them diligently, and found that they were the same men indeede that had preserued Tharsias life. And he gaue great thankes vnto God and them, and imbraced them, & willingly pardoned them their lives.

And for that he knew that the sinister means which they hitherto had insued was caused most by constraint, for want of other trade or abilitie to liue by, he therefore made them all knights, and gaue them plenty of gold and siluer, and indowed them also with great possessions.

The Twenty-Fourth Chapter.

How Apollonius had a yoong sonne and heire by his wife Lucina, likewise of Apollonius age, and how he died: with some other accidents thereunto incident.

WHILE king Apollonius thus passed foorth his time in rewarding his friends which had doone him pleasure in his aduersitie, the part of a thankeful and good natured man, and also vnto his enemies in ministring iustice with mercie, which is the duetie of a vertuous prince, the queene Lucina in the meane season conceiued childe, and grewe euery daie bigger bellied then other. And when the time came that she attended for a good houre, she was deliuered of a faire sonne, whom some of the Ladies that were present saide hee was like Apollonius the father, other some, like king Altistrates the grandfather, and others iudged otherwise, according as is the custome of women to doe, when as (God knoweth) there is no more likenesse betweene them sauing that the childe hath the generall shape and proportion of a man, than is betweene Jacke fletcher and his bolt. Howbeit the boy was called Altistrates, after the grandfathers name, for whome there was much ioy and triumphing, that it had pleased God to send an heire male to gouerne the land, for whose life and preseruation the people daily prayed, that as he was like to succeede his grandfather in place and name, so hee might also be successour to his father and grandfather in honour and vertue, which as they are the true goods, so are they the chiefest inheritance of a king, and to be preferred before the greedie seeking for large dominion and riches, which are the foolish scales whereby Fortune intrappeth us.

But to returne againe to our story, great was the care and prouision for the diligent bringing vp of this yoong gentleman: who as he grew vp more and more euery day to the strength of lusty youth, so his father Apollonius decayed continually through the infirmity of weake old age: Who hauing passed his life with one Ladie the faire Lucina, by whome hee had two beautifull children, the ladie Tharsia and yoong Altistrates, he liued to the age of fourescore and foure yeers, and obtained the empire of three kingdomes, to wit, Tyrus, Antiochia and Pentapolis, whome with the helpe of his sonne in lawe Athanagoras he gouerned peaceably and prosperously. Moreouer, when hee had disposed the affaires of his realmes vnto such of his nobilitie as were in credite about him, although at all times he had recourse vnto his accustomed studies of humanitie, yet then especially he applied his vacant time to his booke, and hee wrote the whole storie and discourse of his owne life and aduentures at large, the which he caused to be written foorth in two large volumes, whereof he sent one to the Temple of Diana at Ephesus, and placed the other in his owne library. Of which historie this is but a small abstract, promising if ever the whole chance to come into my hands, to set it forth with all fidelitie, diligence, and expedition. But when the fatall time was come that Apollonius olde age could no longer be sustained by the benefite of nature, he fell into certaine cold and drie diseases, in which case the knowledge of his physitions could stand him in little steed, either by their cunning or experience. For there is no remedie against olde age, which if the noble skill of phisicke could euer haue found out, doubtlesse it would haue obtained the means to haue made the state of man immortall. Howbeit, God hath determined otherwise; and as he appointed all worldly things to haue an end, so Apollonius had his dying day, wherein in perfect sense, and readie memorie, hee departed this transitorie life in the sweete armes of his louing ladie Lucina, and in the midst of his friendes, Nobles, Allies, kinsfolke, and children, in great honour, and loue of all men. His kingdome of Tyrus he gaue by will vnto Athanagoras and his daughter Tharsia, and to their heires after them for euer: who liued long time togither, and had much issue, both boyes and girles. Unto the queene Ladie Lucina, he gaue the two kingdomes of Antiochia and Pentapolis, for terme of her life, to deale or dispose at her pleasure; and after her decease vnto his sonne lusty yoong Altistrates, and to his heires for euer: But Lucina, as she could not then be yoong, since Apollonius died so old, enioyed not long her widows estate, but pining away with sorrow, and wearing with age, forsooke this present world also, and followed her deare lord into the euerlasting kingdome that neuer shall have end, which so farre exceedeth the kingdome, which forthwith she left vnto her yoong sonne Altistrates to inherite, as heauenly ioyes surmount the earthly, and the bright sunne surpasseth the smallest starre.

FINIS.

3. *The Life of Pericles.*

[*From North's " Plutarch."*]

CÆSAR seeing in Rome one day certaine rich and wealthy strangers, hauing litle dogs and monkies in their armes, and that they made marvellous much of them, he asked thē if the women in their country had no children : wisely reprouing by this question, for that they bestowed their naturall loue and affection vpon brute beasts, which they should with all kindnesse and loue bestow vpon men. Nature in like case also, hauing planted in our minds a naturall desire to learne & vnderstand, we are in reason to reproue those that vainly abuse this good desire, fondly disposing it to learne things vaine and vnprofitable : and to cast behind them in the meane season things honest and necessarie to be learned. For as touching our outward sense, which with passion receiueth impression of the thing it seeth, peraduenture it will be necessarie to consider indifferently the thing seene, whether it will fall out beneficial or hurtfull vnto him : but so fareth it not with our vnderstanding, for euery man may at his pleasure turne and dispose that to the thing he taketh delight in, the reason whereof we must alwaies employ to the best part, and that not only to consider and looke vpon the thing, but also to reape the benefite & commodity of the thing we see. For like as the eye is most delighted with the lightest and freshest colors: euen so we must giue our minds vnto those sights, which by looking vpon them do draw profit and pleasure vnto vs. For such effects doth vertue bring: that either to heare or read them, they do print in our harts an earnest loue and desire to follow them. But this followeth not in all other things we esteeme, neither are we alwaies disposed to desire to do the things we see well done: but contrarily oftentimes, when we like the work, we mislike the workman, as commonly in making these perfumes and purple colours. For both the one and the other do please vs well: but yet we take perfumers and dyers to be men of a meane occupation. Therefore Antisthenes aunswered one very wisely, that told him Ismenias was an excellent player of the flute. But yet he is a naughty man, said he: otherwise he could not be so cūning at the flute as he is. Euen so did Philip king of Macedon say to his sonne Alexander the great on a time: that at a certaine feast had sung passing sweetly, and like a maister of musicke: Art thou not ashamed son to sing so well? It is enough for a King to bestow his leisure sometime to heare musitians sing, and he doth much honor to the Muses to heare the masters of the science otherwhile, when one of them singeth to excell another. But he that personally shall bestow his time, exercising any meane science: bringeth his paines he hath taken in matters vnprofitable, a witnesse against himselfe, to prooue that he hath bene negligent to learne things honest and profitable. And there was neuer any yong gentleman nobly borne, that seeing the image of Iupiter (which is in the city of Pisa) desired to become Phidias: nor

Polycletus, for seeing of Iuno in the citie of Argos:
nor that desired to be Anacreon, or Philemon, or
Archilocus, for that they tooke pleasure somtime to
reade their works. For it followeth not of necessity,
that though the worke delight, the workman must
needes be praised. So in like case, such things do
not profite those which behold them, because they do
not moue affection in the harts of the beholders to
follow them, neither do stir vp affection to resemble
them, and much lesse to conform our selues vnto
them. But vertue hath this singular propertie in all
her actions: that she maketh the man that knoweth
her to affect her so, that straight he liketh all her
doings, and desireth to follow those that are vertuous.
For, as for riches, we only desire to haue them in
possession: but of vertue, we chiefly loue the deeds.
Wherfore we are contented to haue goods from other
men: but good deeds we wold other should haue
from vs. For vertue is of this power, that she
allureth a mans mind presently to vse her, that wisely
considereth of her, and maketh him very desirous in
his heart to follow her: and doth not frame his manners that beholdeth her by any imitation, but by the
only vnderstanding and knowledge of vertuous deedes,
which suddenly bringeth vnto him a resolute desire to
do the like. And this is the reason, why me thought
I should continue still to write on the liues of noble
men, and why I made also this tenth booke: in the
which are contained the liues of Pericles and Fabius
Maximus, who maintained wars against Hannibal.
For they were both men very like together in many
sundry vertues, and specially in curtesie and iustice:
and for that they could patiently beare the follies of
their people, and companions that were in charge of
gouernement with them, they were maruellous profitable members for their country. But if we haue
sorted them well together, comparing the one with

the other: you shall easily iudge that reade our writings of their liues. Pericles was of the tribe of the Acamantides, of the town of Cholargvs, and one of the best and most ancient families of the city of Athens, both by his father and mother. For Xantippus his father (who ouercame in battell the lieutenants of the king of Persia in the iourny of Mygala) maried Agariste that came of Clisthenes, he who draue out of Athens Pysistratus ofspring, and valiantly ouerthrew their tyranny. Afterwardes he established lawes, and ordained a very graue forme of gouernment, to maintaine his citizens in peace and concord together. This Agarist dreamed one night that she was brought to bed of a Lion: and very shortly after she was deliuered of Pericles, who was so well proportioned in all the parts of his body, that nothing could be mended, sauing that his head was somewhat too long and out of proportion to the rest of his body. And this is the onely cause why all the statues and images of him almost are made with a helmet on his head: because the workmen as it should seeme (and so it is most likely) were willing to hide the blemish of his deformitie. But the Attican Poets did call him Schinocephalos, as much as to say as, headed like an onion. For those of Attica do somtime name that which is called in the vulgar toung Scilla, that is to say, an onion of Barbarie, Schinos. And Cratinus the Comicall Poet in his comedy he intituled Chirones, said:

> *Old Saturne he, and dreadfull dire **Debate**,*
>   *begotten haue, betweene them carnally,*
>   *this tyrant here, this heauy iolting pate,*
>   *in court of gods so tearmed worthely.*

And againe also in that which he nameth Nemesis, speaking of him, he saith:

> *Come Iupiter, come Iupiter,*
>   *Come iolt **head**, and come inkeeper.*

And Teleclides mocking him also, saith in a place:

Sometimes he stands amaz'd when he perceiues,
  that hard it were sufficiently to know,
  in what estate his gouernment he leaues.
And then will he be seldome seene below,
  such heauie heapes within his braines do grow.
But yet sometimes out of that monstrous pate,
  he thundreth fast, and threatneth euery state.

And Eupolis in a comedy which he intituled Demi: being very inquisitiue, & asking particularly of euery one of the Oratours (whom he fained were returned out of hell) when they named Pericles the last man vnto him, he said:

Truly thou hast now brought vnto us here that dwell,
  the chiefe of all the captaines that come from darksome
  hell.

And as for musicke, the most authors write, that Damon did teach him musicke, of whose name (as men say) they should pronounce the first sillable short. Howbeit Aristotle saith, that he was taught musicke by Pythoclides. Howsoeuer it was, it is certaine that this Damon was a man of deepe vnderstanding, and subtill in matters of gouernment: for, to hide from the people his sufficiencie therein, he gaue it out he was a musitian, and did resort vnto Pericles as a maister wrestler or fencer: but he taught him how he should deale in matters of state. Notwithstanding, in the end he could not so cunningly conuey this matter, but the people saw his harping and musicke, was only a vizer to his other practise: wherefore they did banish him Athens for fiue yeares, as a man that busily tooke vpon him to change the state of things, and that favoured tyrannie. And this gaue the Comicall Poets matter to play vpon him finely, among which Plato in a comedy of his, bringeth in a man that asketh him :

O Chiron, tell me first : art thou indeed the man,
which did instruct Pericles thus? make answer if
thou can.

He was sometime also scholer to the Philosopher Zenon, who was borne in the citie of Elea, and taught naturall Philosophie, as Parmenides did : but his profession was to thwart and contrarie all men, and to alledge a world of obiections in his disputation, which were so intricate, that his aduersary replying against him, knew not how to answer him, nor to conclude his argument. The which Timon Phliasius witnesseth in these words :

Zenon was subtill sure, and very eloquent,
and craftily could wind a man by way of argument,
if so he were disposed, his cunning to descrie,
or shew the sharpnesse of his wit to practise pollicie.

But Anaxagoras Clazomenian was he that was most familiar and conuersant with him, and did put in him the maiesty and grauity he shewed in all his sayings, and doings, who did farre excell the common course of ordinarie Orators that pleaded before the people : and to be short, he it was that did fashion his manners, altogether to carie that graue countenance which he did. For they called Anaxagoras in his time, Nus, as much to say ; as vnderstanding. Either because they had his singular wit and capacitie in such great admiration, being growne to search out the cause of naturall things : or that he was the first man, who did ascribe the disposition and gouernement of this world, not vnto fortune or fatall necessitie, but vnto a pure, simple, and vnderstanding mind, which doth separate at the first mouing cause, the substance of such like parts as are medled and compounded of diuerse substances, in all other bodies through the world. Pericles made maruellous much of Anaxagoras, who had fully instructed him in the knowledge of naturall things, and of those specially that worke aboue in the ayre and firmament. For he grew not only to haue a great minde and an eloquent tongue, without any affectation, or grosse countrey termes: but to a certaine modest countenance that scantly smiled, very sober in his gate, hauing a kind of sound in his voice that he neuer lost nor altered, and was of very honest behaviour, neuer troubled in his talke for any thing that crossed him, and many other such like things, as all that saw them in him, and considered them, could but wonder at him. But for proofe hereof, the report goeth, there was a naughtie busie fellow on a time, that a whole day together did nothing but raile vpon Pericles in the market place, and reuile him to his face, with all the villanous words he could vse. But Pericles put all vp quietly, and gaue him not a word againe, dispatching in the meane time matters of importance he had in hand, vntill night came, that he went softly home to his house, shewing no alteration nor semblance of trouble at all, though this lewd varlet followed him at the heeles, with words of open defamation. And as he was ready to enter in at his owne dores, being darke night, he commanded one of his men to take a torch, and to bring this man home to his house. Yet the Poet Ion saith, that Pericles was a very proud man, and stately, and that with his grauitie and noble mind, there was mingled a certaine scorne and contempt of other: and contrarily, he greatly praiseth the ciuilitie, humanitie and courtesie of Cimon, because he could fashion himselfe to all companies. But letting passe that which the Poet Ion said: who would that vertue should be full of tragicall discipline, bringing in with it, a certaine satyricall discourse to moue laughter. Now Zenon contrariwise did counsell all those that said Pericles grauitie was a presumption, and arrogancie: that they should also follow him in his presumption. For to counterfeit in that sort things honest and vertuous, doth secretly with time breed an affection and desire to loue them, and afterwards with custome euen effectually to vse and follow them. So Pericles by keeping Anaxagoras companie, did not onely profite himselfe in these things, but he learned besides to put away all superstitious feare, of celestiall signes and impressions seene in the ayre. For to those that are ignorant of the causes thereof, such sights are terrible, and to the godly also fearefull, as if they were vtterly vndone: and all is, because they haue no certaine knowledge of the reason that naturall Philosophie yeeldeth, which in stead of a fearefull superstition, would bring a true religion accompanied with assured hope of goodnesse. Some say a man brought Pericles one day from his farme out of the countrey, a Rammes head that had but one horne, and that the Prognosticator Lampon considering this head, that had but one strong horne in the middest of his forehead, interpreted, that this was the signification thereof. That being two tribes and seuerall factions in the city of Athens touching gouernment, the one of Pericles, and the other of Thucydides: the power of both should be brought into one, and specially into his part, in whose house this signe did happen. Further, it is said that Anaxagoras being present, did cause the Rammes head to be clouen in two peeces, and shewed vnto them that stood by, that the braine of this Ramme did not fill the pan of his natural place, but inclosed it selfe in all parts, being narrow like the point of an egge, in that part where the horne tooke his first roote of budding out. So Anaxagoras was maruellously esteemed at that present by all those that stood by : but so was Lampon, soone after that Thucydides was driuen away, and that the gouernment of the whole common weale fell into the hands of Pericles alone. And it is not to be wondred at (in my opinion) that the naturall Philosopher and the Prognosticator did rightly meete together in troth : the one directly telling the cause, and the other the end of the euent as it fell out. For the profession of the one, is to know how it commeth : and of the other, wherefore it commeth, and to foretell what it betokeneth. For where some say, that to shew the cause, is to take away the signification of the signe : they do not consider that in seeking to abolish by this reason the wonderfull tokens and signes in the ayre, they do take away those also which are done by art. As the noise of basons, the lights of fire by the sea side, and the shadowes of needles or points of dyals in the sunne : all which things are done by some cause and handiworke, to be a signe and token of some thing. But this argument peraduenture may serue better in another booke. And now againe to Pericles. Whilest he was yet but a young man the people stood in awe of him, because he somewhat resembled Pysistratus in his countenance : and the ancientest men of the city also were much afeard of his soft voice, his eloquent tongue, and readie vtterance, because in those he was Pysistratus vp and downe. Moreouer he was very rich and wealthie, and of one of the noblest families of the citie, and those were his friends also that caried the only sway and authoritie in the state : whereupon, fearing that lest they would banish him with the banishment of Ostracismon, he would not meddle with gouernment in any case, although otherwise he shewed himselfe in warres very valiant and forward, and feared not to venter his person. But after that Aristides was dead, that Themistocles was driuen away, and that Cimon being euer in seruice in the warres as Generall in forraine countries, was a long time out of Grece: then he came to leane to the tribe of the poore people, preferring the multitude of the poore communaltie, aboue the small number of Nobilitie and rich men, the which was directly against his nature. For of himselfe he was not popular, nor meanely giuen: but he did it (as it should seeme) to auoid suspition, that he should pretend to make himselfe King. And because he saw Cimon was inclined also to take part with the Nobilitie, and that he was singularly beloued and liked of all the honester sort: he to the contrarie enclined to the common people, purchasing by this meanes safetie to himselfe, and authoritie against Cimon. So he presently beganne a new course of life, since he had taken vpon him to deale in matters of state: for they neuer saw him afterwards at any time go into the citie, but to the market place, or to the Senate house. He gaue vp going to all feastes where he was bidden, and left the entertainement of his friends, their companie and familiaritie. So that in all his time wherein he gouerned the commonweale, which was a long time, he neuer went out to supper to any of his friendes, vnlesse it were that he was once at a feast at his nephew Euryptolemus mariage: and then he taried there no longer, but while the ceremonie was a doing, when they offer wine to the gods, and so he rose from the table. For these friendly meetings at such feastes, do much abase any counterfeit maiestie or set countenance: and he shall haue much ado to keepe grauity and reputation, shewing familiaritie to euery knowne friend in such open places. For in perfect vertue, those things truely are euer most excellent, which be most common: and in good and vertuous men there is nothing more admirable vnto straungers, then their daily conuersation is to their friends. Pericles now to preuent that the people should not be glutted with seeing him too oft, nor that they should come much to him: they did see him but at some times, and then he would not talke in euery matter, neither came much abroad among them, but reserued himselfe (as Critolaus said they kept the Salaminian galley at Athens) for matters of great importance. And in the meane season, in other matters of small moment, he dealt by meanes of certaine Orators his familiar friends, amongst whom Ephialtes (as they say) was one: he who tooke away the authoritie and power from the court of Areopagus, and did giue too much liberty to the people, as Plato said. Vpon which occasion, as the Comicall Poets say, he became so stout and head-strong, that they could no more holde him backe, then a young vnbridled colt: and tooke such a courage vpon him, that he would obey no more, but inuaded the Isle of Evbœa, and set vpon the other Ilands. Pericles also because he would fashion a phrase of speech, with a kind of stile altogether agreable to the manner of life and grauitie he had taken upon him: he gaue himselfe to all matters which he had learned of Anaxagoras, shadowing his reasons of natural Philosophie, with artificiall Rhetoricke. For hauing obtained a deepe understanding by studying of Philosophie, and a readie way effectually to end any matter he vndertooke to prooue, (besides that nature had endued him with an excellent wit and capacitie, as the deuine Plato doth write, to bring any thing to serue his purpose), he did so artificially compasse it with eloquence, that he farre passed all the Orators in his time. And for this cause was he (as they say) surnamed Olympius, as much to say, as heauenly or diuine. But some are of opinion he had that surname, by reason of the common buildings and stately workes he raised vp in the city of Athens, that did much set forth the same. Other thinke it was giuen him for his great authority and power he had in gouernment, as well in wars as in peace. But it is no maruell that this glory was giuen him, considering the many other qualities and vertues that were in him. Howbeit the Comedies the Poets caused to be played in those times (in which there were many words spoken of him, some in earnest, some in sport and ieast) do witnesse that he had that surname giuen him, chiefly for his eloquence. For it is reported, that he thundred and lightned in his orations to the people, and that his tongue was a terrible lightning. And touching this matter, they tell of an answer Thucycides, Milesius son, should pleasantly make concerning the force of Pericles eloquence. Thucydides was a noble man, and had long time contended against Pericles in matters of the commonweale. Archidamus, king of Lacedæmon, asked Thucydides on a time: whether he or Pericles wrestled best. Thucydides made him aunswer: When I haue given him an open fall before the face of the world, he can so excellently denie it, that he maketh the people beleeue he had no fall at all, and perswadeth them the contrarie of that they sawe. Notwithstanding he was euer very graue and wise in speaking. For euer when he went up into the pulpit for orations to speake to the people, he made his prayers vnto the gods, that nothing might escape his mouth, but that he might consider before, whether it would serue the purpose of his matter he treated on: yet are there none of his workes extant in writing, vnlesse it be some few lawes he made, and but very few of his notable sayings are brought to light, saue onely these. He said on a time, that they must take away the citie of Ægina, because it was a strawe lying in the eye of the hauen Piræa. And another time, he said that he sawe the warres a farre off, comming from Peloponnesvs. Another time, as he tooke shippe with Sophocles (his companion in commission with him as Generall of the armie) who commended a faire young boy they met as they came to the hauen: Sophocles, said he, a gouernour must not onely haue his hands, but also his eyes cleane. And Stesimbrotus writeth, that in a funerall oration he made in the praise of those that were slaine in the warre of Samos: he said they were immortall as the gods. For we do not see the goddes (said he) as they be, but for the honour that is done to them, and the great happinesse they enioy, we do coniecture they are immortall: and the same things are in those that dye in seruice, and defence of their countrey. Now where Thucydides doth write the gouernement of the Commonweale vnder Pericles to be as a gouernment of Nobilitie, and yet had apparance of a popular state: it is true that in effect it was a Kingdome, because one alone did rule and gouerne the whole state. And many other say also, he was the first that brought in the custome to deuide the enemies landes wonne by conquest among the people, and of the common money to make the people see playes and pastimes, and that appointed them reward for all things. But this custome was ill brought vp. For the common people that before were contented with litle, and got their liuing painefully with sweat of their browes, became now to be very vaine, sumptuous, and riotous, by reason of these things brought up then. The cause of the alteration doth easily appeare by those things. For Pericles at his first comming, sought to winne the fauour of the people, as we haue said before, onely to get like reputation that Cimon had wonne. But comming farre short of his wealth and abilitie, to carie out the port and charge that Cimon did, entertaining the poore, keeping open house to all commers, clothing poore old people, breaking open besides all inclosures and pales through all his landes, that euery one might with more libertie come in, and take the fruites thereof at their pleasure: and seeing himselfe by these great meanes out-gone farre in goodwill with the common people, by Demonides counsell and procurement (who was borne in the Isle of Ios) he brought in this distribution of the common money, as Aristotle writeth. And hauing wonne in a short time the fauour and goodwill of the common people, by distribution of the common treasure, which he caused to be deuided among them, aswell to haue place to see these playes, as for that they had reward to be present at the iudgements, and by other such like corruptions: he with the peoples helpe, did inueigh against the court of the Areopagites, whereof he neuer was any member. For it neuer came to be his happe to be yearely gouernour, nor keeper of the lawes, nor King of the sacrifices, nor maister of the warres: all which were offices chosen in auncient times by lot. And further, those on whom the lot fell, if they had behaued themselues well in their office, they were called forwards, and raised to be of the body of this court of the Areopagites. Pericles now by these meanes hauing obtained great credite and authoritie amongst the people, he troubled the Senate of the Areopagites in such sort, that he pluckt many matters from their hearing, by Ephialtes helpe: and in time made Cimon to be banished Athens, as one that fauoured the Lacedæmonians, and contraried the commonwealth and authoritie of the people. Notwithstanding he was the noblest and richest person of all the citie, and one that had wonne so many glorious victories, and had so replenished Athens with the conquered spoiles of their enemies, as we haue declared in his life: so great was the authoritie of Pericles amongst the people. Now the banishment wherwith he was punished (which they called Ostracismon) was limited by the law for ten yeres. In which space the Lacedæmonians being come downe with a great army into the country of Tanagra, the Athenians sent out their power presently against them. There Cimon willing to shew the Athenians by his deeds, that they had falsly accused him for fauouring the Lacedæmonians: did arme himselfe, and went on his country mens side, to fight in the company of his tribe. But Pericles friends gathered together, and forced Cimon to depart thence as a banished man. And this was the cause that Pericles fought that day more valiantly than euer he did, and he wanne the honour and name to haue done more in the person of himselfe that day, then any other of all the armie. At that battell also, all Cimons friends, whom Pericles had burdened likewise to fauour the Lacedæmonians doings, died every man of them that day. Then the Athenians repented them much that they had driuen Cimon away, and wished he were restored, after they had lost this battell vpon the confines of the countrey of Attica: because they feared sharpe wars would come vpon them againe at the next spring. Which thing when Pericles perceiued, he sought also to further that the common people desired: wherefore he straight caused a decree to be made, that Cimon should be called home againe, which was done accordingly. Now when Cimon was returned, he aduised that peace should be made betweene both cities: for the Lacedæmonians did loue Cimon very wel, and contrarily they hated Pericles, and all other gouernours. Some notwithstanding do write, that Pericles did neuer passe his consent to call him home againe, before such time as they had made a secret agreement amongst themselues (by meanes of Elpinice, Cimons sister) that Cimon should be sent out with an army of two hundred galleys, to make warres in the king of Persia his dominions, and that Pericles should remain at home with the authoritie of gouernment within the citie. This Elpinice, (Cimons sister) had once before intreated Pericles for her brother, at such time as he was accused before the Iudge of treason. For Pericles was one of the committies, to whom this accusation was referred by the people. Elpinice went vnto him, and besought him not to do his worst vnto her brother. Pericles answered her merily: Thou art too old Elpinice, thou art too old to go through with these matters. Yet when this matter came to iudgement, and that his cause was pleaded: he rose but once to speake against him (for his owne discharge as it were) and went his way when he had said, doing lesse hurt to Cimon then any other of his accusers. How is Idomeneus to be credited now, who accuseth Pericles that he had caused the orator Ephialtes to be slaine by treason (that was his friend, and did alwayes counsell him, and did take his part in all kind of gouernment of the common weale) only for the ielousie and enuy he did beare to his glory: I can but muse why Idomeneus should speake so slanderously against Pericles, vnlesse it were that his melancholy humour procured such violent speech: who though peraduenture he was not altogether blamelesse, yet he was euer nobly minded, and had a naturall desire of honor, in which kind of men such furious cruel passions are seldom seene to breed. But this orator Ephialtes being cruell to those that took part with the Nobilitie, because he would spare or pardon no man for any offence whatsoeuer committed against the peoples authoritie, but did follow and persecute them with all rigour to the vttermost: his enemies laid waite for him by meanes of one Aristodicus Tanagrian, and they killed him by treason, as Aristotle writeth. In the meanetime Cimon died in the Ile of Cyprvs, being generall of the army of the Athenians by sea. Wherefore those that took part with the Nobility, seeing Pericles was now growne very great, and that he went before all other citizens of Athens, thinking it good to haue some one to sticke on their side against him, and to lessen thereby somewhat his authoritie, that he might not come to rule all as he would: they raised vp against him, one Thucydides, of the towne of Alopecia, a graue wise man, and father in law to Cimon. This Thucydides had lesse skille of warres then Cimon, but vnderstood more in ciuill gournement then he, for that he remained most part of his time within the city: where continually inueighing against Pericles in his pulpit for oratiōs to the people, in short time he had stirred vp a like companie against the faction of Pericles. For he kept the gentlemen and richer sort (which they call Nobilitie) from mingling with the common people, as they were before, when through the multitude of the commons their estate and dignitie was obscured, and troden vnder foot. Moreouer he did separate them from the people, and did assemble them all as it were into one body, who came to be of equall power with the other faction, and did put (as a man will say) a counterpoise into the ballance. For at the beginning there was but a litle secret grudge onely betweene these two factions, as an artificiall flower set in the blade of a sword, which made those shew a litle, that did leane vnto the people: and the other also somewhat that fauoured the Nobilitie. But the contention betweene these two persons, was as a deep cut, which deuided the citie into two factions: of which the one was called the Nobilitie, and the other the communaltie. Therefore Pericles giuing yet more libertie vnto the people, did all things that might be to please them, ordaining continuall plaies and games in the citie, many feastes, bankets, and open pastimes to entertaine the commons with such honest pleasures and deuises: and besides all this, he sent yerely an armie of threescore gallies vnto the warres, into the which he put a great number of poore citizens that tooke pay of the state for nine moneths of the yere, and thereby they did learne together, and practise to be good sea men. Furthermore he sent into the countrie of Cherronesvs, a thousand free men of the citie to dwell there, and to deuide the lands amongst them: fiue hundred also into the Ile of Naxos: into the Ile of Andros, two hundred and fiftie: into Thracia, a thousand to dwell with the Bisaltes: and other also into Italy, when the citie of Sybaris was built againe, which afterwards was surnamed the city of the Thvrians. All this he did to rid the citie of a nūber of idle people, who through idlenesse began to be curious, and to desire chaunge of things, as also to prouide for the necessitie of the poore townes-men that had nothing. For, placing the naturall citizens of Athens neere vnto their subiects and friends, they serued as a garrison to keepe them vnder, and did suppresse them also from attempting any alteration or chaunge. But that which delighteth most, and is the greatest ornament vnto the citie of Athens, which maketh strangers most to wonder, and which alone doth bring sufficient testimonie, to confirme that which is reported of the auncient power, riches, and great wealth of Grece, to be true and not false: are the stately and sumptuous buildings, which Pericles made to be built in the citie of Athens. For it is the onely act of all other Pericles did, and which made his enemies most to spite him, and which they most accused him for, crying out vpon him in all counsels and assemblies: that the people of Athens were openly defamed, for carying away the ready mony of all Grece, which was left in the Ile of Delos to be safely kept there. And although they could with good honestie haue excused this fact, saying, that Pericles had taken it from them, for feare of the barbarous people, to the end to lay it vp in a more stronger place, where it should be in better safetie:

yet was this too ouergreat an iniury offerd vnto all the rest of Grece, and too manifest a token of tyrannie also, to behold before their eyes, how we do employ the money, which they were inforced to gather for the maintenance of the warres against the barbarous people, in gilding, building, and setting forth our city, like a glorious woman, all to be gauded with gold and precious stones, and how we do make images, and build vp temples of wonderfull and infinite charge. Pericles replied to the contrary, and declared vnto the Athenians, that they were not bound to make any account of this money vnto their friends and allies, considering that they fought for their safety, and that they kept the barbarous people far from Grece without troubling them to set out any one man, horse or ship of theirs, the mony onely excepted, which is no more theirs that paid it, thē theirs that receiued it, so they bestow it to that vse they receiued it for. And their city being already well furnished, and prouided of all things necessary for the warres, it was good reason they should employ and bestow the surplus of the treasure in things which in time to come (and being throughly finished) would make their fame eternall. Moreouer he said that whilest they continue building, they should be presently rich, by reason of the diuersitie of works of all sorts, and other things which they should haue need of: and to compasse these things the better, and to set them in hand, all maner of artificers and workmen (that would labor) should be set a worke. So should all the townes-men, and inhabitants of the city, receiue pay and wages of the common treasure: and the citie by this meanes should be greatly beautified, and much more able to maintaine it selfe. For such as were strong, and able men of body, and of yeares to cary weapon, had pay and entertainement of the common-wealth, which were sent abroade vnto the warres: and other that were not meete for warres, as craftes-men, and labourers: he would also they should haue part of the common treasure, but not without they earned it, and by doing somewhat. And this was his reason, and the cause that made him occupie the common people with great buildings, and deuises of workes of diuerse occupations, which could not be finished of long time: to the end that the citizens remaining at home, might haue a meane and way to take part of the common treasure, and enrich themselues, as well as those that went to the wars, and serued on the sea, or els that lay in garrison to keepe any place or fort. For some gained by bringing stuffe: as stones, brasse, iuory, gold, ebany, and cypres. Other got, to work and fashion it: as carpenters, grauers, founders, casters of images, masons, hewers of stone, diers, goldsmiths, ioyners working in iuory, painters, men that set in sundry colours of peeces of stone or wood, and turners. Other gained to bring stuffe, and to furnish them, as merchants, mariners, and shipmaisters, for things they brought them by sea. And by land other got also: as cart-makers, cariers, carters, cord-makers, sadlers, coller-makers, and pyoners to make wayes plaine, and miners, and such like. Furthermore euery science & craft, as a captain hauing souldiers, had also their army of the workmen that serued them, labouring truly for their liuing, who serued as aprentises and iourneymen vnder their workemaisters: so the worke by this meanes did disperse abroad a common gaine to all sorts of people and ages, what occupation or trade soeuer they had. And thus came the buildings to rise in greatnesse and sumptuousnesse, being of excellent workmanship, and for grace and beautie not comparable: because euery workeman in his science did striue what he could to excell others, to make his worke appeare greatest in sight, and to be most workmanly done in shew. But the greatest

thing to be wondred at, was their speed and diligence.
For where euery man thought those workes were not
likely to be finished in many mens liues and ages, and
from man to man: they were all done and finished,
whilest one onely gouernour continued still in credite
and authoritie. And yet they say, that in the same
time, as one Agatarchus boasted him selfe, that he
had quickly painted certaine beasts: Zeuxis another
painter hearing him, answered: And I contrarily
do reioyce, that I am a long time in drawing of
them. For commonly slight and sodaine drawing
of any thing, cannot take deepe colours, nor giue
perfect beauty to the worke: but length of time,
adding to the painters diligence and labour in
making of the worke, maketh the colours to continue for euer. For this cause therefore the workes
Pericles made, are more wonderfull: because they
were perfectly made in so short a time, and haue
continued so long a season. For euery one of
those which were finished vp at that time, seemed
then to be very auncient touching the beauty thereof:
and yet for the grace and continuance of the same,
it looketh at this day as if it were but newly done
and finished, there is such a certain kind of flourish-
ing freshnesse in it, which letteth that the iniury of
time cannot impaire the sight therof. As if euery
of those foresaid workes, had some liuing spirit in it,
to make it seeme yong and fresh: and a soul that liued
euer, which kept them in their good continuing state.
Now the chiefe surueyour general of al these works
was Phidias, albeit that there were many other excellent workmasters in euery science and occupation.
For the temple of Pallas, which is called Parthénon
(as a man would say, the temple of the virgine, and
is surnamed Hecatompedon, for that it is a hundred
foote euery way) was built by Ictinus, and Callicrates:
and the chappell of Eleusin (where the secret cere-

monies of the mysteries were made) was first founded by Coræbus, who raised vp the first pillars in order, standing beneath on the ground, and did set them vp vnto the maister chaptrels. But after he was dead, Metagenes, borne in the towne of Xypeta, turned the arches ouer, and then did set the pillars in order also which are aboue: and Xenocles of the towne of Cholargea, was he that made the lanterne or top of the steeple which couereth the sanctuary: but the long wall which Socrates heard Pericles himselfe giue order for the building of it, was done by Callicrates, who vndertooke the worke. Cratinus the Poet, in a comedie he made, laugheth at this worke, to see how slowly it went forward, and how long it was a doing, saying:

Pericles long a go, did end this worke begunne;
  and build it high, with glorious words, if so it had
    bene done.
But as for deedes (in deede) he built nothing at all,
  but let it stand; as yet it stands, much liker for to
    fall.

And as for the Theater or place appointed for musicke, where they heare all musitions play, and is called Odeon: it is very well made within with diuers seates and degrees, and many ranges of pillars, but the top of the roofe is altogether round, which is somewhat hanging downeward round about of it selfe, comming together into one point. And it is said that this was made after the patterne and fashion of King Xerxes royall pauilion, and that Pericles was the first deuiser and maker of it. Wherefore Cratinus in another place of his comedie he maketh of the Thracians, doth play very pretily vpon him, saying:

Pericles here doth come, Dan Iupiter surnamed,
  (and onions head) which hath in his great noddle
    finely framed

*The plot of Odeon, when he deliuered was
from banishment, and dangers deepe, wherein he long
   did passe.*

Pericles was the first that made maruellous earnest labour to the people that they would make an order, that on the day of the feast called Panathenæ, they would set vp games for musicke. And he himselfe being chosen ruler of these games, as iudge to reward the best deseruer : ordained the manner the musitions should euer after keepe in their singing, playing on their flutes, or vpon the citherne, or other instruments of musicke. So the first games that euer were for musick, were kept within the Odeon : and so were the other after them also, euer celebrated there. The gate and entring into the castle was made and finished within the space of fiue yeares, vnder the charge of Menesicles, that was maister of the workes. And whilst these gates were a building, there happened a wonderfull chance, which declared that the goddess Minerua did not mislike the building, but that it pleased her maruellously. For one of the most painefullest worekmen that wrought there, fell by mischance from the height of the castle to the ground, which fal did so sore bruse him, and he was so sick withal, that the phisitions and surgeons had no hope of his life. Pericles being very sory for his mischance, the goddesse appeared to him in his sleepe in the night, & taught him a medicine, with the which he did easily heale the poore brused man, and that in short time. And this was the occasion why he caused the image of the goddesse Minerva (otherwise called of health) to be cast in brasse, and set vp within the temple of the castle, neare vnto the altar which was there before, as they say. But the golden image of Minerua was made by Phidias, and grauen round about the base : who had the charge in manner of all other workes, and by reason of the good will Pericles bare him, he commanded all the other workmen. And this made the one to be greatly enuied, and the other to be very ill spoken of. For their enemies gaue it out abroade, that Phidias receiued the gentlewomen of the citie into his house, vnder colour to go see his workes, and did conuey them to Pericles. Vpon this brute, the Comicall poets taking occasion, did cast out many slaunderous speeches against Pericles, accusing him that he kept one Menippus wife, who was his friend and lieutenant in the warres: and burdened him further, that Pyrilampes, one of his familiar friends also, brought vp foule, and specially peacockes, which he secretly sent vnto the women that Pericles kept. But we must not wonder at those Satyres, that make profession to speake slaunderously against all the world, as it were to sacrifice the iniuries and wrongs they cast vpon honorable & good men, to the spite and enuy of the people, as vnto wicked spirits: considering that Stesimbrotus Thasian durst falsly accuse Pericles of detestable incest, and of abusing his owne sons wife. And this is the reason, in my opinion, why it is so hard a matter to come to the perfect knowledge of the truth of auncient things, by the monuments of historiographers: considering long processe of time, doth vtterly obscure the truth of matters, done in former times. For euery written historie speaking of men that are aliue, and of the time of things, whereof it maketh mention: sometime for hate and enuy, sometime for fauor or flatterie, doth disguise and corrupt the truth. But Pericles perceiuing that the orators of Thucydides faction, in their common orations did stil crie out vpon him, that he did vainely waste and consume the common treasure, and that he bestowed vpon the workes, all the whole reuenue of the citie: one day when the people were assembled together, before them all he asked them, if they thought that the cost bestowed were too much. The people answered him: a greate deale too much. Well, said he then, the charges shall be mine (if you thinke good) and none of yours: prouided that no mans name be written vpon the workes, but mine onely. When Pericles had said so, the people cried out aloud, they would none of that (either because that they wondred at the greatnesse of his minde, or else for that they would not giue him the only honour and praise to haue done so sumptuous and stately works) but willed him that he should see them ended at the common charges, without sparing for any cost. But in the end, falling out openly with Thucydides, and putting it to an aduenture which of them should banish other, with the banishment of Ostracismon: Pericles got the vpper hand, and banished Thucydides out of the citie, and therewithal also ouerthrew the contrarie faction against him. Now when he had rooted out all factions, and brought the citie againe to vnitie and concord, he found then the whole power of Athens in his hands, and all the Athenians matters at his disposing. And hauing all the treasure, armour, galleys, the Iles, and the sea, and a maruellous seigniorie and kingdome (that did enlarge it selfe partly ouer the Grecians, and partly ouer the barbarous people) so well fortified and strengthened with the obedience of nations subiect vnto them, with the friendship of Kings, and with the alliance of diuers other Princes and mightie Lords: then from that time forward he beganne to change his manners towards the people, and not so easily to giue place and frame himselfe to the peoples wils and desires, no more then as it were to contrary winds. Furthermore he altered his ouer gentle and popular manner of gouernement which he vsed vntill that time, as too delicate and too effeminate an harmony of musicke, and did conuert it vnto an imperious gouernment, or rather to a kingly authoritie: but yet held still a direct course, and kept himselfe euer vpright without fault, as one that did, said, and counselled that, which was most expedient for the common-weale. He many times brought on the people by perswasions and reasons, to be willing to graunt that he preferred vnto them: but many times also, he draue them to it by force, and made them against their wils do that, which was best for them. Folowing therein the deuise of a wise phisition: who in a long and changeable disease, doth graunt his pacient sometime to take his pleasure of a thing he liketh, but yet after a moderate sort: and another time also, he doth giue him a sharpe or bitter medicine that doth vexe him, though it heale him. For (as it falleth out commonly vnto people that enioy so great an empire) many times misfortunes did chance, that filled thē full of sundry passiōs, the which Pericles alone could finely steere and gouerne with two principall rudders, feare, and hope: brideling with the one, the fierce and insolent rashnesse of the common people in prosperitie, and with the other comforting their griefe and discouragement in aduersitie. Wherein he manifestly proued, that Rhetoricke and Eloquence (as Plato saith) is an art which quickneth mens spirits at her pleasure, & her chiefest skill is, to know how to moue passions and affections throughly, which are as stops and sounds of the soule, that would be plaid vpon with a fine fingred hand of a cunning maister. All which, not the force of eloquence only brought to passe, as Thucydides witnesseth: but the reputation of his life, and the opinion & confidence they had of his great worthinesse, because he would not any way be corrupted with gifts, neither had he any couetousnes in him. For when he had brought his citie not onely to be great, but

exceeding great and wealthy, and had in power and
authoritie exceeded many Kings and tyrants, yea
euen those which by their willes and testaments might
haue left great possessions to their children: he neuer
for all that increased his fathers goods and patrimony
left him, the value of a grote in siluer. And yet the
historiographer Thucydides doth set forth plainely
inough, the greatnesse of his power. And the Comicall
poets also of that time do report it maliciously vnder
couert words, calling his familiar friends, the new
Pysistratides, saying, how they must make him sweare
and protest he would neuer be King: giuing vs thereby
to vnderstand that his authority was too exceeding
great for a popular gouernement. And Teleclides
(amongst other) saith, that the Athenians had put into
his hands the reuenue of the townes and cities vnder
their obedience, and the towns themselues, to bind
the one, and loose the other, and to pull downe their
wals, or to build them againe at his pleasure. They
gaue him power, to make peace and alliance: they
gaue all their force, treasure, and authority, and all
their goods wholy into his hands. But this was not
for a litle while, nor in a geere of fauour, that should
continue for a time: but this held out forty yeares
together, he being alwayes the chiefe of his city
amongst the Ephialtes, the Leocrates, the Mironides,
the Cimons, the Tolmides, and the Thucydides. For
after he had preuailed against Thucydides, and had
banished him, he yet remained chiefe aboue all other,
the space of fifteene yeares. Thus hauing attained a
regall dignity to commaund all, which continued as
aforesaid, where no other captaines authority endured
but one yeare: he euer kept himselfe vpright from
bribes and mony, though otherwise he was no ill husband, and could warily looke to his owne. As for his
lands and goods left him by his parents, that they mis-
caried not by negligence, nor that they should trouble

him much, in busying himselfe to reduce them to a value: he did so husband them, as he thought was his best and easiest way. For he sold in grosse euer the whole yeares profit and cōmodity of his lands, and afterwards sent to the market daily to buy the cates, and other ordinarie prouision of houshold. This did not like his sonnes that were men growne, neither were his women contented with it, who would haue had him more liberall in his house: for they complained of his ouerhard and straight ordinary, because in so noble and great a house as his, there was neuer any great remaine left of meate, but all things receiued into the house, ranne into accompt, and were deliuered out by proportion. All this good husbandry of his, was kept vpright in this good order, by one Euangelus, steward of his house, a man very honest and skilful in all his houshold prouision: and whether Pericles had brought him vp to it, or that he had it by nature, it was not knowne. But these things were farre contrary to Anaxagoras wisedome. For he despising the world, and casting his affection on heauenly things: did willingly forsake his house, and suffered all his land to run to layes and to pasture. But (in my opinion) great is the diuersitie betweene a contemplatiue life, and a ciuill life. For the one employeth all his time vpon the speculation of good and honest things: and to attaine to that, he thinketh he hath no need of any exteriour help or instrument. The other applying all his time vpon vertue, to the common profit and benefit of men: he thinketh that he needeth riches, as an instrument not onely necessary but also honest. As, looke vpon the example of Pericles: who did relieue many poore people. And Anaxagoras specially among other: of whom it is reported, that Pericles being occupied about matters of state at that time, hauing no leisure to thinke vpon Anaxagoras, he seeing himselfe old and forsaken of the world, laid him

downe, and couered his head close, determining to
starue himself to death with hunger. Pericles vnderstanding this, ran presently to him as a man halfe cast
away, and prayed him as earnestly as he could, that
he would dispose him selfe to liue, being not onely
sory for him, but for himselfe also, that he should
loose so faithfull and wise a counseller, in matters of
state and gouernement. Then Anaxagoras shewed his
face, and told him: O Pericles, those that will see by
the light of a lampe, must put oyle to it, to make the
light burne. Now began the Lacedæmonians to grow
iealous of the greatnesse of the Athenians, wherefore
Pericles to make the Athenians hearts greater, and so
draw their minds to great enterprises: set downe an
order they should send ambassadours to perswade al
the Grecians (in what part soeuer they dwelt in Evrope,
or Asia, as well the litle as the great cities) to send
their deputies vnto Athens, to the generall assembly
that should be holden there to take order for the
temples of the gods which the barbarous people had
burnt, and touching the sacrifices they had vowed for
the preseruation of Grece, when they gaue battel vpon
them: and touching sea matters also, that euery man
might saile in safety where he would, and that all might
liue together in good peace and loue one with another.
To performe this commission, twenty persons were
sent of this ambasiate, euery one of them being fifty
yeares of age and vpward. Whereof fiue of them
went to the Dorians, dwelling in Asia, and to the inhabitants of the Iles, euē vnto the Isles of Lesbos, &
of the Rhodes. Fiue other went through al the
country of Hellespont, & of Thracia, vnto the city of
Bizantivm. Other fiue were commanded to go into
Bœotia, into Phocides, and through al Peloponnesvs,
& from thence by the country of the Locrians, into
the vpland country ioyning to it, vntil they came into
the country of Acarnania, and of Ambracia. And the

other fiue went first into the Isle of Evboea, and from thence vnto the Oetæians, and through all the gulfe of Malea, vnto the Phtiotes, vnto the Achaians, and the Thessalians: declaring to all the people where they came, the Athenians commission, perswading them to send vnto Athens, and to be present at the counsell which should be holden there, for the pacification and vnion of all Grece. But when all came to all, nothing was done, and the said cities of Grece did not assemble, by practice of the Lacedæmonians (as it is reported) who were altogether the let: for the first refusall that was made of their summons, was at Peloponnesvs. This haue I written to make Pericles noble courage to be knowne, and how profound a wise man he shewed himselfe vnto the world. Furthermore, when he was chosen General in the warres, he was much esteemed, because he euer tooke great regard to the safety of his souldiers. For by his good will he would neuer hazard battell, which he saw might fall out doubtfull, or in any thing daungerous: and moreouer, he neuer praised them for good generals, neither would he follow them that had obtained great victories by hazard, howsoeuer other did esteeme or commend them. For he was wont to say, that if none but himselfe did leade them to the shambles, as much as lay in him, they should be immortall. And when he saw Tolmides, the sonne of Tolmæus (trusting to his former victories, and the praise and commendation of his good seruice) did prepare vpon no occasion, and to no purpose, to enter into the countrey of Boeotia, and had procured also a thousand of the lustiest and most valiant men of the citie, to be contented to go with him in that iourney, ouer and aboue the rest of the army he had leauied: he went about to turne him from his purpose, and to keepe him at home, by many perswasions he vsed to him before the peoples face, and spake certaine words at that time,

that were remembred long after, and these they were:
That if he would not beleeue Pericles counsell, yet
that he would tary time at the least, which is the
wisest counseller of men. These words were pretily
liked at that present time. But within few dayes
after, when news was brought that Tolmides self was
slaine in a battel he had lost, neare vnto the citie of
Coronea, wherein perished also, many other honest
and valiant men of Athens: his wordes spoken before,
did then greatly increase Pericles reputation and good
wil with the common people, because he was taken
for a wise man, and one that loued his citizens. But
of all his iourneys he made, being Generall ouer the
army of the Athenians, the iourney of Cherronesvs
was best thought of and esteemed, because it fell out
to the great benefite and preseruation of all the Grecians inhabiting in that countrey. For besides that
he brought thither a thousand citizens of Athens to
dwell there (in which doing he strengthened the cities
with so many good men) he did fortifie the barre also,
which did let it from being of an Ile, with a fortifica-
tion he drew from one sea to another: so that he
defended the country against all the inuasions and
piracies of the Thracians inhabiting thereabouts, and
deliuered it of extreame warre, with the which it was
plagued before, by the barbarous people their neighbours, or dwelling amongst them, who only liued vpon
piracie & robbing on the seas. So was he likewise
much honored and esteemed of strangers, when he
did enuirone all Peloponnesvs, departing out of the
hauen of Peges, on the coast of Megara, with a fleet
of a hundred gallies. For he did not only spoile
the townes all alongst the sea side, as Tolmides had
done before him: but going vp further into the maine
land, farre from the sea, with his souldiers he had in
the gallies, he draue some of them to retire within
their walles, he made them so afraid of him: and in

the country of Nemea, he ouercame the Sicyonians in battell, that taried him in the field, & did erect a pillar for a notable mark of his victorie. And imbarking in his ships a new supply of souldiers which he took vp in Achaia, being friends with the Athenians at that time, he passed ouer to the firme land that lay directly against it. And pointing beyond the mouth of the riuer of Achelous, he inuaded the countrey of Acharnania, where he shut vp the Oeneades within their walles. And after he had laid waste and destroyed all the champion countrey, he returned home againe to Athens: hauing shewed himselfe in this iourney a dreadfull captaine to his enemies, and very carefull for the safetie of his souldiers. For there fell out no manner of misfortune all this iourney (by chaunce or otherwise) vnto the souldiers vnder his charge. And afterwardes, going with a great nauy maruellous well appointed vnto the Realme of Pontvs, he did there gently vse and intreat the cities of Grece, and granted them all that they required of him: making the barbarous people inhabiting thereabouts, and the Kings and Princes of the same also, to know the great force and power of the Athenians, who sailed without feare all about where they thought good, keeping all the coasts of the sea vnder their obedience. Furthermore, he left with the Sinopians thirteene galleys, with certain number of soldiers vnder Captain Lamachus, to defend them against the tyrant Timesileus: who being expulsed and driuen away with those of his faction, Pericles caused proclamation to be made at Athens, that sixe hundred free men of the citie, that had any desire to go, without compulsion, might go dwell at Sinopa, where they should haue deuided among them the goods and lands of the tyrant and his followers. But he did not follow the foolish vaine humors of his citizens, nor would not yeeld to their vnsatiable couetousnesse, who being set on a iolitie

to see themselves so strong, and of such a power,
and besides, to haue good lucke, would needs once
againe attempt to conquer Ægypt, and to reuolt all
the countries vpon the sea coasts, from the empire of
the king of Persia: for there were many of them
whose minds were maruellously bent to attempt the
vnfortunate enterprise of entering Sicilia, which Alcibiades afterwards did much pricke forward. And
some of them dreamed besides, of the conquest of
Thvscan, and the empire of Carthage. But this was
not altogether without some likelihood, nor without
occasion of hope, considering the large bounds of
theire Kingdome, and the fortunat estate of their
affaires, which fell out according to their own desire.
But Pericles did hinder this going out, and cut of
altogether their curious desire, employing the most
part of their power and force, to keepe that they had
already gotten: iudging it no small matter to keepe
downe the Lacedæmonians from growing greater.
For he was alwaies an enemie to the Lacedæmonians,
as he shewed himselfe in many things, but specially
in the war he made, called the holy warre. For the
Lacedæmonians hauing put the Phocians from the
charge of the temple of Apollo, in the city of Del-
phes, which they had vsurped, and hauing restored
the Delphians again vnto the same: so soone as they
were gone thence, Pericles went also with another
army, and restored the Phocians in againe. And
whereas the Lacedæmonians had caused to be grauen
in the forehead of a Wolfe of brasse, the priuiledge the
Delphians had granted them, to be the first that
should make their demands of the oracle: he hauing
attained the like priuiledge of the Phocians, made his
image also to be grauen on the right side of the same
image, of the brasen Wolfe. Now how wisely Pericles did gouerne Grece by the power of the Athenians,
his deeds do plainly shew. For first of all, the coun-

trey of Evbœa did rebell, against whom he brought
the army of the Athenians. And suddenly in the
necke of that, came newes from another coast, that
the Megarians also were in armes against them: and
how they were already entered into the country of
Attica with a great army, led by Plistonax King of
Lacedæmon. This occasion drew him homeward
againe, and so he marched backe with speed into his
country, to make preparation to encounter his enemies, that were already entred into the territories of
Attica. He durst not offer them battel, being so
great a number of valiant soldiers: but hearing that
king Plistonax was yet but a yong man, and was ruled
altogether by Cleandrides counsell and direction
(whom the Ephores had placed about him to counsell
and direct him) he sought priuily to corrupt Cleandrides. When he had won him soone with his money,
he perswaded him to draw backe the Peloponnesians
out of their countrey of Attica: and so he did. But
when the Lacedæmonians saw their army cassed, and
that the people were gone their way, euery man to
his owne city or towne, they were so mad at it, that
the king was condemned in a great sum. The king
being unable to answer his fine, which was so extreme
great, he was driuen to absent himselfe from Lacedæmon. Cleandrides on the other side, if he had not
fled in time, euen for spite had bene condemned to
death. This Cleandrides was Gylippus father, that
afterwards ouercame the Athenians in Sicilia, in whom
it seemed nature bred couetousnes, as a disease inherit-
able by succession from the father to the son. For he
being shamefully conuicted also, for certaine vile
parts he had plaid, was likewise banished from Sparta:
as we haue more amply declared in the life of Ly-
sander. And Pericles deliuering vp the account of
his charge, and setting downe an article of the expence of tenne talents he had employed, or should

employ in needfull causes: the people allowed them
him, neuer asking question how, nor which way, nor
whether it was true that they were bestowed. Now
there are certaine writers (amongst whom the Philosopher Theophrastus is one) who write that Pericles
sent yearely vnto Sparta ten talents, with the which
he entertained those that were in authoritie there,
because they should make no wars with them: not to
buy peace of them, but time, that he might in the
meane season, with better commodity, and that ley-
sure, prouide to maintaine the wars. After that, as
the army of the Peloponnesians were out of the
country of Attica, he returned against the rebels, and
passed into the Ile of Evbœa with fifty saile, and fiue
thousand footmen well armed: and there he ouercame all the cities that had taken armes against him,
and draue away the Hyppobotes, who were the most
famous men of all the Chalcidians, as well for their
riches, as for their valiantnes. He draue away also
all the Hestiæians, whom he chased cleane out of all
the country, and placed in their city, onely the citizens
of Athens. And the cause why he dealt so rigor-
ously with them was, because they hauing taken a
galley of the Athenians prisoner, had put all the men
to death that were in her. And peace being concluded afterwards betweene the Athenians and Lacedæmonians for thirty yeares: he proclaimed open
wars against those of the Isle of Samos, burdening
them, that they being commaunded by the Athenians,
to pacifie the quarrels which they had against the
Milesians, they would not obey. But because some
hold opinion, that he tooke vpon him this warre
against Samos, for the loue of Aspasia: it shall be no
great digression of our story, to tell you by the way,
what manner of woman she was, and what a maruellous gift and power she had, that she could entangle
with her loue the chiefest rulers and gouernors at that

time of the commonweale, and that the Philosophers themselues did so largely speake and write of her. First of all, it is certaine that she was borne in the city of Miletvm, and was the daughter of one Axiochus: she following the steps and example of an old curtisan of Ionia, called Thargelia, gaue her selfe only to entertaine the greatest persons and chiefest rulers in her time. For this Thargelia being passing faire, and carying a comely grace with her, hauing a sharpe wit and pleasant tong, she had the acquaintance and friendship of the greatest persons of all Grece, and wanne all those that did haunt her company, to be at the king of Persiaes commaundement. So that she sowed through all the cities of Grece, great beginnings of the faction of the Medes: for they were the greatest men of power and authoritie of every city that were acquainted with her. But as for Aspasia, some say that Pericles resorted vnto her, because she was a wise woman, and had great vnderstanding in matters of state and gouernement. For Socrates himselfe went to see her sometimes with his friends: and those that vsed her company also, brought their wiues many times with them to heare her talke: though her traine were, to entertaine such as would warme them by her fire. Æschines writeth, that Lysicles a grasier, being before but a meane man, and of a clubbish nature, came to be the chiefe man of Athens, by frequenting the company of Aspasia, after the death of Pericles. And to Platoes booke intituled Menexenus, although the beginning of it be but pleasantly written, yet in that, this story is written truely: that this Aspasia was repaired vnto by diuers of the Athenians, to learn the art of rhetorick of her. Yet notwithstanding it seemeth most likely that the affection Pericles did beare her, grew rather of loue, then of any other cause. For he was maried vnto a kinsewoman of his owne, and that before was Hip-

ponicus wife, by whom she had Callias, surnamed the
rich: and had afterwards by Pericles, Xantippus and
Paralus. But not liking her company, he gaue her
with her owne goodwill and consent vnto another,
and maried Aspasia whom he dearely loued. For
euer when he went abroad, and came home againe,
he saluted her with a kisse. Whereupon in the
auncient Comedies, she is called in many places, the
new Omphale, and sometimes Deianira, and sometimes Iuno. But Cratinus plainly calleth her whore
in these verses:

His Iuno she him brought, Aspasia by name,
  which was indeed an open whore, and past all
    kind of shame.

And it seemeth that he had a bastard: for Eupolis
in a comedie of his called Demosij, bringeth him in,
asking Pironides thus:

I pray thee is my bastard sonne yet aliue?

And then Pironides answered him:

A perfect man long since, he surely had bene found,
  if that this lewd and naughty whore, his vertue
    had not drownd.

To conclude, this Aspasia was so famous, that
Cyrus (he that fought against king Artaxerxes his
brother, for the empire of Persia) called Aspasia
his best beloued of all his concubines, which before was called Milito, and was borne in Phocides,
being Hermotimus daughter. And Cyrus being
slaine in the field, Aspasia was caried to the King
his brother, with whom afterwards she was in great
fauor. As I was writing this life, this story came
to my mind: and me thought I should have dealt
hardly, if I should haue left it vnwritten. But
to our matter againe. Pericles was charged that he

made warres against the Samians, on the behalfe of the
Milesians, at the request of Aspasia : for the two
cities were at wars together, for the citie of Priena,
but the Samians were the stronger. Now the
Athenians commanded them to lay aside their armes,
and to come & plead their matter before them, that
the right might be decided : but they refused it
vtterly. Wherfore Pericles went thither and tooke
away the gouernment of the small number of Nobility,
taking for hostages, fiftie of the chiefest men of the
citie, and so many children besides, which he left to
be kept in the Ile of Lemnos. Some say euery one
of these hostages offered to giue him a talent : and
besides those, many other offered him the like, such
as wold not haue the soueraigne authority put into
the hands of the people. Moreouer Pissuthnes the
Persian, lieutentant to the king of Persia, for the goodwill he bare those of Samos, did send Pericles ten
thousand crownes to release the hostages. But Pericles neuer tooke penny : and hauing done that he determined at Samos, and established a popular gouernment, he returned againe to Athens. Nothwithstanding, the Samians rebelled immediatly after, hauing
recouered their hostages againe by meanes of this
Pissuthnes that stale them away, and did furnish them
also with all their munition of warre. Wherupon
Pericles returning against them once more, he found
them not idle, nor amazed at his comming, but
resolutely determined to receiue him, and to fight for
the seignorie by sea. So there was a great battel fought
betweene them, neare the Ile of Tracia. And Pericles
wan the battel : hauing with 44 saile onely nobly
ouercome his enemies, which were threescore and ten
in number, wherof twenty of them were ships of war.
And so following his victory forthwith, he wan also
the port of Samos, and kept the Samians besieged
within their own citie : where they were yet so bold,

as they wold make sallies out many times, and fight before the wals of the citie. But when there arriued a new supply of ships bringing a greater aide vnto Pericles: then were they shut vp of all sides. Pericles then taking threescore galleys with him, launched out into the sea, with intent (as some say) to go meete certaine ships of the Phœnicians (that came to aide the Samians) as far from Samos as he could: or as Stesimbrotus saith, to go into Cyprvs, which me thinketh is not true. But whatsoeuer was his intent, he committed a foule faulte. For Melissus (the son of Ithagenes, a great Philosopher) being at that time general of the Samians, perceiuing that few ships were left behind at the siege of the city, and that the captaines also that had the charge of them were no very expert men of war, perswaded his citizens to make a sallie vpon them. Wherupon they fought a battel, and the Samians ouercame: the Athenians were taken prisoners, and they sunke many of their ships. Now they being lords againe of the sea, did furnish their city with all maner of munition for wars, whereof before they had great want. Yet Aristotle writeth, that Pericles selfe was once ouercome in a battell at sea by Melissus. Furthermore the Samians, to be euen with the Athenians for the iniury they had receiued of them before: did brand them in the forehead with the stampe of an owle, the owle being then the stampe of their coine at Athens, euen as the Athenians had branded the Samian prisoners before with the stampe of Samæna. This Samæna is a kind of ship amongst the Samians, low afore, and well laid out in the mid-ship, so that it is excellent good to rise with the waues of the sea, and is very swift vnder saile: and it was so called, because the first that was made of this fashion, was made in the Isle of Samos, by the tyrant Polycrates. It is said that the Poet Aristophanes, couertly conveying the stampe of the

Samians, speaking merily in a place of his Comedies, saith:

The Samians are great learned men.

Pericles being aduertised of the ouerthrow of his armie, returned presently to the rescue. Melissus went to meet him, and gaue him battell: but he was ouerthrowne, and driuen back into his city, where Pericles walled them in round about the citie, desiring victorie rather by time and charge, then by danger, and losse of his souldiers. But when he saw that they were wearie with tract of time, and that they would bring it to hazard of battell, and that he could by no meanes withhold them: he then deuided his armie into eight companies, whom he made to draw lots, and that company that lighted vpon the white beane, they should be quiet and make good cheare, while the other seuen fought. And they say that from thence it came, that when any haue made good cheare, and taken pleasure abroad, they do yet cal it a white day, because of the white beane. Ephorus the historiographer writeth, that it was there, where first of all they began to vse engines of warre to plucke downe great wals, and that Pericles vsed first this wonderful inuention: and that Artemon an enginer was the first deuiser of them. He was caried vp and downe in a chaire, to set forward these workes, because he had a lame legge: and for this cause he was called Periphoretos. But Heraclides Ponticus confuteth Ephorus therein, by the verses of Anacreon, in the which Artemon is called Periphoretos, many yeares before this warre of Samos began: and saith this Periphoretos was a maruellous tender man, and so foolishly afeard of his owne shadow, that the most part of his time he stirred not out of his house, and did sit alwaies hauing two of his men by him, that held a copper target ouer his

head, for feare lest anything should fall vpon him.
And if vpon any occasion he were driuen to go
abroad out of his house: he would be carried in a
litle bed hanging neare the ground, and for this cause
he was surnamed Periphoretos. At the last, at nine
moneths end, the Samians were compelled to yeeld.
So Pericles tooke the city & rased their wals to the
ground: he brought their ships away, and made
them pay a marvellous great tribute, whereof part
he receiued in hand, and the rest payable at a
certaine time, taking hostages with him for the assurance of payment. But Duris the Samian dilateth
these matters maruellous pitifully, burdening the
Athenians, and Pericles selfe with vnnaturall cruelty:
whereof neither Thucydides, nor Ephorus, nor Aristotle
himselfe maketh mention. And sure I cannot beleeue it is true that is written: That he brought the
captaines of the gallies, and the soldiers themselues
of Samia, into the market place of the city of
Miletvm, where he made them to be bound fast
vnto boords for the space of tenne dayes, and at the
end of the same, the poore men halfe dead, were
beaten downe with clubbes, and their heads pashed
in pieces: and afterwards they threw out their bodies
to the crowes, and would not burie them. So Duris
being accustomed to ouerreach, and to lye many
times in things nothing touching him, seemeth in this
place out of all reason to aggrauate the calamities of
his countrey, onely to accuse the Athenians, and to
make them odious to the world. Pericles hauing won
the citie of Samos, he returned againe to Athens,
where he did honorably burie the bones of his slaine
citizens in this warre: and himselfe (according to
their manner and custome) made the funerall oration,
for the which he was marvellously esteemed. In
such sort, that after he came downe from the pulpit
where he made his oration, the ladies and gentle-

women of the citie came to salute him, and brought him garlands to put vpon his head, as they do to noble conquerers when they returne from games, where they haue wonne the prize. But Elpinicé comming to him, said: Surely Pericles, thy good seruice done, deserueth garlands of triumph: for thou hast lost vs many a good and valiant citizen, not fighting with the Medes, the Phœnicians, and with the barbarous people as my brother Cimon did, but for destroying a citie of our owne nation and kindred. Pericles to these words, softly answered Elpinicé, with Archilochus verse, smiling:

When thou art old, paint not thy selfe.

But Ion writeth, that he greatly gloried, and stood much in his own conceipt, after he had subdued the Samians, saying: Agamemnon was ten yeares taking of a citie of the barbarous people: and he in nine moneths only had won the strongest citie of the whole nation of Ionia. Indeed he had good cause to glory in his victorie: for truely (if Thucydides report be true) his conquest was no lesse doubtefull, then he found it daungerous. For the Samians had almost bene lords of the sea, and taken the seignorie thereof from the Athenians. After this, the wars of Peloponnesvs being hote againe, the Corinthians inuading the Ilanders of Corphv: Pericles did perswade the Athenians to send aide vnto the Corphians and to ioyne in league with that Iland, which was of great power by sea, saying: that the Peloponnesians (before it were long) would haue war with them. The Athenians consented to his motion, to aide those of Corphv. Whereupon they sent thither Lacedæmonius (Cimons son) with ten gallies onely for a mockerie: for all Cimons family and friends, were wholly at the Lacedæmonians deuotion. Therefore did Pericles cause Lacedæmonius to have so few ships deliuered

him, and further, sent him thither against his will, to
the end that if he did no notable exploit in this
seruice, that they might then the more iustly suspect
his goodwill to the Lacedæmonians. Moreouer whilest
he liued, he did euer what he could to keepe Cimons
children backe from rising: because that by their
names they were no naturall borne Athenians, but
straungers. For the one was called Lacedæmonius,
the other Thessalus, and the third Elius: and the
mother to all them three, was an Arcadian woman
borne. But Pericles being blamed for that he
sent but ten galleys only, which was but a slender
aide for those that had requested them, and a great
matter to them that spake ill of him: he sent thither
afterwards a great number of other galleys, which
came when the battell was fought. But the Corinthians were maruellous angry, and went and complained to the counsell of the Lacedæmonians, where
they laid open many grieuous complaints and accusations against the Athenians, and so did the Megarians
also: alleadging that the Athenians had forbidden
them their hauens, their staples and all trafficke of
merchandise in the territories vnder their obedience,
which was directly against the common lawes and
articles of peace, agreed vpon by oath among all the
Grecians. Moreouer, the Æginetes finding themselues very ill and cruelly handled, did send secretly
to make their mone and complaints to the Lacedæmonians, being afraid openly to complaine of the
Athenians. While these things were a doing, the
city of Potidæa, subiect at that time vnto the Athenians (and was built in old time by the Corinthians)
did rebell, and was besieged by the Athenians, which
did hasten on the warres. Notwithstanding this, ambassadors were first sent vnto Athens vpon these complaints: and Archidamus, king of the Lacedæmonians
did all that he could to pacifie the most part of these

quarrels and complaints, intreating their friends and allies. So as the Athenians had no wars at all, for anie other matters wherewith they were burdened, if they would have graunted to haue reuoked the decree they had made against the Megarians. Whereupon, Pericles, that aboue all other stood most against the reuocation of that decree, and that did stir vp the people, and made them stand to that they had once decreed, and ordered against the Megarians: was thought the originall cause and author of the Peloponnesian warres. For it is said that the Lacedæmonians sent ambassadors vnto Athens for that matter only. And when Pericles alledged a law that did forbid them to take away the table whereupon before time had bene written any common law or edict: Poliarces, one of the Lacedæmon ambassadors said vnto him: Well, said he, take it not away then, but turne the table onely: your law I am sure forbiddeth not that. This was pleasantly spoken of the ambassadour, but Pericles could neuer be brought to it for all that. And therefore it seemeth he had had some secret occasion of grudge against the Megarians: yet as one that would finely conuey it vnder the common cause and cloke, he tooke from them the holy lands they were breaking vp. And to bring this to passe, he made an order, that they should send an herauld to summon the Megarians to let the land alone, and that the same herauld should go also vnto the Lacedæmonians to accuse the Megarians vnto them. It is true that this ordinance was made by Pericles meanes, as also it was most iust and reasonable: but it fortuned so, that the messenger they sent thither died, and not without suspition that the Megarians made him away. Wherfore Charinus made a law presently against the Megarians: that they should be proclaimed mortall enemies to the Athenians for euer, without any hope of after reconciliation. And also if any Megarian should once put his foote within the territories of Attica, that he should suffer the paines of death. And moreouer, that their captains taking yearely their ordinary oath, should sweare among other articles, that twise in the yeare they should go with their power, and destroy some part of the Megarians land. And lastly, that the herauld Anthemocritus should be buried by the place called then the gates Thriasienes, and now called Dipylon. But the Megarians stoutly denying, that they were any cause of the death of this Anthemocritus: did altogether burthen Aspasia and Pericles with the same, alleadging for proofe thereof, Aristophanes verses the Poet, in his Comedie he intituled the Acharnes, which are so common, as euery boy hath them at his toungs end.

> *The young men of our land (to drunken bibbing bent)*
>   *ran out one day vnrulily, and towards Megara*
>   *went:*
> *From whence in their outrage, by force they tooke*
>   *away,*
>   *Simætha noble curtisan, as she did sport and play.*
> *Wherewith enraged all (with pepper in the nose)*
>   *the proud Megarians came to vs, as to their mortall*
>   *foes,*
> *And tooke by stealth away of harlots eke a paire,*
>   *attending on Aspasia, which were both young and*
>   *faire.*

But in very deed, to tell the originall cause of this warre, and to deliuer the troth thereof, it is very hard. But all the historiographers together agree, that Pericles was the chiefest authour of the warre: because the decree made against the Megarians, was not reuoked backe againe. Yet some hold opinion, that Pericles did it of a noble mind and iudgement, to be constant in that he thought most expedient. For he iudged that this commandement of the Lacedæmonians was but a triall, to proue if the Athenians would grant them : and if they yeelded to them in that, then they manifestly shewed that they were the weaker. Other contrarily say, that it was done of a selfe-will and arrogancie, to shew his authoritie and power, and how he did despise the Lacedæmonians. But the shrewdest proofe of all, that bringeth best authoritie with it, is reported after this sort. Phidias the image-maker (as we haue told you before) had undertaken to make the image of Pallas : and being Pericles friend, was in great estimation about him : but that procured him many ill willers. Then they being desirous to heare by him what the people would iudge of Pericles, they intised Menon, one of the workemen that wrought vnder Phidias, and made him come into the market place to pray assurance of the people that he might openly accuse Phidias, for a fault he had committed about Pallas image. The people receiued his obedience, and his accusation was heard openly in the market place, but no mention was made of any theft at all : because that Phidias (through Pericles counsell and deuise) had from the beginning so laid on the gold vpon the image, that it might be taken off and weyed euery whit. Whereupon Pericles openly said vnto his accusers, take off the gold and wey it. The glory of his works did purchase him this enuy. For he hauing grauen vpon the scutchion of the goddesse, the battell of the Amazons, had cut out the protraiture of himselfe maruellous liuely, vnder the person of an old bald mã, lifting vp a great stone with both his hands. Further, he had cut out Pericles image, excellently wrought and artificially, seeming in manner to be Pericles selfe, fighting with an Amazon in this sort : the Amazons hand being lift vp high, holdeth a dart before Pericles face, so passing cunningly

wrought, as it seemed to shadow the likenesse and
resemblance of Pericles: and yet notwithstanding
appeareth plainely to be Pericles selfe on either side
of the portraiture. So Phidias was clapt vp in prison,
and there died of a sicknes, or else of poison (as
some say) which his enemies had prepared for him:
and all to bring Pericles into further suspition, and
to giue them the more cause to accuse him. But
howsoeuer it was, the people gaue Menon his free-
dome, and set him free for paiment of all subsidies,
following the order Glycon made, and gaue the captains charge they should see him safely kept, and
that he took no hurt. And about the same time
also Aspasia was accused, that she did not beleeue in
the gods: and her accuser was Hermippus, maker of
the Comedies. He burdened her further, that she
was a bawd to Pericles, and receiued citizens wiues
into her house, which Pericles kept. And Diopithes
at the same time made a decree, that they should
make search and enquirie for heretikes that did not
beleeue in the gods, and that taught certaine new
doctrine and opinion touching the operations of
things aboue in the element, turning the suspition
vpon Pericles, because of Anaxagoras. The people
did receiue and confirm this inquisition: and it was
moued also then by Dracontides, that Pericles should
deliuer an account of the mony he had spent, vnto
the hands of the Prytanes, who were treasurers of the
common fines and reuenues, and that the Iudges de-
puted to giue iudgement, should giue sentence within
the citie vpon the altar. But Agnon put that word
out of the decree, and placed in stead thereof, that
the cause should be iudged by the 15. hundred Iudges,
as they thought good, if any man brought this action
for theft, for battery, or for iniustice. As for Aspasia,
he saued her, even for the very pity & cōpassion
the Iudges took of him, for the teares he shed in

making his humble sute for her, all the time he
pleaded her case: as Æschines writeth. But for
Anaxagoras, fearing that he could not do so much
for him: he sent him out of the city, & himselfe did
accompany him. And furthermore, seeing he had
incurred the ill will of the people for Phidias fact, and
for this cause fearing the issue of the iudgment: he
set the wars a fire againe, that alwaies went backward,
and did but smoke a litle, hoping by this means to
weare out the accusations against him, and to root
out the malice some did beare him. For the people
hauing waighty matters in hand, and very dangerous
also: he knew they wold put all into his hands alone,
he hauing won already such great authority and reputation among them. And these be the causes why
he would not (as it is said) suffer the Athenians to
yeeld vnto the Lacedæmonians in any thing: howbeit
the truth cannot certainely be knowne. But the
Lacedæmonians knowing well, that if they could weed
out Pericles, and ouerthrow him, they might then
deale as they would with the Athenians: they commanded them they should purge their city of Cylons
rebellion, because they knew well inough that Pericles
kin by the mothers side were to be touched withall,
as Thucydides declareth. But this practise fell out
contrary to their hope and expectation, that were sent
to Athens for this purpose. For, weening to haue
brought Pericles into further suspition and displeasure,
the citizens honoured him the more, and had a better
affiance in him then before, because they saw his
enemies did so much feare and hate him. Wherefore,
before King Archidamus entred with the army of the
Peloponnesians into the country of Attica, he told
the Athenians, that if King Archidamus fortuned to
waste and destroy all the country about, and should
spare his lands and goods for the old loue and
familiaritie that was betweene them, or rather to giue

his enemies occasion falsly to accuse him: that from
thenceforth, he gaue all the lands and tenements he
had in the country, vnto the common wealth. So it
fortuned that the Lacedæmonians with all their
friends and confederates, brought a maruellous army
into the countrey of Attica, vnder the leading of
King Archidamus: who burning and spoiling all the
country he came alongst, they came vnto the towne
of Acharnes, where they encamped, supposing the
Athenians would neuer suffer them to approach so
neare, but that they would giue them battell for the
honour and defence of their countrey, and to shew that
they were no cowards. But Pericles wisely considered
how the daunger was too great to hazard battell, where
the losse of the citie of Athens stood in perill, seeing
they were threescore thousand footmen of the Peloponnesians, and of the Bœotians together: for so
many was their number in the first voyage they made
against the Athenians. And as for those that were
very desirous to fight, and to put themselues to any
hazard, being mad to see their country thus wasted
and destroyed before their eyes, Pericles did comfort
& pacifie them with these words: That trees being
cut and hewne downe, did spring againe in short
time: but men being once dead, by no possibilitie
could be brought againe. Therefore he neuer durst
assemble the people in counsell, fearing lest he should
be inforced by the multitude, to do something still
against his will. But as a wise Pilote, when he seeth
a storme comming on the sea, doth straight giue
order to make all things safe in the shippe, preparing
euery thing ready to defend the storme, according to
his art and skill, not hearkening to the passengers
fearefull cries and pitifull teares, who thinke themselues cast away: euen so did Pericles rule all things
according to his wisedome, hauing walled the city
substantially about, and set good watch in euery

corner: and passed not for those that were angry and offended with him, neither would be perswaded by his friends earnest requests and entreaties, neither cared for his enemies threats nor accusations against him, nor yet reckoned of all their foolish scoffing songs they sung of him in the citie, to the shame and reproch of his gouernment, saying that he was a cowardly captaine, and that for dastardlinesse he let the enemies take al, and spoile what they would. Of which number Cleon was one that most defamed him, and began to enter into some pretie credite and fauour with the common people, for that they were angry, and misliked with Pericles: as appeareth by these slaunderous verses of Hermippus, which were then abroade:

O King of satyres thou, who with such manly speach,
    of bloudy warres and doughty deeds, dost dayly to vs
        preach:
Why art thou now afraid to take thy launce in hand,
    or with thy pike against thy foes, couragiously to
        stand?
Since Cleon stout and fierce, doth dayly thee prouoke,
    with biting words, with trenchant blades, and deadly
        daunting stroke.

All this nothwithstanding, Pericles was neuer mooued any thing, but with silence did patiently beare all iniuries and scoffings of his enemies, and did send for all that a nauie of a hundred saile vnto Peloponnesvs, whither he would not go in person, but kept himselfe at home, to keepe the people in quiet, vntill such time as the enemies had raised their campe, and were gone away. And to entertaine the common people that were offended and angry at this war: he comforted the poore people againe, with causing a certaine distribution to be made amongst them of the common treasure, and diuision also of the lands that were got by conquest. For after he had driuen all the Æginetes out of their countrey, he caused the whole Ile of Ægina to be deuided by lot amongst the citizens of Athens. And then it was a great comfort to them in this aduersitie, to heare of their enemies hurt and losse in such manner as it did fall out. For their army that was sent by sea vnto Peloponnesvs, had wasted and destroyed a great part of the champion country there, and had sacked besides many small cities and townes. Pericles selfe also entring into the Megarians countrey by land, did waste the whole country all afore him. So the Peloponnesians receiuing by sea as much hurt and losse at the Athenians hands, as they before had done by land vnto the Athenians: they had not holden out warres so long with the Athenians, but would soone haue giuen ouer (as Pericles had told them before) had not gods aboue secretly hindred mans reason and pollicie. For first of all there came such a sore plague among the Athenians, that it tooke away the flower of Athens youth, and weakened the force of the whole citie besides. Furthermore the bodies of them that were left aliue being infected with this disease, their hearts also were so sharply bent against Pericles, that the sicknesse hauing troubled their braines, they fell to flat rebellion against him, as the patient against his phisition, or children against their father, euen to the hurting of him, at the prouocation of his enemies: who bruted abroade, that the plague came of no cause else, but of the great multitude of the country men that came into the city on heaps, one vpon anothers necke in the heart of the sommer, where they were compelled to lie many together, smothered vp in litle tents and cabines, remaining there all day long, cowring downewards, and doing nothing, where before they liued in the countrey in a fresh open ayre, and at libertie. And of all this (say they) Pericles is the only cause, who procuring this war, hath pent and shrouded the country men together within the walles of a citie, employing them to no manner of vse nor seruice, but keeping them like sheep in a pinfold, maketh one to poison another with the infection of their plague sores running vpon them, and giuing them no leaue to change aire, that they might so much as take breath abroad. Pericles to remedy this, and to do their enemies a litle mischief, armed a hundred and fifty ships, and shipped into them a great number of armed footmen and horsemen also. Hereby he put the citizens in good hope, and the enemies in great feare, seeing so great a power. But when he had shipped all his men, and was himselfe in the admirall ready to hoise sayle: sodainely there was a great eclypse of the Sunne, and the day was very darke, that all the army was striken with a maruellous feare, as of some dangerous and very ill token towards them. Pericles seeing the maister of his gally in a maze withall, not knowing what to do, cast his cloake ouer the maisters face, and hid his eyes, asking him whether he thought that any harme or no. The maister answered him, he thought it none. Then said Pericles againe to him: There is no difference betweene this and that, sauing that the body which maketh the darknesse is greater, then my cloake which hideth thy eyes. These things are thus disputed of in the schooles of the philosophers. But Pericles hoising saile notwithstanding, did no notable nor speciall service, answerable to so great an army and preparation. For he laying siege vnto the holy citie of Epidavrvm, whē euery man looked they should haue taken it, was compelled to raise his siege for the plague that was so vehement: that it did not only kill the Athenians themselues, but all other also (were they neuer so few) that came to them or neare their campe. Wherefore perceiuing the

Athenians were maruellously offended with him, he
did what he could to comfort them, and put them in
heart againe: but all was in vaine, he could not
pacifie them: for by the most part of voices, they
depriued him of his carge of General, and condemned
him in a maruellous great fine and summe of money,
the which those that tell the least, do write, that it
was the summe of fifteene talents: and those that say
more, speake of fiftie talents. The accuser sub-
scribed in this condemnation, was Cleon, as Idomeneus, or Simmias say, or as Theophrastus writeth:
yet Heraclides Pōticus saith, one Lacratidas. Now
his common griefes were soone blowen ouer: for the
people did easily let fall their displeasure towards
him, as the waspe leaueth her sting behind her with
them she hath stung. But his owne priuate affaires
and household causes were in very ill case: both for
that the plague had taken away many of his friends
and kinsemen from him, as also for that he and his
house had continued a long time in disgrace. For
Xantippus (Pericles sonne and heire) being a man of
a very ill disposition and nature, and hauing married
a young woman very prodigall and lauish of expence,
the daughter of Isander, sonne of Epilychus, he
grudged much at his fathers hardnesse, who scantly
gaue him mony and but a litle at a time. Whereupon
he sent on a time to one of his fathers friends in
Pericles name, to pray him to lend him some money,
who sent it vnto him. But afterwardes when he came
to demaund it againe, Pericles did not onely refuse to
pay it him, but further also he put him in sute. But
this made the young man Xantippus so angrie with
his father, that he spake very ill of him in euery place
where he came: and reported in way of mockery,
how his father spent his time when he was at home,
and what talke he had with the Sophisters, and the
maister Rhetoritians. For a mischaunce fortuning on

a time, at the game of the throwing of the dart, who should throw best, that he that threw, did vnfortunately kill one Epitimius a Thessalian: Xantipous went pratling vp and downe the towne, that his father Pericles was a whole day disputing with Protagoras the Rhetoritian, to knowe which of the three by law and reason should be condemned for this murther. The dart: he that threw the dart: or the deuiser of the game. Moreouer Stesimbrotus writeth, that the brute that ranne thorough the citie, how Pericles did keepe his wife, was sowne abroade by Xantippus himselfe. But so it is, this quarrell and hate betwixt the father and the sonne continued without reconciliation vnto the death. For Xantippus died in the great plague, and Pericles owne sister also: moreover he lost at that time by the plague, the more part of his friendes and kinsfolkes, and those specially that did him greatest pleasure in gouerning of the state. But al this did never pull downe his countenance, nor any thing abate the greatnesse of his mind, what misfortunes soeuer he had sustained. Neither saw they him weep at any time, nor mourne at the funerals of any of his kinsmen or friends, but at the death of Paralus, his yongest and lawful begotten sonne: for, the losse of him alone did onely melt his heart. Yet he did striue to shew his naturall constancie, and to keepe his accustomed modestie. But as he would haue put a garland of flowers vpon his head, sorrow did so pierce his heart when he saw his face, that then he burst out in teares and cried amaine: which they neuer saw him do before all the dayes of his life. Furthermore the people hauing proued other captaines and gouernours, and finding by experience that there was no one of them of iudgement & authority sufficient, for so great a charge: in the end, of themselues they called him againe to the pulpit for orations to heare their counsels, and to the state of a captaine also to take charge of the state. But at that time he kept himselfe close in his house, as one bewailing his late grieuous losse and sorrow. Howbeit Alcibiades, and other his familiar friends, perswaded him to shew himself vnto the people: who did excuse themselues vnto him, for their ingratitude towards him. Pericles then taking the gouernement againe vpon him, the first matter he entred into was: that he prayed them to reuoke the statute he had made for base borne children, fearing least his lawful heires would faile, and so his house and name should fal to the ground. But as for that law, thus it stood: Pericles when he was in his best authoritie, caused a law to be made, that they onely should be counted citizens of Athens, which were naturall Athenians borne by father and mother. Not long time after, it fortuned that the king of Ægypt hauing sent a gift vnto the people of Athens, of 40. thousand bushels of corne, to be distributed among the citizens there: many by occasion of this law were accused to be base borne, & specially men of the baser sort of people, which were not knowne before, or at the least had no reckoning made of them, and so some of them were falsly and wrongfully condemned. Whereupon so it fell out, that there were no lesse than fiue thousand of them conuicted and sold for slaues: and those that remained as free men, and were iudged to be naturall citizens, amounted to the number of fourteene thousand and fortie persons. Now this was much misliked of the people, that a law enacted, and that had bene of such force, should by the selfe same maker and deuiser of the same be againe reuoked and called in. Howbeit Pericles late calamitie that fortuned to his house, did breake the peoples hardened hearts against him: who thinking these sorrowes smart, to be punishment enough vnto him for his former pride, and iudging that by Gods diuine iustice and permission, this plague and losse fell vpon him, and that his request also was tollerable: they suffered him to enrole his base borne sonne in the register of the lawfull citizens of his family, giuing him his owne name, Pericles. It is the selfesame Pericles, who after he had ouercome the Peloponnesians in a great battell by sea, neare vnto the Iles of Arginvses, was put to death by sentence of the people, with other captaines his companions. Now was Pericles at that time infected with the plague, but not so vehemently as other were, but more temperatly: which by long space of time, with many alterations and chaunges, did by litle and litle decay and consume the strength of his body, and ouercame his senses and noble mind. Therefore Theophrastus in his morals declareth, in a place where he disputeth, whether mens manners do chaunge with their misfortunes, and whether corporall troubles and afflictions do so alter men, that they forget vertue, and abandon reason: that Pericles in his sicknesse shewed a friend of his that came to see him, I cannot tell what a preseruing charme, that the women had tied (as a carkanet) about his necke, to let him vnderstand he was very ill, since he suffered them to apply such a foolish bable to him. In the end, Pericles drawing fast vnto his death, the Nobilitie of the citie, and such his friends as were left aliue, standing about his bed, beganne to speake of his vertue, and of the great authoritie he had borne, considering the greatnesse of his noble acts, and counting the number of his victories he had wonne (for he had wonne nine foughten battels being Generall of the Athenians, and had set vp so many tokens and triumphs in honour of his country) they reckened up among themselues all these matters, as if he had not vnderstood them, imagining his senses had bene gone. But he contrarily being yet of perfect memorie, heard all what they had said, and thus he began to speake vnto them: That he maruelled why they had so highly praised that in him, which was common to many other captaines, and wherein fortune dealt with them in equalitie alike, & all this while they had forgotten to speake of the best and most notable thing that was in him, which was, that no Athenian had euer worne blacke gowne through his occasion. And sure so was he a noble and worthy person. For he did not onely shew himselfe merciful and courteous, euen in most weightie matters of gouernment among so enuious people and hatefull enemies: but he had this judgement also to thinke, that the most noble acts he did were these, that he neuer gaue himselfe to hatred, enuy, nor choler, to be reuenged of his most mortal enemy, without mercy shewed towards him, though he had committed vnto him such absolute power & sole gouernment among them. And this made his surname be Olympius (as to say, diuine or celestiall) which otherwise for him had bene too proud and arrogant a name, because he was of so good and gentle a nature, and for that in so great libertie he had kept cleane hands and vndefiled: euen as we esteeme the gods authors of all good, and causers of no euill, and so worthy to gouerne and rule the whole monarchy of the world. And not as Poets say, which do confound our wits by their follies, and fond fainings, and are also contrary to themselues, considering that they call heauen (which containeth the gods) the everlasting seate, which trembleth not, and is not driuen nor moued with winds, neither is darkned with cloudes, but is alwayes bright and cleare, and at all times shining equally with a pure bright light, as being the onely habitation and mansion place of the eternall God, onely happy and immortall: and afterwards they describe it themselues, full of dissentions, of enmities, of anger, and passions, which do nothing become wise and learned men. But this discourse peraduenture would be better spoken of in some other booke. Now the troubles the Athenians felt immediatly after Pericles death, made them then lament the losse of so noble a member. For those who vnpatiently did brooke his great authoritie while he liued, because it drowned their owne: when they came after his death to proue other speakers and gouernours, they were compelled then to confesse, that no mans nature liuing could be more moderate nor graue, with lenitie and mercy, then was his. And that most hated power, which in his life time they called monarchie, did then most plainely appeare vnto them, to haue bene the manifest ramper and bulwarke of the safety of their whole state and common-weale: such corruption and vice in gouernement of the state did then spring vp immediately after his death, which when he was aliue, he did euer suppresse and keepe vnder, in such sort, that either it did not appeare at all, or at the least it came not to that head and libertie, that such faults were committed, as were vnpossible to be remedied.

TIMON OF ATHENS.

THE novel here given from Painter's "Palace of Pleasure," was not included in the former edition; yet it was evidently seen by our poet, and probably was of service to him. With the "Life of Timon" from North, may be read the short passing notice of him, which occurs in Plutarch's "Life of Mark Antony," already (iii. 399-400) printed as an illustration of "Antony and Cleopatra," and the "Life of Alcibiades" in North.

The old play of "Timon" will form part of the second series, or Foundation-Dramas.

Mr Hunter ("New Illustrations," ii. 142) remarks, "He (Shakespeare) has contrived to introduce everything that Plutarch says of Timon in the two lives in which he occurs, Alcibiades and Mark Antony. He seems also to have been acquainted with Lucian's Dialogue." But I concur with Douce here as to Lucian: "We are at liberty to doubt how far Apemantus [the character in the play so-called] is a copy from Lucian, or rather to believe that he is a highly-finished portrait after a very slight sketch by Plutarch ("Illustr." ii. 69).

1. *The Life of Timon.*

[*From Painter's "Palace of Pleasure,"* 1566, vol. i.]

—o—

The Twenty-Eighth Nouell.

Of the straunge and beastlie nature of Timon of Athens, enemie to mankinde, with his death, buriall, and Epitaphe.

AL the beastes of the worlde do applye theimselues to other beastes of theyre kind, Timon of Athens onely excepted : of whose straunge nature Plutarche is astonied, in the life of Marcus Antonius. Plato and Aristophanes do report his marueylous nature, because hee was a man but by shape onely, in qualities hee was the capitall enemie of mankinde, which he confessed franckely vtterly to abhorre and hate. He dwelt alone in a litle cabane in the fieldes not farre from Athenes, separated from all neighbours and company : he neuer wente to the citie, or to any other habitable place, except he were constrayned : he could not abide any mans company and conuersation : he was neuer seen to goe, to any mannes house, ne yet would suffer them to come to him. At the same time there was in Athenes another of like qualitie, called Apemantus, of the very same nature, differente from the naturall kinde of man, and lodged likewise in the middes of the fields. On a day they two being alone together at dinner, Apemantus said vnto him: "O Timon what a pleasant feast is this, and what a merie companie are wee, being no more but thou and I." "Naie (quoth Timon) it would be a merie banquet in deede, if there were none here but my selfe."

Wherein he shewed how like a beast (in deede) he was: for he could not abide any other man, beinge not able to suffer the company of him, which was of like nature. And if by chaunce hee happened to goe to Athenes, it was onelye to speake with Alcibiades, who then was an excellente captaine there, wherat many did marueile: and therefore Apemantus demaunded of him, why he spake to no man, but to Alcibiades. "I speake to him sometimes, said Timon, because I know that by his occasion, the Atheniens shall receiue great hurt and trouble." Which wordes many times he told to Alcibiades himselfe. He had a garden adioyning to his house in the fields, wherin was a figge tree, whereuppon many desperate men ordinarily did hange themselues: in place whereof, he purposed to set vp a house, and therefore was forced to cutte it downe, for which cause hee went to Athenes, and in the markette place, hee called the people about him, saying that hee had newes to telle them: when the people vnderstoode that he was about to make a discourse vnto them, which was wont to speake to no man, they marueiled, and the citizens on euery parte of the citie, ranne to heare him: to whom he saide, that he purposed to cutte downe his figge tree, to builde a house vpon the place where it stoode. "Wherefore (quoth he) if there be any man amonges you all in this company, that is disposed to hang himselfe, let him come betimes, before

it be cutte downe." Hauing thus bestowed his
charitie amonges the people, hee retourned to his
lodging, wher he liued a certaine time after, without
alteration of nature; and because that nature
chaunged not in his life time, he would not suffer
that death should alter, or varie the same: for like
as he liued a beastly and chorlish life, euen so he
required to haue his funerall done after that maner.
By his last will, he ordeined himselfe to be interred
vpon the sea shore, that the waues and surges might
beate and vexe his dead carcas. Yea, and that if it
were possible, his desire was to be buried in the
depth of the sea: causing an epitaphe to be made,
wherin was described the qualities of his brutishe
life. Plutarche also reported an other to be made by
Calimachus, much like to that which Timon made
himselfe, whose owne soundeth to this effect in Eng-
lishe verse.

> *My wretched catife dayes,*
> *Expired now and past:*
> *My carren corps intered here,*
> *Is faste in grounde:*
> *In waltring waues of swel-*
> *ling sea, by surges cast,*
> *My name if thou desire,*
> *The gods thee doe confounde.*

2. *Account of Timon of Athens.*

———o———

[*From* "*A Discourse of the Felicity of Man*," *by Sir Richard Barckley*, 4o., 1598.]

ANOTHER company there were of a most strange disposition, that would not only murmur and grudge at the nature and condition of men, but were as hateful enemies to their own kind, supposing that Nature had set up man as a butt or mark, against which she would discharge all the bullets of her wrath and indignation; amongst which sort of men was one called Tymon, a philosopher of Athens, who professed himself openly an enemy of mankind, and performed it in effect. But he would never dwell or keep among men, but withdrew himself into the deserts, and led his life among beasts, that he might not be seen of men; and, passing his life in this solitary sort, he would speak to no man, saving only with Alcibiades, a valiant gentleman of Athens, neither with him for any love he had to the man, but for that he did foresee that he would be one day a plague and scourge

to men, and especially to the Athenians; and it was
not sufficient for him to abhor and detest the company of men as furious wild beasts, but he sought all
the means he could, if it could have been possible, to
destroy mankind, and for that purpose he set up a
great many gibbets in his garden, that desperate folks
and such as were weary of their lives might hang
themselves; and after certain years, meaning to enlarge his little cottage where he dwelt, he determined
to cut down those gibbets for his building; and being
loath the lack of them should be any hindrance to his
citizens' death, he went to Athens, and openly in the
market place he caused the people to be assembled
that he might deliver some news to them, who, knowing his humour that used to speak to no man, ran to
the place out of all parts, expecting attentively some
strange matter. When they were come together, he
cried out with his hoarse voice, "My citizens of
Athens, if any of you be disposed to hang yourselves
do it quickly, for I mean shortly to cut down the gibbets for my necessary building." And when he had
ended his charitable motion, he departed home to his
house without speaking any word more, where he
lived many years, continuing in the same opinion,
detesting the miserable state and condition of men.
And when Tymon perceived that death approached,
he took order for his burial to be at the low-water
mark in the very brink of the sea, that the waves
might not suffer any man to come near him to see his
bones or ashes, and caused this epitaph to be written
upon his tomb, made Latin thus :—

> Hic sum post vitam miseramque inopemque sepultus;
> Nomen non quæras; Dii, lector, te male perdant.

And as another of his condition that lived solitarily
in the woods, eschewing likewise the company of
men, came to him to supper; in the midst of

the banquet, O Tymon (quoth he) what a pleasant supper is this that hath no more guests than thou and I. So were it (said Tymon) if thou were away. He was so hateful to the condition of men that he could not endure the company of him that was of his own disposition.

THE TAMING OF A SHREW.

THE old comedy with this title, and on this subject, which preceded Shakespeare's, and which he had undoubtedly before him, is inserted in *Part the Second*. Its interest for us is enhanced by the more than possibility that in its original shape it received certain touches from Shakespeare's hand at the time when he was bestowing a considerable share of his attention on the alteration of existing dramas, before he entered on the composition of pieces, in which he depended chiefly on the inspiration of his own genius.

The ballad of the "Curst Wife lapt in Morel's Skin" seemed scarcely worth its room, as it is printed in Hazlitt's "Popular Poetry;" but although it has nothing in common with Shakespeare's play, and is a lamentable piece of doggrel, there was such a desire to collect together all the probable Aids and Lights to the works of the great poet, that it has been admitted.

As regards Shakespeare's indebtedness to another source— the "Suppositi" of Ariosto, as translated by George Gascoigne, and performed at Gray's Inn in 1566, the reader should consult Mr Hunter's work (i. 352); and it may be sufficient to add, that the English version of the "Suppositi" has been rendered accessible in Hazlitt's edition of Gascoigne.

The "Waking Man's Fortune" is reprinted from the "Shakepeare Society's Papers," vol. ii., where it is described as a small fragment of an otherwise unrecovered publication; and whether it be identical or no with the lost story-book of Richard Edwards, cited by Warton, it gives us the tale of the Tinker, which makes the Induction to the drama, and which we trace back to the "Arabian Nights." It is common to many collections, and Mr Hunter relates the curious anecdote, relevant and apposite to it, of the Marquis of Worcester.

1. *Story of the Induction.*

(i.) VANITY OF THE WORLD AS REPRESENTED IN STATE.[1]

———o———

[*From Goulart's "Admirable and Memorable Histories,"* 1607, *p.* 587-9.]

PHILIP called the good Duke of Bourgondy, in the memory of our ancestors, being at Bruxells with his Court and walking one night after supper through the streets, accompanied with some of his fauorits: he found lying vpon the stones a certaine Artisan that was very dronke, and that slept soundly. It pleased the Prince in this Artisan to make triall of the vanity of our life, whereof he had before discoursed with his familiar friends. Hee therfore caused this sleeper to be taken vp and carried into his Pallace : hee commands him to bee layed in one of the richest beds, a riche Night-cap to bee giuen him, his foule shirt to bee taken off. and to have an other put on him of fine Holland : when as this Dronkard had disgested his Wine, and began to awake : behold there comes about his bed, Pages and Groomes of

---

[1] [This is the same story as "The Waking Man's Dream" differently told. It also related by Burton in his "Anatomy of Melancholy," 1624. See Hazlitt's Warton, iv. 218-19.]

the Dukes Chamber, who drawe the Curteines, make
many courtesies, and being bare-headed, aske him if
it please him to rise, and what apparell it would please
him to put on that day. They bring him rich apparrell. This new Monsieur amazed at such curtesie,
and doubting whether hee dreampt or waked, suffered
himselfe to be drest, and led out of the Chamber.
There came Noblemen which saluted him with all
honour, and conduct him to the Masse, where with
great ceremonie they giue him the Booke of the Gos-
pell, and the Pixe to kisse, as they did vsually vnto
the Duke: from the Masse they bring him backe
vnto the Pallace: hee washes his hands, and sittes
downe at the Table well furnished. After dinner, the
great Chamberlaine commandes Cardes, to be brought
with a great summe of money. This Duke in Imagination playes with the chiefe of the Court. Then
they carrie him to walke in the Gardein, and to hunt
the Hare and to Hawke. They bring him back vnto
the Pallace, where hee sups in state. Candles beeing
light, the Musitions begin to play, and the Tables
taken away, the Gentlemen and Gentle-women fell
to dancing, then they played a pleasant Comedie,
after which followed a Banket, whereas they had presently store of Ipocras and precious Wine, with all
sorts of confitures, to this Prince of the new Impression, so as he was drunke, & fell soundlie a sleepe.
Here-upon the Duke commanded that hee should
bee disrobed of all his riche attire. Hee was put
into his olde ragges and carried into the same place,
where he had been found, the night before, where hee
spent that night. Being awake in the morning, hee
beganne to remember what had happened before, hee
knewe not whether it were true in deede, or a dreame
that had troubled his braine. But in the end, after
many discourses, hee concluds that all was but a
dreame that had happened vnto him, and so enter-

tained his wife, his Children and his neighbors, without any other apprehension. This Historie put mee in minde of that which Seneca sayth in the ende of his 59. letter to Lvcilivs. No man saies he, can reioyce and content himselfe, if he be not nobly minded, iust and temperate. What then? Are the wicked depriued of all ioye? they are glad as the Lions that haue found their prey. Being full of wine and luxury, hauing spent the night in gourmandise, when as pleasures poored into this vessell of the bodie (beeing to little to conteine so much) beganne to foame out, these miserable wretches crie with him of whome Virgill speakes,

Thou knowest, how in the midest of pastimes false & vaine,
We cast and past our latest night of paine.

The dissolute spend the night, yea the last night in false ioyes. O man, this stately vsage of the aboue named Artisan, is like vnto a dreame that passeth. And his goodly day, and the years of a wicked life differ nothing, but in more and lesse. He slept foure and twenty houres, other wicked men some-times foure and twenty thousands of houres. It is a little or a great dreame: and nothing more.

(ii.) *The Waking Man's Dream.*

---o---

It strikes me that I have found the original of the Induction to "The Taming of the Shrew;" and my object in forwarding the present paper is that some member of the Shakespeare Society should throw farther light upon the subject.

Warton, in his "History of English Poetry," iv. 117, edit. 1824, informs us that a collection of comic stories by Richard Edwards, dated 1570, and printed in black letter, contained the incidents of the Induction in question. This fact does not depend upon the statement of Collins that he had the book, but upon the assertion of Warton that he himself had seen it. He adds, that the library was dispersed, and nobody seems to have heard since of the volume. It would be singular if the amusing collection made by Edwards, and published in 1570, were never reprinted; and I apprehend that I have now in my hands a portion of a reprint of it, containing the very tale on which the Induction to Shakespeare's "Taming of *the* Shrew," and to the older "Taming of *a* Shrew," was founded. It is a mere fragment of a book, and contains no more than this story, so that we can only judge of its date by its type and orthography: the type and orthography appear to me to be as old as about the year 1620 or 1630, and it begins upon p. 59, and ends upon p. 67. Of the orthography the reader will be able to form an opinion from what follows; and, having been a student of old books for the last twenty or thirty years, I think I can speak positively to the date of the type, which is rather large Roman letter, much worn and battered. The words, "the fifth event," at the commencement, show that four stories preceded it, but by how many it was followed it is impossible to decide. I should not be surprised if the old language of 1570 had been in some degree modernized in 1620 or 1630, but upon that point it is not necessary for me to offer an opinion.

If my conjecture be correct, that Edwards's story-book of 1570 was reprinted fifty or sixty years afterwards, and that my five leaves are a portion of that reprint, we have arrived at the source of the Induction to "The Taming of *a* Shrew;" for I take it for granted that Shakespeare's comedy was constructed upon the older play, in which the Induction stands, in substance, as it is given by our immortal dramatist. I subjoin a *verbatim et literatim* copy of my fragment, and I shall be happy to receive any farther information regarding it, either through "The Shakespeare Society's Papers," or otherwise.

H. G. NORTON.

LIVERPOOL, *March* 4, 1845.

THE WAKING MAN'S DREAME.

The Fifth Event.

THE Greek proverbe saith, that a man is but the dreame of a shaddow, or the shaddow of a dreame: is there then anything more vaine then a shadow, which is nothing in it selfe, being but a privation of light framed by the opposition of a thicke body unto a luminous? is there any thing more frivolous then a dreame, which hath no subsistence but in the hollownesse of a sleeping braine, and which, to speake properly, is nothing but a meere gathering together of Chimericall Images, and this is it which makes an ancient say, that we are but dust and shadow: our life is compared unto those, who sleeping dreame that they eate, and waking find themselves empty and hungry; and who is he that doth not find this experimented in himselfe, as often as he revolves in his memory the time which is past? who can in these passages of this world distinguish the things which have been done from those that have beene dreamed? vanities, delights, riches, pleasures, and all are past and gone ; are they not dreames ? What hath our pride and pompe availed us? say those poore miserable soules shut up in the infernall prisons: where is our bravery become, and the glorious show of our magnificence? all these things are passed like a flying shadow, or as a post who hastens to his journeyes end. This is it which caused the ancient Comicke Poet to say that the world was nothing but an universall Comedy, because all the passages thereof serve but to make the wisest laugh : and, according to the opinion of Democritus, all that is acted on this great Theater of the whole world, when it is ended, differs in nothing from what hath bin acted on a Players stage : the mirrour which I will heere set before your eyes will so lively expresse all these verities, and so truly shew the vanities of all the greatnesse and opulencies of the earth, that although in these Events, I gather not either examples not farre distant from our times, or that have beene published by any other writer, yet I beleeve that the serious pleasantnesse of this one will supply its want of novelty, and that its repetition will neither bee unfruitfull nor unpleasing.

In the time that Phillip Duke of Burgundy (who by the gentlenesse and curteousnesse of his carriage purchaste the name of good) guided the reines of the country of Flanders, this prince, who was of an humour pleasing, and full of judicious goodnesse, rather then silly simplicity, used pastimes which for their singularity are commonly called the pleasures of Princes : after this manner he no lesse shewed the quaintnesse of his wit then his prudence.

Being in Bruxelles with all his court, and having at his table discoursed amply enough of the vanities and greatnesse of this world, he let each one say his pleasure on this subject, whereon was alleadged grave sentences and rare examples : walking towards the evening in the towne, his head full of divers thoughts, he found a Tradesman lying in a corner sleeping very soundly, the fumes of Bacchus having surcharged his braine. I describe this mans drunkenesse in as good manner as I can to the credit of the party. This vice is so common in both the superior and inferiour Germany, that divers, making glory and vaunting of their dexterity in this art, encrease their praise thereby, and hold it for a brave act. The good Duke, to give his followers an example of the vanity of all the magnificence with which he was invironed, devised a meanes farre lesse dangerous than that which Dionysius the Tyrant used towards Democles, and which in pleasantnesse beares a marvellous utility. He caused his men to carry away this sleeper, with whom, as with a blocke, they might doe what they would, without awaking him; he caused them to carry him into one of the sumptuosest parts of his Pallace, into a chamber most state-like furnished, and makes them lay him on a rich bed. They presently strip him of his bad cloathes, and put him on a very fine and cleane shirt, instead of his own, which was foule and filthy. They let him sleepe in that place at his ease, and whilest hee settles his drinke the Duke prepares the pleasantest pastime that can be imagined.

In the morning, this drunkard being awake drawes the curtaines of this brave rich bed, sees himselfe in a chamber adorned like a Paradice, he considers the rich furniture with an amazement such as you may imagine: he beleeves not his eyes, but layes his fingers on them, and feeling them open, yet perswades himselfe they are shut by sleep, and that all he sees is but a pure dreame.

As soone as he was knowne to be awake, in comes the officers of the Dukes house, who were instructed by the Duke what they should do. There were pages bravely apparelled, Gentlemen of the chamber, Gentleman waiters, and the High Chamberlaine, who, all in faire order and without laughing, bring cloathing for this new guest: they honour him with the same great reverences as if hee were a Soveraigne Prince; they serve him bare headed, and aske him what suite hee will please to weare that day.

This fellow, affrighted at the first, beleeving these things to be inchantment or dreames, reclaimed by these submissions, tooke heart, and grew bold, and setting a good face on the matter, chused amongst all the apparell that they presented unto him that which he liked best, and which hee thought to be fittest for him: he is accommodated like a King, and served with such ceremonies, as he had never seene before, and yet beheld them without saying any thing, and with an assured countenance. This done, the greatest Nobleman in the Dukes Court enters the chamber with the same reverence and honour to him as if he had been their Soveraigne Prince (Phillip with Princely delight beholds this play from a private place); divers of purpose petitioning him for pardons, which hee grants with such a continuance and gravity, as if he had had a Crowne on his head all his life time.

Being risen late, and dinner time approaching, they asked him if he were pleased to have his tables covered. He likes that very well. The table is furnished, where he is set alone, and under a rich Canopie; he eates with the same ceremony which was observed at the Dukes meales; he made good cheere, and chawed with all his teeth, but only drank with more moderation then he could have wisht, but the Majesty which he represented made him refraine. All taken away, he was entertained with new and pleasant things: they led him to walk about the great Chambers, Galleries, and Gardens of the Pallace (for all this merriment was played within the gates, they being shut only for recreation to the Duke and the principall of his Court): they shewed him all the richest and most pleasantest things therin, and talked to him thereof as if they had all beene his, which he heard with an attention and contentment beyond measure, not saying one word of his base condition, or delaring that they tooke him for another. They made him passe the afternoone in all kinds of sports; musicke, dancing, and a Comedy, spent some part of the time. They talked to him of some State matters, whereunto he answered according to his skill, and like a right Twelfetide King.

Super time approaching, they aske this new created Prince if he would please to have the Lords and Ladies of his Court to sup and feast with him; whereat he seemed something unwilling, as if hee would not abase his dignity unto such familiarity: nevertheslesse, counterfeiting humanity and affability, he made signes that he condiscended thereunto: he then, towards night, was led with sound of Trumpets and Hoboyes into a faire hall, where long tables were set, which were presently covered with divers sorts of dainty meates, the Torches shined in every corner, and made a day in the midst of a night: the Gentlemen and Gentlewomen were set in fine order, and the Prince at the upper end in a higher seat. The service was magnificent; the musicke of voyces and instruments fed the eare, whilest mouthes found their food in the dishes. Never was the imaginary Duke at such a feast: carousses begin after the manner of the Country; the Prince is assaulted on all sides, as the Owle is assaulted by all the Birds, when he begins to soare. Not to seeme uncivill, he would doe the like to his good and faithfull subjects. They serve him with very strong wine, good Hipocras, which hee swallowed downe in great draughts, and frequently redoubled; so that, charged with so many extraordinaryes, he yeelded to deaths cousin german, sleep, which closed his eyes, stopt his eares, and made him loose the use of his reason and all his other sences.

Then the right Duke, who had put himselfe among the throng of his Officers to have the pleasure of this mummery, commanded that this sleeping man should be stript out of his brave cloathes, and cloathed againe in his old ragges, and so sleeping carried and layd in the same place where he was taken up the night before. This was presently done, and there did he snort all the night long, not taking any hurt either from the hardnesse of the stones or the night ayre, so well was his stomacke filled with good preservatives. Being awakened in the morning by some passenger, or it maye bee by some that the good Duke Philip had thereto appointed, ha! said he, my friends, what have you done? you have rob'd mee of a Kingdome, and have taken mee out of the sweetest and happiest dreame that ever man could have fallen into. Then, very well remembring all the particulars of what had passed the day before, he related unto them, from point to point, all that had happened unto him, still thinking it assuredly to bee a dreame. Being returned home to his house, hee entertaines his wife, neighbours, and friends, with this his dreame, as hee thought: the truth whereof being at last published by the mouthes of those Courtiers who had been present at this pleasant recreation, the good man could not beleeve it, thinking that for sport they had framed this history upon his dreame; but when Duke Philip, who would have the full contentment of this pleasant tricke, had shewed him the bed wherein he lay, the cloathes which he had worne, the persons who had served him, the Hall wherein he had eaten, the gardens and galleries wherein he had walked, hardly could hee be induced to beleeve what hee saw, imagining that all this was meere inchantment and illusion.

The Duke used some liberality towards him for to helpe him in the poverty of his family; and, taking an occasion thereon to make an Oration unto his Courtiers concerning the vanity of this worlds honours, hee told them that all that ambitious persons seeke with so much industry is but smoake, and a meere dreame, and that they are strucken with that pleasant folly of the Athenian, who imagined that all the riches that arrived by shipping in the haven of Athens to be his, and that all the Marchants were but his factors: his friends getting him cured by a skilfull Physitian of the debility of his brain, in lieu of giving them thanks for this good office, he reviled them, saying that, whereas he was rich in conceit, they had by this cure made him poore and miserable in effect.

Harpaste, a foole that Senecaes wife kept, and whose pleasant imagination this grave Phylosopher doth largely relate, being growne blind, could not perswade herselfe that she was so, but continually complained that the house wherein she dwelt was dark, that they would not open the windowes, and that they hindred her from setting light, to make her beleeve she could see nothing: hereupon this great Stoick makes this fine consideration, that every vitious man is like unto this foole, who, although he be blind in his passion, yet thinks not himselfe to be so, casting all his defect on false surmises, whereby he seeks not only to have his sinne worthy of excuse and pardon, but even of praise : the same say the covetous, ambitious, and voluptuous persons, in defence of their imperfections; but in fine (as the Psalmist saith), all that must passe awaye, and the images thereof come to nothing, as the dreame of him that awaketh from sleepe.

If a bucket of water be as truly water, as all the sea, the difference only remaining in the quantity, not in the quality, why shall we not say, that our poore

Brabander was a Soveraigne Prince for the space of fowre and twenty houres, being that he received all the honours and commodities thereof: how many Kings and Popes have not lasted longer, but have dyed on the very day of their Elections or Coronations? As for those other pompes, which have lasted longer, what are they else but longer dreames? This vanity of worldly things is a great sting to a well composed soule, to helpe it forward towards the heavenly kingdome."

2. *A Merry Jest of a Shrewd and Curst Wife Lapped in Morel's Skin, for her Good Behaviour.*

————o————

[THE following humorous tale in verse has no especial relation in its incidents to Shakespeare's "Taming of the Shrew," and consequently none to the older comedy reprinted in the present work; but it is of a similar character, and has always been mentioned in connection with both: it is therefore appended, in order that the ancient materials existing in the time of our great dramatist, and most likely well known to him, may be at one view before the reader. Regarding the merit of " The Wife lapped in Morels Skin," as a piece of popular poetry, there can be no dispute. The author of it is unknown: at the end, we read " Finis, quoth Mayster Charme her," but that is evidently an assumed name.

The poem was included by Mr Utterson, in 1817, in his two excellent and amusing volumes; but our edition has been made from a fresh collation (for which we are indebted to Mr Halliwell) with the original copy (wanting one leaf) in the Bodleian Library, so that it differs in no other respect than that we have not adopted the black-letter type. When Mr Utterson republished it, he apprehended that the entry in the Stationers' Registers, in 1594, referred to it; for, in 1817, the copies of the old "Taming of *a* Shrew," of 1594 and 1596, had not been discovered. It is to the first of these, unquestionably, that the memorandum in the Stationers' Registers relates.

It was long supposed that only two copies of " The Wife lapped in Morels Skin" were known; but this now appears to be a mistake, although it is certainly a production of great rarity. It came from the press of Hugh Jackson, without date, but about 1550 or 1560, under the following title:—

"Here begynneth a merry Ieste of a shrewde and curste Wyfe, lapped in Morrelles Skin, for her good behauyour.—Imprinted at London in Fleetestrete, beneath the Conduite, at the signe of Saint Iohn Euangelist, by H. Jackson."

The only differences in the colophon are, that the word "Saint" is represented by the capital initial, and that the printer's Christian name is given at length. The popularity of the poem is not to be doubted; and in Laneham's celebrated "Letter from Kenilworth," 1575, "the wife lapt in Morels skin" is enumerated as one of the stories which Captain Cox had "at hiz fingers endz."—See Collier's "Bridgewater Catalogue," p. 163.—*Collier*.]

LYSTEN, friendes, and holde you still,
 Abide a while and dwell:
A mery Iest tell you I will,
And how that it befell.
As I went walking vpon a day,
Among my friendes to sporte:
To an house I tooke the way,
To rest me for my comforte.

A greate feaste was kept there than,
And many one was thereat:
With wyues and maydens, and many a good man,
That made good game and chat.
It befell then at that tyde
An honest man was there:
A cursed Dame sate by his syde,
That often did him dere.

His wife she was, I tell you playne,
This dame, ye may me trowe:
To play the maister she would not layne
And make her husband bowe.
At euery word that she did speake,
To be at peace he was full fayne,
Or else she would take him on the cheeke,
Or put him to other payne.

When she did winke, he durste not stere,
Nor play where euer he wente,
With friend or neighbour to make good chere,
Whan she her browes bente.
These folke had two maydens fayre and free,
Which were their daughters dere:
This is true, beleeue you me,
Of condicions was none their pere.

The yongest was meeke, and gentle ywys,
Her Fathers condicion she had:
The eldest her mothers withouten misse,
Sometime franticke, and sometime mad.
The father had his pleasure in the one alway,
And glad he was her to behold:
The mother in the other, this is no nay,
For in all her curstnesse she made her bolde.

And at last she was in fay,
As curst as her mother in worde and deede,
Her mischieuous pageauntes sometime to play,
Which caused her fathers heart to bleede:
For he was woe and nothing glad,
And of her would fayne be rid:
He wished to God that some man her had,
But yet to maryage he durst her not bid.

Full many there come the yongest to haue,
But her father was loth her to forgoe:
None there came the eldest to craue,
For feare it should turne them to woe.
The Father was loth any man to beguile,
For he was true and iust withall,
Yet there came one within a while,
That her demaunded in the Hall.

Another there came right soone also,
The yongest to haue he would be fayne,
Which made the fathers heart full woe,
That he and the yongest should part in twayne.

But the mother was fell, and might her not see,
Wherefore of her she would haue bene rid :
The yong man full soone she graunted pardy,
Greate Golde and syluer with her she bid.

Saying, full soone he would her haue,
And wedded they were, shorte tale to make :
The Father sayd, so God me saue,
For heauinesse and sorrowe I tremble and quake.
Also his hearte was in greate care,
How he should bestowe the eldest y wys,
Which should make his purse full bare :
Of her he would be rid by heauens blisse.

As hap was that this yong man should
Desyre the eldest withouten fayle :
To maryage, he sayd, full fayne he would,
That he might her haue for his auayle.
The father sayd with wordes anon,
Golde and syluer I would thee giue :
If thou her marry, by sweete Saynt John,
But thou shouldest repent it all thy liue.

She is conditioned, I tell thee playne,
Moste like a Fiend, this is no nay :
Her Mother doth teach her, withouten layne,
To be mayster of her husband another day.
If thou shouldest her marry, and with her not gree,
Her mother thou shouldest haue alway in thy top :
By night and day that shouldest vex thee,
Which sore would sticke then in thy crop.

And I could not amend it, by God of might,
For I dare not speake my selfe for my life :
Something among, be it wrong or right,
I let her haue all for feare of strife.
If I ought say she doth me treate,
Except I let her haue her will,
As a childe that should be beate
She will me charme : the Deuill her kill.

Another thing thou must vnderstande,
Her mother's good will thou must haue also:
If she be thy friend, by sea or by lande
Amisse with thee then can it not go.
For she doth her loue with all her minde,
And would not see her fare amisse:
If thou to her dareling could be kinde,
Thou couldest not want, by heauens blisse.

If thou so the mother now wilt seeke,
Behaue thy selfe then like a man:
And shew thy selfe both humble and meeke,
But when thou haste her, doe what thou can.
Thou wotest what I sayd to thee before,
I counsayle thee marke my wordes well:
It weare great pitty, thou werte forelore,
With such a deuillishe Fende of hell.

I care not for that, the yong man sayd:
If I can get the mothers good will,
I would be glad to haue that mayde,
Me thinketh she is withouten euell.
Alas! good man, I am sorry for thee,
That thou wilt cast thy selfe away,
Thou art so gentle and so free:
Thou shalt neuer tame her, I dare well say.

But I haue done, I will say no more,
Therfore farewell, and goe thy way:
Remember what I sayd to thee before,
And beware of repentaunce another day.

How the yong man departed from the Father, and sought to the Mother for to haue the mayde to mariage.

Now is the yong man come to the dame,
With countenaunce glad, and manners demure:
Saying to her, God keepe you from blame,
With your dere daughter so fayre and pure.

She welcommeth agayne the fayre yong man,
And bid him come neare, gentle friende:
Full curteously he thanked the good dame than,
And thought her wordes full good and kinde.

Then he began, I shall you tell,
Unto the mother thus to say,
With wordes fayre that become him well,
For her deare daughter thus to pray:
Saying, good dame, now by your leaue,
Take it for none euell though I come here,
If you to me good leaue would giue,
With you right fayne would I make good chere.

The dame sayd: syt downe, a while abyde,
Good chere anon than will we make:
My daughter shall sit downe by thy syde,
I know well thou commest onely for her sake.
You say full true forsooth, sayd he,
My minde is stedfastly on her set:
To haue that mayde fayre and free,
I would be fayne, if I coulde her get.

The mother thanked him for his good will,
That he her daughter so did desyre:
Saying, I hope you come for none euell,
But in good honesty her to requyre.
For if ye did, I will be playne,
Right soone it shoulde turne you vnto griefe,
And also your comming I would disdayne,
And bid you walke with a wylde mischiefe.

But surely I take you for none of those,
Your condiscions shew it in no wise:
Wherefore me thinke you doe not glose,
Nor I will not counsell you by mine aduise.
For I loue my Daughter as my harte,
And loth I were, I will be playne,
To see her suffer payne and smarte,
For if I did my harte were slayne.

If that thou shouldest another day
My daughter haue, and her good will,
Order her then vnto her pay
As reason requireth, it is good skill.
In women sometime great wisdome is,
And in men full little it is often seene,
But she is wise withouten mis,
From a yong child vp she hath so beene.

Therefore to her thou must audience giue
For thine owne profite, when she doth speake,
And than shalt thou in quiet liue,
And much strife thus shalte thou breake.
Howe sayest thou, yong man, what is thy minde?
Wouldest thou her haue, my doughter dere?
Than to her thou must be kinde,
And alway ready to make her good chere.

For an C. li. of money haue thou shalte,
Of Syluer and eke of Golde so round,
With an C. quarters of Corne and malte,
And xl. acres of good ground;
If thou wilt liue with her like a man,
Thou shalt her haue, and this will I giue,
And euer after while I can,
Be thy good Mother as long as I liue.

And I will speake to my daughter for thee,
To know if it be her will also:
If she be content, my daughter free,
Then together may ye go.
The mother demaunded her daughter than,
If that she could fynde in her minde,
With all her harte to loue that yong man,
So that he to her would be kinde?

She sayd, yea, mother, as you wyll,
So will I doe in worde and deede:
I trust he commeth for none yll,
Therefore the better may we speede.

But I would haue one that hath some good,
As well as I, good reason is :
Me thinke he is a lusty blood,
But gooddes there must be withouten misse.

The yong man was glad these wordes to heare,
And thanked the mother of her good will,
Beholding the Mayden with right mild cheare,
And prayed her hartely to be still :
Saying to her then in this wise,
Mine heart, my loue, my dearling deare,
Take no displeasure of my enterprise,
That I desyre to be your peare.

I am not riche of Gold nor fee,
Nor of great marchandise, ye shall vnderstand,
But a good Crafte I haue, pardee,
To get our liuing in any land :
And in my heart I can well fynde,
You for to loue aboue all other,
For euermore to you to be kynde,
And neuer forsake you for none other.

Lyke a woman I will you vse,
And doe you honour, as ye should doe me :
And for your sake all other refuse,
As good reason is it should so be.
By my trouth, but well you say,
And me thinke by your countenaunce ywis,
That ye should not another day,
For no cause deale with me amis.

And in you I hope pleasure to take,
If ye woulde be gentle as ye should,
And neuer none other for your sake,
To marry for a M. pound of gold.
But sometime ye must me a little forbeare,
For I am hasty, but it is soone done :
In my fume I doe nothing feare,
Whatsoeuer thereof to me become.

And I cannot refrayne me in no wise,
For I haue it by nature a parte y wis.
It was wont to be my mothers guise,
Sometime to be mayster withouten misse:
And so must I, by God, now and than,
Or else I would thinke it should not be well,
For though ye were neuer so good a man,
Sometime among I will beare the bell.

And therefore tell me with wordes playne,
If ye can be pacient what time it is,
To suffer me with a little payne,
Though that you thinke I doe amisse?
Or else say nay, and make a shorte ende,
And soone we shall asonder departe:
Then at your liberty you may hence wend,
Yet I doe loue you with all my harte.

The yong man was glad of her loue, in fay,
But loth he was master her for to make,
And bethought him what her father before did
  saye,
When he on wooing his iorney did take:
And so consented to all her will,
When he aduised him what he should doe.
He sayd, ye may me saue or spill,
For ye haue my loue, sweete heart, and no
  moe.

The mother, hearing this, for the father
  sente,
Shewing to him what was befall:
Wherewith he was right well content,
Of all their promises in generall.
Upon this greement they departed then,
To prepare all thinges for the feast:
Glad was the bride and her spouse then,
That they were come to this beheast.

*How the Bryde was maryed with her Father and
Mothers good wyll.*

The day approched, the time drue neare,
That they should be wedded withouten misse :
The Bryde was glad and made good cheare,
For she thought to make greate ioye and blisse,
As that day to tryumphe with games and sporte,
Among her friendes a rule to beare :
And eake with his friendes that thether should resorte,
Thinking that no body might be her peare.

The bridegrome was glad also, in fay,
As man might be vpon the molde,
And to himselfe thus gan he say,
Now shall I receyue an heape of golde,
Of poundes many one, and much goods besyde,
To reioyce my sorrowes, and also my smarte :
I know not her peare in this country so wyde,
But yet I feare alway her proude harte.

She is so syb to the mother, withouten fayle,
Which hath no peare that I know :
In all mischiefe she dare assayle,
The boldest Archer that shooteth in a bow.
But no force, I care not, I wote what I thinke,
When we be wed and keepe house alone
For a small storme I may not shrinke,
To run to my neighbour to make my mone.

Soone to the church now were they brought,
With all their friends them about,
There to be maryed as they ought,
And after them followed a full great rout,
With them to offer, as custome is,
Among good neighboures it is alway seene :
Full richly deckte, withouten mis,
And she thought herselfe most likest a Queene.

Incontinent when the Masse was done,
Homeward forsooth they tooke the way:
There followeth after them right soone,
Many a tall man and woman full gay.
The fathers and mothers next of all,
Unto the Bridgrome and Bryde also:
As to them then it did befall,
With them that tyde so for to go.

How the Bryde and her friendes came from the Church, and were of the Brydegroome at their feast honestly serued.

When they came home the bordes were spread,
The Bride was set at the hye dysse:
Euery one sayd, she had well sped
Of such a fayre husband as serued her mysse.
The friendes sate about her on euery syde,
Each in their order, a good syght to see,
The Bryde in the middest, with much pryde,
Full richely beseene she was pardye.

The mother was right glad of this sight,
And fast she did her daughter behold,
Thinking it was a pleasaunt wight,
But alway her Fathers heart was cold:
When he remembred what might befall
Of this yong Daughter, that was so bold,
He could nothing be merry at all,
But moned the yong man full many a fold.

Beholde, how often with countenaunce sad
Saying to himselfe, alas, this day!
This yong man proueth much worse then mad,
That he hath marryed this cursed may.
Where I haue counsayled him by heavens blisse
That he should not meddle in no wise,
Least he repented, withouten misse,
That euer he made this enterprise.

But seeing it is thus, selfe doe selfe haue,
He is worse then mad that will him mone;
For I will no more, so God me saue,
But God send him ioy, with my daughter Jone.
She is as curste, I dare well swere,
And as angry y wis as euer was waspe:
If he her anger she will him tere,
And with her nayles also him claspe.

What auayleth it to say ought now?
The deede is done, no remedy there is:
Good cheare to make, I make God auowe,
Is now the best, withouten misse;
For now is the time it should so be,
To make good game and sporte in fay,
In comforting all this company,
That be assembled here this day.

The father and mother were dilligent still
To welcome the friendes both more and lesse:
The yong man did also his good will
To serue them well at euery messe.
Wherein the mother great pleasure tooke,
And so did the father eake truely,
The Bride gaue a friendly looke,
Casting on him a wanton eye.

Then was the Brydegrome reioysed sore,
Alway our Lord thanking of his great grace,
Hauing in minde times many a score,
That his Bryde shewed him such a fayre place.
The mynstrelles played at euery bord,
The people therewith reioysed right well,
Geuing the Bridegrome their good word,
And the bryde also, that in bewty did excell.

The time past forth, the dinner was done,
The tables were taken vp all:
The Brydegroome welcommed them euery ech one,
That were there in the hall.

They thanked him then, and the bryde also,
Of their greate cheare they had,
And sware great othes, so mote I go,
They were neuer at feast so glad.

Now we will remember you or we depart,
As vse and custome doth requyre :
He thanked them with all his harte,
So did both dame and syre.
The Bryde to the table agayne was set,
To keepe countenaunce than in deede :
The friendes that were together met
Be gyfted them richely with right good speede.

The father and the mother fyrst began,
To order them in this wise.
The Brydegrome was set by the Brydes syde than,
After the countrey guise :
Then the father the fyrst present brought,
And presented them there richly in fay,
With deedes of his land in a boxe well wrought,
And made them his heyres for aye.

He gaue them also of malte and corne
An hundred quarters and more,
With sheepe and oxen, that bare large horne,
To keepe for household store.
And then came the mother, as quick as a bee,
To the Brydegrome with wordes smart,
Saying sonne, so mote I thee,
I must open to thee my harte.

She gave them also both carte and plow,
And bade them alway to doe well,
And God should send them good ynow,
If they did marke what she did tell.
Before the people in this Hall
I will say and to thee rehearse :
An hundred pound now geue thee I shall,
But harken fyrst vnto my vearse.

Thou hast here my daughter deare,
A pleasaunt thing it is :
In all the countrey I know not her peare,
So haue I parte of blisse ;
For she is wyse and fayre with all,
And will nothing cast away :
I trow there be now none in this hall,
That better can saue all thing in fay.

Nor better doth know what doth behoue
Unto an house or huswiuery,
Then she doth, which causeth me to moue
This matter to thee so busily.
She can carde, she can spin,
She can thresh, and she can fan :
She can helpe thee good to win,
For to keepe thee like a man.

And here is an hundred pound in Golde
To set thee vp, thy crafte to vse :
Wherefore I am playne, I would thou should
In no maner of wise thy selfe abuse,
To striue with my daughter or her to intreate,
For any thing that she shall doe
Here after, my child therefore to beate,
It should turne playnely to thy greate woe.

O ! my deare mother, take no displeasure,
Till you haue cause what so befall,
But vse your selfe alwaye by measure,
For other cause none haue you shall.
My wyfe and I full well shall gree,
I trust to God in throne :
She is my loue, and euer shall be,
And none but she alone.

O ! my deare sonne, thou makest me glad,
Which before was full of sorrowe :
For my deare daughter I was full sad,
But now I say, our Lord to borrow,

Thou geuest me good comfort : now fare wel care,
Here is thy hundred pound :
I pray God geue thee well to fare,
And kepe thee whole and sound.
I thanke you dere mother, the yong man sayd,
Of your good gifte and daughter deare :
Me thinkes she is the worthiest mayde,
In all this Lande, withouten peare.
I hoape to liue with her alway
So gentelly, that she shall fynde,
And you her mother, I dare well say,
In euery season gentle and kynde.

The people, standing them to behold,
Regarded the wordes of the Brydegrome than,
And sayd, he aunswered with wordes cold,
Which became full well the good yong man.
And then they prest forth ech after other,
With golde and syluer, and riche giftes eake ;
And many a scorne they gaue the mother,
But euer they praysed the yong man meeke.

To whome he gaue thankes with all his mighte,
As honesty requyreth him to doe :
He ordred himselfe alway aright,
Yet they thought all he should haue woe ;
For he was matched so ywys,
That he could not wante for sorrow in fay,
But alway hampred, withouten misse,
Of mother and daughter, for euer and aye.

When all was done they gan depart,
And tooke their leaue full friendly thoe,
Thanking ech other with all their harte,
And on their way home they gan go.
The father and mother thanked them all,
The Bryde and Brydegrome also, without mis,
Did thank the company in generall,
Departing from them with ioy and blisse.

Then they went home while it was day,
And lefte the Bryde and Brydegrome there,
And they that did abide there, in good fay,
They made at euen agayne good cheare.
And after supper they did make good sporte,
With dauncing and springing as was the vse :
Yong people by other there did resorte,
To no mans hynder nor confuse.

After that all sportes were ended and done,
And that the bryde should goe to bed,
About the hall they daunced soone,
And suddaynly away the bryde was led,
To take her rest with her dere spouse,
As reason would it should so be :
Euen as the cat was wonte with the mouse
To play, forsoth euen so did he.

The next morning, if that ye will heare,
The mother did come to their bedsyde,
Demaunding them what was their cheare,
And the Bryde began her head to hyde;
Saying to her, as one ashamed,
I wys, deare mother, I would ye were gone :
Or ye came heare I was not blamed
For being in his armes heare all alone.

Myne own deare daughter, be not displeased,
Though I doe let you of your disport :
I would be loath ye were diseased,
But you shall haue a cawdell for your comforte.
A while I will goe and let you alone,
Till ye be ready for to ryse.
And sodaynely the mother was from them gone
To make the cawdell after the best wise.

When that the mother departed was,
They dallyed togither and had good game :
He hit her awry; she cryed, alas!
What doe ye man? hold vp for shame.

I will sweete wife, then gan he say,
Fulfill your mynde both loud and still;
But ye be able, I sweare in fay,
In all sportes to abide my will.

And they wrestled so long beforne,
That this they had for their greate meade:
Both shyrt and smock was all to torne,
That their vprysyng had no speede.
But yet the mother came agayne,
And sayd to her daughter, how doest thou nowe?
Mary, mother, betweene us twayne,
Our shyrtes be torne, I make God auowe.

By Gods dere mother, she sware than,
This order with vs may not continue:
I will no more lye by this man,
For he doth me brast both vayne and sinew.
Nay, nay, deare mother, this world goeth on wheeles:
By sweete Saynt George ye may me trowe,
He lyeth kicking with his heeles,
That he is like to beare me a blow.

My owne deare daughter, if thy smock be asonder,
Another thou shalte haue then, by this light:
I pray thee hartely doo thou not wonder,
For so was I dealt with the fyrst night
That I by thy father lay, by the roode,
And I doe thee with wordes playne:
Me thought neuer night to me so good,
As that same was when I tooke such payne.

Why, mother, were ye then glad
To be thus delt with as I am now?
Me thinke my husband worse then mad,
For he doth exceede, I make God auow.
I could not lye still, nor no rest take,
Of all this night, beleue ye me:
Sometime on my syde, and sometime on my backe,
He rode and layd me, so mote I thee.

And from the beds head vnto the beds feete,
A cloth we had not vs for to decke,
Neyther our couerlet, nor yet our sheete,
That I pray God the deuell him checke;
For I am ashamed, my mother deare,
Of this nightes rest, by God in throne:
Before our friendes I dare not appeare,
Would to Gods passion I had layne alone!

Nay, nay, deare daughter, be not ashamed,
For here is nothing done amis:
They be more worthy to be blamed,
That hereof thinketh shame y wys;
For this is honesty for thee and vs all,
And a new smock I will thee fet;
And eke for thee, my sonne, I shall
For thy true laboure a new shyrte get.

And soone of these they were both sped,
The daughter, and eake the sonne also:
Full quickly they rose out of their bed,
And with their mother they gan go
Abroade among their friendes all,
Which bid them good lucke, and eake good grace:
The cawdell was ready there in the Hall,
With myrth and glee for their solace.

Thus ended the feast with sporte and play,
And all their friendes, each with other,
Did take their leave and went their way,
From Bryde, and Brydegrome, with father and mother;
Which right hartely did thanke them tho,
So did the Bryde, and Brydegrome eke;
Yet when the friendes were all ago,
This yong folke abode with the mother all the weeke.

The father was glad to see them agree,
So was the mother, by heauen queene;
And sayd eche to other, so mote I thee,
I thought not so well it should haue beene

Betweene them twayne as it is now;
And therefore alone here shall they bide:
We will leaue them all, I make God auowe,
And go to dwell in our house harde beside.

At shorte conclusyon they went their way,
Leuing their children all that was there,
And come not agayne of many a day,
For their deare daughter to inquere.
Thus they bode together than:
He set vp his shop with haberdash ware,
As one that would be a thriuing man,
To get great goods for his welfare.

And after that he tooke greate payne
To order his plowes and cattell also:
He kepte both boye, and also swayne,
That to the carte and plow did goe.
And some kept neate, and some kept sheepe,
Some did one thing, some did another,
But when they came home to haue their meate,
The wife played the deuell then, like her mother.

With countenaunce grim, and wordes smart,
She gave them meate, and bad them brast.
The pore folke that come from plow and carte,
Of her lewde wordes they were agast;
Saying eche to other, what dame is this?
The deuill I trow hath brought vs here:
Our mayster shall know it, by heauens blisse,
That we will not serue him another yeare.

The good man was fourth in the towne abroade,
About other thinges, I you say:
When he came homewarde he met with a goade,
One of his carters was going away:
To whome he sayde, Lob, whether goest thou?
The carter spyde his master than,
And sayd to him, I make God auow,
No longer with thy wife abide I can.

Mayster, he sayd, by Gods blist,
Our dame is the deuell, thou mayst me beleeue:
If thou haue sought her, thou haste not miste
Of one that full often thee shall greeue.
By God, a man thou canst not haue
To go to carte, ne yet to plow,
Neyther boy, nor yet knaue,
By Gods deare mother I make God auow,

That will bide with thee day or night.
Our Dame is not for vs, for she doth curse:
When we shall eate or drinke with right,
She bannes and frownes, that we be all the worse.
We be not vsed, where euer we wende,
To be sorely looked on for eating of our meat.
The deuell, I trow, vs to thee send:
God helpe vs a better maystres to get.

Come on thy way, Lob, and turne agayne;
Go home with me, and all shall be well:
An Oxe for my meyny shall be slayne,
And the hyde at the market I will sell.
Upon this together home they went:
The good man was angry in his minde,
But yet to his wife, with good intent,
He sayd, sweete heart, you be vnkinde.

Entreate our meyny well alway,
And geue them meate and drinke ynough;
For they get our liuing euery day,
And theirs also, at carte and plough.
Therefore I would that they should haue
Meate and drinke to their behoue;
For, my sweete wife, so God me saue,
Ye will doe so, if ye me loue.

Gyue them what thou wilt, I doe not care,
By day nor night, man, beleeue you me:
What euer they haue, or how they fare,
I pray God euell mote they thee.

And specially that horeson that doth complayne,
I will quite him once if euer I liue;
I will dash the knaue vpon the brayne,
That euer after it shall him greeue.

What! my deare wife, for shame, be still;
This is a payne such wordes to heare:
We can not alwayes haue our will,
Though that we were a kinges pere.
For to shame a knaue what can they get?—
Thou art as lewde, for God, as they,
And therefore shalt thou serue them of meate,
And drinke also, from hence alway.

What! wife, ye be to blame,
To speake to me thus in this wise:
If we should striue, folke woud speake shame,
Therefore be still in mine aduise.
I am loth with you to striue,
For ought that you shall doe or say.
I sweare to Christ, wife, by my liue,
I had rather take Morell, and ryde my way,

To seeke mine aduenture, till your moode is past.
I say to you these manners be not good,
Therefore I pray you that this be the last,
Of your furious anger that semeth so wood.
What can it auayle you me for to greeue,
That loueth you so well as I doe mine harte?
By my trouth, wife, you may me beleeue,
Such toyes as these be would make vs both smarte.

Smarte in the twenty fayning Deuelles name!
That liste me once well for to see:
I pray God geue the[e] euell shame!
What shouldest thou be, werte not for me?
A ragge on thine arse thou shouldest not have,
Excepte my friendes had geuen it thee:
Therefore I tell thee well, thou drunken knaue,
Thou arte not he that shall rule me.

O! good wife, cease, and let this ouerpasse:
For all your great anger and hye wordes eake,
I am mine owne selfe, euen as I was,
And to you will be louing, and also meeke;
But if ye should doe thus, as ye doe begin,
It may not continue no time ywys:
I would not let for kyth nor kin,
To make you mend all thinges that is amys.

Make me! mary, out vpon the dreuill,
Sayest thou that? wilte thou beginne?
I pray God and our Lady, that a foule euill
Lyghten vpon thee and all thy kinne.
By Gods deare blest, vex me no more,
For if thou doe thou shalte repente;
I haue yet somewhat for thee in store.
And with that a staffe in her hand she hent.

At him full soone then she let flee,
And whorled about her as it had bene a man:
Her husband then was fayne perdy
To voyde her stroake, and goe his way than.
By Gods deare mother, then gan she sweare,
From henceforth I will make thee bow;
For I will trim thee in thy geare,
Or else I would I were cald a sow.

Fye on all wretches that be like thee,
In worde or worke both lowde and still!
I sware by him that made man free,
Of me thou shalte not haue thy will,
Now nor neuer, I tell thee playne,
For I will haue Golde and riches ynow,
When thou shalte goe iagged as a simple swain,
With whip in hand at carte and plough.

Of that, my deare wife, I take no scorne,
For many a goodman with minde and harte
Hath gone to plough and carte beforne
My time y wys, with payne and smarte,

Which now be rich, and haue good at will,
Being at home, and make good cheare;
And there they intend to leade their life still,
Till our Lord doe sende for them heare.

But now I must ryde a little way:
Deare wife, I will come right soone agayne.
Appoynt our dinner, I you pray,
For I doe take on me great payne:
I doe my best, I sweare by my life,
To order you like a woman y wys;
And yet it cannot be withouten strife,
Through your lewde tongue, by heauens blisse.

Ryde to the Deuell, and to his dame,
I would I should thee neuer see!
I pray to God send thee mickle shame,
In any place where euer thou be.
Thou wouldest fayne the mayster play,
But thou shalte not, by God I make thee sure:
I sweare I will thy Peticote pay,
That long with me thou shalt not endure.

How the good man rode his way, till he thoughte her anger was past; and then he retourned home agayne.

The good man was sorry, and wente his way
About his busynes, as he was vsed,
And to himselfe thus gan he say:
Lord God, how was I thus abused!
When I tooke this wife I was worse then mad,
And yet can I blame my selfe and none other,
Which maketh me sigh and often be sad,
Repenting full sore, by Gods deare Mother.

Fye vpon goods withouten pleasure!
Betweene man and wife that cannot agree,
It is a payne far passing measure,
Such stryfe to see where as loue should be:

For there was neuer man y wys
So hampred with one wife as I am now,
Wherefore I thinke, withouten misse,
She shall repent it, I make God auow.

Except she turne and change her minde,
And eake her conditions euerichone,
She shall fynde me to her so vnkinde,
That I shall her coyle both backe and bone,
And make her blew and also blacke,
That she shall grone agayne for woe;
I will make her bones all to cracke,
Without that she her condicions forgoe.

I was neuer so vexte this time beforne,
As I am now of this wife alone;
A vengeaunce on her that euer she was borne.
For she maketh me often full woe begon!
And I cannot tell where me to tourne
Nor me to wende, by God in faye,
Which cause me often for to mourne,
Or yet to know what for to say.

I am worse then mad or wood,
And yet I am loth with her to begin;
I feare me I shall neuer make her good,
Except I do wrap her in black Morels skin,
That can no more drawe at plough ne carte.
It shall be to late to call for her kinne,
When she beginneth once for to smarte,
For little ease thereby she shall winne.

Morell is olde, he can labour no more,
Nor doe no good but alway eate;
I trowe, I haue kept him thus long in store,
To worke a charme that shall be feate.
The horeson is blynde and lame also,
Behynde and before, he cannot stere;
When he from the stable to the streete should go,
He falleth downe ryght than in the myre.

Yet I am loth him for to kyll,
For he hath done me good seruice or nowe;
But if my wife fulfyll not my wyll,
I must him flea, by God I trowe.
But at thys poynt nowe will I be :
I wyll be mayster, as it is reason,
And make her subiect vnto me,
For she must learne a newe lesson.

Her father did warne me of this beforne,
How I should it finde in euery degree,
But I did take it for halfe a scorne,
And would not beleeue him then, perdee.
But now I perceaue it very well
He did it for good will y wis;
Wherefore I thinke that Morels fell
Must mend all thing that is amis.

Thus he that will not beleeue his friend,
As her deare father was vnto me,
He is worthy for to fynde
Alway greate payne and misery.
But I may not choose him to beleeue,
For the deede doth proue himselfe in fay;
Euer she is redy me for to greeue.
And thinkes to continue so alway.

But now I will home to proue her minde,
And see what welcome I shall haue;
She may be to me so vnkinde
That she shall repent it, so God me saue :
For if I should of her complayne,
Folke would me mock, and giue me scorne,
And say, I were worthy of this payne,
Because it was shewed me so well beforne.

*How the goodman was welcommed when he retourned
home agayne.*

The good man came ryding to the gate,
And knocked as he had bene wode;
His seruaunt right soone did meete him thereat,
And bid him welcome with right milde moode.
The mayster sayd, what doth my dame now?
Is she as frantick yet as she was?
Than will I tame her, I make God auow,
And make her sing full loude alas.

Where arte thou, wife? shall I haue any meate,
Or am I not so welcome vnto thee,
That at my commaundement I shall ought get,
I pray thee hartely soone tell thou me?
If thou doe not serue me, and that anon,
I shall thee shew mine anger y wis:
I sweare by God, and by saynt John,
Thy bones will I swaddle, so haue I blisse.

Forth she came, as brym a bore,
And like a dog she rated him than,
Saying thus, I set no store
By thee, thou wretch, thou arte no man:
Get thee hence out of my sight,
For meate nor drink thou gettest none heare;
I sweare to thee by Mary bright,
Of me thou gettest here no good cheare.

Well, wyfe, he sayd, thou doste me compell
To doe that thing that I were loath:
If I bereaue Morell of his old fell,
Thou shalte repente it by the fayth now goath:
For I see well that it will no better be,
But in it thou must, after the new guyse.
It had bene better, so mote I thee,
That thou haddest not begon this enterpryse.

How the good man caused Morell to be flayn, and the hide salted, to lay his wife therein to sleepe.

Now will I begin my wife to tame,
That all the world shall it know;
I would be loth her for to shame,
Though she do not care, ye may me trow.
Yet will I her honesty regard,
And it preserue, where euer ye may,
But Morell, that is in yonder yarde,
His hyde therefore he must leese in fay.

And so he commaunded anon
To slea old Morell, his great horse;
And flea him then the skin from the bone,
To wrap it about his wiues white coarse.
Also he commaunded of a byrchen tree
Roddes to be made a good great heape;
And sweare by deare God in Trinity,
His wife in his seller shold skip and leape.

The hyde must be salted, then he sayd eake,
Bycause I would not haue it stinke;
I hope herewith she will be meeke,
For this I trow will make her shrinke,
And bow at my pleasure, when I her bed,
And obay my commaundementes both lowde and
  still;
Or else I will make her body bleede,
And with sharp roddes beate her my fill.

Anon with that to her he gan to call;
She bid abide in the diuelles name;
I will not come what so befall:
Sit still with sorrow and mickle shame.
Thou shalte not rule me as pleseth thee,
I will well thou know by Gods deare Mother,
But thou shalt be ruled alway by me,
And I will be mayster, and none other.

Wilte **thou be** mayster, deare wife? **in** say,
Then must we wrestle for the best game;
If thou it win, then may **I** say,
That I haue done my selfe greate shame.
But fyrst **I** will make thee sweate, good Jone,
Redde blood euen to the heels adowne,
And lappe thee in Morels skin alone,
That the blood shall be seene euen from **the**
    crowne.

Sayest thou me that, thou wretched knaue?
It were better thou haddest me neuer seene;
I sweare to thee, so God me saue,
With my **nayles** I will scratch out both thine
    eyen,
And therefore thinke not to touch me once,
For, by the masse, if thou begin that,
Thou shalte be handled for the nonce,
That **all** thy braynes on the ground shall squat.

Why then there is no remedy, I see,
But needes I must doe euen as I thought,
Seing it will none other wise be,
I will thee not spare, by God that me bought;
For now I am set thee for to charme,
And make thee meeke, by Gods might,
Or else with roddes, while thou arte warme,
I shall thee scourge with reason and right.

Now, good Morels skin,
Receiue my curst wife in.

How the curst wife in Morels skin lay,
Because she would not her husband obay.

Now will I my sweete wife trim,
According as she deserueth to me:
I sweare by God, and by saynt Sim,
With byrchen roddes well beate shall she be,

And after that in Morels salte skin
I will her lay, and full faste binde,
That all her friendes, and eake her kyn,
Shall her long seeke or they her fynde.

Then he her met, and to her gan say,
How sayest thou, wife, wilte thou be mayster **yet?**
She sware by Gods body, and by that day,
And sodaynly with her fyst she did him hit,
And defyed him, dreuill, at euery worde,
Saying, precious horesone, what doest thou thinke
I set not by thee a stinking torde,
Thou shalt get of me neyther meate nor drinke.

Sayest thou me that wyfe? quoth he than.
With that in his armes he gan her catche,
Streyght to the seller with her he ran,
And fastened the dore with locke and latche,
And threwe the key downe him besyde,
Askyng her than if she would obay?
Than she sayde nay, for all thy pryde,
But she was mayster, and would abyde alway.

Then, quoth he, we must make a fraye:
And with that her cloths he gan to teare,
Out vpon thee, horesone! than she did saye,
Wilte thou robbe me of all my geare?
It cost thee naught, thou arrant theefe:
And quickly she gat hym by the heade;
With that she sayde, God giue thee a mischiefe,
And them that fed thee fyrst with breade.

They wrestled togyther thus they two,
So long that the clothes asunder went,
And to the grounde he threwe her tho,
That cleane from the backe her smock he rent.
In euery hand **a** rod **he** gate,
And layd vpon her a right good pace;
Asking of her what game was that?
And she cryed out, horeson, alas! **alas!**

What wilte thou doe? wilte thou kill me?
I haue made thee a man of nought:
Thou shalte repente it, by Gods pitty,
That euer this deede thou haste y wrought.
I care not for that, dame, he did say,
Thou shalt giue ouer or we departe
The maystership all, or all this day
I will not cease to make thee smarte.

Euer he layde on, and euer she did crye,
Alas! alas! that euer I was borne!
Out vpon thee, murderer, I thee defye,
Thou hast my white skin, and my body all to
    torne:
Leaue of betyme, I counsayle thee.
Nay, by God, dame, I saye not so yet,
I sweare to thee, by Mary so free,
We begyn but nowe: this is the first fyt.

Once agayne we must daunce about,
And then thou shalt reast in Morels skyn.
He gaue her than so many a great cloute,
That on the grounde the bloud was seene.
Within a whyle, he cryed, newe roddes, newe!
With that she cryed full lowde alas!
Daunce yet about, dame, thou came not where it
    grewe,
And sodainely with that in a sowne she was.

He spyed that, and vp he her hente,
And wrang her harde then by the nose:
With her to Morels skin straight he wente,
And therein full fast he did her close.
Within a while she did reuiue,
Through the grose salt that did her smarte:
She thought she should neuer haue gone on
    liue
Out of Morels skin, so sore is her harte.

When she did spy that therein she lay,
Out of her wit she was full nye,
And to her husband then did she say,
How canst thou doe this vilany?
Nay, how sayest thou? thou cursed wife,
In this foule skin I will thee keepe
During the time of all thy life,
Therein for euer to wayle and weepe.

With that her moode began to sinke,
And sayd, deare husband, for grace I call;
For I shall neuer sleepe nor winke
Till I get your loue, whatso befall:
And I will neuer to you offend,
In no maner of wise, of all my lyue;
Nor to doe nothing that may pretend
To displease you with my wittes fyue.

For Father, nor Mother, whatsoeuer they say,
I will not anger you, by God in throne,
But glad will your commaundementes obay,
In presence of people, and eake alone.—
Well, on that condicion thou shalt haue
Grace, and fayre bed to reste thy body in;
But if thou rage more, so God me saue,
I will wrap thee agayne in Morels skin.

Then he tooke her out in his armes twayne,
And beheld her so pitteously with blood arayed:
How thinkest thou, wife, shall we agayne
Haue such businesse more? to her he sayd.
She aunswered nay, my husband deare,
Whyle I you know, and you know me,
Your commaundementes I will, both far and neare,
Fulfil alway in euery degree.

Well then, I promise thee, by God, euen now,
Betweene thee and mee shall neuer be strife;
If thou to my commaundementes quickly bow,
I will the[e] cherish all the dayes of my life.

In bed she was layde, and healed full soone,
As fayre and cleare as she was beforne;
What he her bid was quickly done,
To be diligent y wys she tooke no scorne.

Then was he glad, and thought in his minde,
Now haue I done my selfe great good,
And her also, we shall it finde,
Though I haue shed parte of her blood
For as me thinke she will be meeke,
Therefore I will her father and mother
Byd to guest now the next weeke,
And of our neighboures many other.

How the good man did byd her Father and Mother to guest, and many of his neyghbours, that they might see his wiues pacyence.

Great payne he made his wife to take,
Agaynst the day that they should come;
Of them was none that there did lack,
I dare well say vnto my doome.
Ye, father and mother, and neighbours all,
Dyd thether come to make good cheare:
Soone they were set in generall,
The wyfe was dilligent as did appeare.

Father and mother was welcome then,
And so were they all, in good fay:
The husband sate there like a man,
The wyfe did serue them all that day;
The good man commaunded what he would haue,
The wyfe was quick at hand.
What now! thought the mother, this arrant knaue
Is mayster as I vnderstand.

What may this meane, then she gan thinke,
That my daughter so dilligent is?
Now can I nother eate nor drinke,
Till I it know, by heauen blisse.

When her daughter came agayne
To serue at the borde, as her husband bad,
The mother stared with her eyen twayne,
Euen as one that had ben mad.

All the folke that at the boord sate,
Did her behold then euerichone;
The mother from the boord her gate,
Following her daughter, and that anone,
And in the kitching she her fand,
Saying vnto her in this wise:
Daughter, thou shalte well vnderstand,
I did not teach thee after this guyse.

A, good mother! ye say full well,
All thinges with me is not as ye weene:
If ye had bene in Morels fell
As well as I, it should be seene.
In Morels fell! what deuill is that?
Mary, mother, I will it you show;
But beware that you come not thereat,
Lest you your selfe then doe beshrew.

Come downe now in this seller so deepe,
And Morels skin there shall you see,
With many a rod that hath made me to weepe,
When the blood ranne downe fast by my knee.
The mother this beheld, and cryed out alas!
And ran out of the seller as she had bene wood;
She came to the table where the company was,
And sayd, out, horeson! I will see thy harte blood.

Peace, good mother! or so haue blisse,
Ye must daunce else as did my wyfe,
And in Morels skin lye, that well salted is,
Which you should repent all the dayes of youre lyfe.
All they that were there held with the yong man,
And sayd, he dyd well in euery maner degree:
Whan dynner was done, they departed all than,
The mother no lenger durst there be.

The Father abode last, and was full glad,
And gaue his children his blessyng ywys,
Saying, the yong man full well done had,
And merely departed wythouten mys.
This yong man was glad ye may be sure,
That he had brought hys wyfe to this.
God gyue vs all grace in rest to indure,
And hereafter to come vnto his blisse.

Thus was Morell flayne out of his skin,
To charme a shrew, so haue I blisse.
Forgeue the yongman, if he did sin,
But I thinke he did nothing amisse :
He did all thing euen for the best,
As was well prooued then.
God saue our wiues from Morels nest,
I pray you say all, amen.

Thus endeth the iest of Morels skin,
Where the curst wife was lapped in ;
Because she was of a shrewde leere,
Thus was she serued in this maner.

FINIS, QUOTH MAYSTER CHARME HER.

Imprinted at London in Fleetestreete, beneath the Conduite, at the signe of S. Iohn Euangelist, by Hugh Iackson.

He that can charme a shrewde wyfe
  Better then thus,
Let him come to me, and fetch ten pound,
  And a golden purse.

END OF VOL. IV.